OPENING
CLOSED
GUARD

OPENING
CLOSED
GUARD

THE ORIGINS OF JIU-JITSU IN BRAZIL

THE STORY BEHIND THE FILM

ROBERT DRYSDALE

Opening Closed Guard: The Origins of Jiu-Jitsu
in Brazil: The Story Behind the Film
Copyright © 2020 Robert Drysdale

ISBN-13 9798680602287

Independently published through Kindle Direct Publishing
https://KDP.amazon.com

Portions of this book were originally published on GTR:
Global-Training-Report
www.Global-Training-Report.com

Edited by Scott Burr
Layout and cover design by Scott Burr
Connect with Scott online at www.EnclaveJiuJitsu.com

All images, unless otherwise noted,
© Robert Drysdale / Message in a Bottle, LLC
For cover photo legend and credits, see Appendix III

For more information about the film *Closed Guard: The Origins of
Jiu-Jitsu in Brazil*, visit www.ClosedGuardFilm.com

DEDICATION

This book is dedicated to the two loves of my life, Athena Rose Drysdale and Clio Cristina Drysdale, as well as all Jiu-Jitsu practitioners in the world who strive for unity and wish the Gentle Art to be the most practiced martial art in the world.

—

Part of the proceeds from this book will go to Jiu-Jitsu for the People, a nonprofit organization active in Mexico, Brazil, and the U.S. helping underprivileged children, law enforcement personnel, and military veterans through the practice of Jiu-Jitsu. For more information, and to learn how you can get involved, visit www.JJ4TP.org.

Thou, Nature, art my goddess; to thy law
My services are bound. Wherefore should I
Stand in the plague of custom, and permit
The curiosity of nations to deprive me,
For that I am some twelve or fourteen moonshines
Lag of a brother? Why bastard? wherefore base?
When my dimensions are as well compact,
My mind as generous, and my shape as true,
As honest madam's issue? Why brand they us
With base? with baseness? bastardy? base, base?
Who, in the lusty stealth of nature, take
More composition and fierce quality
Than doth, within a dull, stale, tired bed,
Go to th' creating a whole tribe of fops
Got 'tween asleep and wake? Well then,
Legitimate Edgar, I must have your land.
Our father's love is to the bastard Edmund
As to th' legitimate. Fine word—'legitimate'!
Well, my legitimate, if this letter speed,
And my invention thrive, Edmund the base
Shall top th' legitimate. I grow; I prosper.
Now, gods, stand up for bastards!

—William Shakespeare, *King Lear*, Act 1, Scene 2

CONTENTS

AUTHOR'S NOTE REGARDING MAIN TEXT AND INTERVIEWS

The interview transcripts were edited by the author to make them more succinct for the reader. Repetitive answers were deleted, as were off-topic comments. Some similar answers were combined into one, while others were moved out of the original order to give the interview a better "flow" for the reader. Some unsubstantiated claims were kept to give the reader a sense for the scope of the official narrative and the prevailing misconceptions in the art, but every effort was made by the author to address these claims in the main text. The author cannot, however, guarantee that all unsupported claims made by the interviewees are labelled as such. Readers who wish to vet these claims for themselves are encouraged to read the works by Pedreira, Serrano, and Cairus, which they will find referenced throughout the book.

Throughout the text I make use of a variety of different ways to refer to "Jiu-Jitsu," reflecting the changes the word has gone through over the past century. "Jū-Jutsu" refers specifically to the pre-Meiji styles that predate Kodokan's Judo. I refer to the style that early Japanese immigrants were teaching in Brazil as either "Judo/Jiu-Jitsu" or "Jiu-Jitsu/Judo." "Jiu-Jitsu" is used throughout the text as a general term, but primarily refers to the art that was being practiced in Brazil between the beginning of that art's split from the Judo matrix and the beginning of the usage of the name "Brazilian Jiu-Jitsu/BJJ" in the age of Royce Gracie, the Ultimate Fighting Championship (UFC), and the worldwide boom that we are currently witnessing (roughly the period between the 1950s and 1990s). The term "BJJ" refers exclusively to the art practiced in the modern, post-UFC/IBJJF era (post '93/'94). "Vale Tudo" refers to the Brazilian variant of "no holds barred" competition, while the terms "Mixed Martial Arts/MMA" refer to the modern (post-UFC) variant.

Opinions expressed by the interviewees are their own, and do not necessarily reflect those of the author.

All Portuguese-to-English translations are by the author. Japanese-to-English translations are by Google Translate, and are edited by the author.

ACKNOWLEDGEMENTS

In telling this story we wanted to present as unbiased a history as the sources allowed. I knew that there would be some gray area in all of this, and that it would ultimately fall on me to decide what to include, what to leave out, and which shades of the story got told. It was a process that required me to do my own research, understand diverging opinions and interpretations, check my own biases repeatedly, question previous interpretations, unpack the deeply-seated misconceptions that had been planted in the minds of martial arts enthusiasts in general, and Brazilian Jiu-Jitsu (BJJ) practitioners in particular (myself included), all while trying to condense one hundred years' worth of characters and world events into ninety minutes or less... and with no experience in film-making. All of this to finally explain what really happened: how Jiu-Jitsu took root in Brazil, who really planted it there, and how it split from Judo.

Fortunately, there were many whose knowledge far exceeded my own, and who were eager to help me tell this story. Thanks are due to our team: Jay Coleman, Steve Jeter, Daniel Jeter, and Fabio Takao. Thanks are also due to Roberto Pedreira, both for his infinite patience and for his suggestion that I write an article about my memories of making the film—an article which ultimately grew into this book. Thanks to Marcial Serrano for his enthusiasm and his determination to bring this story to light, to José Tufy Cairus for his pioneering research and consulting, to Max Masuzawa for his support on the Japan leg of this journey, to Elton Brasil for being Armando Wriedt's right-hand man until his passing, and to Brazilian researcher Elton Silva, author of *Muito Antes do MMA,* for supplying us with videos, pictures, and his own knowledge and insights about the history of grappling in Brazil. To Rodrigo Gracie, for opening the doors of his academy for us to interview his cousin, Royce; to Andre Fernandes and Marcelo Siriema for so willingly making the interview with Carlos Gracie, Jr. possible. Also, thanks to Scott Burr for helping me edit and package this book, as well as for his priceless advice in assisting me with my first book.

I would also like to extend my thanks to our interviewees: Chris Haueter (one of the first American Black Belts), Carlos Gracie, Jr. (son of Carlos Gracie and founder of the International Brazilian Jiu-Jitsu Federation (IBJJF)), Armando Restani (Red Belt under Gastão Gracie, Jr.), Luiz Otavio Laydner (Black Belt, researcher, and author of *With the Back on the Ground: From Early Japanese in America to MMA—How Brazilian Jiu- Jitsu Developed*), Shiguero Yamasaki (Japanese immigrant to Brazil, Red Belt), Mario Yamasaki (UFC referee and BJJ Black Belt), Oswaldo Carnivalle (Red Belt under George Gracie), Roberto Leitão (godfather of Brazilian Catch Wrestling, or Luta Livre), Andre Pederneiras (renowned BJJ and MMA coach), João Rezende (Red Belt under Oswaldo Fadda), Hélio Fadda (Red-Belt and nephew of Oswaldo Fadda), João Alberto Barreto (Red Belt under Hélio Gracie), Robson Gracie (Red Belt, patriarch of the Gracie Family and son of Carlos Gracie, Sr.), Gotta Tsutumi (Executive Director of the Pan-Amazonian Nipo-Brazilian Association), Carlos Loddo (Brazilian researcher), Armando Wriedt (Red Relt under Hélio Gracie), Kyra Gracie (BJJ Hall of Famer), Sensei Matsubara (Kosen Judo instructor and Professor of Economics and Sociology at Tokyo University), Sensei Naoki Murata (Judo 8th Dan and curator of the Kodokan museum), Yuuhei Unno (Kosen instructor at Kyoto University and graduate student of the history of Kosen Judo), Takeshi Itani (Kosen instructor at Kyoto University and graduate student), Sensei Inoue (contemporary Fusen-Ryu teacher), Yuki Nakai (BJJ pioneer in Japan and president of the Japanese Federation of Brazilian Jiu-Jitsu), Pedro Valente (Hélio Gracie student and Black Belt) for sharing sources and first-hand experiences with Hélio, Guilherme Valente (Hélio Gracie Black Belt and researcher), Royce Gracie (UFC Hall of Famer), Danieli Bolelli, (martial artist, author, and professor), Antonio Vieira (last living student of Luis França), and Darlyson Lira (member of the Sá lineage).

Special thanks are due as well to the Kodokan, for not only helping give birth to BJJ but for their willingness to grant us an interview inside their museum.

Last but not least, special thanks are due to Mairbek and Zaurbek

Khasiev for their belief in and support of this project. It is because of you that we were able to tell the story for those whose voices had been drowned out by the loud speakers of relentless marketing.

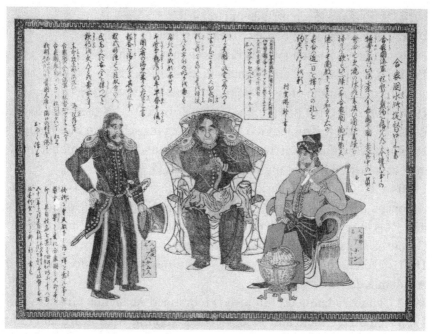

Japanese rendering of Commodore Perry's visit to Edo. Source: Library of Congress.

TIMELINE

1854 - Commodore Perry's armed fleet persuades the Shogun to open Japan's ports to commerce with the United States.

1882 - Between 1882 and 1889, Jigoro Kano establishes a system of martial arts that comes to be known as Kodokan Judo.

Late 1800s and early 1900s - Stagnating economic conditions causing poor living conditions and high unemployment push Japanese people to search elsewhere for a better life. Many Japanese immigrate to the Americas.

1904-05 - Russo-Japanese War

1908 - Judo/Jiu-Jitsu practitioner Sada Miyako arrives in Brazil.

1913 - Mario Aleixo is teaching Jiu-Jitsu in Rio de Janeiro. He claims to have learned the art from Sada Miyako. Later, in 1915, he would also claim to have learned the art from Mitsuyo Maeda.

1914 - Mitsuyo Maeda arrives in Brazil.

1916 - Mitsuyo Maeda begins to teach in Belém do Pará.

1920 - Mitsuyo Maeda awards rank to five Brazilians.

1921 - "Oscar" Gracie and Donato Pires dos Reis have a match. Both are referred to in the press as being students of Jacyntho Ferro.

1928 - Donato Pires dos Reis invites Carlos to be his assistant to the Police of Belo Horizonte; Geo Omori opens his school in São Paulo.

1929 - Carlos Gracie arrives in São Paulo and has a demonstration match, followed by a grappling match, with Geo Omori.

1930 - Geo Omori and Carlos Gracie fight a second time; Carlos Gracie opens his first academy in São Paulo; In September, Donato Pires dos Reis opens the Academia de Jiu-Jitsu with Carlos and George Gracie as assistant instructors.

1931 - Donato and Carlos have a falling out, and Donato leaves the Academia de Jiu-Jitsu.

1932 - The Academia de Jiu-Jitsu is rebranded Academia Gracie.

1933 - George Gracie and Tico Soledade fight in what is arguably the first Vale Tudo [MMA] match in Brazil.

1935-36 - Hélio Gracie and Yassuiti Ono have two no-points matches that officially end in draws, but that are dominated by Ono.

1951 - Hélio Gracie fights Kato twice and Masahiko Kimura, each time in front of a massive audience.

1954 - An in-house tournament at the Gracie Academy uses a point system that will become the foundation for the modern BJJ tournament system.

1967 - Establishment of the Federação de Jiu-Jitsu da Guanabara.

1991 - Vale Tudo challenge between Luta Livre and Jiu-Jitsu is televised on national TV in Brazil.

1993 - Royce Gracie and the UFC make their debut.

1994 - Establishment of the Confederação Brasileira de Jiu-Jitsu, later known internationally as the International Brazilian Jiu-Jitsu Federation (IBJJF).

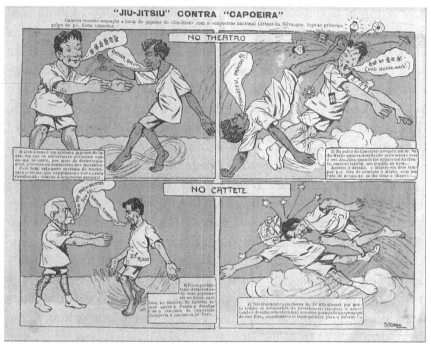

Brazilian cartoon depicting the loss of Jiu-Jitsu practitioner Sada Miyako, in a fight against a Capoeira called Mestre Cyriano. Inset is an analogy of the fight with the politics of the time. Source: Brazilian National Library

INTRODUCTION

"Truth is the quality that moves us forward, expands our horizons, and—ultimately—sets us free. We should never fear it. Those who do, do so perhaps because they have something to hide. Perhaps they worry that the relentless light of truth may expose the inadequacies or worse, the deliberate deceptions, in their own words."
—Rorion Gracie, *Gracie Jiu-Jitsu in Action, Vol. 2*

What is the origin of Brazilian Jiu-Jitsu? Is it merely a by-product—a rebel offspring—of Judo? What was the nature and content of the art that Mitsuyo Maeda, a.k.a. "Count Koma," and other Japanese taught in the Amazon? Was it Judo? Jiu-Jitsu? Was it Maeda's own

9

personal fight-tested style, built on a foundation of Judo and informed by his dozens and dozens of matches around the world? What was the bridge between the art he learned at the Kodokan and the Brazilian style that claims him as its godfather: a style now practiced by millions worldwide (and growing bigger every day)? Should Maeda even be at the center of this story? And what role did Carlos and Hélio Gracie play in all of this? Did they "invent" BJJ? Would BJJ exist without them? And, if so, what—if anything—did they create? And why does this history matter to the average BJJ practitioner today?

There is a popular adage that "those who don't know history are doomed to repeat it"—that by observing the missteps of our forbearers we may discern ways to avoid them. But this understanding misses a more vital aspect of history and the lessons it has to teach: it postulates the present and the past as separate islands in time, causally related and yet functionally distinct. If we stop and consider this for a moment, however, we discover its flaws: we are no more separate from history, in terms of our circumstances or our orientation within them, than we are from the stretch of road we've traveled for the last hundred miles.

Simply put: the present *is* its history. Where a thing is and where it's going are inextricable from where it has been and where it is coming from. It is simply a fluke of perception that we feel ourselves somehow separate from this trajectory. The fact is that we are born into a progress that started long before us, and whose composition and direction will determine our experience as surely as a current carries us into shore or further out to sea. We are where we are *because of where we have been*, the present is the present *because of the past*, and in order to understand ourselves we must understand the nature of this journey.

Yet there is a more vital imperative at work. The writer George Orwell famously observed, in his dystopian masterpiece *1984*, that "who controls the past controls the future. Who controls the present controls the past." Time and time again history, for all of its apparent inevitability, can be and has been hijacked by those with the power to distort its narrative. We like to believe that we ourselves are immune, but history shows us that such things are, in fact, reoccurring. We all fall victim to our own biases: a people who don't know where they came from don't truly know where they are, and a people who don't know where they are can be led anywhere. To know one's own history is to free oneself from this state of susceptible ignorance: it is, in fact, the only way to know the nature of the ground beneath your feet.

—

Even armed with earnest intent, however, the history of BJJ is hard to grasp. History is the product of countless events great and small, and—even in the absence of ill intent—the records that remain must necessarily reflect the characteristics of the observers who made them as much as the observed events themselves. This is simply inevitable: no matter the honesty of a group of individuals, people differ in their focus and their interpretation of the world and its events, and accordingly their views on and accounts of those events—historical or otherwise—are likely to differ to a commensurate degree. Bias—whether innocent or self-serving, whether arising from ignorance or financial incentive, vanity, egomania, or some combination of these—more often than not steers narratives towards convenient or self-serving conclusions and interpretations and away from an honest account.

Nor is the historian himself immune: Mathematicians have the privilege of knowing that the number seven is exactly that; that its definition exists objectively, outside the influence of an observer's interpretation. Historians, on the other hand, seek to navigate and decipher the complexity of past events and the myriad interpretations and diverging narratives surrounding them without any such assurance that, in the end, a fact will be established that stands free from all ambiguity. Accordingly, in historical inquiry, we are taught that the word "truth," should be avoided, if used at all; we satisfy ourselves instead by making it our guiding principle, attempting to reach the most reasonable conclusions possible with the scraps of information with which we are left, while taking care not to fall into the relativist black hole. The historian is not allowed the "truth" as a final destination, at best, it is a guiding principle: a self-aware and skeptical attempt to reach what could be called the most reasonable conclusions possible with the scraps of information with which we are left. We satisfy ourselves that, at best, we may orbit around the historical "truth," even if we never get close enough to fully and decisively define it.

As observers of history we succumb to these same biases and often deviate from the gravitational pull of our desired historical object and lose our orbit in favor of the same passions to which our protagonists fall victim. Outright selection of the favorable facts and willful neglect of the inconvenient ones become the modus operandi of those who lose their orbit but, unaffected by their disorientation, go on registering these events regardless. This is where the discipline of history quickly takes a dishonest turn—a turn from which it is so difficult to recover. It is as if our nature beguiles us with a tendency to lie and deceive (ourselves first and foremost) whenever it is advantageous; it is only through an enormous effort of the will that we can escape that to which we are held.

Nonetheless, we do our best and continue on our path toward our historical object. We hold to our earnest desire to know even the inconvenient truths and we discern to the best of our abilities while using the remnants we have: that not all professed truths are created equal, and that some of these have more to say and teach than others. We seek to ask the right questions knowing that the wrong ones may cause us to miss vital information that may lie outside the scope of our inquiry. Or, worse: cause us to mine out data affirming previously-held biases, leading us deeper into our own preferred narratives and farther from our object. And without ever losing this north, we make the colossal effort to acknowledge, account for, and sidestep our own persistent biases.

—

The history of BJJ—the events themselves and the stories that have been told and retold about them—don't escape these pitfalls. No history does. People are people, and history will reflect their virtues as well as their flaws. I have put myself in the shoes of Carlos Gracie more than a few times and asked myself: If I were broke, ambitious, in need of credibility and trying to make a name for myself in the hub of Japanese immigration in Brazil, and I were asked who I learned Jiu-Jitsu from, what answer would I have given? I might have been tempted to give the name of the most famous practitioner of my hometown—a name that everyone would immediately recognize, even in a place as far away as São Paulo—as the sole author of this apprenticeship. Doing so would grant me immediate credibility, though it would also mean denying credit to those it was due. I'd like to believe that I would have been too self-aware, and unable to leave out acknowledging my real teacher, but I was not in his shoes so I can only wonder. As for Hélio Gracie's claim that he "invented" BJJ[1], I am

---

[1] The following is an interview with Hélio Gracie that appeared in a feature on the channel *Estilo Radical* in 2007. I came across this interview and was able to purchase the rights from the original owner. The brief but—for our purposes—interesting interview is included below. If nothing else, it presents a portrait of the man during the final iteration of his BJJ "myth of creation":

Interviewer: *How did the idea of bringing Jiu-Jitsu to Brazil come about?*

Hélio Gracie: *Jiu-Jitsu did not come to Brazil. I created Jiu-Jitsu. Because who created this Jiu-Jitsu was me. There was no such Jiu-Jitsu. My brother practiced a little Judo. I was not used to Judo because it depended on a little skill, strength, and I was very weak and I looked for the strokes that I could see from Judo, I perfected and created Jiu-Jitsu. The Jiu-Jitsu that exists in the world is mine. I created it, because it doesn't depend on strength, you know?*

Interviewer: *Was the beginning of Vale Tudo also here in Brazil?*

Hélio Gracie: *I have the impression that I was the first person to do a Vale Tudo against Fred Evert, vice-champion of the world. But this was a long time ago, I was 18, I don't know.*

Interviewer: *Did Carlos Gracie begin teaching you?*

Hélio Gracie: *Carlos didn't teach me. Carlos did Judo. I did not do Judo because it depended on physical ability and I didn't have that ability, I created it with techniques that were in Judo and I improved them and made Jiu-Jitsu. The existing Jiu-Jitsu was created by me.*

Interviewer: *Many have the curiosity of learning how Jiu-Jitsu was born.*

Hélio Gracie: *What happens is that the Jiu-Jitsu that I created, because my brother did Judo, I didn't do Judo because I didn't have any physical qualities. Judoka has to be a strong guy, he has to know how to fall, he has to have qualities and I didn't have one. So I "pulled," developed this fight to the ground. This Jiu-Jitsu that exists today, the Jiu-Jitsu Gracie, was created by me for that reason, because I could not do Judo. I took some of the Judo that I had and improved it for my physique. I was always very light, very weak and made an art that does not depend on strength.*

in far less of a quandary about what I would have done in his shoes. It is one thing to stretch history and omit your real teacher from your story simply because he wasn't Japanese: it is something else entirely to omit your own brother and teacher and "invent" a new history in denial of the hundreds of people who laid the groundwork upon which your entire martial arts experience took place.

Perhaps this is simply the way of things: history tends to remember the bold and ambitious, those who are willing to pay any price and do anything to be remembered, and forget the humble, the noble, and the modest. We refer to men such as the Greek/Macedonian Alexander as "The Great" rather than "The Terrible" or "The Megalomaniac." We ascribe to George Washington the sole glory of victory but we aren't taught that the American Militias—who Washington considered "an exceeding dirty and nasty people [evincing] an unaccountable kind of stupidity"—played a far more important role in winning the Revolutionary War than that with which they are credited. And, even when a historical protagonist is justly recorded in accordance with his actions, as in the case of someone like Hitler, others—such as Adenauer, who do the less dramatic work of cleaning afterwards—are seldom as widely noted or remembered.

These epithets and recordings (as well as the lack of these recordings) aren't necessarily contingent on the laudable as well as reprehensible actions of these protagonists, but rather on who holds the pen of historical remembrance at the end of it all. And what is true of the larger scope of world history holds just as true when it comes to our favorite pajama game. This is why men like Hélio Gracie and Mitsuyo Maeda draw exclusive focus while men like Geo Omori, George Gracie, and Georges Mehdi need historians to remind the dispirited that a life of commitment does echo in history: that their deeds live on through us and our practice of the arts they helped shape.

Though I always held a certain amount of skepticism towards the popular narrative of BJJ's history, I learned rather late the full extent to which it had—like other histories—been revised, rearranged, edited, redacted, and outright fabricated. You would think that someone like me—who not only has been deeply involved in Jiu-Jitsu for his entire adult life but who also has a deep and abiding passion for history—might have investigated the subject earlier, but such was not the case. I can't give you a good reason why: despite having spent much of my youth and adulthood reading in the humanities and training BJJ as a way of life, it just never occurred to me to combine the two. My energy was focused elsewhere: into developing my Jiu-Jitsu, into competitions, into building my school, into Mixed Martial Arts. It wouldn't be until my retirement from professional fighting that my two passions would become irrevocably intertwined.

Looking back now with the knowledge of what followed—knowing the circuitous journey, the countless hours and the thousands of miles traveled, not to mention the seemingly ever-deepening labyrinth of differing accounts and conflicting histories to which it would lead—the question that started my inquiry seems absurdly simple. A student in one of my Jiu-Jitsu classes asked me why I didn't have pictures of Carlos and Hélio Gracie on my gym wall, as was common practice in so many other BJJ schools. My answer to him was that I simply didn't know that much about BJJ's history, and for one reason or another I'd never bothered looking into it.

"OK," he replied, "but weren't you a history major?"

Challenge accepted.

My general attitude toward the official narrative—that Carlos Gracie had been a favored student of the Japanese Master Mitsuyo Maeda, also known by the stage name "Conde Koma" ("Conde" means "Count" and "Koma" is short for "Komaru," which means "problem" or "trouble" in Japanese); that Carlos taught the art to his younger brother Hélio who, being small and weak, had to develop an approach to the material that favored position and leverage over brute force; that it was Hélio's innovations that birthed the distinctive style now known worldwide as "Gracie" or "Brazilian" Jiu-Jitsu—was always one of skepticism. Still, this official narrative had taken on a life of its own and hardened into gospel truth, bolstered by age and relentless repetition, and in the process that followed I was surprised to discover how thoroughly this narrative was ingrained even in me, despite my avowed skepticism; it wasn't until near the end of our production, in fact, that I felt like I was finally able to view these events from a point of view free of the official narrative's gravity. (Even the most skeptical of skeptics, it seems, will succumb to the tendency to believe something free of scrutiny at some point... Though these failures prove the value of the course, and remind us to redouble our efforts.)

To answer my student's question, I began where my memory immediately led me. I have a habit (admittedly, a somewhat rude one) of taking a peek at a person's bookshelf upon entering their home. You can learn a lot about someone based on what books they read... or what books they don't read. As I said, this might be rude—it might be a bit judgmental—but I can't help it. And, as I've found, nothing creates a connection faster than discovering that you and the person whose home you're visiting share a common interest, a favorite book, or a favorite writer. So, it cuts both ways. For the purpose of this book and our documentary, my habit worked in our favor: a few years back I'd visited the home of one of our Zenith-affiliated schools in Spring Hill, Tennessee. While staying with my host and friend, Ray Casias, and while indulging this old habit of mine, I reached out to a thick blue volume titled *Choque: The Untold Story of Jiu-Jitsu in Brazil, Volume 1* by Roberto Pedreira. I briefly skimmed it, and I remember thinking to myself that I had no idea that there was anything like this out there, especially in English rather than Portuguese. It hadn't occurred to me until that point that I had never seen anything regarding the history of BJJ that wasn't an internet or magazine article that, in one way or another, recycled the same Maeda-Carlos-Hélio narrative. Still, as I said, the history of BJJ wasn't on my radar at that time. I skimmed the book and put it back on Ray's shelf, filing away the title and the author for another time. Now I was glad I had: *Choque* seemed like the perfect place to start. I did an online search and quickly found the same volume on Amazon. Continuing my search, I found another volume, this one in Portuguese and titled *Geo Omori: O Guardião Samurai* (*Geo Omori: The Guardian Samurai*) by Marcial Serrano. I quickly read through the two volumes and was glad to discover that Volumes 2 and 3 of *Choque* were also available on Amazon, and that Marcial Serrano also had many other published works on the history of Jiu-Jitsu in Brazil.

A further internet search led to a variety of other published works which, for the most part, lacked reliable sources and often led back to internet articles and/or interviews with members of the Gracie family, all of whom simply repeated the history as told by Carlos (or Hélio). In fact, the best independent primary sources seemed to be those uncovered and presented by Pedreira and Serrano in their books (most of these were materials archived in the Brazilian National Library). There were, however, two notable exceptions: The Ph.D. dissertation by José Tufy Cairus, titled *The Gracie Clan and the Making of Brazilian Jiu-Jitsu: National Identity, Performance and Culture: 1905-1993* and an article written by the same author titled "Modernization, Nationalism, and the Elite: The Genesis of Brazilian Jiu-Jitsu 1905-1920." Both cited sources that appeared in neither Pedreira nor Serrano's works. This, despite the fact that both of these men drew on a rich and wide catalog of sources in their volumes. As I was to learn, Tufy (he goes by his middle name) began researching for his dissertation prior to the Brazilian National Library digitizing their archives (around 2012): he did his research by traveling throughout Brazil looking for primary sources in their physical archives. In doing so, he discovered a small but dedicated community of researchers who had always been skeptical towards the official narrative of BJJ's history, and who had been steadily researching the history of our sport all along. Tufy would go on to discover documents and newspaper articles that had never been digitized, that still exist only in their physical archives.

I had only scratched the surface, and already the picture that was forming was far more involved, interesting, nuanced, and complicated than the linear, top-down "myth of creation" (as Luiz Otavio Laydner, one of our interviewees, would call it) which described the birth of BJJ in the popular consciousness. It was becoming clear that we had all been told a substantially incomplete story, one full of omissions and distortions, and that here, as is so often the case, reality was far more interesting than fiction.

—

At this point I was hooked. The combination of my two main passions had me firing on all cylinders. It's one thing to learn about a new subject or skill: it's something else altogether to suddenly find that the world you thought you knew, the world that felt utterly familiar, is actually an unknown frontier waiting to be discovered. I very quickly learned that the story of Brazilian Jiu-Jitsu did not begin with Carlos or Hélio Gracie—or even, for that matter, with Mitsuyo Maeda. Roberto Pedreira writes in *Craze: The Life and Times of Jiu-Jitsu* that the history of modern Jiu-Jitsu really begins with Commodore Perry's gun-boat diplomacy towards the Shogun in 1854—with the forced and rapid modernization of Japan, and the creation of Judo in response to and in the context of the political and cultural upheaval that followed; that it was shaped by the events of the Russo-Japanese War (with Japan's victory becoming a marketing tool for the original Jiu-Jitsu "craze"), and carried outward to the world with a wave of expatriating Japanese immigrants to arrive in Brazil during the Amazon rubber boom of the early 20th century, where it eventually took on its own distinct flavor as Brazilians (the Gracie family primarily) capitalized on the Kodokan's neglect of ground-fighting and carved out a niche for themselves outside the rapidly expanding style formulated by Jigoro Kano, the father of Judo.

At some point in this process I began to realize that I had come to this inquiry at a unique and privileged moment: that I was living in what would inevitably turn out to be a small window of time, perhaps a decade long, between the digitization of the Brazilian National Archives, which greatly expanded the quantity and variety of materials available to researchers, and the moment when many, if not all, of the original Grandmasters—the first generation of Brazilian practitioners—would have passed away. It was a "Goldilocks" moment, if you will: not too soon and not too late. I knew, however, that the window was closing: that if I wanted to do something I would have to do it soon, and the idea for a documentary tracing the untold history of Jiu-Jitsu in Brazil was born.

This book is the story of that film's production. *Closed Guard: The*

INTRODUCTION

Origins of Jiu-Jitsu in Brazil was three years in the making, and the finished film is the product of the passion of many dedicated researchers, historians, and talented film-makers, the belief of a BJJ aficionado who was willing to stake this project and place the required funds in the hands of a complete stranger (yours truly) over a handshake, and the ambition of someone (again, me) who knew less than everyone else involved, but was well-positioned to help put it all together.

—

Writing this book was fairly easy, given that it is largely composed of recollections that were still fresh in my mind, along with interpretations and conclusions I came to over the course of the film's three-year production. Structuring the book, however, proved to be slightly more challenging. Apart from telling the story of what was an incredible and eye-opening three-year journey, part of the idea in writing this book was to give a home to the overwhelming amount of material we collected during the production which, due to the constraints of filmmaking, didn't make it into the final cut. As it would turn out, though, print storytelling has its own constraints. Accordingly, I have elected to include edited interview transcripts within each interviewee's chapter. This material, while lengthy, is simply too valuable to just sit on a hard drive somewhere, and I know that practitioners and enthusiasts in general will be interested in the full interviews.

It is also important to note that the events discussed throughout these chapters follow the chronology of the production—the order in which they were revealed to our team—and not the chronology of BJJ's history. It was in light of this, and in an effort to mitigate any confusion this might cause, that I included a timeline at the beginning of the book of some of the most relevant events throughout BJJ's history for the reader to use as a reference.

As I said, I have also included my own impressions and conclusions about BJJ and its history where such impressions and conclusions are related or relevant to an interviewee's responses. These include articles that I previously published on the Global Training Report (GTR) website. These conclusions were made based on facts that were revealed or that were already well known, and/or my own understanding of fighting as a practitioner and coach. You are, however, free to disagree with them.

From left to right: A letter of appreciation from the immigration (or related) asso-ciation to Mitsuyo Maeda, dated November 10, 1940; a letter from the Home Min-istry (naimusho, 内務省) to Mitsuyo Maeda expressing the Japanese government's appreciation for Maeda's work in Brazil; An honor awarded posthumously to Mitsuyo Maeda dated November 15, 1959. Shown to the production team by Abel, Maeda's daughter Clivia's husband.

CONCEPTION AND GOAL

"I think that in the future I can do something [different], so I focus on that, rather than the past. Have I always done the right thing? No. Have I done some things that were wrong? Perhaps. But I can't change the past. But I can evidently better my future and I can craft my present into having greater value through my actions."

—Grandmaster Oswaldo Carnivalle, student of
George Gracie and the Ono Brothers

Roberto Pedreira and Marcial Serrano's books and Tufy's disserta-tion revealed a story that the BJJ community and the martial arts community at large didn't know: a story which, I was certain, they would be stunned to learn. Much of what they'd written shook the foundations of martial arts in Brazil, including not only the develop-ment of BJJ but also of "Valendo-Tudo," later branded MMA to an anglicized audience. Still: the books were published. The information was out there, and few people knew about it. It seemed that the truth was at risk of disappearing not behind a lie, but rather behind the at-tention deficit that the internet and smartphones have instilled in an entire generation. Well, then: if they wouldn't read it, I was confident that they would be interested enough to watch a documentary that told the story.

What was particularly interesting to me was how widespread and deeply ingrained the popular narrative was: Mitsuyo Maeda, the itinerant Japanese prodigy, finds his way into the Brazilian Amazon. A Scottish descendant and circus owner named Gastão Gracie helps Maeda establish himself there. A friendship is formed between the two men and Gastão, upon learning that Maeda is a Japanese champion teaching Jiu-Jitsu classes, requests that Maeda train his unruly son Carlos. Maeda, foreseeing a future champion, passes on the mysteries of the art to Carlos, who in turn passes it on to his younger brother Hélio (or, depending on the account, no passing on was necessary: Hélio simply learned the art from watching his brother teach), and the two create a legacy that forever changes the face of martial arts... and the world.[2] It wasn't just that Roberto Pedreira, Marcial Serrano, and Tufy Cairu's work challenged this narrative: they also expanded and enriched it, with other stories and characters absent from the Maeda-Carlos-Hélio matrix. Men like Jacyntho Ferro, Donato Pires dos Reis, George Gracie, and Geo Omori were completely excluded from the original account, yet they were clearly instrumental in the development of what we now call BJJ—more so, in fact, than Carlos Gracie himself in those early days. (Interestingly, one of our interviewees and patriarch of the Gracie family, Robson Gracie, not only knew of Jacyntho Ferro (Ferro died in February of 1929, while Robson was born in 1935), but mentioned that his father spoke highly of him. Our historians, however, questioned this: they thought that perhaps Robson was just telling us what he thought we wanted to hear. We will never know.)

———

At this point my documentary idea was still in its infancy, and

---

[2] The story of how Carlos Gracie met and was trained by Maeda is repeated throughout the internet and follows more or less the account above. Also see Reila Gracie's biography of her father *Carlos Gracie: O Criador de uma Dinastia* for the same account. Hélio's account of how he learned Jiu-Jitsu evolved over time: first his brother Carlos taught him everything, then he learned it from observing, and finally, in the Rorion Gracie era, he "invented" it.)

didn't impinge on my life as a BJJ coach in any way. For the time being, life continued as normal. On my seminar trips I always try to use the quiet time in-flight to catch up on my reading (interchanging that with catching up on sleep), and after reading and rereading every sourced book I could find on the history of BJJ (the few I have already mentioned), I suddenly remembered that I had an old Judo book sitting unread in my study. It was an old book by Oda Tsunetane that had fallen into my hands a few years back by way of a family member.

My great uncle, Lewis, was son to Lewis Preston Harris, who had been a Lieutenant-Colonel in Hawaii during the Pearl Harbor attack (the elder Lewis was the one who coined the phrase "Remember Pearl Harbor," used as a propaganda slogan for Uncle Sam after the Japanese attack). I only had the opportunity to meet Great-Uncle Lewis twice: once in my grandmother's living room, where he gifted me the book, and once in a nursing home in San Diego, where he lived out his last days. A bit of an adventurer who never grew roots, Lewis had been an active member of the anti-war/hippie movement at Berkeley during the Vietnam War. He was also an avid reader; when Lewis learned that I was into martial arts, he gave me the only martial arts book he had in his collection: *Judo on the Ground* by Oda Tsunetane (I would learn later that Tsunetane was very influential in the development of Kosen Judo, the ground-oriented version of Judo, in Japan). Lewis also gave me his father's military knife from his time in Hawaii, his father's shoulder pads with rank, and a collection of World War II uniform patches that I have framed in my study. Among these is a patch bearing a Nazi Swastika which still, all these years later, never fails to put me in a dark and thoughtful mood when I consider the extent of human irrationality and the perils of mass psychology.

Standing in my grandmother's living room, I honestly didn't think much of the book: it wasn't until much later that I realized what a treasure it was, and I added it to my small but prized collection of old Jiu-Jitsu books. Now I was glad that I had. Still, unfortunately, the book was of limited usefulness in my current pursuit: it contains what we would call "fundamentals" in BJJ today, but does not say much about either the history of Kosen Judo or of Oda himself; history, it seems, is seldom interesting while it is happening.

Another family-related coincidence: shortly after Reila Gracie (Roger Gracie's mother) wrote her father's biography *Carlos Gracie: O Criador de uma Dinastia*, in 2008, she reached out to my father about translating her book into English. My father had on many occasions done translations for BJJ-related publications and websites (*Gracie Magazine* and *Tatame Magazine*), and his contact information had somehow reached Reila. For whatever reason the deal didn't work out, but my father still had the copy of that book that she had mailed him during their initial discussions. Interestingly, when he first read the book, my father tried repeatedly—and failed repeatedly—to get me interested in it. Now, though, I was beyond eager. I picked up the book from my father's home in Las Vegas and got into it right away. After reading Serrano, Tufy, and Pedreira, though, I couldn't help but notice the almost complete lack of sources in the Carlos biography. The whole book consisted of information given by family members and family friends, with the occasional—and always favorable—newspaper article thrown in. Oral history has its merits, and it certainly deserves recording, but its shortcomings are many and obvious: simply put, people lie and people forget things. The former may rise from shifting affiliations or financial, emotional, or social incentives, the latter from the simple and scientific fact that memory becomes less reliable as time goes by, though a narrator may be too proud to admit what he or she does not actually remember. Whichever the case, the end result is the same: a distorted view of the true event.

In some academic circles, such skepticism toward oral history is frowned upon: some cultures, it is argued, maintain and venerate their own oral histories, and it is only in the context of Western historical inquiry—a field historically dominated by white men, with their preference for the written and the quantifiable—that these accounts are cast as "questionable" and "less-than." However, while it is undoubtedly true that, in some instances, the questioning of these oral accounts may be grounded in white male prejudice, this possibility does nothing to diminish the issues outlined above (that people forget, misremember, and outright lie), and thus does nothing to improve the overall reliability of oral accounts. To right the perceived wrong by asserting in practice that oral accounts are just as reliable as written history, and should be considered equally valid, seems to me a disservice to the historical discipline. Written accounts, at least, stay consistent through time, and there is simply no equating a fact which can be substantiated with contemporaneous material and an oral account, no matter that account's source. This is the standard to which our pursuit of the historical object must be bound; otherwise we risk becoming— at worse—little more than propagandists ourselves.

In light of this, it is interesting to note that BJJ's history, up to very recently, had been almost exclusively the product of oral accounts, namely Carlos', which later suffered further twists and embellishments by Rorion and Hélio Gracie (in that order), while other influential family members either remained silent or repeated the new "truth"; this alone against the silence left by those Brazilian and Japanese practitioners whose accounts never made it past their graves.

I had always been most interested in the period between Maeda's arrival in Belém and the moment where BJJ branched and emerged definitively as its own distinctive style; to my disappointment, however, I found that Reila's book had little to say about that period (though this is perhaps understandable, given that she was merely relaying what her father had told family members and friends, and possibly herself as well). At the very least, the version seems heavily biased towards Reila's father and family. Take, for example, the way she talks about Jacyntho Ferro. She words it very carefully, so as to not allow the reader to draw the obvious conclusion: "Na ausência do mestre, continuou a praticar com seu auxiliar, Jacinto Ferro, que dava aulas para os irmãos Oswaldo e Gastãozinho." ("In the absence of the Master, [Carlos] continued to practice with his assistant, Jacinto Ferro, who taught his brothers Oswaldo and Gastãozinho.") (Gracie 2008, pg. 39). Given Carlos' young age at the time and Jacyntho's prominence as not only a famed athlete in the city of Belém but also as Maeda's right-hand man, this account—that Jacyntho trained alongside Carlos and taught Carlos' younger brothers Oswaldo and

Gastão, Jr., but not Carlos himself—seems highly improbable. In fact, given the circumstances, it is far more likely that Carlos was a student of Jacyntho, who had been a student of Maeda and who had taken over the club due to Maeda's absence (Maeda, possibly tired of a life dedicated to fighting and looking toward more financially rewarding endeavors, was heavily involved with Japanese immigration at the time, as is maintained even in Carlos' story of his own father's meeting with Maeda).

Despite its problems, Reila's biography deserves credit for at least a couple of reasons. Though it builds on unsubstantiated claims and is unreliable in many instances (such as the account of Carlos' fight against Catch Wrestler Manuel Rufino dos Santos, in which Carlos officially lost, or the account of the fight against the Capoeira Samuel, of which there is no record anywhere outside of the family's oral history), she does give the reader a very insightful glimpse into the dynamics of the family and their relationship to Jiu-Jitsu and themselves. Her accounts of family feuds, of the political and economic landscape, of Carlos' relationship with his brothers and his obsession with health, a unique diet, and the supernatural, all paint a vivid picture of the context in which BJJ began to develop (this picture is sometimes even a little too vivid for my taste). At any rate, Reila attempts to paint what she seems to feel is a fair and full portrait of her father, and I suspect that most of the family would have been happier had she not opened the books on family history and Carlos' personal beliefs. Despite Reila's loving presentation, much of Carlos' behavior—the way he used his spiritual beliefs to manipulate people, particularly his greatest benefactor Oscar Santa Maria, as well as many women, not to mention his rampant promiscuity—is far from commendable. Still, it is clear that, in Reila's view, these things (and others, like her father's dealings with a spiritual entity from Peru called "Mago Egídio Lasjovino") should not be left unsaid and buried in time (it seems clear, rather, that in her mind this presentation of Carlos' preoccupation with the supernatural would elevate her father, and potentially cast him as some sort of holy man in the eyes of martial arts practitioners worldwide). Despite the limitations of her research and the fundamental bias innate to the project's aim (namely, the restoration of Carlos Gracie's name and standing), it is clear that Reila endeavored to present what she considers to be the truth of the matter.

—

A trend was emerging. No matter where I looked, the information that was available about this crucial period in Jiu-Jitsu's history all came back to one source: Carlos. Almost everything I found concerning this early period came back to the story told by the leader of the Gracie Clan. Yet the more I learned about the context of those claims the less reliable they seemed: in fact, given the timing and logistics, not to mention all he had to gain from this association, the bedrock claim that he had apprenticed under Maeda was starting to seem suspect. And if that claim was untrue, what else in the story could stand above suspicion?

I was nursing a growing sense that time was not on my side. I couldn't help thinking that, if the Brazilian National Library had digitized their files prior to the passing of the first generation of practitioners from Belém, the martial arts community would have access to far more accurate first-hand accounts of these early years. Had practitioners such as Dr. Matheus Pereira, Waldermar Lopes, Rafael Gomes, Guilherme Dela Rocque, Donato Pires dos Reis, not to mention Jacyntho Ferro himself, been able to tell their stories and have them recorded, Carlos Gracie would not be the only source of information for this most crucial period in the history of BJJ (as I was to learn, Donato, at least, had a thing or two to say about Carlos Gracie's version of events). It was becoming clear that if I wanted to do something—if I wanted to learn, record, and present the true history from the men who had lived it—then I needed to act quickly.

From left to right: Tufy, Marcial, Fabio, and the author discussing the film.

THE TEAM

"The history of our Jiu-Jitsu needs to be told, but without any fantasies."

—Grandmaster João Alberto Barreto,
one of the first students of Hélio Gracie and author

This production wouldn't be just a new project, it would also be a reawakening of an old passion: history. As a child, even though I was obsessed with everything combat related, I was sure that archaeology was my calling; even back then, the thought of digging through dirt to find old relics was enticing. BJJ had put all of that on the back burner: from the moment I found BJJ when I was 16 until my retirement almost twenty years later, there was only one thing in front of me. Everything else was just noise.

Now, though, newly retired from competition and charged up by my reawakened passion for history, I enrolled in a graduate program at UNLV. My plan was to study the history of martial arts. The program wasn't meant to be anything other than a side project: my intention from the beginning was to take one or two classes per semester and not rush anything. Unfortunately, the whole endeavor quickly revealed itself to be a bureaucratic nightmare. I soon discovered that, even at the graduate level, professors will attempt to steer you towards their comfort zones, preferences, and areas of expertise, and away from your passions. I thought of changing my field of study to Latin American history, which wasn't met with much enthusiasm either. The situation quickly became unworkable when, four semesters into my MA, I was told that credits I had previously earned studying in Brazil were not valid after all. Even though I appreciate the pragmatism and rigorous standards of academic work, the bureaucracy and petty egotism I encountered are things I simply can't stomach. Wisdom, regardless of its origin, should breed humility. I don't propose a solution to any of this but, at any rate, it was a big bummer.

Around this time, I got word that my old friend and business partner, Sean Rigo, was passing through Vegas for work. We went out for sushi, and I mentioned to him that I was thinking about putting together a documentary about the history of BJJ. Before I could even finish the thought, he interrupted and asked if I had read *Choque*. Surprised that he knew the book, I told him that not only had I read it, but that it was one of the books that had inspired the idea for the film. Rigo then told me he had actually met Roberto Pedreira once while visiting Rio, and could give me his email address.

That first email I sent Pedreira is reproduced below. It is the first in what would become a long exchange, one which would see Pedreira take on the role of consultant and advisor for not only my own research but also for the film itself.

Hello Professor,

My name is Robert Drysdale, I am an American-Brazilian who has trained Jiu-Jitsu both in the United States and in Brazil, where I grew up and went to school.

I was awarded my Black Belt by Leonardo Vieira (Ricardo Vieira's older brother) in 2004. I currently live and teach in Las Vegas, NV. I am writing to you in regards to your book Choque.

I hold a BA in History. A passion that precedes my interest in combat. However, early in my teen years, I was introduced to BJJ which, essentially, took my life over. And it wasn't until recently that I have regained my interest in academics. To be more precise, a student of mine asked me "why was it that I didn't have a picture of Carlos and/ or Hélio Gracie on my gym's wall." My answer was that I knew close to nothing about the inception of our art in Brazil and that I remained skeptical as to its development.

This question, immediately got me wondering about this topic and the possibility of better understanding it. It was then that I remembered hearing about your book by a student who read its first edition. I went on to buy all three volumes and was glad to learn that there was such an extensive, thorough, and comprehensive work on the history of martial arts in Brazil.

Your work went on to inspire me to pursue a Master's program at UNLV where I plan on researching into the life of Mitsuyo Maeda, more specifically, his travels through Latin America and its purpose(s).

I have recently retired from a professional MMA career and plan on dedicating much of my time and energy to new projects, including this one, since it brings together my two inclinations in life: history and Jiu-Jitsu. And for that your work has given me much to be thankful for.

Best regards,
Robert Drysdale

I'd taken the first steps, but I had more than a few left to go. I found Marcial Serrano on Facebook, and I was able to get contact information for José Tufy Cairus through a mutual friend, BJJ World Champion Hannette Staack. I sent them both messages similar to the one I'd sent Pedreira. All three were very friendly in their replies, and all three said that they would be willing to help in any way that they could. Tufy was living in the south of Brazil and teaching at the Instituto Federal Catarinense; Serrano was living a semi-retired life in São Carlos, a few hours outside of São Paulo, and still dedicating much of his free time to researching and writing about the history of Jiu-Jitsu in Brazil (at the time of this writing Serrano has published a total of thirteen books on the history of Jiu-Jitsu, all in Portuguese). Their support and willingness to help gave me even more confidence in the project: despite my enthusiasm, I knew that I couldn't manage a movie production and everything it would entail on my own.

The email exchange with these researchers continued for months until, in late 2016, I reached out to Serrano and asked if we could meet in person. I would be visiting my family in Brazil, and his hometown is not too far from where I spent most of my formative years and where much of my maternal family still lives. He suggested that I meet instead with his friend and fellow researcher Fabio Takao who, he said, was more active than he was in this research and who, by coincidence, would be driving back from a canine convention (pit bulls are Takao's other passion, outside of BJJ and its history) and passing through my hometown of Itu the same week that I would be there.

I contacted Fabio and we arranged a place to get together and discuss any possible overlapping in our interests. We met over açai, the Amazonian fruit-turned-dessert that is now so widely associated with BJJ, in an old gallery-mall in Itu, a place that brought back many childhood memories for me (such as waiting in line for three hours to watch *Titanic* with my first girlfriend... twice she made me do this). I was excited to meet Fabio: the prospect of meeting with someone who had been studying the origins of our art for so long gave me hope that soon I would find some more of the information I'd been searching for... or that, at the very least, I would get pointed in the right direction. Lucky for me, Fabio was more than willing to help.

Fabio Takao is a Japanese descendant and a BJJ Black Belt; at the time of our meeting, he had already been deeply involved in researching the history of Jiu-Jitsu in Brazil for well over a decade. He also has a sarcastic and witty sense of humor, which made talking to him

easy and fun. Along with his wit, he brought with him a small collection of old Jiu-Jitsu books to show me: a true gift, considering that I
had only recently parachuted into this circle of researchers. He was
very familiar with all of the materials with which I'd been acquainting
myself, and I was happy to hear that our interpretations of the facts
based on these materials were lining up, particularly our shared sense
that BJJ arose as a distinct style due to Judo's limited emphasis on
ground-fighting (*ne-waza*) in its official ruleset and practice, and not
because of a revolution of techniques made by Brazilians in general
and the Gracie family in particular. This was just one point among
many where we agreed: we shared similar views on the role that
Catch Wrestling played in BJJ's development, the importance of the
circus, as well as an acknowledgment and understanding that, for
much of the 20th century, the groundwork of the Japanese far surpassed that of the Brazilians (the Kosen Judo style came up repeatedly during our discussion).

Through his research Fabio knew not only all of the living Grandmasters in Brazil, many of whom he had already interviewed for his
own archives (the list is long, and includes such names as Armando
Restani (Black Belt under Gastão Gracie, Jr. and now Red Belt), Oswaldo Carnivalle (Black Belt under George Gracie and now Red
Belt), Armando Wriedt (Black Belt under Hélio Gracie and now Red
Belt), Hélio Fadda (Black Belt and nephew of Oswaldo Fadda and
now Red Belt), but also many of the researchers whose work would
be instrumental in this project, and who we would later interview for
the documentary (Luiz Otavio Laydner, Carlos Loddo, and Gotta
Tsutsumi, the head of the Nipo-Amazonian Institute in Belém). He
had also exchanged emails with Tufy in the past.

My conversation with Fabio, and his insights about not only the
research but also the community of amateur and professional historians pursuing it, revealed an unexpected complication. Apparently, the
small community of researchers in Brazil had begun as an online chat
group, a group which would later—in a fashion mimicking the dynamics and politics of their subject of study—splinter into factions of
fierce rivalry. At first this struck me as silly… until I remembered the

countless tribal schisms in which I had passionately participated during my BJJ journey. What at first I considered laughable and childish behavior from grown men quickly became food for thought when I considered my own actions in the arena of BJJ politics. It made me wonder what an alien visitor of superior intelligence would think of the human race and its tendency to corrode everything from sports to politics to religion to even the study of martial arts with this sort of behavior. We would probably appear as some sort of intergalactic comedy to them, something akin to the way warring and campaigning ant factions seem to us. But of course I didn't know the details of these feuds, so I tried to steer away from any judgment and kept my thoughts to myself.

I liked Fabio right away, and I was encouraged by the fact that our ideas and interpretations lined up in so many ways. I was further encouraged that his frustrations echoed my own: that nobody knew the true history, while everybody "knew" the popular myth; this despite the fact that the full history is now widely available in Tufy and Pedreira and Serrano's works. It had also occurred to him, he said, that maybe the way to get this story out to a broad audience wasn't through books, but through a film: a film that would not only tell the history but also point audiences back toward the more detailed histories available in the books. My thoughts exactly. We agreed that we would continue to cooperate and brainstorm ways to make our idea for a documentary film a reality. The overall mood was one of excitement tempered by our understanding that, in order for us to pull this off, we would need the right pieces to fall into place. As it turned out, it wouldn't take long for that to happen.

Shortly after our first meeting, Fabio put me in contact with a Black Belt from Virginia named Jay Coleman. Jay isn't your average American BJJ instructor: he comes from the Francisco Sá lineage, and his style, school, and perspective all reflect his unique pedigree. Sá was a student of the Japanese immigrant Takeo Yano, and also of George Gracie for a period; his lineage took root in the impoverished and arid Brazilian northeast, and stands out today for its more traditional approach to Jiu-Jitsu. By this I don't only mean that they have retained the respectful manners of a Judo school, but also that they maintain a self-defense-focused approach to the art: something of a rarity in an era when "Brazilian Jiu-Jitsu" is synonymous with the competition-focused style now practiced in the majority of schools. Like Fabio, Jay is a history enthusiast and a collector of old martial arts books; he is also a very talented artist.

After reaching out to Jay and spending a few hours with him on the phone discussing the possibility of making a documentary film, it seemed that things were starting to come together: it looked to me that between myself, Jay, and Fabio, we had a good enough rapport going to actually pull this off. Jay brought a lot to the table: aside from being a Black Belt from a very unique Brazilian lineage, he also had experience choreographing fights for films and had connections with a talented film crew consisting of Steve Jeter, an award-winning filmmaker and cinematographer, Steve's brother Daniel, a talented editor, and Brad Zerivitz, an experienced producer who worked as a videographer for the Red Cross and who also trains under Jay.

The pieces were beginning to fall into place: I was familiarizing myself with the research that was currently available, I was connecting and meeting with the relevant historians, many of whom were eager to help me tell this story, and I'd found an experienced film crew who all held an interest in martial arts. We didn't quite have everything we needed, but the project was taking shape. We made plans to meet in person by way of a seminar I would teach at Jay's gym in Virginia in early 2017.

The gym, located in Fredericksburg, Virginia, had a pleasant, "old-school" feel to it. Jay did his best to keep the gym as Japanese and traditional as the 21st century allowed. After the seminar Jay, Steve, and I went out for sushi, and we spoke at length about piecing a documentary together and how we would do this. We had the outline of a plan and the foundation of a team, but the project—at that time was tentatively titled *Brazilian Jiu-Jitsu: The Untold History* (I had also considered calling it simply *The Story of Arte Suave*)—still needed money. We discussed the possibility of crowd-funding within the BJJ and martial arts community, but decided that it was unlikely we would be able to raise the kind of money we needed. We talked about doing a low-budget production with whatever we could crowd-fund, but decided finally that we would be unable to do the story justice with this approach. There was no way around it: our team wasn't complete. We needed a patron.

From left to right: Mairbek Khasiev and the author at the ACB compound in Grozny; Mairkek, the author, and Bek driving the author back to the airport; the Medal of Honor gifted to the author by Mairberk Khasiev.

THE LAST PIECE TO THE PUZZLE

"Don't worry about the money, as long as you tell the truth."
—Mairbek Khasiev

This period was marked by the continuous excitement of doing something new and meaningful. We were going to teach audiences the true story of BJJ's largely unknown and fascinating history, introduce them to events and pioneers and characters they'd never heard of or imagined existed, and give credit to those whose names and voices had been lost to the onslaught of time and relentless self-marketing. Phone calls and emails were going back and forth daily, with all of the team members brainstorming ideas. A solid concept began to emerge: modeling ourselves on Anthony Bourdain's *Parts Unknown*, we would travel through Brazil and Japan to interview the Grandmasters and the historians where they lived, gather B-Roll footage, and wrap up each topic we tackled with conclusion remarks made by me before heading off for the next location.

Of these items, only the last one—my conclusions and commentary—gave me pause. Other than Fabio I was the most knowledgeable about BJJ's history, but given that we wanted the film's narrator to speak English Fabio wasn't an option. I was the man for the job. Even though this seemed like the best course of action, I couldn't help but feel a little uncomfortable with the idea. For the most part I am not shy in front of a camera, and even with my relatively rudimentary knowledge of the story I felt confident that I could speak about it. My discomfort was due to my awareness that there were people who had dedicated thousands of hours to this research, and who were much more qualified than me to speak on it (though I would later learn that this point was moot: many of these experts were camera shy and difficult to interview). Add to that the fact that I didn't want anyone thinking the documentary was just a crass attempt to put me in the spotlight as the face on an anti-Gracie agenda. At any rate the film needed a narrator, and amongst our team I was the man for the job. Eventually I would make my peace with being the face for the film, and with the fact that my connections and accomplishments in the BJJ world could help us promote it. Over the course of the film's three-year production, I would go on dozens of podcasts to talk about our project. (All of these concerns would prove moot as well: later in the production we decided not to make a *Parts Unknown*-style documentary, and chose instead to present the story with another narrator.)

Still, at the time even this fundamental question about the nature of the documentary seemed like a background issue: my willingness or reluctance to be the voice of the film wouldn't make a bit of difference if the financing didn't come together. We needed an angel investor if any of this was going to become a reality. We needed someone who was not only passionate about BJJ but who also had the funds and the desire, and who believed in the importance of our project. Our plan was to create a low budget teaser that would give the investor a glimpse of the important material we wanted to share while also demonstrating that, even without a budget, we had a team that was ready and able to deliver a quality product. We set up another meeting in Virginia, again organized around a seminar at Jay's gym, and went to work in the off hours, filming an interview with me and a reenactment of Maeda's training with other Japanese in the Belém academy. Jay's beautiful and classically-styled school fit the bill perfectly.

For my interview, we selected a few of the topics that we felt would get the investor interested and excited: a) How Maeda was not the first Japanese to teach in Brazil; b) How there were in fact Brazilians—namely Mario Aleixo—teaching the Japanese method prior to Maeda's arrival in 1914; c) The sorely-neglected role played by George Gracie in the development of the Brazilian styles of BJJ and Vale Tudo; d) The role of the circus, fixed fights, and Catch Wrestling; e) How and why BJJ had splintered off Judo; f) The Gracie preference for shorter gis as an attempt to weaken the Japanese advantage in throws; and g) How there was no evidence that the Gracie Brothers had ever been promoted to Black Belt by anyone (nor, it should be mentioned, was there any evidence that Oswaldo Fadda had, either).

We knew that this last point was going to be a bombshell in the BJJ community, and that the vocal anti-Gracie camp would attempt to use this knowledge to discredit Carlos and Hélio. I want to emphasize that our intention with this project was never to discredit anyone, regardless of their surname, but rather to give everyone their due credit. Of course, we knew that this would also mean taking some wind out of the sails of the characters with whom the public was more familiar. We also knew that, in Carlos and Hélio's eyes, they were representatives of something new (or maybe they were the saviors of something older than Judo itself) and therefore there would have been no one to promote them. Even though Hélio had been allegedly promoted to a Judo Black Belt by a man called Kotani in Brazil, he and his brother had created an entirely new hierarchy outside of the Kodokan. Still, this was nothing new: according to Roberto Pedreira (*Craze Volume 1,* Chapter 5), Jigoro Kano himself was awarding diplomas of his newly-created system to his students even before he had received a Kito-Ryu diploma himself (this was, it is interesting to note, the only martial arts diploma he ever possessed). In this sense, at least, Carlos and Hélio were following an established tradition.

The "Who promoted Carlos and Hélio Gracie to Black Belt?" question would not only be part of this first teaser, but would also be one of the questions we asked all of the Grandmasters and historians we interviewed (though we ended up not using those answers in the documentary: we simply couldn't talk about everything we wanted to, and instead had to stick to the most relevant facts pertaining to the development of BJJ away from Judo). Though we didn't end up using it in the documentary, the question featured prominently in the teaser; we felt it was necessary in order to "spice things up," create excitement, and secure the investment.

The interview process was a rude awakening for me. I flew to Virginia, Jay picked me up from the airport, and we went straight to a friend's house so we could begin. We didn't have a script: the idea was for me to "wing it." Jay, Steve, and Brad were setting up the cameras and lights while I sat comfortably in a chair by the pool and thought about what I was going to talk about. I felt relaxed and ready to go. And then, when it was time... I froze, both literally and figuratively. It was winter, 2017, and coming from the Mojave Desert the Virginia cold and my nervousness made my teeth chatter the whole time. Finally Steve took me inside to warm up, drink a beer (which I don't even like drinking), and relax a bit. It didn't help: we tried another take and I bombed again. I couldn't understand it. Generally speaking, I am not camera shy. Either because I was too tired from the trip, too cold, or too nervous, we decided to call it a night. We were going to try again after the seminar and before the reenactment was set to shoot.

The second attempt went much better than the first. I was able to get all the main points across and talk about the importance of the new research that had been made available. The reenactment also went well, and I was particularly happy with how much our "Maeda" resembled the original. Content with the result, I flew back home and Steve and Brad got down to editing.

Truth be told, we didn't have enough material to put together a good teaser. Between my interview and the reenactment of Maeda we had some decent footage, but I felt I lacked the credibility as a researcher—a problem when you're taking on a narrative that is both widely accepted and almost a century old. Fabio and Marcial would add a lot of credibility to our teaser, so I suggested that we pay someone to interview them down in Brazil. Though Fabio was willing, our lack of funds meant that we ultimately had to make do with Fabio filming himself with his own camera against an improvised white background.

Having a teaser is one thing: getting it in front of the right people is something else altogether. But I had a plan. In February 2017 I was working as a commentator for Absolute Championship Berkut (ACB), a Chechen organization that was making an enormous effort to help popularize BJJ in the Russian Caucasus, Eastern Europe, and Central Asia. My relationship with ACB began when I was called in as a last-minute replacement and asked to commentate alongside Frank Mir, who did the commentary for the MMA version of the same show. It would be the start of a more or less consistent side job, which was fine by me: as the land of arguably the best Wrestlers in the world, the Caucasus had always been a place of particular interest to me, and I was thrilled to have the opportunity to travel there and experience the region.

I want to also mention that, in my opinion, those ACB shows were the best professional BJJ events ever produced. Everything from the production to the quality of fighters to the treatment everyone received was top level. BJJ practitioners from the slums of Brazil were treated like royalty and flown in to compete in faraway places like Doha, Qatar; Almaty, Kazakhstan; Warsaw, Poland; Moscow, Russia... It was a dream of an organization. Events were held monthly and the fighters were paid handsomely—so handsomely, in fact, that it threw the entire BJJ market on its head. ACB not only posed a threat to other professional organizations, it posed a threat to every BJJ-related business outside of gyms. As I understood it, their intention wasn't to take over the sport, but rather to boost the presence of BJJ in a region of the world that had been a hub for elite grappling of all styles—from traditional Freestyle and Greco-Roman Wrestling to Sambo, Judo, and other folk styles of Wrestling from Central Asia that are too numerous to name here and that, at any rate, escape my limited knowledge on the topic—for centuries. As I see it (or, better put, as I desire to see it), Brazilian Jiu-Jitsu is on its way to becoming the most widely practiced martial art in the world, and it was being artificially introduced into a region of the world with which it had previously been unacquainted through large injections of cash from enthusiastic supporters of the art. In my eyes, the fact that BJJ has inspired such enthusiasm and investment in a region halfway across the globe is clear evidence that BJJ is or soon will be Brazil's largest cultural export—a fact which makes the question of its true history all the more pressing.

It had occurred to me that the owners of ACB might be interested in funding our project, and that, in a lot of ways, they were a perfect fit for us: they were BJJ fans, they had the funds, and didn't have any ties to any of the multiple political clans that permeated the BJJ scene in the Brazil-U.S. axis. I quickly made up my mind that they were the ideal investors, and that it was very unlikely that I would find anyone so well-suited for the role. I figured this was my one best shot at doing my part to help retell BJJ history, so I began writing a business plan.

Editing of the teaser took longer than expected, but given the frequency of ACB's events (I was flying in to commentate events monthly, at this point) I wasn't too worried about it. I was a bit worried, however, when I finally saw our finished product. Brad had largely been responsible for editing the teaser, and the video he sent me seemed flat.

It was early days, and already there were signs that our team wasn't of one mind when it came to our vision for the project. For myself and Fabio the idea was to tell the history as accurately as possible, regardless of the consequences and the flak we might catch on the back end. We also favored a more straightforward style that prioritized information over aesthetics. Brad and Steve, on the other hand, favored a more neutral and less confrontational approach, and placed a great deal of emphasis on aesthetics. I realized that this discord had the potential to be an issue moving forward, but I also realized that these divergent approaches could complement each other and become a point of potential strength… if we could keep it together.

At any rate, I conveyed to Brad and Steve that I felt we wouldn't be able to sell an investor on the project unless the teaser hooked them: that, at least during this initial phase, we needed to be a little more aggressive to secure the investment. I reminded them that our goal wasn't to attack anyone or diminish anyone's standing, that it was to give due credit to all involved in the process of BJJ splitting off from Judo, and that we couldn't let the fear of upsetting those loyal to the official narrative ground our film before it even had a chance to take flight.

With all of this in mind I made some adjustments to the teaser script, and ended it with a bang: Fabio asks the question, "Who promoted Carlos and Hélio to Black Belt?" and Marcial answers, "They promoted themselves." Smash cut to the title card (by this point we were calling the film *Closed Guard: The Origins of Brazilian Jiu-Jitsu*) and then, finally: "In memory and honor of those who also helped make Brazilian Jiu-Jitsu possible." It wasn't an enormous improvement from the first version, but it definitely had more "bite." Steve and Brad added the necessary Russian subtitles, and we were almost ready to present the plan.

I had been working on a presentation with projections showing relevant information about the project: the purpose, the budget, the travel plans, and everything else that went into our business plan. The problem was that I had never written a business plan before, let alone a budget for a documentary film. I did my best, but eventually my girlfriend at the time intervened. She helped me with the plan while Brad rewrote the budget entirely. If I wasn't the man to write it all up, I was confident at least in my ability to present it.

The owner of ACB, Mairbek Khasiev, seldom attended the BJJ events. He focused more on being the face of the MMA side of the production, while his son, Zaurbek Khasiev handled the events that I was commentating for. I would have an opportunity to show the teaser to Zaurbek at the next ACB event, this one to be held in Rio de Janeiro in September 2017.

The show was held at the Parque Olímpico in Rio de Janeiro—an incredibly beautiful venue, and the most stunning display of infrastructure I have ever seen in Brazil. I approached Zaurbek before the show and told him that I had been working on a documentary film about the untold history of BJJ, that I'd like to run the idea by him, but that I needed more time to fully present the project. Could we talk about it over dinner after the show? "Zaur," as his friends call him, was more than receptive. We made plans to connect later. It was time for me to do my part of the job.

To be frank, I was more than surprised to discover how open to the idea Zaur was. I had no idea what to expect, but I took as a good sign that he brought along a number of friends as well as an interpreter, Bek, who spoke fluent English and helped us enormously through not only this episode, but the whole process to follow. Zaur loved the idea, but told me that ultimately the decision would fall to his father. He said it would be best if I presented the project to him myself the next time I was in Russia.

To me, the mere fact that I had not been blown off completely felt like a victory. Though I was convinced that the Khasievs were our ideal investors, I'd had no way of knowing whether they would feel the same way. At worst I'd considered the whole endeavor a long shot. Now I was one successful pitch in, and would have a chance to present our project to the boss himself.

The next month, after another great event in Doha, Qatar, flights from Doha to Moscow and from Moscow to Grozny, Chechnya, deposited me on the doorstep of my meeting with Mairbek. I was traveling with Bek and some other members of the ACB production team who all lived in Grozny, and despite being eager to talk to them and get to know them better, the language barrier made it difficult to develop a friendship with any of them. The Chechens had always struck me as a very cohesive group of people, tightly knit and bound not only by religion and language but also by history and brotherhood. I respect this, and even though I knew little of their culture and history I appreciated the honor culture and the respect they had for fighters.

I was dropped off at a nice hotel in Grozny and told that I would meet with Mairbek the following evening (really the next morning for my jet-lagged brain). Between the time change and my anxiety over the presentation I didn't sleep at all: I stayed awake all night going through the presentation in my mind and making minor adjustments to the business plan. The closest thing to a business pitch that I had ever done was pleading with my gi sponsors for an increase in how many gis I would receive annually: I never went to business school or film school and I'd never read a single book on either topic. My entire experience in business was limited to running BJJ schools... and that was barely, and with lots of help. All I'd known my entire adult life was BJJ, MMA, and coaching. Still, I knew I could speak passionately about something I believed in; I would find out soon whether or not that passion would be able to breach the language barrier.

The next evening a driver and Bek picked me up from the hotel and drove us to Mairbek's compound on the outskirts of Grozny. The compound was unlike anything I'd ever seen. It was like a well-guarded fortress out of a movie. It had a fully equipped training hall with mats, heavy bags, weights, and a cage. There was also a large building under construction which was to serve as housing for the fighters who trained there. It even had its own restaurant. This was where our meeting was to take place: I was led inside and pointed to the corner, where Mairbek sat alone watching TV while he waited for me.

I'd met Mairbek before at the ACB shows, but this was the first time I'd actually spoken to him (that is: through Bek). Luckily Zaur had already relayed some of the information about our project and its purpose. I introduced myself, gave him a little bit of my background, and explained the purpose of the film. I opened up my laptop and showed him our teaser, then followed it up with the presentation of our business plan: our projections of the film's potential reach, its repercussions and profitability, et cetera. I emphasized how the "official" narrative had been distorted for a variety of reasons, and different important figures discredited and omitted, and that it was our desire to tell the story of those whose stories had not been told. I could see the excitement in Mairbek's eyes (I have wondered since if, because he is a Chechen nationalist, Maribek felt a certain affinity with the story we were trying to tell: Chechens are not ethnic Russians—they differ in religion, language, and culture—and yet they are part of the Russian Federation; due to this, I wondered if perhaps he felt a certain affinity with those whose stories have not been heard). I hadn't even finished my presentation when Mairbek cut straight to the chase.

"How much do you need?" he asked.

I pulled up the page that explained our budget, scrolled to the bottom where the items were totaled, and showed him the number. Mairbek looked at it, spoke to Bek, and Bek translated. I couldn't believe it, but Mairbek had just promised us more than we were asking for. I warned him that documentary productions rarely make back their initial investment, that this was not only a niche production aimed at martial arts enthusiasts but also a risk given that there was nothing like it on the market, and we had no way of knowing how an audience would react. As soon as I said it I wished that I hadn't: for those few moments while Bek translated I was kicking myself, wondering if I had just tanked the entire project. Fortunately for us, Mairbek was undeterred.

"Don't worry about the money," he replied, "as long as you tell the truth."

I couldn't believe what I was hearing. It was better than I could ever have hoped for. Our dream was going to become a reality.

We met up again the next morning. Mairbek came to my hotel and we discussed some further details, and he presented me with a Medal of Honor as a gift (I would later learn that it is a very high honor for a foreigner to receive a Medal of Honor). We spoke about MMA, BJJ, life, and family. It was a great conversation, the perfect ending to a brief but wonderful trip, and I left with a high impression of not only Mairbek but also of the Chechen people as a whole. When you say "Chechnya" anywhere in the West, the first thing that comes to mind for many people is the war with Russia and terrorist activities. In my time there I found them to be a very traditional and family-oriented people, proud of their history, their religion, and their customs: a people who hold a deep respect for fighters and their various arts and who, perhaps because of their history, and luckily for us, hold a strong belief that history should be accounted accurately. Mairbek drove me to the airport himself (at about double the speed limit), walked me through a private security area, and waited with me in a private lounge until the time came for me to board. He walked with me all the way past the gate and to the narrow stairs leading up to the aircraft. I

45

had flown from Las Vegas to Chicago to Doha to Moscow to Grozny; now I was flying from Grozny to Moscow to Beijing to Los Angeles, where I would board my final flight back to Las Vegas. All of this in five days' time, about half of which was spent either in an airport or on a plane. I was tired but happy. I'd accomplished my mission: with the funding in place we actually had a shot at retelling BJJ's history. My flight back was mostly spent trying to catch up on all the sleep I'd been missing. As I dozed off it struck me that Mairbek had never signed the agreement I'd brought: he'd placed his trust in me and his faith in the film—and over the years, would wire me money as needed—with nothing but a handshake deal between us. I made a promise to myself that I was going to repay that trust by making the best film I could, by presenting an account of the history that was to the greatest extent possible free from bias (except for those biases that were unknown to us), and by being as true to the facts as our sources allowed.

U.S.

Chris Haueter, one of the first American BJJ Black Belts

CHRIS HAUETER

"Think of the Gracie family as akin to rock 'n' roll. They're the Beatles. And did they invent rock 'n' roll? No, but they certainly blew it up."

—Chris Haueter, one of the first American BJJ Black Belts

One of the most difficult things about writing the script for the film was composing the varied and overlapping threads into an intelligible chronology. For example: if we mention fixed fights, which ran all throughout BJJ's history, at what point should we introduce them? Introduce them too early and you risk talking about something that feels random and irrelevant to the story; introduce them too late and you risk giving the audience the feeling that they are leap-frogging back and forth in time, ruining any sense of narrative. Writing this book has been less difficult, in that the chronology it follows is that of the documentary production and not that of BJJ's development in Brazil. Nevertheless, I find it ironic that the interviewee who, if we were to follow the chronology of BJJ's development, would have been dead last (as he represents the development of BJJ after it left Brazil and came to the U.S.), turned out to be the very first person we interviewed.

Chris Haueter is one of the earliest practitioners of BJJ, and one of the first BJJ Black Belts, in the U.S. Originally I hadn't liked the idea of interviewing anyone who wasn't a Red Belt, who hadn't lived through at least some of the events we were discussing, or who wasn't a researcher who could speak with authority about the period we were covering. Steve and Jay's persistence about the point, though, would convince me that it would be helpful to give the audience some familiar faces to help bridge the gap between the distant past and more recent developments with which our viewers would be more familiar. It was a lesson I would continue to learn throughout the production of the film: we would not succeed unless we made a film that had the viewer's experience, and not just my own preference, as its guiding principle. Historical inquiry is interested only in accuracy and completeness; film, on the other hand, is a medium for entertainment. A documentary about the history of BJJ would have to strike a balance between the two.

The recent history of BJJ, though somewhat peripheral to our stated focus, is fascinating in its own right, and we would have been hard-pressed to find a better person than Chris to talk about it. If we view Judo as an evolutionary stage—a variation of Jiu-Jitsu that arose out of the turmoil of the Meiji period—then it seems equally fair to view BJJ as the continuation of this same evolutionary process: Jigoro Kano, Judo's founding father, adapted techniques from the two schools with which he was familiar, Tenjinshinyo-Ryu and Kito-Ryu, and also from Sumo and Western Wrestling, compiling them into a style which changed and grew as it became not only a martial art but also a physical and moral educational method for children. Later still, under different social and cultural pressures in Brazil, it would continue to change until it resembled not so much Judo as it did an entirely new sport. Finally, in the '90s, it would reach the massive American audience, who would continue to reshape it according to their own preferences and priorities. As one small but telling example: I remember moving back to the U.S. from Brazil in 2008 and having people ask me for my "BJJ curriculum," and having no idea what they were talking about. It wasn't until someone showed me a Karate curriculum that I finally understood what they meant. The structured approach to martial arts is something the American market (and later, the world market) expected from BJJ, but it wasn't something BJJ instructors were ready to deliver just yet.

This wasn't the only change. These new markets wanted classes to start on time, wanted belt tests, wanted standardized uniforms. Instructors began doing the things that had proven to be most profitable for other styles, bringing BJJ much closer to how "traditional martial arts" schools were run in the U.S. (though, to be fair, despite these market adaptations BJJ has remained remarkably less affected than some other traditional martial arts styles, particularly in regards to promotion and other styles' seemingly endless appetite for more and more rank belts).

Over time, and outside of the core techniques, these changes left little of the art that originally departed Japan: Brazilians dramatically changed the art to fit with the surf culture of Rio de Janeiro; more recently, segments of the English-speaking world have done their part to reshape it by creating a professional Jiu-Jitsu scene modeled after that of Pro Wrestling and Boxing. This is particularly interesting when we consider that Kano changed the name of his style from Jiu-Jitsu to Judo precisely because of Jiu-Jitsu's association with professional fights, circuses, and fixed fights. In fact one could argue that, in many ways, BJJ in the 21st century has become the opposite of what Kano was trying to create.

The Anglicization of BJJ is perhaps most notably exemplified by the "Sub-Only" competition formats, where all points are removed, and in the parallel trend to call what is practiced either "American Jiu-Jitsu" or simply "Jiu-Jitsu," the former being popular among those who learned primarily or exclusively from other American practitioners. I won't expand on these but will note that, in my view, it is a discomfort with the idea of immigrant Brazilians running the show that lies at the heart of these movements. Simply put, the Anglo world doesn't seem to like non-English-speaking peoples at the head of the sport they love so much. Whether this is the inevitable backlash of a people accustomed to a globalized cultural dominance in every regard that matters to them, I can't say. In my view it is not, however, a coincidence that the same people who fiercely oppose IBJJF's leadership refuse to use the "B" in "BJJ." It is notable that this opposition, typically rallied behind the charge that the IBJJF is a money-grubbing organization that is disinterested in the overall well-being of the sport, seems at the very least reluctant to level the same critique at Dana White and the UFC (though the comparison, in terms of profits, is obviously unfair with IBJJF). It is also possible that the split now emerging in the sport may simply be a natural phenomenon, a result of the fact that the art has grown tremendously and without any guiding organization or structure (at least until recently: more on this in the next chapter): that when a group of people grows too large it is natural for it to fragment into factions and sub-divisions. There's simply no kitchen large enough when so many people want to be the Head Chef.

However we feel about this trend, it is interesting to note that the coordinated effort by segments of the English-speaking world to carve out a space outside of the IBJJF in fact closely resembles what the Gracie Brothers did to the Japanese so many years ago: if you can't beat them then you modify the rules in your favor, all while promoting yourself and your style as the "real Jiu-Jitsu."

This recent attempt to split Jiu-Jitsu is often justified by the claim that practitioners in the English-speaking world are now "leading innovation" in the art... To which my response would be that "innovation" has always been the norm in Jiu-Jitsu: the only thing that is unusual is that people believe there is something *unusual* going on. The only change over the years has been in the number of competitors/practitioners and the number of competitions being held, followed by the rapid spread of newly-adapted techniques, largely thanks to the internet, which when combined rapidly accelerate technical development. The notion that there is more, or superior, "innovation" taking place thanks to people who happen to be born in a hospital north (or south) of the equator doesn't even merit discussion. "Innovation" is invariably a product of competition: the more of it there is the faster these developments take place. Geography plays no role in this.

Perhaps the most interesting aspect of this phenomenon is the way in which the "Americanization" of BJJ has been exported back to Brazil: at least during my early years in BJJ, the sort of shameless self-promotion now common in the American BJJ scene would have earned you reprimands from your professors and flak from your teammates; nowadays, however, it is common to see Brazilian practitioners borrowing the successful marketing tactics of their northern brothers, particularly in terms of self-promotion through social media marketing. Bearing in mind that even the type of self-promotion originally employed by the Gracie Brothers is at odds with how most Brazilians practice martial arts, this new trend represents a significant cultural shift—and not one for the better. I suspect that Kano would not have been impressed with the current state of the offshoot of his creation; still, the present—like the past—seems to be in the hands of those with the best—or at least the most relentless—marketing tools at their disposal.

As one of the first students of and Black Belts in BJJ in America, Chris Haueter has had a front-row seat for almost the entire history of BJJ's stateside evolution. But someone like Chris is a key piece to this story for another reason: he was also an eye-witness to the second greatest revolution the martial arts world has ever seen.

It is unquestionable that our very understanding of martial arts today owes an enormous debt to Sensei Jigoro Kano. It was Kano who was savvy enough to comprehend the enormous changes that Japan was going through in his time, in terms of both its relation to its traditional past as well as in its somewhat forced and rapid assimilation of Western ideas; it was Kano who shrewdly adapted elements—both technical and cultural—of a fading and frowned-upon "martial" culture in Japan and formed them into the mold set forth by the Japanese

Ministry of Education—a stroke of genius which essentially created the construct within which all other styles of combat around the world could (and would) be practiced by civilians. From Kano onwards martial arts would be a tool not merely for combat but for educating civilians of all walks of life. It could be argued that the introduction of martial arts into Hollywood films helped the public become acquainted with martial arts as a whole, but—at least in technical terms—there was nothing extraordinary happening here. And even when we consider someone like Bruce Lee, a man who was certainly ahead of his time in terms of his understanding of true combat, the role he played in the history of the development of the martial arts pales in comparison to what Royce Gracie did in '93.

Chris Haueter was a backstage witness to this revolution, and I often wonder if he fully comprehends how fortunate he was to be in the right place at the right time. Having such a privileged vantage point, viewing these events as they happened, must have been quite an experience. It is my belief that, for as long as the modern practice of martial arts exists, the events that Chris witnessed (and the Gracie family and Jiu-Jitsu in general) will stand at the center of any conversation about the history of martial arts. Having witnessed these events ourselves from afar, as well as the process of rapid evolution they set forth, both in BJJ and MMA, we would do well to acknowledge our own privileged place in time… and recommit ourselves to working together to play our own part in the history we are living.

— Chris Haueter —

Could you begin by introducing yourself?

I am Chris Haueter, a Jiu-Jitsu Black Belt. I should probably say Brazilian Jiu-Jitsu Black Belt, to separate it from Japanese Jujitsu. I'm an aging Black Belt who was in the right place at the right time, and I discovered this art that's now blown up all over the world.

What got you into Jiu-Jitsu?

I was a 24-year-old former Wrestler, lifelong martial artist when I had my first private in the back of Rorion's garage with Royce Gracie. I was one of those lifelong martial artists who have that same ubiquitous tale I hear all the time: I grew up watching kung-fu movies. When I was young, I was an insecure stuttering kid who was unaware that I even had athletic skills. Due to various circumstances of my childhood and life, I craved power.

What was it like discovering BJJ?

You know it's easy to judge the past, right? And when we're looking at the past, because we know its outcome, we can see how it all went down. And at that time, when I first discovered Brazilian Jiu-Jitsu, then called Gracie Jiu-Jitsu, it really was like magic. It was techniques and moves that were elegant and simple, no duh. No other art could compare, whether it was Wrestling or Judo. They would loosely do what we do. And it was a big surprise. I had found gold, and I knew I had found the martial art that was going to take off. I didn't know how much it would take off, and oddly enough—the first few years pre-UFC, I was a purple belt when UFC 1 happened—it was like you couldn't beg guys to come in and do this thing. You had to prove it. And you look back on the Gracie challenge, it might seem a little bit arrogant or rude. But I can understand why they had to push this challenge thing in one sense, if you want to teach martial arts. Students wanna do stuff that looks flashy. High kicks, high punches and all that stuff. And with jujitsu the grappling arts never looked very flashy. It looked really boring, predictable and readable and so they had to push that aspect of it.

What were the early days of training like?

There were three sleeping bags on the mat with new fresh guys from Brazil there who would show me all the new stuff out of Brazil. There was this explosion of moves and approaches, techniques, new theories. The open guard/closed guard debate was raging. Open guard was not good because it did not add value itself to MMA or real situations.

How did you think Royce's performance would go in UFC 1?

I knew beyond a shadow of a doubt that Royce would win those, as long as he could close the gap and clinch. Because in the olden days the worry was, it was like you had an AR, and the other styles had a musket. If they got you with that one shot, you lost. Once it ended up on the ground, he would win. The odds skyrocketed to 95 percent regardless of the weight class of his opponent. And if you could bridge that gap, you had multiple shots. And so you kind of felt like you could see martial arts as an arms-race. The arms-race period really occurred in the '90s. It's what I call the Rio explosion, akin to the Cambrian explosion on evolutionary biology.

Why do you think it was so hard to sell grappling to the world?

In olden days, real Wrestlers were starving because people wouldn't watch. This is why it evolved into this Wrestling, fake drama thing.

What is the role of mythology in martial arts?

Our human brains want to see drama and a story. We want a story, we want myth. We do it in Jiu-Jitsu all the time. We want to believe that there is some mythical origin of martial arts. Even if part of us knows it's not real, there's part of our brain that wants the story of the origin myth. In martial arts, more than any other physical activity, we create larger-than-life myths about the reality of it. You don't see that in football or in ballet.

Why is there so much partisanship in martial arts?

You know how people in politics will be conservative or liberal?

Ultimately the middle way is balance. And for anything that seems good, you can find a bad part of it. That's true for religion, for politics and ideologies and all that stuff. And in martial arts that same polarizing conflict is happening all the time.

What is the role of the Gracie family in all of this?

Think of the Gracie family as akin to rock 'n' roll. They're the Beatles. And did they invent rock 'n' roll? No, but they certainly blew it up.

What are the origins of BJJ?

I don't even know if I've heard people say that the Gracies never even met Maeda. Who knows? Who cares? The art is still there. The "music" is still there.

*The author and Carlos Gracie Jr. at the IBJJF HQ; From left to right: Jay Cole-
man, Marcelo Siriema, Andre Fernandes, Steve Jeter and author. Watching over
us, Carlos and Helio Gracie; The author gifts Carlos Gracie Jr. a copy of* **Choque**
by Roberto Pedreira.

CARLOS GRACIE, JR.

*"Our goal has remained the same throughout: The global develop-
ment of Jiu-Jitsu until it becomes the most widely practiced martial
art in the world."*

—Carlos Gracie, Jr.
President of the IBJJF and Founder of Gracie Barra

Carlos Gracie, Jr.—or "Carlinhos," as Brazilians call him—is the
President of both the Confederação Brasilieira de Jiu-Jitsu (CBJJ) and
the International Brazilian Jiu-Jitsu Federation (IBJJF), as well as the
leader of Gracie Barra, the largest BJJ team in the world. Though he
is sometimes thought of as only the heir to his father's dynasty, this
view simply misses the extent of the influence he has had in recent
decades: it is my belief that Carlinhos is, in fact, even more important
to the history of BJJ than his father.

This sounds like a stretch until we consider our own tendency to re-
vere those whose lives are crystalized in an idealized past while holding
contempt for the present, its actors, and their accomplishments (a tendency which clouds a pragmatic view of history in the making in defer-
ence to a canonized past). Viewed dispassionately and in sum, the question stands on its merits: In the scope of BJJ's recent history, who has
done more to influence the art than Carlinhos Gracie?

For example:

In private conversation with the man many consider to be the god-father of modern BJJ, Carlinhos explained to me his role in the origin of the team affiliation system decades ago. The BJJ scene in Rio de Janeiro had become territorial, as members of the Gracie family grew into adulthood and began to show ambitions of starting their own schools outside of the original Gracie Academy, and out from under the controlling and territorial eyes of Hélio.

Carlinhos' brothers, Carlson and Rolls Gracie, would splinter off from their uncle's academy and begin brands of their own (with, at one point, two different "teams" training in the same building). Despite their Uncle Hélio's controlling nature (and his not liking the competition), he couldn't stop them. Carlson's charisma, skill, and coaching ability did not necessarily make him a good businessman, though, and when Rolls Gracie left this world prematurely due to a hang gliding accident, it fell to their younger brother and assistant instructor Carlinhos to take over Rolls' gym.[3]

At some point, one of Carlinhos' oldest students, ADCC champion Alexandre "Soca" Carneiro, voiced his desires to open a BJJ school in Rio de Janeiro. However, his loyalty prevented him from parting abruptly and without his teacher's consent. Carlinhos, wisely seeing that he could not justifiably stop a man who held the same passion as him from making a living, made the following suggestion: open your own school, call it Gracie Barra, and make sure it isn't across the street from your former home academy. The affiliation system, so typical of BJJ and so at odds with how things were done in other martial arts styles, had been created.

This simple innovation would have an enormous impact on how BJJ grew in the years that followed, and it alone would have established Carlinhos' standing as a key figure in the history of the Gentle Art. It was, however, only the beginning: in 1994 Carlinhos took one

---

[3] I would come to deeply regret not being able to insert characters such as Rolls and Carlson Gracie into our film, as they were clearly cornerstones of BJJ during a crucial period of its history: a period which we, unfortunately, wouldn't be covering in this film (though maybe in a future one...)

of the most crucial steps in establishing BJJ as a sport outside of Judo: the founding of the CBJJ. Despite the fact that tournaments organized by the Guanabara Federation had existed since 1967, BJJ still lacked the structure it needed to become an international sport. From timed ranks to unified rules to trained and professional referees to competition norms, the CBJJ—and later the IBJJF—would create the platform on which BJJ could and would expand worldwide.

I had witnessed this evolution firsthand, from the now legendary and nostalgic Tijuca Tenis Clube to the Walter Pyramid in Long Beach University where the IBJJF's World Championships are currently held. Their evolution as an organization in many ways facilitated the evolution of BJJ itself: there had always been a sense that BJJ was meant to grow beyond its Brazilian borders, but would have to go through some major organizational changes to achieve it. The IBJJF brought—and embodied—that change.

It is important to take note here of a crucial difference between Judo and BJJ. Judo grew out of a small room in Tokyo, and largely out of the mind of a single man with a broad vision. Kano codified a curriculum, a canon, a moral philosophy, not to mention a competition rule and regulation set, long before his art arrived on the world stage. Judo, in other words, grew outwards from an original small cell. Its Brazilian variant, on the other hand, proliferated widely, rapidly, and organically, to arrive at a critical mass that was simply beyond the structural capacity of whatever de facto organizational tendencies had evolved with it. Simply put, BJJ needed to build (or assert) the sort of structure that Judo had from the outset after having already experienced worldwide growth... and that was no simple task. Even though the CBJJ came into being just one year after the first UFC, it would take over a decade before they could come near the level of consistency, organization, and professionalism so typical of other martial arts organizations. They were still playing catchup to the unprecedented growth the sport had experienced globally.

(It could be argued that all of this came too late, and that the lack of cohesion the sport still experiences today is a side effect of this tardiness. The present-day multiplicity of BJJ events, rulesets, and formats stands in stark contrast to Judo, which has managed to remain surprisingly cohesive and within a single hierarchy over the past century. Still, the present is not the end of the process, and it must be noted that it wasn't until the visionary and business-minded Carlinhos began the CBJJ that the sport began to resemble an organized league; that nowadays the IBJJF World Championship resembles the Olympics; that every year more and more schools adopt the IBJJF's standards; that as a trend these efforts are, by and large, succeeding.)

Before meeting with Carlinhos, I had the opportunity to sit down with Marcelo Siriema, the man who is largely the brains behind the IBJJF's growth. We talked briefly about the evolution of the sport, and the IBJJF's role in it. He told me that early on he approached a friend who organized events in Japan, and asked him what their protocol was for when a competitor was late for the commencement of their division. His Japanese counterpart, he said, seemed confused by the question: in Japan there was no waiting. A competitor who was late to the mat was immediately disqualified.

At this time the biggest BJJ competition in the world, the Mundials, then held at the Tijuca Tenis Clube in Rio, was characteristically run with plenty of reliance on "jeitinho brasileiro" (a term I will loosely translate as the "Brazilian little-way" and which denotes an approach characterized by an expectation that many things will be solved last-minute, and without any real planning). Competitors who were slightly over weight for their division got a pass, there were more relaxed standards for the length and hygiene of gis, divisions rarely started on time, and referees were far less well-trained than they are now. Fundamentally shifting that culture wouldn't be easy, and it wasn't until competitors started being disqualified over things like old belts, dirty gis, and being an ounce over weight that the organizers gained the respect they needed to establish a world-class event, and establish BJJ as a world-class sport. Regardless of what one thinks of IBJJF, it is undeniable that they are the leading force behind BJJ's growth, and we have men like Carlinhos, Marcelo Siriema, and Andre Fernandes to thank for that.

Our team met with Carlinhos at the IBJJF headquarters in Burbank, California. The bridge was made by Siriema and Andre who, admirably very protective of their Professor, sat there for the entirety of the interview (it lasted over four hours), listening. I was excited about this interview for a variety of reasons, not the least of which was the fact that I was getting the chance to spend time with the leading mind behind BJJ. Though I had known Carlinhos for years from various BJJ competitions, this was the first time I was actually sitting and talking with the man who had helped make BJJ more than just a part of the culture of the South Zone in Rio, and more than merely a variant of Judo. In many ways, Carlinhos was the person responsible for helping shape the world from which I make a living today.

Before the interview I got to spend some time discussing BJJ history with Carlinhos, and the role his father played in it, in a conference room on the top floor of IBJJF's headquarters. He was familiar with Geo Omori as a man his father had fought, and he relayed his father's version of events: that Carlos had broken Omori's arm in their first bout. I tried to explain, as humbly and tactfully as possible, that this match was likely fixed, due to the fact that Carlos was acting as Omori's manager in Rio de Janeiro shortly after their bout—something of which Carlinhos was unaware. I tried to do this as respectfully as possible, as I didn't want to introduce an air of hostility and thus ruin the interview, and so I explained to him that these fixed matches were common: that in fact Maeda himself had been deeply involved in them, and that they were necessary to help promote fighting to an audience that was by and large too uneducated about grappling to understand what they were seeing. This knowledge wasn't met with any hostility: rather Carlinhos seemed genuinely surprised... though he also seemed to feel that what I'd told him didn't change the end result, because it didn't. I let the issue stand, though later I presented Carlinhos with a copy of the first volume of *Choque* by Roberto Pedreira. If he wanted to know more, I figured, now he had the resource at his fingertips.

While Steve and Jay were still setting up their equipment, Carlinhos and I went to Whole Foods to grab some lunch and discuss the interview. I'm not sure Carlinho's choice of a wrap was in accord with his father's diet, or if the elder Carlos would have approved, but it was certainly green and looked promising. And, at any rate, it felt like a fitting moment to signal, even in a small way, that for us to chart our own growth we must break with the old ways of our fathers.

— Carlos Gracie, Jr. —

What is your name and how were you introduced to Jiu-Jitsu?

My name is Carlos Gracie, Jr. I am an 8th degree Red-and-White belt. I will be 62 years old next month, in January, 2018. I started doing Jiu-Jitsu when I was a kid. In my family everyone talked about Jiu-Jitsu ever since I was born. I was born surrounded by Jiu-Jitsu. But I think I started to get really interested in being a Jiu-Jitsu instructor after I started pursuing a Jiu-Jitsu career at the age of about 15. So I've been teaching Jiu-Jitsu for around 45 years. Jiu-Jitsu is my life and I want to help people to do Jiu-Jitsu. That's my goal.

What was it like growing up in the Gracie family? Any favorite memories?

Growing up in the Gracie family was really something special for me, you know? A lot of times it creates a lot of pressure, because it requires certain behaviors, certain attitudes, a certain development that you have to show. There's a lot of pressure on everyone that's born in the Gracie family, I believe, but I think it was something special for me. It was very important for me. The best memories I have, being born in the Gracie family, are of my childhood. Living in a house out in the country with approximately thirty kids together, within certain rules, living a different life than most people lived. It was as if we lived in a boarding school within our own family, where we had rules, a special diet, and we were required to follow those norms very seriously. You were punished if you didn't follow the rules. This became deeply rooted in my personality. Because of this memory, I've always believed in doing things for the group, and living as a group, more than living individually.

What was an important moment in your career?

Having trained and competed in Wrestling, my brother Rolls introduced to us Wrestling coaches, through a contact he made here in the United States. The most important of them was Bob Anderson. I think it added a lot to my Jiu-Jitsu and really improved my takedowns and broadened my vision, you know? It taught me control and helped me in developing my Jiu-Jitsu. Certain positions became more efficient. I think Wrestling helped me a lot.

What was the inspiration for the creation of CBJJ/IBJJF?

After becoming a teacher and having my own school, I began analyzing and I saw that athletes from other sports had the chance to travel around the world to compete, while those of us doing Jiu-Jitsu, including myself, had only competed, traveled and left Brazil for a Sambo championship. I came to compete here in California. That was because my brother Rolls acquired contacts, after meeting Bob Anderson, and came to compete in Sambo. So I noticed how great that was and that Jiu-Jitsu practitioners didn't have these kinds of experiences. I began trying to talk to people who were in charge of different organizations. I tried to show them and spread Jiu-Jitsu, not just in little championships in small schools. I noticed that people didn't have a vision for that and they weren't prepared. So, I started creating, doing things... If you want to do something, do it yourself, don't wait around for others. I started putting together an organization, I created an organization, the Barra da Tijuca Jiu-Jitsu Association, and I started organizing championships around there. Later, I created the Brazilian Confederation, and I started organizing national championships. After that, I created the international federation. I started organizing international championships along with the growth of Jiu-

Jitsu in the United States. That opened the door for us to create a championship. So, I created the first Pan American Championship, which was the first international Jiu-Jitsu championship for Jiu-Jitsu. From then on, things took off and we expanded around the world accompanying the growth of Jiu-Jitsu. One thing helped the other. Jiu-Jitsu grew in one place and we would get a championship going, expand Jiu-Jitsu there, and to this day that is what we continue doing. We go to places where Jiu-Jitsu is just getting started and needs some incentive. We organize championships in these places. In a short period of time Jiu-Jitsu takes off and starts developing there.

What was the reaction after the first Jiu-Jitsu Brazilian Nationals?

The first Brazilian Jiu-Jitsu championship in most cases had a very positive reaction. It showed us it was possible to do something of that magnitude and people loved it and it turned into something very important for Jiu-Jitsu. It gave us a Brazilian championship title. A title that we didn't have until then. People came from all over Brazil, mostly from Rio de Janeiro. But there were also academies from other parts of Brazil. It was an excellent championship in small gyms that were packed and the response was strong. Of course, it caused some jealousy among those who were directing Jiu-Jitsu at the time and those who were leading its development, you know? The truth is we took it to a higher level with the championships. It caused the organization to stand out. It was unprecedented and created a strong repercussion, respect, and credibility for having organized that. So I think it was of huge importance within this process of developing Jiu-Jitsu.

What is the goal of CBJJ/IBJJF?

The growth of the organizations in the Brazilian Confederation and the IBJJF. Our goal was always just one, you know? The global development of Jiu-Jitsu and turning Jiu-Jitsu into the most widely practiced martial art sport in the world. That's our goal and that's what we intend to achieve. And we continue pursuing that same goal. Our objective is to make it the most widely practiced martial art sport in the world. That is our challenge, that's our objective, and I believe we can do it for several reasons. We are on the right path. Even in the beginning our goal was the same. We are now farther ahead, we are getting there, closer than ever. This goal will continue to be ours until we achieve it. Jiu-Jitsu came to conquer the world as the most practiced martial art in the world.

What are the best memories of your father?

The best memories that I have of my father were living with him for practically forty years. I had more and more great memories through my learning in life. I place more value on that, how important he was and how much he taught me in life. Back then I learned, but I didn't know the motives he had for teaching me. I also don't know if he was preparing me for something special, but I can see that his teachings, the conversations we had, were things that were passed on from a Master to a student. I see my father as a Master. Nowadays in Jiu-Jitsu when a person receives a Black-and-Red belt, he gets the title of a Master. I have this title of Master for having this Red-and-White belt, but Master—the only one I recognize as a Master, a true Master—was my father. Although he didn't teach me practical Jiu-Jitsu lessons, he was a Master in terms of life. He taught me, he directed me, so that I could reach the maximum potential possible, make achievements and to follow this important path in my life. So I see him as a true Master. I believe a Master has wisdom, and this person has to be a person with a vision, capable of teaching. A Master for me is a person with a vision that really has meaning and that can improve humanity. I believe that Masters are individuals who have come to make a difference in the world. A person may be a Master in martial arts; he can teach you to fight and perform techniques, but it is completely different when there is a Master who makes a difference and makes humanity better. I think all of us Masters, and I include myself in that, are tools that work for the greater good of humanity. We are tools. And maybe one day, one of us may become something that can teach others so that they can make that difference in the world. So I see my father as one of them. I see very few Masters in the world. I see Gandhi as a Master, a great Master in the world. And I see other great Masters, some of them religious. I don't want to mention all of them. I mention Gandhi for having achieved things, for being able to change a large part of humanity, to do things, to influence people without having to start wars or use weapons, for his peace and influence. I see my father—that my father became something like that. Something that could—in a small, a much smaller situation, much smaller in size—[do] something comparable, at the end of his life. Like Gandhi's ideas. Turning Jiu-Jitsu into a tool that could improve the world, help the world live in peace and to bring humans together, to create friendship among people through martial arts. Changing the lives of millions of people in the world. I believe that is the objective he set out to achieve and wanted to pass on to us. I think all of us within our capacity, each one of us, consciously or unconsciously, do our work in the world this way. The people who stayed with Jiu-Jitsu, who can teach Jiu-Jitsu, are always improving people, improving them within their capacity, within their knowledge, and changing humanity a little. Within the academies there is a brotherhood, there's no racism, no difference in status. Inside [the academy] everyone is a brother, everyone is a friend. A rich person trains with a poor person, and the friend of the poor respects the poor for having a higher ranking than him. So it builds a very strong link of friendship between people, which can only happen in an academy, on the mat. This gradually improves the world, it builds friendship. It improves humanity little by little. With Jiu-Jitsu we can do our work to improve humanity. I believe my father had this vision. Even though he had many children, he had everyone training Jiu-Jitsu. I think he foresaw this and prepared us to [follow] this path.

What is your opinion of your father's biography written by Reila, your sister?

My sister's book makes out my father to be a religious guy. I see him more as a person that was a mystic. Not just a religious person, he didn't talk much about religion. He spoke about life, missions, and our subconscious capacities to improve ourselves internally, to perfect ourselves on the inside, and that life didn't end at death. He would say that death didn't exist, that we were here to spend time to learn, to do our work. Everything happens for a reason. So he saw things that each one of us had and our mission in life. And he saw that clearly and showed us that there was a spiritual force that drives all of us on, it drives humanity to evolve. Those people had the duty and influence to do their best and to set the best example. One important thing he did for me once. When I was a kid, 17 or 18, I hung out with some guys. I was from Teresopolis, and I moved to Rio de Janeiro, to Copacabana. One time, a maid from the house saw this group smoking marijuana and I was there. She went to my house and said that Carlinhos was there and they were smoking marijuana. So he called me over one day to talk and said, "My son, you have a mission in life to be a Jiu-Jitsu teacher and you will be a Jiu-Jitsu teacher, a person that influences people, and your actions will be very important in the influence you have over other people. You were not called to be an ordinary person that can do anything he wants. People are watching you and looking at you as an example. So, everything you do in life, will have repercussion in other people, it will influence other people. You are responsible for the development of others. So you have to be very careful with the things you do in life and what you're doing, to be a positive influence and not a negative influence." That really touched me in such a way that I never smoked marijuana again in my life, I don't drink, and I have tried to do things right, and I have tried to keep my life to be an example for my students, and I have spoken out about these things. I have never had anything to hide. I have shared my experiences, my errors and my successes. And that... Instead of arguing with me, and raising his voice, he just showed me the truth. He gave me a book to read at that time, "Mental Magic." That book taught me a lot about what we are about. That book "Mental Magic" showed me will power and imagination. Will power and imagination must work together. If you have lots of imagination, but you don't have the will power to achieve it, you're just a dreamer. If you have will power, but you don't have a dream, you're a guy who does things but has nothing to achieve. So, the combination of the two, to dream and to achieve with will power, is our human potential. He said that marijuana numbs your neurons and left you dreaming a lot and you would lose your will power and that people who smoked marijuana would lose, having only their dreams and would not achieve anything. That really terrified me and that book really showed me that. From then on, I began to dream and to accomplish the things I did. Thanks to his teachings and those things, everything I have accomplished to-day has been done with imagination and will power working together. So, I see this... This was the counsel of a Master, something that changed, he saw the possibilities that I could achieve. He didn't pro-hibit anything or argue with me. He just showed me the right path. I would either be prepared to accept it and follow it or I wouldn't be, and I wouldn't do it. I try to do these things, I have always tried to do these things with my students, to show this to them. Some have ac-cepted and followed it, while others didn't show any trust and weren't prepared to learn it and kept on doing what they wanted to do. Those that accepted it have had their accomplishments and were able to achieve their dreams and the imaginations they wanted to do. Others fell behind and have not achieved anything.

What is the importance your father had for Jiu-Jitsu?

My father's importance in Jiu-Jitsu around the world, I think that without him Jiu-Jitsu would have died and today all of us would be doing Judo, and Jiu-Jitsu would not exist. I believe the organization of Judo in my vision, which was to substitute Jiu-Jitsu, would have been successful and Jiu-Jitsu would have died as it died in Japan be-cause the old generation, there was no need, Jiu-Jitsu was a defense necessity for the Japanese people. When the war changed and became the Bhutan War, there was no longer this need. Therefore, Judo took over and those that knew Jiu-Jitsu died and didn't pass it on, because there was no longer a need. So Japanese Jiu-Jitsu died and just became Judo and other martial arts there. Today, Japanese Jiu-Jitsu had to come to Brazil, learn the Jiu-Jitsu they had forgotten, go back to Japan and restart the whole project that they themselves ended for one reason or another. Nobody know what it was.

What was the relationship between Carlos and Hélio like?

The relationship between Carlos and Hélio was the relationship of a father and son. Hélio considered my father to be his father. My father was the one who raised Hélio. When Hélio came to live with my father he was 11 years old. His father was sick, but when my grandfather passed away, Hélio was 11 and my father became his father. The older brothers stayed together. My father's other older brothers may have seen my father as a brother, but Hélio was seen as son. In fact, one brother who was very close to my father, George, died. Oswaldo died and George followed his path. He didn't agree much with my father's guidelines. Gastão also followed his path, went to São Paulo, set up his life there and Hélio continued living and being raised by my father, following the guidelines and objectives that were to be made and Hélio was a fundamental part in the continuation of my father's project that my father set out to do.

What was the biggest name in the Gracie family of all time?

To talk about the biggest name of all time in the Gracie family in MMA and Jiu-Jitsu is something very difficult, because each one had their importance at their particular time. If that guy at that time had failed, it may have affected the development of Jiu-Jitsu. I believe they all had a crucial importance in this point. I don't think you could take one name and speak of just one. It would be very difficult and it wouldn't be fair to all of them.

What was your relationship with your brother Carlson like?

My relationship with my brother Carlson during my life was always a relationship... I always liked Carlson because Carlson was a very calm guy. And the personal relationship with him in the house... I really liked Carlson's companionship. I had a lot of fun with Carlson and messed around with Carlson. We would laugh and he would mess with us... We played together. Carlson was a player. We played poker and he liked to go play poker. He joked around. He messed around with everyone. He liked messing with every one of us. We would laugh and mess with him, too. It was a relationship a lot like that, really cool, until the day I got to the point where I was his rival on the mat, at the academy. I took over the academy from Rolls. It turned into a competition potential academy, which started making him worry because he wanted to be the man. He had huge rivalry with my Uncle Hélio. My Uncle Hélio used to say that his Jiu-Jitsu was a rough Jiu-Jitsu. And he wanted to prove that my students can beat your students. All of that was fought out in the championships. And who were the Gracie Academy students at that time? They were us, the Gracie Academy only had private students, and there were no groups or classes. Carlson was a team of competitors. Carlson created competition Jiu-Jitsu, Jiu-Jitsu in groups, which never existed, just private classes. Carlson was the first guy who taught in groups in the Gracie family. So who at the championships, who would fight against Carlson's students? We did... The students at the Gracie Academy were the ones who fought against his students. On a personal side, he would go to the house, he was always there, had lunch there, dinner there, spent lots of time there, and on the weekends he would go to Teresopolis, on holidays he would go to Teresopolis. He would mess around with us, "Hey, my student is going to get you, this guy's going to get you, whatever..." I didn't get along very well with his students because he would mess with me so much and I would get upset with those guys. And he would say he was going to squash us or something. So I trained with everything I had to try and beat Carlson's students, and I would make fun of him. I saw Carlson as a teacher who was a rival set on preparing others to get me. That was my perspective and the perspective of others. That was Rickson's, Royler's,

Crolin's, Rilion's, Rorion's, and Relson's opinion as well. Everyone! That Carlson's students were our rivals. And he would argue with Uncle Hélio about that. He would prepare his students to beat Rickson, that kind of thing... Until one day, in the beginning it was that kind of rivalry. Later, I became a teacher. I set up my own academy. Rolls was Carlson's rival in this war of students. They opened an academy together, then they split up, and later had a huge rivalry. Rolls' academy was the one that fought head-to-head with Carlson's. Rolls died and I took over. Carlson used to win the championships because his academy was older and he had more Black Belts. But my academy and his, we would go on fighting, fighting, and fighting, and when it came to brown belt, it would be farther apart. In the blue and purple belt it was really pretty equal. When it came to brown, he started winning... He would win because he had more brown belts than I had. Among the Black Belts, he was far ahead. But, in time, my academy started having more brown and Black Belts and it started equaling and equaling, and eventually Gracie Barra began beating his academy. We took the lead in the championships. This started a big rivalry with him and with me, you know? Not personal but between academies. After that, I became president of the confederation, I took on the status of a leader, an organizer of Jiu-Jitsu. But, at the same time, I never wanted to go over their heads. I always considered them older Masters and teachers than me. I always respected them, but I had a bigger vision of how Jiu-Jitsu should be run and how the championships should have respect, not allowing the teachers' influence, wanting to offer opinions in fight decisions. I started giving credit to the judges, and started to create rules and I had to face them, because they wanted to go above these rules and wanted to do those kinds of thing, because they wanted to do this kind of thing. So, this created a certain rivalry among everyone there.

What was your relationship with your brother Rolls like?

My relationship with Rolls... There was the Gracie Academy and the teachers at the Gracie Academy were my Uncle Hélio, who would show up once in a while—he had a few students—and Rolls and Rorion, were the two teachers. There were two mats and each of them taught classes. I trained there, helped them, I lived in Uncle Hélio's house with them, so I stayed around helping. I helped Rolls, and I helped Rorion. I learned Jiu-Jitsu helping them. Actually, what I felt with Rolls... I had a better relationship, I felt that Rolls was a guy that loved me more. I had more confidence in Rolls' love. I believe in Rolls more than in Rorion and the others there. I noticed that Rolls was a guy who had a better relationship... I stayed with him, and I started feeling more influence from him and my questions about Jiu-Jitsu... I chose him to be my teacher. It's like the dog who chooses its owner, and I chose him to be my leader, the guy I wanted to follow, the guy I admired more, who was the person I believed in. I saw in him the qualities to be my leader, and I began following his leadership.

What did Hélio think of Rolls cross-training with other styles?

Uncle Hélio was totally against it. Rolls, in my opinion, was considered the first athlete within Jiu-Jitsu. We were Jiu-Jitsu practitioners. Uncle Hélio was the one who thought that nobody needed to work out and do other outside sports. All you had to do was just train all day and you get good. That was his mentality. My brother, train. All day, train as much as you can, spend all day on the mat, and nobody needed to do anything else. That was his vision... He trained for hours and hours and hours. But when Jiu-Jitsu became more of a sport Jiu-Jitsu, with time and points, a certain time to fight, to be an athlete was an advantage, because sometimes the guy couldn't beat you, he couldn't submit you in ten minutes, but he could force his game in ten minutes and beat you... He made it to the end and won the fight. To be able to handle it and not let his physical dominance take over, you would have to have physical conditioning and be strong as well. Not just technique. You have to have explosion, muscle mass, and go with a more offensive Jiu-Jitsu. And Rolls was the first within Jiu-Jitsu to realize that and want that. He wasn't content with getting a guy in his category and feeling weaker than that guy. He would say,

71

"My brother, why am I weaker than him? I can have more technique or I can be stronger, too. I can have a better offensive game than his. Why do I have to accept that?" He didn't accept any superiority that someone could have over him in a fight. So he started looking to prepare even better to be an athlete.

What can you tell us about Georges Mehdi?

Georges Mehdi... What I know about Georges Mehdi was that he came from Europe as a Judoka. I don't know if he came as a Judoka and learned Jiu-Jitsu... went to Japan and later returned to Brazil or if he had gone to Japan before entering the Gracie Academy. He had been to Japan, because he came good in Judo. He was a good Judoka. People said that Georges Mehdi was a Judo instructor. He had a great knowledge of throws. He came to the Gracie Academy and started training there. I don't know if he had money to pay or what it was... He stayed there as a janitor at the Gracie Academy. He worked at the Gracie Academy. He lived there... He lived at my uncle's house. And he trained at the Gracie Academy every day as a sparring partner, all day. In fact, Waldemar Santana was also a janitor. These guys that were janitors spent the whole day at the academy [and] got better because they spent the whole day training. They weren't students. They were there the whole day learning. Georges Mehdi got good at Jiu-Jitsu. One day, I don't know why, for some reason he left and opened up his own academy. But he set up a Judo academy. Maybe Uncle Hélio didn't let him open a Jiu-Jitsu academy. Or Uncle Hélio didn't like him for leaving the academy. I don't know what that relationship was like. I just know that Uncle Hélio didn't like Georges Mehdi very much and didn't speak very highly of Georges Mehdi. I looked at Georges Mehdi as a rival because he had a Judo academy at that time. And we all thought Judo tried to hide Jiu-Jitsu, that Judo wanted to take the place of Jiu-Jitsu, and we saw... There was this mentality. But I know that Georges Mehdi, he became very famous within Judo. I know that... not because of his throws in Judo, but because he would finish any Judoka that went there. In the land of the blind, the guy with one eye is king. He spent many years at the Gracie Academy, set up his academy and all the Judo guys wanted to learn a little about what he called ne-waza. He didn't say the name Jiu-Jitsu. They would go there to learn from Georges Mehdi. And he would get the guys from the Brazilian national team, the new guys, and finish off everyone. Everyone was so impressed. Georges Mehdi, Georges Mehdi, Georges, Mehdi. Because he finished off those Judo guys there, and nobody knew what was what. He would go there and he knew Judo well. The guys just knocked them down easily. So, in training there, he started winning the Brazilian championships and Georges Mehdi became very famous in Brazil as a Judoka, which was the guy who everyone went to prepare to learn a little on the ground with Georges Mehdi. So this is the story that I have of Georges Mehdi.

What was the relationship between your father and his brothers like?

My father's relationship with his brothers, as far as I know and my father told me: Oswaldo was very close to my father. I think he was the closest brother, the second brother. He was always with my father there. George and Gastão were pretty much like that, but Oswaldo was very close and Uncle Hélio was very small. Oswaldo died from typhus at that time. My father, when he set up his academy, went to Rio de Janeiro, São Paulo, and his brothers came with him. Hélio was small. My father's relationship with Hélio was father to son. The other brothers lived with my father, but I think over time they decided to follow their own paths and Hélio stayed with my father. Uncle Hélio's relationship with the other brothers was no big deal. He trusted my father. The two stayed together and the others grew far apart. Uncle George began teaching classes all over Brazil, but he was an adventurer. He would go to one place, then stay there, set up an academy, teach some people, then to another and wouldn't put down roots anywhere. My father and my uncle were set on Rio de Janeiro. They opened an academy, set up fights and students, and made Jiu-Jitsu grow in Rio de Janeiro. Uncle George kept moving, moving, and mov-

ing, and wouldn't stay in any one place, got older, began losing inter-est, returned to Rio. He had no academy, no structure. He stayed there and got back in touch with my father. He began visiting us. That was the time that I had contact with him. I thought he was interesting, I really liked to be with him. A nice guy. He liked my dad and respected him a lot. Uncle Hélio would say that, but there was a certain cour-tesy among them, you know? He didn't relax much. He wasn't too re-laxed, and with my father he was more that way. My father was more relaxed with him. Until the day he dies, Uncle Gastão went to São Paulo and had two kids. His children had an academy, but all of a sudden, they gave up and set up a shooting school. They didn't follow Jiu-Jitsu with an objective. The ones who followed Jiu-Jitsu with an objective were those who were influenced by my father and pursued that dynasty. The others stopped. Their children, my cousins, who were their children, started and trained Jiu-Jitsu with me a little, but later disappeared, took other professions, and lost interest in Jiu-Jit-su. So, the truth for that part of the family: Uncle George's son doesn't train Jiu-Jitsu. Uncle Gastão's son doesn't train Jiu-Jitsu nowadays, Gastãozinho doesn't train Jiu-Jitsu either. Gastãozinho doesn't train, so if Jiu-Jitsu were to depend on them to continue for-ward, it would be over, it would have died. Dad, Uncle Hélio, and this generation who came later, who were influenced by my dad's ideal-ism, were the ones who kept Jiu-Jitsu alive. They were the ones who made Jiu-Jitsu expand around the world.

Tell us about the evolution of positions like the triangle, arm-bar and Ezequiel.

These three positions, the triangle, the arm-lock, and the arm in-side the leg. These three techniques had a huge influence on Jiu-Jitsu. That is: the triangle, arm-lock, holding the leg with your hand on the leg, and the Ezequiel, the choke, had a big influence in the technical development of Jiu-Jitsu, after they came around, right? That's be-cause they were techniques that were very efficient and put the old style in danger, Jiu-Jitsu passing defense. So I practically started learning the triangle, I remember it very well, I was a purple belt. Up until purple belt nobody did a triangle in Jiu-Jitsu.

When did you see a triangle for the first time?

In the '80s. This was in the '80s. But I really can't explain it too well. No, I was a purple belt. I earned my Black Belt in 1976. I got my Black Belt in 1976. This was in the early '70s. In the '70s, early '70s, I was a purple belt. So actually this came from Professor Osvaldo Alves. He was a guy from the Brazilian national Judo team, who began learning Jiu-Jitsu from my brother Reyson and Antonio de Padua, who had an academy in Copacabana. He demonstrated this triangle technique, which came from Kosen Jiu-Jitsu, which I watched later on in a video of older Jiu-Jitsu fighters in Japan. I saw them putting on a triangle in this tape. I thought, "Wow, this was back in their day, why wasn't it ever done in Jiu-Jitsu?" I mean, some techniques, even if the Japanese knew about them, maybe the Japanese hadn't taught it to foreigners. Maybe Koma didn't teach that technique to my father. He hid some techniques. Koma himself probably hid some techniques from my father, because he wasn't a legitimate Japanese. And if this was part of the Kosen Judo, in the Jiu-Jitsu Kosen, Koma should have known that.

Who was Ezequiel?

Ezequiel was a Judoka from the Brazilian national team who showed up to train one day at my academy, Gracie Barra Academy in the Barra da Tijuca, taken by one of our students there. "Hey, there's a Judoka that wants to train here!" He just came by to train. And when he began training, he passed the guard, he took his head like this, as if he were going to move in the guard, which nobody did in Jiu-Jitsu. A guy takes hold of his head in the guard and you end up going for his back. But he held on, he was a really strong guy, he held on there, and pushed your leg out with his hand and then the guy would go to his hand to defend. He would take hold of your head like this and when he went with his hand to defend he came over here and choked you, which was called Ezequiel, from in the guard. Then, the guy would take that choke and his reaction would be to back off. When you moved away, you choked him even more, because he was moving away. And he was really strong. The Judokas always had that quality, because the standup training in Judo is a constant action force training and it makes you really strong. The Judokas who immigrated to Jiu-Jitsu, all of them who immigrated to Jiu-Jitsu were great Jiu-Jitsu competitors due to their physical conditioning, you know? Including Jacaré, Barbosinha, and others who had good careers within Jiu-Jitsu, because their physical conditioning was sometimes superior to those who trained Jiu-Jitsu. And this Ezequiel was a strong guy. He got some guys there, and it was like, What is that? Hey, did you see that Ezequiel? Since it didn't have a name, it didn't have anything, just Ezequiel who was doing it, we would say where's Ezequiel? Who did that Ezequiel? Ezequiel? They gave it the name of the choke, Ezequiel, because Ezequiel was the one doing it. Ezequiel didn't invent this. This came with the thing that came from there... He learned it there. But he was the one who did it. Just like the De la Riva Guard. The De la Riva guard where you put your foot down below, behind the thigh. This is older than my grandmother. You see Kosen Judo doing that. I do that, and I have done since I was a blue belt. But De la Riva took this guard and created this style of guard as his guard. And since he was the guy who went to the championship, he used that kind of guard that nobody could pass, it was efficient. Did you see that De la Riva Guard? They gave it the name, De la Riva Guard because De la Riva used it efficiently. That doesn't mean he invented it. He was just the guy who used it very well and developed a game on that kind of guard, that kind of thing.

How was the opening of gyms by Carlson and Rolls?

Speaking of the rivalry that existed between the family and competition. What happened is, Carlson had the main academy, which was the Gracie Academy founded by my father and run by Uncle Hélio.

Everyone, all the Gracies taught classes there and worked there. Actually my Uncle Hélio worked there, and they worked for my Uncle Hélio. My father was my uncle's partner but he didn't butt in there. The one who got involved and spoke up was my Uncle Hélio. He was the manager of the academy. Everyone was under the direction of Professor Hélio Gracie there. Carlson left, took off, I don't know, had an argument there, left and opened his own academy. Reilson left. Reilson was the first to leave and opened his own business. Later Carlson left and went to Copacabana. He set up his academy. His academy opened and started teaching in groups. Carlson was the first Gracie to teach in groups in an academy. He was the one who created this methodology to teach in groups. After a few years, Rolls left and he and Carlson had a conversation. Let's go into a partnership, open a large academy, and set up a better business, join me. Rolls wanted his independence as well and to get away from the direction there. To vent his own aspirations. He moved and became Carlson's partner there in Copacabana to open a larger academy. But after six months working together, they had a business argument over money, business, and couldn't agree to be able to work together. They said, "Brother, we are in this academy here, right now, what we can do is this, let's divide. I have my students and you have yours. Monday, Wednesday, and Friday, I will teach at this main dojo, and Tuesday, Thursday you teach at the one below, and I use it for private classes. Tuesday, Thursday, and Saturday you teach and we switch. We had just one front desk. One front desk for the two of us. People showed up, "Do you want to train? Sure! With Rolls or Carlson?" You had to choose. You went to this one or the other one. And that's how things went. Actually, they went to the championship. In the past, everyone came out together to fight the others. We would... It was like, the people from the city came who were Rorion's students. That was Uncle Hélio's academy and Rorion was the head guy, we got together with Rolls' students and joined with Carlson's students... We had an eliminatory to represent the Gracie Academy against any other academy. But, the argument, the fighting in the eliminatory was so big that we said, "OK brother, you go in with your students, and I will go in with mine."

They separated. So, Rolls' students and Rorion's students at the academy... We would put together an eliminatory and enter together, and Carlson was separate. We joined up with Carlson's students. To the time when... The time came when Rolls and Rorion had a misunderstanding. Rorion go in for yourself. I am going in for myself, and Carlson for himself. Anyway, there was the Gracie Academy, Gracie Jiu-Jitsu Club, which was Rolls, and the Carlson Gracie Academy. Each one representing one. So the Gracie family divided up in the championship. Each one with his group. Actually, the biggest fight was between the three of us. Right? The championship always went to the final and these three academies going after each other as finalists. And the rivalry was huge. Carlson wanted his students to beat everyone else. Rolls wouldn't take that, so my student is better than your student, and at home the argument, all the fighting went on to a match at the competition. And the students all had their minds made up, for one not to lose, no way brother. You've got to win! It was a really personal thing. This created a real rivalry among the students. So we all trained in that same building. Carlson with his students, but there wasn't much talking to Carlson's students. Not much conversation at all, enemies. Hey, hey, how are you? Hey, Hi... Some talked and others didn't. They knew they were going to face off in the championship. They respected each other, but not much talk at all. No training together, no chatting. Separate groups. That's how things worked at the time.

Why was the story of George Gracie not told?

Uncle George's story may not have been told well, since he distanced himself from the circle that began developing Jiu-Jitsu, which was dad and Uncle Hélio. Uncle George stayed out of it. People talked about Uncle George. Dad talked about him sometimes, my mother spoke to people about Uncle George. Many said that Uncle George's fighting was more exciting than Uncle Hélio's. But nobody got into Uncle George much, maybe because Uncle George, in my father and Uncle Hélio's mind, had been a bad example for not fol-

lowing and not staying there following the directions that dad had determined. Uncle George was a little rebellious. He was a guy who you just couldn't control too much. So I think that's why people didn't mention him, so as not to give publicity to a rebel. They wanted everyone disciplined, following the discipline there. If they had publicized a rebel, it would have created more rebels. Maybe that's the reason why nobody talked much about Uncle George.

What was George Gracie like?

Uncle George, wasn't a guy that would stay in one place too long. He was an adventurer. He wanted to go someplace, do something, go on to another place, and then to another. So he spent a lot of time around the countryside of Brazil, putting together fights, opening academies, teaching... He left there and went on to another place. He didn't stay rooted in any one place and didn't set up a certain school where he had followers and created a lineage. He went all over disseminating, planting seeds, and people went along. There were some important people, like Octavio de Almeida in São Paulo, Nahum out in the countryside of São Paulo. I had contact with Octávio de Almeida Jr. and Professor Nahum—Master Nahum, I had more contact with him—but with others, I didn't have much contact. He was in Minas, created a few students there, some teachers in Minas Gerais. Later I had a few contacts like that. But Uncle George was just that way. He was very well known across the countryside of Brazil But he was a little distant from us in the city, so sometimes we wouldn't hear much about him. I just heard more about Uncle George when later on I put the Brazilian Jiu-Jitsu Confederation together, and I started to relate to Jiu-Jitsu all over Brazil. Then I picked up more of Uncle George's lineage... Guys would come along and say, "No, I was George's student. I am a student of a student of George." So I started realizing George's importance in the countryside and in the development of Brazil, Jiu-Jitsu in Brazil around the countryside of Brazil. Up until then, I didn't know much about it.

Was he important for Jiu-Jitsu in Brazil?

I had more contact with the lineages that Uncle George left in Jiu-Jitsu after creating the Brazilian Jiu-Jitsu Confederation, and I started relating with teachers outside Rio de Janeiro. Teachers who had schools in Brazil, the countryside of Brazil, came and said they were a student of Uncle George. So that's when I began to realize the importance Uncle George had on the development of Jiu-Jitsu in Brazil, throughout the countryside of Brazil. He was in many places that none of us had been before. We didn't know that Jiu-Jitsu was there. Uncle George went through those places disseminating Jiu-Jitsu, opening schools, creating disciples, and I noticed the importance he had in the development of Jiu-Jitsu as well.

What was the beginning of your father's teaching career like?

One of his students—I don't know his name, I just know this guy invited my father to go [teach the police in Minas Gerais]. I can't remember his name. So he went there to teach Jiu-Jitsu there in Minas Gerais to the police. He got into a confrontation with a policeman who didn't believe... These guys laughed when my father got there, frightened. My father said, "I arrived there scared, it looked like I was yellow with tuberculosis. This big strong gringo, a police teacher, looked at me and said, 'Hey! Who is this clown? What is he going to teach here?' Then they put me out there to fight this guy. So, I had to fight him and nobody believed anything. I started fighting this guy, put my foot in his stomach, and got him in an arm-lock. I took his arm and he let out a scream. Everybody there got scared. So from then on, they started believing in me. I stayed in Minas, and after Minas, I went to São Paulo. I opened an academy in São Paulo, and to impress I put it in the newspaper. Then there was this fight with Geo Omori, and I ended up moving to Rio de Janeiro and got settled in Rio de Janeiro." This is pretty much a synthesis of his trajectory when he left Belém. More or less that's what he told me.

What would you have changed in terms of CBJJ and IBJJF?

Look, in terms of the CBJJ and the IBJJF, I wouldn't have changed anything because it was all done just as it should have been done at the time. There wasn't any other way to do it. Jiu-Jitsu was a feudal environment. So there wasn't any other way to do it. I don't see any other way and the IBJJF also couldn't have been done any other way, and I think I would do it all again the same. I would have kept it all.

Why do you think that self-defense has disappeared from Jiu-Jitsu?

Look, this is something they talk a lot about nowadays, and I disagree with this way of thinking today. I see Jiu-Jitsu as one thing. So, here's what happened... The first Jiu-Jitsu organization created in the world was created by my uncle. It was the Jiu-Jitsu Confederation of the State of Guanabara. He created it along with a student and created the rules for sport Jiu-Jitsu. I fought in championships, Rorion, Rolls, everyone who fought in Jiu-Jitsu championships fought under these rules of sport Jiu-Jitsu, the Jiu-Jitsu Federation of the State of Guanabara. Later it became the Jiu-Jitsu Federation of the State of Rio de Janeiro because there was no more state of Guanabara and it turned into the state of Rio de Janeiro. After that it became the confederation and later, IBJJF, right? Personal defense Jiu-Jitsu... It was a thirty-six class Jiu-Jitsu. It was the kind of Jiu-Jitsu that when a guy, no experience, that knows nothing about Jiu-Jitsu, he learns Jiu-Jitsu positions just to get into the world of Jiu-Jitsu. Just to give him a connection with the world of Jiu-Jitsu. So he learns holds, striking defense, back defense grips, mount escape, back escape, how to mount, how to execute these basic things in Jiu-Jitsu. This takes thirty-six lessons. After that, he goes into the technical learning field, which is two guys who know Jiu-Jitsu fighting each other. That's when the Jiu-Jitsu development begins. You have learned to mount, right? But now the guy is not going to let you mount. How are you going to handle defense from the mount to mount? In these thirty-six classes *there's none of that. It teaches you to mount, to escape from below, land on all fours, to sweep, two or three sweeps, and to choke. It gives you basic Jiu-Jitsu to be able to start learning to train. After these thirty-six classes you are ready to understand Jiu-Jitsu in order to train Jiu-Jitsu. But you are a beginner. If you get a guy that's graduated higher than you in Jiu-Jitsu there's nothing you can do to him, and he can get you in all these things. So from then on you start learning Jiu-Jitsu, which is the Jiu-Jitsu of those who know how to fight against those who know how to fight. The guy doesn't let you pass his guard. How are you going to handle passing his guard to pass the guard? Then it starts, you do this, do that. A chess match. As it gets more difficult, you have to learn more. Each time you have to do these things. Those who show up today and say, "No, because Jiu-Jitsu tactics are leaving out the personal defense Jiu-Jitsu!" What personal defense am I leaving out? A-B-C? Maybe! But, what about you, having a Jiu-Jitsu Black Belt, a Jiu-Jitsu world champion, do you really think someone off the street without experience is going to give you a choke you can't get out of? Even if you have never taken the little class on choke defense? Do you think someone in the UFC will tap on a simple choke? It's just that those guys have never taken a choke defense class in their lives, but they know how to fight and they have the means to fight. What kind of guy if he takes thirty-six class hours of personal defense, is going to tap with a guy like that? Because the guy already knows everything. These thirty-six classes are just for you to defend yourself against someone with no experience, who doesn't know how to fight at all, get you in a choke in the street and you get out of the simple choke. If you get a Judoka's movement and he gives you a Judoka, and you as a Black Belt, you will have a hard time getting out with all the classes of personal defense you have. So if you don't have specific training, have a trained neck, have all your skills trained, all your movements to change from one position to another, accustomed to being squeezed to get out, you will never get out of a Judoka's hold in your life. Because I have practical experience and I know that. Because I have seen this happen since I first started training Jiu-Jitsu. So when a guy talks about sport Jiu-*

Jitsu... These guys are fighting there... Damn, fighting Jiu-Jitsu and tying people up in knots. The guys says, "Hey, he's not prepared to fight, to defend himself on the streets, he can't protect himself on the streets. He is not prepared to fight in the UFC because he's going to take on guys at his level who are fighting." But if they prepare for a year or two they are able to fight, because they will have to learn, not personal defense A-B-C, because this personal defense A-B-C, is not going to change them much at all. What's going to change them is the standup, takedown, strike defense from guys who are specialists and a high level of training. So when someone comes along to tell me this Jiu-Jitsu they're doing is sport Jiu-Jitsu: no way, my brother, it's highly competitive Jiu-Jitsu, high level, and these guys are prepared for anything. Just not prepared to go to the UFC, but they are prepared to defend themselves on the street against anyone, except a high level MMA professional. There you have to be a high level MMA professional that knows Jiu-Jitsu, which is normally everyone that is also a Black Belt in Jiu-Jitsu. So, for me, it's just a lot of talk.

What is the role your family played in resisting Judo's expansion?

I believe the Gracie family vision to hold up the Jiu-Jitsu flag was because of what Koma must have said to my father, "Judo no! Jiu-Jitsu!" My father used to say that. Koma said, "Judo no! Jiu-Jitsu!" And my father stayed with Jiu-Jitsu. It was offered to my Uncle Hélio and my father to change the name of the school from Jiu-Jitsu to Judo, which is what happened in Brazil. Jiu-Jitsu schools, which at the time were Japanese, which were called Jiu-Jitsu, changed to Judo. Including Onu's school. Every Jiu-Jitsu school in Brazil, which were ninety-nine percent Japanese, changed over to the -do system, Judo. The only one that stayed there was my father's academy that said no, because Koma told me not to change, so why would I change? That's where they wanted to challenge us. All of my Uncle Hélio's Jiu-Jitsu fights with the Japanese were an attempt to discourage and say that Judo was better and they began representing Judo. At that point, I would tie or lose, until Kimura came, and Kimura said that he would consider the fight lost if he didn't win in two minutes. The entire Maracanãzinho jumped up when the two minutes were up and turned into fourteen minutes. So, it really was a victory for Jiu-Jitsu, my uncle's fight with Kimura, because Kimura said that if anyone outside Japan could last more than two minutes with him, he would call it his loss. And this guy, Kimura, weighing 90-some kilos fought a guy with 62 kilos, the time came, he fought for fourteen minutes. One round and fourteen more minutes into the next round. This was the climax of Jiu-Jitsu. It's what strengthened it. From then on, it was prohibited for any Japanese to fight against a Gracie. Leave the Gracies alone, brother. Each time they fight, they're getting more fame. So, there were no more fights against the Japanese. Kimura was the last one. There never was another fight, Japanese against Jiu-Jitsu. Never spoken of again. It was over! Don't mess with those guys there. So we kept going!

Has your father ever said that he was promoted to Black Belt by Count Koma?

I don't remember. That never... I never questioned that. Never was because, actually my father told me, he never trained with anyone else. He just told me about his story with Koma. My father's story was that he was promoted to Black Belt by Koma... I never heard any other story or similar questioning. My father just connected with his teacher and that was Koma. Having trained there, leaving there as Koma's student. I don't think I ever asked, never saw, and I don't think I ever heard any other subject other than that.

What is the importance of the UFC and CBJJ for the growth of Jiu-Jitsu?

This development in '93 by Royce having won the UFC, having made the Brazilian Jiu-Jitsu Confederation, I believe that gave international recognition. Royce broke down the international barrier for the world's interest in Brazilian Jiu-Jitsu. I believe that Royce's victory there had this aspect. The world came to know Jiu-Jitsu. The confederation got organized to offer the world a Jiu-Jitsu in which we could show Jiu-Jitsu techniques to the world and prepare people to go into the world, people with names, rankings, in order to go out into the world representing and opening Jiu-Jitsu schools, developing Jiu-Jitsu around the world. So there were two important points in vision. If my father had any idea about how this would happen. My father saw this, he would say, "Your subconscious knows everything." He was a guy who through his meditation, would always leave his conscious and go into his subconscious. This happened many times in his life. He talked to me about that. I think that this... maybe consciously he didn't have, but subconsciously he knew that this thing would end up happening. That this was the way. This would be it.

BRAZIL

Grandmaster Armando Restani before the interview; Master Marcial Serrano and Grandmaster Armando Restani; Steve and Fabio collect B-Roll in the Liberdade neighborhood in São Paulo.

ARMANDO RESTANI

"What I would really like is for [practitioners] to create a life not of victories or titles... but of becoming a better person through sport."
—Grandmaster Armando Restani, student of Gastão Gracie, Jr.

I am of the firm belief that as a parent, friend, coach, training partner, or citizen, the way to convey your loving support is with constructive criticism. Telling people what they want to hear doesn't make you a good parent, coach, friend, or citizen: it makes you a cheerleader. With that said, I have always tried to have this sort of loving relationship with everyone and everything in my life... which doesn't always go well. Many people prefer the "feel good" approach, and my "constructive criticism" method has, admittedly, created many problems in my personal life. Nonetheless, I don't believe I'm incorrect. As I see it, life is about achievement, improvement, and performance, and these require constant critical reflection. Surround yourself with people who tell you what you want to hear, and you are unlikely to solve your issues and get past your hang-ups.

The same holds true for the places we care about. Never have I encountered a place with such happy, creative, and energetic people as those in Brazil. Yet these same citizens seem largely complacent with the fact that their country remains, in many ways, a colonial society festering with corruption. Brazil was the last country in the Americas to end slavery; it has never gone through any significant land-reform; its Republic and "Revolutions" are vertical (top-down) movements led by traditional colonial elites and their descendants. Poverty is everywhere, and corruption is so rampant and ingrained in the culture that one wonders how the country even functions. Add to these a cultural preference for "jeitinho brasileiro" and "malan-dragem" (a word that lacks a direct equivalent in English, but which might be translated as "a cunning way of dealing with people and the world"), and it's not hard to see how being Brazilian can be frustrating at times—particularly when you stop and consider the ways in which this giant of a country remains in the shadow of its older brother to the north: free to do as it is told, but not free to do as they have done.

Being born in the U.S. and growing up in Brazil, with a Brazilian mother and an American father, I had a unique seat on the fifty-yard line of this geopolitical quagmire. I grew up in the midst of debates like, "Who invented the airplane? Was it the Wright Brothers or San-tos Dumont?" (The answer depends on what you mean by "airplane," though this simple fact hasn't stopped many people from falling down this rabbit hole, having never even agreed on what they are arguing about... a common theme in many arguments, including those about the history we were trying to tell.)

I have learned to love Brazil and Brazilians deeply, and if I am critical of them it is only in the most caring of ways, and only because I feel that they take their immense potential for granted. Nevertheless, I am happy that I spent my formative years in Brazil (and just as glad that I have the privilege to now live in the U.S.): happy that I learned "malandragem" and "jeitinho brasileiro" (though now I struggle to beat those things out of me), attempted soccer (with mediocre results) and the Brazilian womanizing game (with less than mediocre results); above all, and given the direction that life took me, I am happy that my experience helped me to understand BJJ as a worldwide cultural phenomenon.

Now, though, traveling back to the country in which I was raised, one question kept running through my head: Why the "B" in "BJJ"?

Or, to put it another way: What is the nature of this strange marriage between Japan and Brazil?

It has always been fascinating to me how quickly the Japanese warmed to Brazil. I cannot think of cultures that are more distinct in their manners. As a college professor would always tell me in our private discussions, "Toda generalização é burra" ("All generalizations are dumb"), but it doesn't take a sociologist to notice that there are some major differences between how the average Brazilian and the average Japanese behave on a daily basis. Still, somehow the Japanese seem to fit in with Brazil. Maybe it's because the two countries are so different, or maybe it's because the emigres had few choices: the 1924 Exclusion Act forbade any Asian from immigrating to the U.S. Whatever the original reason, the two cultural are now deeply enmeshed: Brazil is home not only to the biggest Japanese population outside of Japan, but also to cities where Japanese is spoken as a second language and where newspapers are written entirely in Japanese.[4]

Interestingly, my childhood best friend and neighbor was named William Maeda (not, to my knowledge, directly related to the famed Maeda of our film) and his family went from humble immigrant beginnings to becoming one of the largest tomato producers in the world in the span of only one generation (to give you a sense of their work ethic). In other words, the Japanese impacted Brazil in more ways than just bringing martial arts to the land of Samba, Bossa Nova, Carnaval, and soccer, and this impact can be felt across the country.

We wanted to explore this cultural fusion: the relationship between the Japanese immigration and the Brazilian culture is, after all, at the very heart of how BJJ came to be. Fabio would prove to be instrumental in this: not only because he knew all the relevant characters,

---

[4] As a side note, and to give you a scope of the Japanese presence in Brazil: after Japan surrendered to the Allies during World War II, many ultra-nationalists Japanese living in Brazil and belonging to an organization called "Shindo Renmei" were in absolute denial of the Japanese surrender. Their logic was that since the Emperor was god himself he could not, by definition, lose. What they were reading and hearing, then, was clearly war propaganda. The Shindo Renmei went on a killing spree of anyone, Brazilian or Japanese, who would dare write or say anything about Japan having lost the war. This went on for months. And, in a move perhaps emblematic of their deep loyalty to their homeland, they did this killing with their Katana swords.

but also because he went far beyond his intended role of historical consultant and became our production manager in Brazil. He organized flights, booked hotels and car rentals, and coordinated all of the interviews. We had decided to bring Tufy along as a second consultant; we needed to interview him anyway, so we decided that he would be part of the São Paulo and Rio de Janeiro portions of our trip.

This would be no leisurely vacation: we had *a lot* of ground to cover. Jay and Steve flew down on Saturday to join Fabio and Marcial and interview Armando Restani, a Black Belt under Gastão Gracie, Jr. (Carlos' younger brother, and senior to Hélio) and today a Red Belt. I was set to arrive on Sunday: I regretted not being there for our first interview, but I was happy to hear that it went well and that we were able to capture some footage of one of the last students of Gastão Gracie, Jr. still living today.

A Black Belt since 1968, Restani had developed a reputation in São Paulo for still being active in BJJ competitions well into his 70s. (Among other things, I wished I'd had the opportunity to sit down with him and ask him what kept him going, since at 38 my body was constantly demanding a break from the mats. I suspect, however, that I already knew the answer: longevity in BJJ has little to do with recovery methods or training methodology; it simply requires more of that same ingredient from which champions are made.)

That same day, Fabio took Steve and Jay to gather some B-roll in the Bairro da Liberdade, the traditional Japanese neighborhood in São Paulo. I didn't realize how important the collection of this B-Roll would be later into the film, nor how fun it was to watch Steve collect the footage: to me, it felt like a crash-course in photography and filmmaking.

Still, good B-Roll wouldn't do much to help us tell the history. The tale of BJJ isn't a simple one: it is full of ambition, commitment, rivalry, jealousy, courage, and passion, and we wanted to leave out nothing significant. Men like Restani, Wriedt, Barreto, and Carnivalle were our link to that past, and their vital role gave the whole production an added sense of urgency: these Masters were all approaching their 80s and some, their 90s, and I couldn't stop thinking about how these

Masters might not be around tomorrow, and we might miss out on the opportunity to hear what they had to say. These men, as I saw it, were living BJJ treasures, and we needed to extract as much information from them as we could before it was too late. We needed to learn as much as possible and get the full story out on how BJJ developed, instead of letting time create even more questions for the future. And, even if we failed to accomplish our mission, we felt at the very least that these pioneers needed to be honored, and their stories recorded for the ages. History is quick to forget, and we wanted to make sure a testament remained to remind the younger generation of practitioners of the shoulders upon which they stood.

— Armando Restani —

What is your name and how long have you trained Jiu-Jitsu?

My name is Armando Restani, I'm 75 years old, and I've been practicing Jiu-Jitsu since 1960. I started in athletics. I competed in collegiate championships encouraged by the college's physical education teacher. I excelled in tournaments and got a taste for competitions. Later I began to train Boxing with Master Valdemar Zumbano and then weightlifting. I started to train [Jiu-Jitsu] in 1960 at the age of 18 at Gracie Academy of Gastão Gracie Filho. At that time, there were no Jiu-Jitsu competitions [in São Paulo]. There was only the Federation of the State of Rio de Janeiro, presided over by Master Hélio Gracie.

How did Jiu-Jitsu Tournaments begin in São Paulo?

The championships in the state of São Paulo began in the middle of the '70s through the Master Otávio de Almeida Senior, who was the teacher of Master Moises Muradi. Master Moises Muradi made official the Jiu-Jitsu Federation of the State of São Paulo that began with official championships in the '90s. I started participating in the championships in 1993. Then came the Brazilian, Pan- American, and World Championships.

How was your beginning in the sport?

I started to train Jiu-Jitsu because at that time I had a girlfriend, who ended up being the mother of my son. She was very beautiful and I wanted her to do self- defense because she was always harassed on the streets. She said, "I will practice, but as long as you come with me." So we started together. The Master thought that I had the ability to become a fighter and teacher, and invited me to take a specialization course and specialize in teaching at his academy.

How were classes under Gastão Gracie, Jr.?

Classes at the Gastão Gracie Filho gym were individual or in groups of a maximum of three students. I was doing it with my girlfriend, Miriam. He lent the kimonos to us and we did not need to bring our own. We wore the kimonos and the next class they would already be washed and ironed.

Where was his academy?

The academy of Gastão Gracie Filho was in São Paulo, in the Jardim Europa neighborhood, on the Avenida Cidade Jardim.

What was the methodology like?

First you had a basic course of thirty-six self-defense classes. Choke escapes were taught, necktie from the back escape, wrist grab escape, leg-locks, arm-bar, front and back defense against knife and revolver, punch and kick defense, et cetera.

What were competitions like during that period?

There were no sports competitions between the academies [in São Paulo. They began to be conceptualized by the Master Otavio de Almeida Senior. Even the diplomas of the championships were made by the Paulista Boxing Federation, because the Federation of Jiu-Jit-su did not still have a legal recognition. An example is the certificate of champion of the Master Moisés Muradi at the time with 14 years was of the [Paulista] Boxing Federation signed by the Master Otavio de Almeida.

Who promoted you to Black Belt?

In 1968 I was awarded a Black Belt in Jiu-Jitsu by Gastão Gracie Neto.

When did you begin teaching?

I started giving Jiu-Jitsu classes as soon as I awarded a Black Belt, in 1968.

Were there other teachers?

There was Professor Hiroshi Nogami, the Master Gastão Gracie Neto, when I joined the team.

Could you tell us more about the methodology at the time?

I followed Gracie's methodology. When the student entered the gym he started with the basic system of personal defense that was the chokes, neck-ties, et cetera.

What was Gastão like as a person?

Master Gastão Gracie Filho was a very pleasant person, friendly with everyone, and he was always a very simple person.

How was Gastão Gracie Neto [the Third]?

Master Gastão Gracie Neto followed in his father's footsteps and had the same teaching principles. He began teaching classes for television artists. At the time there was a show on TV Record that was an icon in Brazilian television, and we made appearances on this program.

What was the difference between Jiu-Jitsu and Judo at the time?

The difference basically was that Judo was about takedowns and immobilizations. Jiu-Jitsu trained for takedowns and the fight on the ground. Immobilization did not win the fight. We understood that when the opponent was immobilized he could still continue fighting, so we continued until we applied a choke or an arm-bar.

Hélio and Carlos Gracie, did they make it to São Paulo to train at Gastão's academy during your time?

Not during my time, no. They did some demonstrations and fights. Hélio fought, but not at the academy, no.

Did Gracie family members used to come to São Paulo?

Eventually yes. Not the brothers, but the younger generation. Carley, Rorion, and Rolls came to visit the academy in São Paulo.

Until when did you compete in sport Jiu-Jitsu?

I competed in sport Jiu-Jitsu until recently. I stopped [in 2015], a year and a half ago, because I had to have a prosthesis in the hip, and now I am waiting for medical authorization to fight again. That is my greatest desire.

Do you still teach classes?

I continue to teach, but not specifically Jiu-Jitsu, because as a weightlifter, I show the movements and the person performs. Jiu-Jitsu *specifically has become more difficult, because I would have to do demonstrations and today I cannot do a hip escape, for example.*

Your students now, are they old, do they still visit you?

Older students keep in touch as friends, but I do not mentor them in terms of fighting. The students I support are weightlifters. They live in condos that have fitness rooms. I arrive and communicate through the intercom and I proceed to advise on the movements that must be made with the weightlifting equipment.

How many Black Belts did you promote?

I promoted several Black Belts. However, later I left the Gracie Academy. A long time ago. After that I did not promote anyone else. From that time I have some names in my memory, but it is not something recent.

In all these years of practice, what are your best memories in Jiu-Jitsu?

The memories I have of Jiu-Jitsu are countless, such as the warmth from the fans, the support I had and still have of Master Moisés Muradi and Master Raul Vieira e Souza, and the vibration. All this is priceless. I achieved my success thanks to them, because in fact I only managed to get where I arrived today through the support that I had from Master Moises and Master Raul, and this I can't deny. I make a point of always affirming it.

Why do you think that most people know Hélio Gracie but not the other brothers?

The importance of Hélio Gracie is greatly emphasized, because he was a fighter and appeared in the newspapers challenging people, fighting and projecting much more than the brothers. His brother

Carlos, for example, who is the eldest of the family, and who even taught him and the other brothers the art of Jiu-Jitsu, does not appear so much because of it. The spotlight was directed more at Hélio, because he fought and beat much heavier and stronger opponents. He got publicity, which made him look like he was the only one, but that was not the case. There was a whole team behind him.

What is the importance of Gastão Gracie, Jr. in your opinion?

The importance of Gastão Gracie Filho was that he was dedicated to teaching. His motto was this: "Not seeking to create fighters, seeking to create men." Even the method that had been printed in the academy pamphlets was: "The Gracie Method educates for life."

Do you have any memory of some difficult moment in Jiu-Jitsu?

In Jiu-Jitsu, of course, all fights are difficult and none are easy. But instead of discouraging me, it stimulated me. Because when you are overcome by someone, you will train more to be able to surpass that opponent who beat you. So although defeat is a discouragement for many, for me was an incentive for improvement. By the time I got to face that fighter again, I could beat him. Not only in Jiu-Jitsu, but throughout my sporting life. The trophies and medals I achieved were not through discouragement, but through the encouragement to get to the place where I am today.

Would you have done anything different within your life inside Jiu-Jitsu?

Nothing different. I would try to do better, but I would not do anything different, because Jiu-Jitsu and the sport in general is my life. I think if there is reincarnation, I'm coming back as a sportsman.

What message would you like to leave students and practitioners today?

Well, what I would really like is for them to become a better person through sport, not for them to chase a life of victories or titles. What I really wanted to do was to make sport a way for the student to have a life, not only of victories or titles as I have, but rather a way of being better through sport.

Upper left: Master Marcial Serrano before the interview; Upper right: From left to right, Marcial Serrano, Oswaldo Carnivalle, and the author; Lower: top row, left to right: sound guy [unknown], Tufy, Jay, Steve; bottom row, left to right: Fabio, Marcial, and the author.

MARCIAL SERRANO

"Today, at the age of 73, I feel almost accomplished as a person, as a family man. I am fulfilled. As a Jiu-Jitsu lover, I'm almost done. I will only be completely fulfilled when... this rich history of Jiu-Jitsu is reborn as a phoenix that has risen from its ashes."

—Grandmaster Marcial Serrano, author

The next morning we met up with Marcial Serrano at the hotel where we were all staying. The hotel manager was kind enough to allow us to use their conference room on the upper floor, where we would have privacy for the whole day. The energy in the room was great and while the researchers introduced themselves to one another and talked BJJ history, Steven and Jay got down to the technical work of setting up lights and cameras and figuring out their shots. There was an overall air of optimism and excitement in the room, a sense that this was the beginning of a turning point: that after our film was released the history of BJJ would be understood in a completely new light. We had the team and the means to accomplish this: now it was up to us to make it a reality.

Marcial is not only the most published author in terms of BJJ history, but he is also a 7th degree Coral Belt. He is one of many researchers in Brazil who have dedicated much of their free time to studying BJJ history and retelling it to the world. Relentless in his research and publishing of BJJ history, his rhetoric is more anti-Gracie than most. And, although I agreed with him on many of his conclusions, some I felt the need to be more conservative about. Marcial was quick to remind people that he was a Judo and Jiu-Jitsu student at heart, and not an academic. He denied the label of "historian" and insisted that he was a "pesquisador" (researcher) instead. He had spent the last several years researching and writing voraciously, eager to tell the story of his Master, Oswaldo Carnivalle, a student of George Gracie (and someone we would also interview during this trip). His enthusiasm and dedication were inspiring: regardless of what anyone thinks of him or his writings, he has made a commitment to search out the true roots of BJJ. The direct way in which he writes differs dramatically from how academics are expected to write and, though I understand the need for rigorous standards of editing, I don't feel that this deviation discredits Marcial in the least. He had spent thousands of hours researching and writing and, even before our film, played an important role in correcting BJJ history in the country where it all began. As I have already written, it was his book (alongside Pedreira and Tufy's works) which first inspired the film we were working on.

Personally, I have always liked him. Even in advanced age, Marcial had a youthful energy about him: he joked, laughed, and blended in with just about anyone easily. It was as if his spirit was still that of a 20-year-old, full of optimism and hope. I can't help but wonder if he is optimistic by nature, or if it is something that time and experience have taught him. I wish I had asked him that day. Instead I focused on the task at hand, asking questions about George Gracie and Maeda.

Strangely enough, the official narrative which Marcial has spent so much time questioning never took root in Brazil as it did in the English-speaking world. This is perhaps understandable in that it was in the U.S., not Brazil, that the origin story of BJJ would be told unremittingly. Still, it is worth noting that I have never seen pictures of Maeda, Carlos, and Hélio Gracie on the wall of any gym in Brazil. Brazilians either don't care or they don't believe the official narrative. The mythological proportions that stories of Rickson Gracie would reach in the U.S. are generally met with skepticism in Brazil. Unbeknownst to most English-speaking peoples, no Brazilian up until very recently has ever referred to BJJ as "Jiu-Jitsu Brasileiro," but invariably as "Jiu-Jitsu." (I am reminded of a trip I took to Thailand, and the moment when I asked the waiter for "Thai-Tea." He replied sarcastically and coldly: "You mean tea?") It was only after the North American BJJ boom of the mid-'90s that Brazilians began associating the terms "Brazilian" and "Jiu-Jitsu." In fact, most Brazilians (myself included) had never even heard of "Jiu-Jitsu" at all growing up. Taekwondo, Karate, Kung-Fu, and Judo were all highly popular, but Jiu-Jitsu was almost an alien word to us. (Perhaps part of this has to do with geography: I grew up in São Paulo, and BJJ has always been more popular in Rio de Janeiro and Manaus.) It wasn't until Royce Gracie became a sensation in the U.S. that this would change. This is interesting when you consider the general assumption that BJJ is as popular in Brazil as Thai Boxing is in Thailand, or Judo is in Japan. This is simply not the case: the BJJ boom took place in Brazil at more or less the same time as it did around the world. The difference was that Brazil had more Black Belts to teach it. There were many who would disappear from the mats during the silent decades (that is, silent for BJJ) of the '60s, '70s and '80s. Mostly for financial reasons, these practitioners would go on to begin new careers completely outside of BJJ practice, only to return when the booming demand produced the opportunity. As if nothing had changed, these disciples of the "Gentle Art" began anew their martial arts journey after years—and in some cases, decades—of hiatus (some of these old practitioners even came back requesting belt-stripes for all the years they lost pursuing other professions). Such is the way it goes: economic concerns outrank idealism and passion in so much of our lives, and our martial arts practice, unfortunately, does not escape this.

— Marcial Serrano —

Could you introduce yourself and talk about your beginning in martial arts?

My name is Marcial Serrano, I'm from the city of São Paulo, capital. I'm 73 years old. I was born on November 22, 1944. My first contact with fighting was with Judo, which was then fashionable for kids to practice: Judo [for the sons] and ballet [for the] daughters. So, like every boy at the age, I went to practice a fighting sport and practiced with one of the Judo icons, the Master Messias Rodarte in the district of Penha.

Being a Master in both, could you talk about the differences between Judo and BJJ?

The difference is that in Judo you projected using the seoi-nage, for example, to finish or made the immobilization, and in Jiu-Jitsu, no. You made the transition to the floor. On the floor you ended up finishing with chokes or locks. So, it was more dynamic and I do not say it was better but more appropriate for the season, because it was self-defense.

Could you tell us a little bit about the differences between BJJ in Rio and São Paulo?

Rio de Janeiro was already three years ahead of São Paulo. The first championships began in 1973 [in São Paulo]. There was even an interesting case in one newspaper. We had a great Master here whose name was Pedro Hemetério. He had the nickname "Okra," because he was slippery, he struggled a lot and went to the opponents back with ease, so he was called "Okra." He wanted to enter the championship. He introduced the students as being his students from the company Vigor. Vigor is a large dairy company in São Paulo. He presented from eighteen to twenty students. The interesting thing is that I was entering the DEF [Departamento de Educação Física] and I saw this large number of young people getting off the bus, all very sunburned. Then we knew they were from Rio and heard a commotion. Robson [Gracie] was present. He heard a general uproar because Master Octavio de Almeida, Master Orlando Saraiva, and Master Carnivalle barred the Cariocas because they were not students of Vigor. There was a challenge between Rio de Janeiro and São Paulo. I remember that Rio de Janeiro won eight fights out of eighteen, I think. São Paulo tied eight and won two. At that time, I asked Master Carnivalle why this difference. He told me that he estimated that in Rio de Janeiro there were about seven hundred practitioners in condition to enter a championship, and in São Paulo there were a maximum of two hundred between the academies of Saraiva, Octavio de Almeida, and Carnivalle. That's why they have a greater number of quality athletes, and because they are three years ahead in sports competitions.

What do you think is happening to BJJ today?

I recognize the evolution of BJJ in the ground game. I usually use a catch phrase that is: "Let's go back to the origins without losing the acquired evolution." Today I usually show this on Facebook because I try to value the current moment that is real. I'm not nostalgic.

What is the importance of this evolution?

How important is that? The UFC and these fights have brought

more people to the academies. Today the practitioners are true ath-
letes. They are elite players. Fighters you start the fight standing,
which I think is wonderful. They do not pull guard at the beginning of
the fight.

What we cannot lose is what we had in traditional Jiu-Jitsu, which
is the self defense and the standing part, and not only dedicate our-
selves to sport BJJ.

What is the importance of the UFC for BJJ?

If we did not have the UFC, I do not know if Jiu-Jitsu would have
survived.

Could you tell us a little about the history of Japanese immigra-
tion to Brazil?

In 1910 we have a record of Jiu-Jitsu being taught in the public
force of the state of São Paulo, current Military Police. It was a group
of French Masters who left because of World War I in 1914. Some
lieutenants continued the training. Prior to 1910 we had Japanese
immigration arriving in Brazil. The first colony arrived in 1908 by the
port of Santos and many of these immigrants practiced in Japan the
Jiu-Jitsu. This Jiu-Jitsu ended up being taught in the interior of São
Paulo where there was arable land. In 1914 and 1915 we have the
first records of Mitsuyo Maeda, Count Koma, arriving in Brazil and
performing shows in theaters. In 1924, in the second Japanese immi-
gration to Brazil until 1928, we had the Masters we call Masters of
the notorious knowledge, who was Ono in 1928, the Ono brothers. It
was Takeo Yano in 1934, in 1936 the Master Ryuzo Ogawa. We had
Geo Omori at the end of 1928 for the beginning of 1929. They were
really who brought modern Jiu-Jitsu to Brazil.

Can you tell us a little bit about Jacyntho Ferro and Donato
Pires dos Reis?

We have heard of it and there are also many reports recorded in the newspapers of the day about Jacyntho Ferro. Jacyntho Ferro was a sprinter, was an athlete. There are records that from 1921 he was already a teacher of Jiu-Jitsu linked to Mitsuyo Maeda, the Count Koma. At the same time we also see Donato Pires dos Reis. We have a record of a 1921 report where Count Koma presents a group of students in the show. Among these students are Oscar Gracie and Donato Pires dos Reis as students of Jacyntho Ferro, who would be a student of Count Koma. There is a question whether Maeda was their direct teacher. The doubt I have and not from other researchers is whether they were not Satake's students and Maeda used them for his shows. Donato Pires dos Reis was the teacher for three months in the special police of Minas Gerais with Carlos Gracie. And then in 1930 he opened his first gym in Rio de Janeiro, and took Carlos Gracie and also took George Gracie.

What can you tell us about Maeda, Count Koma?

Count Koma was featured in our history of Jiu-Jitsu as the fighter of the thousand fights. Invincible. What is perceived for those practicing the art is that he did show-fights because they were in theaters for the society of the time. The lay public imagined that those fights were real. For us art-savvy, there is no possibility that a Kodokan Master like Count Koma will challenge someone from the audience and not win in the first minute or win in the first second of the fight. So the fights were demo shows. Propagation of art. It was a show-art.

What can you teach us about the relationship between Carlos Gracie and Maeda?

Further investigating the connection between Carlos Gracie and Mitsuyo Maeda, Count Koma. Carlos claims in 1929 when he was attempting a position as the self-defense instructor of the São Paulo police he gives the first names of the troupe of Maeda and binds himself to Count Koma. So, we know the story that Carlos Gracie was a student of Count Koma, but that now deeply searching today, with the ease of internet searches of the old newspapers of the time that are digitized in the digital library of the National Library of Rio de Janeiro, we have more than seven hundred thousand digitized items on all subjects. And the story of Count Koma and his students is very rich and we cannot find anything to prove [that Carlos trained with him]. We did not find any photo, no comments that justify [that story]. In contrast, we have two statements of 1934 from Donato Pires dos Reis, who was [Carlos'] teacher for three months in the police of Belo Horizonte in Minas Gerais. Due to Carlos' professional fight with another Wrestler, Donato made a comment not liking the presentation of the way Carlos was exposing Jiu-Jitsu. He says that Carlos had no right to expose Master Mitsuyo Maeda that way. Soon after, in the same year, in the newspaper O Globo *also appears an article of Donato Pires speaking of Carlos Gracie, and he says that Carlos Gracie did not meet Count Koma, that he himself had been a student of Count Koma, and shows the reporter a paper, a document. Except that there is no photographic record of this document. We do not know if it is a certificate or if it is only a letter stating that he had been a student [of Maeda]. And yet he says he is the only one. In other reports, it appears that he would not be a direct student of Count Koma, but of Jacyntho Ferro, who was a student of Count Koma. There is something to be deeply researched, some document to find if Donato was actually a direct pupil of Count Koma, or indirectly through Jacyntho Ferro. Now he makes it very clear that Carlos Gracie did not meet Count Koma.*

Did Carlos reply to these accusations?

Carlos always responded, because he had direct contact mainly in the newspaper A Noite, *he always responded to everything. He did not answer [to this]. What did he do [instead]? He joined with the brothers and assaulted Donato Pires dos Reis. This report he made in* O Globo *is due to the aggression he suffered at the hotel in Catete, in Rio de Janeiro. And Carlos never defended himself. So it's hard to say based solely on a verbal statement, with no concrete evidence, no linkage that actually proves [Carlos' story]. It was only orally told by [Carlos] and challenged by the one who was his teacher, who was Donato Pires dos Reis.*

Your final thoughts about BJJ and its history Professor?

Today, at the age of 73, I feel almost accomplished as a person, as a family man. I am fulfilled. As a Jiu-Jitsu lover, I'm almost done. I will only be completely fulfilled when I see this manmade art, the greatest system of self-defense and sport ever created by man, with its story recounted truthfully, clearly. And it's the moment for that. Other researchers, other historians will take this story forward, and I am sure that within a very short time this rich history of Jiu-Jitsu will be reborn as a phoenix that has risen from its ashes.

Dr. José Tufy Cairus; From left to right: Tufy, Fabio, Shiguero Yamasaki, Mario Yamasaki, and Jay Coleman

JOSÉ TUFY CAIRUS

"[D]espite all the troubles, the financial troubles of the Gracies, that kind of... financial decline, they kept intact this elitist mindset. This idea of being superior. Of whatever they do, they think they are and could do better than others. And in Brazil especially, you have to come to know a bit about the Brazilian culture. [The Gracies] are white, they are scions or descents of this aristocratic family from the 19th century."

—*Dr. José Tufy Cairus, Judo Black Belt and historian*

Tufy would be our next interviewee. From the first time I wrote to him and we began speaking, it was obvious that we had a lot in common: our conversation ranged over everything from Jiu-Jitsu to world history to Brazilian and international politics, and I felt that I had found not only a historical consultant but also a lifelong friend. Tufy wrote his Ph.D. dissertation on the history of the Gracie family and its relation to BJJ as a vehicle for their "patrician ethos" (my favorite phrase to come up during the entire production), dirtying his hands in the old archives prior to the digitizing of the Brazilian National Library.

Tufy was raised in Rio de Janeiro, not too far from the Gracie Academy. His father was a well-known Judo instructor with many ties to the local BJJ community, and Tufy knew personally many of the characters that came up in our conversations. He had plenty of stories about growing up in the South Zone in Rio, the arena for the original "pit-boys" (as the BJJ troublemakers became known in Brazil). Further, as a professional historian (one of only two we would be interviewing, the other being Danieli Bolelli), he could speak with more authority than anyone else we interviewed on events that didn't directly pertain to BJJ but that impacted its existence in one way or another, such as the Russo-Japanese War, the influx of Japanese immigrants to Brazil, and the rubber boom of the Amazon.

I have wondered, though I've never actually asked him, what his motivation was for writing his Ph.D. on BJJ and the Gracie family. I've wondered if it had to do with his Judo background, and a desire to confirm what famed Brazilian Judoka Georges Mehdi always claimed: that the art being practiced in Brazil was, in fact, "all Judo." Maybe it had something to do with the fact that he also came from a family of martial artists. I suspect, however, that the true reason lies elsewhere: that, like with so many of these amateur investigators who have dedicated so much of their free time to this pursuit (with various degrees of effort and subsequent success), he is driven by a love for the historical object—something I can understand and respect.

Tufy was aware that there had been a renaissance of research after he finished his Ph.D. in 2012; he felt however that, for the most part, it mainly served to augment what he had already written. For myself, I loved seeing how world events (the Shogun's unwillingly opening of Japanese ports to the U.S. in 1854, the Russo-Japanese War, Japanese immigration and the rubber boom in the Amazon) completed the story we were trying to tell. It is easy to fall into the trap of reducing any history down and only focusing on the "main" characters, simplifying the story to its most obvious actions and actors. This approach ignores the often equally important world events that provide context for, and often directly influence, these protagonists and their actions. What we were learning was something that is obvious to any keen observer of history: it is impossible to separate the story of BJJ's split from Judo from the world events that created the environment in which its protagonists acted.

Our interview with Tufy enriched my understanding and made me realize even more than I had before that the history of BJJ goes beyond martial arts: that, really, its history is intrinsically woven into the history of globalization in the 20th century. We should be thankful that there are so many like Tufy out there who have dedicated so much of their time to this study—especially at a time when very few people were interested in learning any of this, and the official narrative was held as gospel truth. We need to remind ourselves that there is no great reward for studying history and adding to any narrative, and that when any deviation or change is proposed it is often to the detriment of the one who challenges the established narrative.

No great risk, perhaps, but neither are there great returns. Writing history is immense work and an effort that seldom grants proportionate gain and profitability. Thus the motivation must lie elsewhere, closer to the passions that give wind to action through writing. But the honest observer must remind himself or herself that passions run both ways, towards and from the orbit of the historical object. In this sense, writing history becomes either an act of justice or an act of self-advancement, with all shades in between.

— Dr. José Tufy Cairus —

Can you introduce yourself?

My name is José Tufy Cairus, and I was born and raised in Rio de Janeiro. My father was a martial artist as well. He was like a pioneer in Kodokan Judo in Brazil. Kind of first generation of Brazilians [to] learn directly from the Japanese in São Paulo's Kodokan Judo. So basically I was born and raised around martial arts. I'm a Kodokan Judo Black Belt. Academically I hold a B.A. in History, an M.A. in African History, and a Ph.D. in Latin American History from York University, Toronto, Canada.

Who was Sada Miyako?

So Sada Miyako arrived in Brazil in 1908 and was hired by the Brazilian Navy to teach the cadets and the Navy Jiu-Jitsu. Also, I found records for Sada Miyako teaching the Army cadets in the south of Brazil. And he stayed for some time, teaching in the Brazilian military, until a very interesting passage where he fought in a prize fight, a challenge, public challenge with a local Capoeira in Brazil. And in the fight the Capoeira beat Sada Miyako.

How did Brazilians perceive Jiu-Jitsu back then?

Brazilians start to pay more attention to Japan after the Russo-Japanese War. It's not by coincidence that they, the Brazilian government, finally decide to start to encourage the Japanese immigration to Brazil. That starts in 1908, so three years after the Russo-Japanese War. First of all, we have to understand that martial arts, Japanese martial arts, is something unknown in the West. So the idea is of Japanese, these very exotic people, performing a very exotic something right? A stunt, let's say. And I think they relate this exotic performance to the circus, and also the Japanese at the time they used to perform in the circus in the Western world.

Why were these Japanese migrating to the Amazon?

Well, Japanese immigration to Brazil started back in 1908, right? But especially in São Paulo. Why São Paulo? Because São Paulo is the powerhouse in the economy in Brazil. So usually immigrants— Japanese were not the only ones—felt compelled to immigrate to São Paulo. There was more opportunity, more jobs, because São Paulo is the center of the Brazilian economy. To go to the Amazon, to settle in the Amazon... the problem is the weather, the jungle, and other issues. [It's] not easy for immigrants to settle in the Amazon. The Japanese were the only ones, the only immigrants, foreign immigrants, to settle in the Amazon, attracted by this booming economy based on the export of natural rubber.

What was Maeda's relationship with the Kodokan after he left Japan?

Maeda was somehow estranged with the Kodokan Judo headquarters in Tokyo. Especially because Maeda's career in prize fighting wasn't something that was encouraged by Jigoro Kano, the creator of Kodokan Judo. And Maeda wasn't the only one estranged from Kodokan Judo headquarters. Other Japanese martial artists traveling in the West who performed in prize fighting also became estranged from the ideal of Jigoro Kano. Jigoro Kano used to say that the only honorable means of making money for a Kodokan Judo instructor is teaching. Prize fighting was not something considered honorable by Jigoro Kano. So this particular issue of the timing of the ranking promotion, the belt promotion, of Maeda and other Japanese having stopped as long as they were performing in prize fighting. Around the time of Maeda performing in Central America, in Mexico and Cuba, the belt promotion stopped. Also, Maeda stopped using the term Judo. From that point onwards, [he] only used the term Jiu-Jitsu. You have to understand the Japanese mind. He was being punished by Kodokan headquarters. Maeda stopped using the term Judo in prize fighting to preserve the reputation of his school, and his Master, Jigoro Kano. From that point onward [he] only used [the name] Jiu-Jitsu, which is a generic name that could mean a hundred [other] schools of Jiu-Jitsu in Japan, as to not compromise the reputation of Jigoro Kano and his school. Belt promotion resumed after Maeda stopped prize fighting and began the process of becoming a representative of the Emperor and the Empire in Brazil. Then the belt promotion resumed. From that moment onward Mitsuyo Maeda started to represent the interests of Japan in the Amazon.

Why was he thought to be an intelligence agent for the Japanese Empire?

[It] makes sense when the Americans accuse Maeda of being a spy. I don't know if he was a spy, but he worked for the Japanese govern-

ment. That's true. Within the eyes of the American intelligence or something, [it] seems that Maeda is a spy. Because it was very common at the time for the Americans to have this stereotype about the Japanese. That every Japanese working abroad are not only workers but are potential spies for the Japanese government. So the idea of the Japanese, whatever they are, [is that] they work for the Japanese in thinking of future war or something. They informed the Japanese [Empire of] everything that's going on. I don't know if he was a spy. But certainly he worked for the Japanese government.

Were there many other Japanese martial artists that immigrated to Brazil?

In the 1930s there was one boat full of Japanese immigrants [that] came to Brazil that's a special case. [It's] very interesting. It is a boat carrying Japanese immigrants, [and] there is a dojo set up on the boat. So they come from Japan to Brazil. It's a long journey, right? [And they're] practicing Jiu-Jitsu and Judo. And among them there is a high percentage of Black Belts. The Japanese spent like forty days on this trip to Brazil, and they organize a tournament while at sea. And ten percent of the Japanese immigrants in that vessel—the Maru out of Buenos Aires—are martial arts practitioners. So if you take that one boat as an example, you can just picture how many Japanese martial arts came to Brazil in the first three decades of immigration.

Given the scope of the true history, the narrative of how Maeda taught Carlos who taught Hélio seems overly simplistic. How did this narrative take shape?

First there is a boom, there is a growing interest for Jiu-Jitsu in Brazil, and then there is growing interest in Jiu-Jitsu abroad, outside of Brazil. So the narrative, the Gracies' narrative for a long time, I wouldn't care much for. Because it's a martial arts practice of just a bunch of guys in some neighborhoods of Rio de Janeiro. But once it became something exported, something widespread in Brazil, then it becomes an issue. There's a growing interest, and then comes the Gracie narrative. The Gracie narrative became something more elaborate in that sense. It's what in academic terms we call the invention of a tradition. They invent a past, they invent a tradition. It's a concept developed by an historian, Eric Hobsbawm. They invent a narrative for marketing purposes. To sell off the idea that the Gracies had the monopoly on this knowledge of Japanese Jiu-Jitsu. That they had the knowledge and they are the ones who reinvented Jiu-Jitsu in Brazil. They created a more sophisticated and elaborate narrative to just fill the demand.

Was this narrative unfair with other protagonists?

It's important to give voice to those who participated in the collective creation of Brazilian Jiu-Jitsu. Who usually are left out of the official narrative of the start of Jiu-Jitsu.

What gave the Gracie Brothers impetus to be so ambitious in regards to their role in martial arts?

You have to understand who the Gracies are in the first place. The Gracies are falling aristocrats. They become a very important and wealthy family in the 19th century in Brazil, but in the beginning of the 20th century they underwent some kind of economic dire straits. They're on the decline, an economic decline, and in consequence of course they're also in social decline. The thing that you have to bear in mind is that, [throughout this,] the Gracies are able to keep their social network. Even broke, financially broke, they kept that social network. This will become important later on, when the Gracies return to Rio de Janeiro from the Amazon with this new kind of knowledge that they acquired in the Amazon, this Jiu-Jitsu. And they decide to use Jiu-Jitsu [to] try to find some economic and social redemption.

Can you tell us more about these social networks?

In times of nationalism, the Gracies' network—the social networks that endured their economic down turn—they were very important, because they managed to be involved with the state. They started teaching Jiu-Jitsu to the Brazilian dictator, Getúlio Vargas', body-guards. So they become part members of the so-called special police, created to protect the Brazilian dictator. So the Gracies—and this is what I claim in my dissertation—despite all the troubles, the financial troubles of the Gracies, that kind of financial decline, they kept intact this elitist mindset. This idea of being superior. Of whatever they do, they think they are and could do better than others. And in Brazil especially, you have to come to know a bit about the Brazilian culture. The Gracies find themselves in this kind of privileged spot at that time. They are white, they are scions or descendants of this aristocratic family from the 19th century.

But they would later lose this privileged position when the military come into power, right?

There were two kind of dictatorship regimes in Brazil. [There was] the dictatorship that went from 1937 to 1945, under Getúlio Vargas. The Gracies enjoyed the benefits and the protection of this nationalistic dictatorship. And then the other dictatorship in Brazil, [the one] that started as a military dictatorship, is different. Getúlio Vargas was a civilian, like a strong man. But in 1964 it was different. It was military. The officers took power in Brazil. And that changed everything for the Gracies. Because the Gracies always benefited from the styles of the national icons since the 1930s, 1940s, 1950s. But when the armed officers the army took power in '64 it's a different breed. A different kind of dictatorship. The army officers are essentially middle class. They come from the middle class. And also, the Japanese Kodokan Judo became an Olympic sport in 1964. The Tokyo Olympics. There was a rise in prestige of Kodokan Judo after the Olympics. And it wasn't by accident that Brazil hosted the world Judo championship in 1965.

Why did you decide to write your dissertation on this topic?

[It is] something very personal. I had to go back in the history of Brazilian Jiu-Jitsu, and maybe I'd find something that, at some point, would create some kind of tension between me and the people that I know. The Gracies that I know, the Gracies that are part of my world. And I knew that at some point [my research] would clash [with] the Gracie official narrative. That created some kind of dilemma for me at the time. And my father passed away at the time. So it took me a while to decide to finally write a dissertation about Brazilian Jiu-Jitsu. But in the end I said, "I have to do it." [I felt I had] to give voice to the unheard voices that people left out of the process of the official narrative.

Do you think any Gracie read your dissertation?

I just cannot say to what extent the Gracies really read the dissertation or not. That's a thing that is important about this documentary. You're playing a very important role, because the documentary will reach places that my dissertation cannot reach. A large audience. I think that's important.

How much did Judo influence BJJ?

For years and years and years Judo played a very important role in influencing Brazilian Jiu-Jitsu. And then they have the reverse: Judo is changed because of the growth of Brazilian Jiu-Jitsu. Judo has tried to go back to the fundamentals, back to the ground game. Perhaps change the rules, because they lost this knowledge in ground combat, and this emphasis on ground combat. It is reinvented in Brazil and then it goes back to Japan. For me it's fantastic, it's a fantastic thing that you see this globalization of martial arts. And remember, Brazilian Jiu-Jitsu is not something created like the other Asian martial arts.

Can you talk a little bit about the rivalry between the Gracie Brothers with the Japanese?

In my opinion [it had to do with the fact that] the Japanese had the technical edge over them. They were just trying to defend themselves when facing the Japanese, which is crucial to understanding the style of Brazilian Jiu-Jitsu as a defensive system on the ground. Because the [BJJ] rules say, you only win if your opponent quits or taps out. There are no scored points or anything. So it's essential to make your opponent surrender.

What is the overall role of the Gracie family in your view?

There is a lot of criticism, but anyway they promote the martial art. They created the UFC, they created all of the stuff. And the [Japanese immigration] happened in so many different places. Right? The Jiu-Jitsu, well, look how styles of Jiu-Jitsu just disappeared. It happened in Brazil, it happened in São Paulo among the Japanese. They changed, they shifted, changing Jiu-Jitsu to Judo. Later on, it happened in France. There's a local style of French Jiu-Jitsu [that was] just swept [away by] Judo during the post-war period. So to understand [BJJ's success today], you have to go back to the Gracies. Right? The Gracies had what we call in [academic] history "agents." Individual agents.

Upper left: Luiz Otavio Laydner (right) with Jay Coleman (left); Upper right, left to right: Luiz Otavio Laydner, Fabio, Marcial, and the author; Bottom: Luiz Otavio Laydner.

LUIZ OTAVIO LAYDNER

"Well, Brazilian Jiu-Jitsu developed into a different martial art in a Darwinian style, let's say, in the sense that isolation makes it different from traditional Kodokan Judo."
> —Luiz Otavio Laydner, BJJ Black Belt and author

Our last interview of the day would be with Luiz Otavio Laydner, author of *With the Back on the Ground* (available in English on Amazon) and a student of the man for whom an entire guard system was

named: Ricardo De la Riva. Laydner came highly recommended by
Fabio as knowledgeable, well-spoken, and—lucky for us—fluent in
English. His book hypothesized that the "guard" position arose as a
reaction to the particular challenges the Japanese practitioners faced
when pitted against the bigger Wrestlers from the West, particularly
when a gi wasn't made available; Maeda himself, having been at the
center of these challenge matches many times, would have become
acutely aware of the importance of the "guard" position as a defensive
tactic against heavier opponents. I wanted to hear more about this idea
and explore it in the context of BJJ's overall growth and development.
It has been widely assumed, and sometimes claimed, that the "guard"
position is a Brazilian creation; according to Laydner, this simply
wasn't true at all. In fact, the "guard" position—including forms and
approaches like the "De la Riva"—was well known in Japan during
the early days of the Kodokan. This alone suggests a high-level
ground-grappling scene in Japan, and a competitive scene at that
(even if only competitive in practice): a complex solution is the product of a complex problem and, if this is true, the conclusion of a De la
Riva guard is unlikely to be reached without thousands of hours of
competitive practice. The simple fact is that you don't develop highly
sophisticated techniques by simply imagining them: these developments are the product of an attempt to solve a new problem by building on old solutions. In other words, at least in martial arts, inventions
and discoveries are the product of the serendipity that comes from
problem solving in the heat of combat, not a product of the imagination alone in a state of physical inertia.

Laydner's theory made tactical sense: even in today's competitions
it is common for a practitioner to use the guard position as a tool
against a heavier opponent, whose size makes the top position an almost foregone conclusion. A smaller Japanese, faced off against a
larger Western Wrestler and armed with the core techniques of guard
fighting from his training at the Kodokan, would seek to meet his
challenges with the techniques at his disposal, thus employing (and in
so doing, developing) his guard. The innovation had happened, it had
just happened much earlier than was claimed in the mainline BJJ nar-

rative. The organic development that occurred in Brazil, by comparison, was done much later, and likely relied heavily on the innovation of Japanese practitioners already familiar with the guard position.

At any rate, it is unquestionable that the guard position is one of the defining elements of our practice—for better or worse, depending on how you feel about the fact that "guard pulling" and the guard position itself provide constant fodder for critics of "sport BJJ" and BJJ in general. Once, during a private conversation with IBJJF's lead strategist, Marcelo Siriema, I tried to convince him to change the rules so that "guard-pulling" was penalized with a minus one (-1) point. My rationale went something like this: a) The IBJJF would incentivize the "martial" aspect of the art if it created a rule-set that pushed competitors toward a more "standing" and takedown-oriented approach, particularly in the lighter divisions where takedowns have essentially disappeared in high-level competition; b) The criteria would not have to be created, since it already exists within the ruleset: namely, if two competitors are on the ground and the top one disengages and backs out, the referee automatically punishes him with a minus one (-1) point. In light of this, the non-punishment of guard-pulling seemed to me a double-standard as well as a contradiction.

In reality, my argumentation had the shape of a long and premeditated speech that, at least in my head, allowed for no possible rebuttal. I was, however, unprepared for the argument I received in reply. "But Robert," Siriema said simply, "people like to pull guard." Touché. Siriema went on to explain that, in his view, the "guard" position was one of the main reasons for BJJ's success around the world, as it made it possible for smaller and less athletic individuals to put up an even fight within a tournament ruleset and not have to wrestle anyone down. I didn't agree with him—I believe that BJJ should be led by what practitioners "need" and not what they "want"—but I understood his point completely and acknowledged that it was a good one, as it coincided exactly with my experience as a gym owner. Whenever I announced that we would be practicing takedowns the next day, my class inevitably turned into a small group-private session of members that had not attended class the previous day and who had not, apparently, received the memo either (one of many instances in which business-oriented thinking affects our martial arts practice... Something of which we are all, despite our best intentions, guilty).

Despite Laydner's claims, I am not convinced that Maeda and his compatriots in Brazil had developed sophisticated guards themselves (though there is evidence that more sophisticated guard technique, including open guard technique, was present at the Kodokan); however, it does seem likely that, at least against Wrestlers and heavier opponents, they would have ended up on the bottom and been compelled to fight from there as best they could.

I would have liked to discuss the subject more, but, as it turned out, Laydner was the researcher with whom I had spent the least amount of time. He seemed like a fair-mannered person, calm, humble, and intelligent, and with more time I would have enjoyed getting to know him better. Interestingly, going over his interview, I took note that many of our conclusions in regards to the origins of BJJ were very similar, and again felt it a shame that we didn't get a chance to explore what other interpretations we might have in common. As it worked out we met up with him in the evening, after his day job, when he was tired and ready to go home, and we didn't want to keep him for too long. His remarks were filled with good observation and, like Tufy, he spoke English well enough that we could interview him in his second language. After our farewells, we wrapped on a long day of filming.

— Luiz Otavio Laydner —

Can you introduce yourself?

My name is Luiz Otavio Laydner and basically I started Jiu-Jitsu back in the '80s, last century. And I started with Master Ricardo De la Riva, when he actually left the Carlson Gracie team to start his own academy in Copacabana. At that time I started practicing. I went from white to Black Belt with Master De la Riva. Today I live in São Paulo and I train here. But, sadly, not as much as I would like to.

When and why did you begin researching BJJ history?

I started becoming interested in researching back at the very beginning. One of the first classes that I attended, after the training session, I sat beside the mat and asked a colleague, 'How actually did Jiu-Jitsu become Jiu-Jitsu?' What's the sport, what's this martial art, and how it differs from Judo. And he basically told me the traditional story that everyone knows about Jiu-Jitsu.

After all, was Maeda a Judoka or not? Did he have any experience in any other Jiu-Jitsu school?

Maeda is a traditional Kodokan Judoka. There is no link whatsoever that links Maeda to any other Jiu-Jitsu school in Japan. When Maeda arrived at the Kodokan, the takeover of Jiu-Jitsu by Kodokan Judoka was complete. So in this aspect he was a traditional Judoka, a traditional Kodokan Judoka.

If he was a Kodokan Judoka, why was he still using the term Jiu-Jitsu?

Actually, Maeda did use the term Judo in the very beginning in his first travels. He did use Judo, as well as Jiu-Jitsu. We must remember that, outside of Japan, Judo and Jiu-Jitsu—the differences between both terms—was not clear for anybody. In the very beginning when traveling, Maeda tried to use the term Judo and tried to explain to his audience, in which aspects Judo was different from the traditional Jiu-Jitsu schools back in Japan.

Was Maeda involved in fixed fights?

Many of the Maeda fights, probably most of the Maeda fights, were rigged. Basically, [they were] for entertainment purposes. [The] true fight, the actual fight, fighting in real life, is ugly. Just for example: it took years for the UFC guys to develop rules that would make a real fight palatable.

Can we verify the relationship between Carlos Gracie and Mitsuyo Maeda "Count Koma"?

I never saw any evidence, hard evidence, of Carlos training under Maeda. There is a good case for the relationship of Gastão Gracie, Carlos' father, and Maeda. They were in the same place. They were involved in fighting in [the] circus. So, there's a good case for Carlos to know Maeda. And, in that case, to suggest that his son trained with Maeda. So [Brazilian practitioners] were basically a group of people training Judo under Maeda in the region of Belém do Para. Another possibility is that Carlos actually trained with one of Maeda's pupils. And, like we have today, sometimes you have an academy and you have the Master of the academy, and you also have teachers that teach on behalf of the Master.

Was BJJ influenced by other martial arts?

We can tell for sure that BJJ had the influence of another martial art, because it happens to this day. Unlike the traditional Judo, Jiu-Jitsu—Brazilian Jiu-Jitsu—is not linked to any canon or any list of techniques. So it's an open style of martial art, where you can incorporate the techniques of other martial arts as you wish.

Is the official narrative of how BJJ came to be accurate?

I think the traditional story of Brazilian Jiu-Jitsu is what you call a "myth of creation." Every time a human being creates something, it tends to attach a mythology to it. The traditional story of Brazilian Jiu-Jitsu is basically part of the mythology that was created almost together with the martial art. And it is important in a sense to create a theme, or something that helps people to properly understand the martial arts in a more spiritual concept.

How did BJJ develop outside of its Judo matrix?

Well, Brazilian Jiu-Jitsu developed into a different martial art in a Darwinian style, let's say, in the sense that isolation made it different from traditional Kodokan Judo. In the '30s, if you asked any practitioner, Gracie or not, they did not have the perception that they were practicing a new or different martial art.

What is the importance of Geo Omori in relation to BJJ and the Gracie Brothers?

So even though Maeda brought what we call Jiu-Jitsu or Judo to the north of the country, actually Omori was more involved in developing it together with the Gracies in the '30s in the late '20s.

What happened in the matches between Carlos Gracie and Geo Omori?

Actually, there's a lot of controversy in the fights between Geo Omori and Carlos Gracie. They had a demonstration that was supposed to be a fight, but Omori hurt his hand [before the fight, so] it became a pure demonstration [instead]. [This was] in São Paulo. After that they had the first real fight. Where, even though there was no clear winner in this fight, Omori had some almost broken arm-lock applied by Carlos Gracie. And [there was] a lot of controversy in this fight, because Omori stated that this fight was fixed.

Was the Gracie Academy founded in 1925?

To the best of my knowledge, there is no evidence of a Gracie Academy in 1925. It was founded in Rio de Janeiro in September 1930 by Donato Pires and had as instructors Carlos and George Gracie.

What is the relevance of Hélio Gracie to BJJ?

Hélio Gracie was one of the main characters that did participate in the development of Brazilian Jiu-Jitsu, but for sure he's not the only one. He was very important in two aspects, the first one is that, as George Gracie his brother mentioned in 1940, he never did participate in rigged fights. Every fight that Hélio did participate in was for real. And the second thing is that the obstinacy of Hélio Gracie allowed Jiu-Jitsu to avoid being incorporated into traditional Kodokan Judo in Brazil in the '50s and the '60s. So, in that aspect, he was very, very important.

Who promoted the Gracie Brothers to Black Belt?

Probably no one promoted the Gracie brothers to Black Belt. I think we need to understand that at that time the grading system in Brazil was very fluid. It was not very objective, so it's very likely that at the time they promoted themselves. There's nothing wrong with that. It's something that was not uncommon in that period of time. So, it's very unlikely that they were ever promoted by someone.

What was the importance of the Gracie family in the history of martial arts in Brazil?

I think the Gracies were successful in keeping the combat philosophy that was traditional in Japan in the early days of the Kodokan, but [that] over time the Kodokan managed to end. And basically they were able to keep this combat philosophy untouched over the decades, and it helped [BJJ] to avoid being incorporated into Kodokan Judo.

—

Our first day had been long and, for me, surprisingly tiring. We'd been in the same room all day, and all we'd had to do was change settings for each interviewee, which Steve and Jay managed themselves.

In the abstract it just didn't seem like a lot of work; if you'd asked me how long interviewing three people would take prior to this, my answer would have been two to three hours. Not the case: this had been a fifteen-hour day. It was my first real lesson in filmmaking—but it wouldn't be my last. Far from it, in fact.

Upper left: Grandmaster Behring being interviewed; Upper right: Steve Jeter filming Grandmaster Behring on the balcony; Bottom: Grandmaster Flávio Behring

FLÁVIO BEHRING

"What was important in the breaking of [Brazilian] Jiu-Jitsu from Judo was exactly the path that was traced by the Gracie family. Because what came to Brazil was nothing more than Kano Jiu-Jitsu and therefore the Judo he had transformed."

—Grandmaster Flávio Behring, student of Hélio Gracie

When we entered into this project we knew we had a good story to tell; what we didn't know was how much the story would grow and develop as the production went on. After reading Roberto Pedreira, Tufy Cairus, and Marcial Serrano, I felt I was fairly acquainted with the most relevant facts we were going to discuss in the documentary. Now, though, after only a couple of days of interviews, we had learned things that fundamentally reshaped our understanding of characters like Maeda, Carlos, and Hélio, and how they fit into the large and fascinating landscape of Judo's strange life in Brazil... and we were far from finished.

Our next interview would be with Flávio Behring, the leader of the Behring clan and father to the legendary Marcelo Behring, who would meet such a tragical fate so early in life. (In his prime Marcelo was one of the most prolific grapplers in Brazil; the first time I heard his name was on an old VHS tape I had the opportunity to watch as a white belt. I was training at a gym called "4 Tempos" in Itu under Otávio de Almeida, Jr. The tape was from the early '90s, and showed Marcelo Behring teaching a seminar in São Paulo and showing some of the new techniques that were being developed and practiced in Rio. Some of it was fairly simple and fundamental by today's standards: if memory serves me correctly, he was at one point describing a "triangle choke.")

Flávio Behring, alongside João Alberto Barreto, is one of the first two Brazilians to teach BJJ (that is, the variant of Judo they were all practicing and that later we would call "BJJ") in the United States. The first time I saw him was back in 1999. I was a 16-year-old white belt competing at the Campeonato Paulista ("Paulista" denotes something or someone from the state of São Paulo) de Jiu-Jitsu, and he was refereeing at the event. At one point during the tournament one of the matches didn't go the way one of the coaches wanted, and a scuffle ensued. I remember being appalled by how the brown belt coach (who, incidentally, had made a name for himself as a "pit-boy" and a Vale Tudo fighter in São Paulo) could be so disrespectful to someone who was clearly his senior. But I also admired how Flavio held himself through the exchange: stoic, firm, respectful, and full of class, even in the face of such disrespect from a relative newcomer to the sport (and someone who, in my eyes, was acting like an ape desperate for attention).

This, my second encounter with Flavio Behring, would be under vastly different circumstances. An old training partner of mine and one of my best friends in Brazil, Alfredo Miras, is both a BJJ addict and an overnight multimillionaire from his shampoo business. I reached out to him and explained that we needed a place to conduct our interview. Alfredo gladly made himself and his penthouse available. Coincidentally, one of the pieces of artwork in Alfredo's home was a red glass flame that strongly resembled the Behring Jiu-Jitsu logo; background chosen, we got down to interviewing the Grandmaster.

Flávio lived a good portion of his youth inside the Gracie Academy, learning directly from Hélio Gracie, and we were looking forward to learning what we could about Hélio as a person, his teaching methods, and in what ways the Gracie family's methodology differed from that of Judo. We were also hoping for an insight into what role that Vale Tudo played in the practice and development of the art. We were curious to learn what differences there were between the narrative we had been told and the reality of the dynamics inside the original Gracie Academy from someone who was actually there during some of the most significant moments in the Academy's—and the art's—history.

Master Behring was one of the most well-spoken of all of our interviewees, and also one of the most sympathetic to our mission. He was so sympathetic, in fact, that at the end of the interview we felt comfortable asking him if, as a favor, he would request an interview with Georges Mehdi on our behalf (Mehdi had developed a reputation for being secluded and reluctant to give interviews): a favor which he cheerfully granted. As it would turn out, though, no matter how much he insisted on our behalf, Mehdi would not budge. According to him he was "a no one" ("mas eu não sou ninguém") who "had nothing to say" ("não tenho nada a dizer"). Needless to say we were disappointed by this, but I had no idea how much this disappointment would grow in me over time: the more I learned about Mehdi the more I felt that he was the type of Grandmaster I wanted to meet and learn from. Mehdi had, by some accounts, been a driving force behind the evolution of BJJ after his return from Japan, where he trained for six months.

Throughout our brief experience with him, Master Behring confirmed his reputation as a soft-spoken gentleman and a class act. He shared vital information with us regarding the early days of the Gracie Academy as well as his thoughts on self-defense and the state of BJJ today. Like with many others of these Grandmasters, I would have enjoyed spending more time talking with him about his views on BJJ, and on life in general.

— Flavio Behring —

Could you introduce yourself and tell us how you started in Jiu-Jitsu?

My name is Flavio Behring, full name Flavio Schmidt Behring, family of German origin on both sides. I started Jiu-Jitsu in 1947, in the home of Hélio Gracie. I am 80 years old, and have seventy years of Jiu-Jitsu practice.

Tell us some more about your beginnings in Jiu-Jitsu?

I started training Jiu-Jitsu at Hélio Gracie's house. I had a respiratory failure. I suffered from asthma and my father was looking for some sport that I could practice and that could bring some improvement. He was a friend of Hélio and took me to his house in an attempt to help me. And that's how I started at Hélio Gracie's house, in a little room that he had lined with canvas and mattresses.

Could you tell us of the episode in which Hélio picked you up from school?

When Hélio Gracie came to pick me up from school, it was a curi-

ous episode because I was called a coward because I had been slapped in the face and not had any kind of reaction. I was 13 years old at the time. So Hélio went to school knowing my psychological need, because I was completely depressed, and he went to school to get me. When he entered the school, he was well known and people were impressed and said, "Hélio Gracie is here." And he very skillfully said, "I came to get one of the instructors of my academy, Flavio Behring." Some questioned the fact that I had been slapped in the face and Hélio said, "But I do not authorize Flavio to fight anyone." So that was the episode where he picked me up at school took me home. I had lunch and then went to the gym. It was then that I started to take off in Jiu-Jitsu, when he introduced me to João Alberto Barreto, who was 16 years old, and who became my teacher.

How did BJJ separate from Judo?

What was important in the breaking of Jiu-Jitsu from Judo was exactly the path that was traced by the Gracie family. Because what came to Brazil was nothing more than Kano Jiu-Jitsu, and therefore the Judo he had transformed.

What were the classes at the Gracie Academy like?

[The training] began with self-defense, and then became more sport. [The sport] was the unfolding of what had been learned on the basis of self-defense. Then the "rolling" came in. But it depended on the profile of the student, as there were students who could not do the sport part. But the whole point was self-defense.

What is the importance of this new research and these new discoveries for our history?

The importance is the fact of a true origin, a true form. For the moment under the right time period of form of the right form and the greater consciousness of all of us. I believe that people do not even seem interested, but if you report it will certainly create an interest and that interest will foster a condition of a deeper knowledge. I am a supporter of the scientific, academic need for you to work the development of the art grounded mainly in the bio-mechanical part. If you do not you will be out of alignment with the future. Today's information of historical consistency is of paramount importance. Now, I believe that in reality it will not change anything. It will let it be known that there were facts that are different from those that are told. As for the impact of this within the universe of Jiu-Jitsu practitioners, it will be very small. I think that the impact within the family can probably occur to the extent that something about the family history is demystified.

What is your sense of the role Carlos Gracie played in BJJ's history and development?

One thing I emphasize is that Carlos Gracie was a genius because if he had little contact time with Mitsuyo Maeda, with that little time he created this [art that is a] monster nowadays. He was the foundation of all that is there. I mean, a great, great genius. So I think Carlos Gracie and subsequently Hélio Gracie were two geniuses who managed to shape up something they had very little time to learn.

Tell us about your first trip teaching Jiu-Jitsu in the U.S.

The first time Jiu-Jitsu arrived in the United States from a formal point of view was in 1963. That is, Gracie Jiu-Jitsu. Joao Alberto and I made a trip to the United States at our peril and did several demonstrations and exhibitions and challenges starting at the Washington Naval Academy in Annapolis. Later, in New York, we did several presentations in colleges and universities and in the New York Athletic Club in Central Park. We made some fights and challenges and [it was] the challenges that were interesting, because they were [real] fights. A kind of free fight, to show how Jiu-Jitsu could involve other segments of martial arts. And it was interesting and the result was very positive. That was the first, in 1963. I cannot pin down the month, but it was that year for sure. It's curious. The first informal arrival was probably, I do not know if anyone else did, but in 1955 I went to the United States to study at a university in the southern United States in Lafayette, Louisiana called the South West Louisiana Institute. I was there with another Brazilian, Chermon, I remember his name, we were working out. We were rolling in the Wrestling area. At one point the football team was training indoors because outside it was very cold and raining, and they got curious and approached and asked what we were doing, if it was Wrestling. I said it was Jiu-Jitsu and I invited them to come in and train. I started to show positions to them, but there was not much time on both sides because they trained a lot and I had to study. But anyway, maybe informally this time was the first time.

What were the technical adaptations made by the Gracie family?

The most developed part was [on] the ground. That is the part in which there was a fairly large progression. Now, all martial arts have influence of other martial arts. Jiu-Jitsu as a martial art originating in Japan and Kano [made] these well-established foundations. So there was no distortion. What was actually there were some adjustments. The Gracies had a rather sharp view which was as follows: adaptation to their morphology.

What is the role of Vale Tudo in Jiu-Jitsu?

The role of Vale Tudo in the history of Jiu-Jitsu is very interesting because it was the way to demonstrate the superiority of technique, or rather of the art.

Do you remember the first time you saw a triangle choke?

In my vision and my personal experience, inside the Gracie Academy I do not remember seeing or practicing the triangle. There was

131

something done that resembled the triangle: sankaku jime, which is a strangulation with the legs. So this was an adjustment that was made from what was brought by Judo. Undoubtedly the sankaku jime had a Judo influence, without a doubt. Like almost everything, because the origin of everything we practice is Japan, it is the Kano school, some things have undergone transformations, but the essence and the fundamentals are the same. The juji gatame is the same thing, the armbar, the triangle, the chokes.

Who promoted Carlos and Hélio to Black Belt?[5]

That's a good question. Who promoted Carlos and Hélio Gracie to Black Belt? I do not know, frankly I do not know. So much so that they wore blue belts. It was a navy blue, it was not a Black Belt. The Black Belt [was] adopted or created in Gracie Jiu-Jitsu in the '70s, but before that was Navy Blue Belt that was for the instructors, who were Carlos and Hélio, and later the teachers of the level of João Alberto, Carlson, Vígio, Armando. They never wore the Black Belt. That is the reality. The belts were established in the '70s, when the first federation of Rio de Janeiro was founded. Then belts were created. Until then it was something done at will. Everyone graduated. It is no different from today.

Anything remarkable that you remember Hélio telling you?

It's a phrase that Hélio spoke to me on my first day and that I think synthesizes everything. The phrase is: "You can do it, do not hesitate."

---

[5] Carlos and Hélio are known to have worn Black Belts as early as the 1950s.

Upper left: Grandmaster Shiguero Yamasaki; Upper right: Grandmaster Shiguero Yamasaki; Lower left: Grandmaster Shiguero Yamasaki being interviewed by Fabio; Lower right: Mario Yamasaki

SHIGUERO AND MARIO YAMASAKI

"The first thing a Judo Master needs to do is to captivate the trust of their students. Don't focus on orders. You need to gain their trust with simplicity, so that you can teach something about life... To show humility because [Judo's] power is in showing simplicity, and not imposing."

—Shiguero Yamasaki, Judo Grandmaster

Shiguero and his son Mario Yamasaki were next. The interview would take place on the matted area of BodyTech, a gym inside a

133

shopping mall in São Paulo, and this made finding a place to set up for the interview particularly challenging: for us to have any hope of getting decent footage the lighting and external sounds had to be under absolute control, a task that was easier said than done in a shopping mall.

The interviewing process itself was fairly simple, and I actually found it to be quite fun; the logistics surrounding the interviews were another story altogether. Coordinating everyone's busy schedules with a space that was both available and appropriate for an interview was proving to be more of a challenge than we'd anticipated. Once all of that was accomplished, though, the interviewing itself was a pleasure. Interviewing was an art with which I was only just becoming acquainted, but I was genuinely enjoying the process. Still, I had to admit that Fabio was better at it than me. While in Brazil we'd decided that Fabio would do the interviews in Portuguese and I would do the interviews in English. He had done this many times before during his years researching BJJ, and he knew just how to extract the "gems" out of people. It was all still new to me: I'd been on the opposite side of that microphone, but now I was learning how the other half lives in real time.

Fabio, Jay, and I had tailored questions to each of our interviewees. These questions were designed to not only explore the story that each interviewee had to tell but also to extract good soundbites. Still, as I said, I was learning the ropes. One trick I was learning was to not have the interviewee talk too much about the topic before the interview started, but rather "warm them up" with unrelated small talk (again, admittedly, Fabio is much better at this than I am). The idea was to relax the interviewee as much as possible, while beginning to develop the sort of mood we wanted for the interview. I was learning how this could be done with tone, vocal rhythm, and contextual framing; most importantly I was learning to engage interviewees emotionally and get them to speak from the heart, rather than just tell us what they thought we wanted to hear. (It was interesting to find, also, that this method seemed most effective with the Grandmasters; with the historians I found that the trick was to establish a more intellectual and serious tone.)

In many ways, Shiguero Yamasaki embodied the unknown side of the story we were trying to tell. He is a member of the Japanese-Brazilian community, as well as a Red Belt Judoka; he trained with the Ono Brothers (the original rivals of the Gracie family); he was present and involved in the Brazilian grappling arts community when Kato, Yamaguchi, and Kimura made their first visit to Brazil in 1951 (he was actually present for Kato's second fight with Hélio). Finally, he was a witness throughout the era of the rivalry between Judo, largely represented by the Japanese community in São Paulo, and the version of Judo being carved out in Brazil, largely represented by the Gracie Brothers in Rio de Janeiro.

Shiguero's son, Mario, was relevant because we had decided from the beginning that we wanted some "not-so-old-school" characters in the film who, we hoped, would bridge the gap between the old-timers and the younger BJJ audience. We were worried that it would be alienating to the audience to only show people that the average BJJ practitioner had never even heard of. Mario bridged the gap perfectly: his family and their history rooted him in the broader history of both Judo and BJJ, while his perennial presence as a ring referee made him immediately recognizable to fans of MMA and the UFC.

— Mario Yamasaki —

Can you introduce yourself?

My name is Mario Yamasaki. I'm from São Paulo, Brazil.

Where did the techniques in BJJ come from?

I believe all the techniques in Brazilian Jiu-Jitsu came from olden-days Judo.

Is the groundwork in BJJ more sophisticated than the ground-work in Judo?

Well, I believe that [Brazilian] Jiu-Jitsu became more sophisticated because before the war, in Judo in Japan, they could do ne-waza, tachi-waza. After the war, in Japan, some parts of Judo were prohibited. So Judo kind of had to change into the sport Judo that it is today. So I believe the Gracies brought back [what had been removed].

What was it like growing up as Japanese-descendant Judoka, and watching the growth of BJJ?

I saw Brazilian Jiu-Jitsu really grow when I was young. People from Rio used to come to the Judo tournaments in São Paulo, and they had a couple of Jiu-Jitsu guys in the team, and [the Jiu-Jitsu guys] were aggressive, all different than Judo. You know, the discipline and all that is different. And people from Judo used to say, "Those people are no good, they're no good." Everybody used to tell me that Jiu-Jitsu is dirty. You can't do Jiu-Jitsu, you have to stick to Judo. And so it fascinated me because, you know, they used to beat some Judo guys, good Judo guys. I grew up in the Judo community here. They hated Jiu-Jitsu. I felt that when I moved from Judo to Jiu-Jitsu, because the Jiu-Jitsu community didn't want to accept me, because I came from Judo. And the Judo community didn't want to accept me back, because I went to Jiu-Jitsu. So I was right in the middle of the war between Judo and Jiu-Jitsu.

What are some of the cultural differences between the two arts?

You know, the contention, I don't think was Japanese. I think it's the culture. The Japanese were really trying to close, not to let anybody else in. Because they think that Judo is "clean." They didn't want to have anything else coming in. They're very strict, very narrow-minded. Jiu-Jitsu is open minded. You can learn and introduce to Brazilian Jiu-Jitsu anything that you can do to make your game better. So I think it was just a part of the Japanese [culture] that didn't want to get Jiu-Jitsu infused into Judo.

How did the Gracies steer their style away from Judo?

I believe [the Gracies] were ahead of a lot of people. They are thinking always ahead and they are very good at marketing, and so they started challenging people to prove that a small guy could beat a big guy. And I think that's the reason it blew up here, because [Brazilians] like to fight. They like to fight, they like to see challenges. And they started challenging people on the streets, and that's when they became the pit-boys, and all that. To prove that Jiu-Jitsu is the best martial art in the world.

Tell us about the episode in which you met Marcelo Behring, and how you got into BJJ.

When Marcelo Behring came to São Paulo, he came to challenge me. I was teaching in the gym. Standing up I threw him a lot of times, but on the ground I couldn't even move. Every time I went to the ground, every time to the ground, tap. And I was really good in Judo. My family went to the Olympics, and all that. I used to train with the national team, so I was really a badass here. But then, when Marcelo Behring came, I was submitted a lot of times. And I thought to myself, I need to learn this art. That's when I switched.

—

— **Shiguero Yamasaki** —

Can you introduce yourself and tell us a little bit about your history?

My name is Shiguero Yamasaki. I was born in the city of Lins on October 3, 1933, and started in Judo at the age of 6. Today I am 9th degree Red Belt in Judo, promoted by the Paulista Federation and recognized internationally. I was an international Judo referee and I have refereed several international tournaments, world championships, and also at the Olympic Games in Barcelona. I was also in South Korea, where I was a special guest to referee an international Judo tournament in Korea. I'm from the second generation, called "Nisei." My parents were born in Kumamoto. My father was a lieutenant of the Japanese Army and fought in World War I, and came to Brazil to work in the coffee plantations in the northwest of the state of São Paulo.

I started [Judo] with 6 years of age in the city of Tremembé, in Central Brazil, on a farm. Training was done not on mats, but on rice straw covered with tarpaulin. There was a lot of dust in our Judo training! I learned something there. I then came to São Paulo, where I started to train in Budokan with sensei Ogawa. I received my Black Belt when I was 14 years old. I was selected to train with the Judo World Champions, who were here.

You met and trained with Kato and Kimura before their matches with Hélio Gracie, right? Could you tell us a little about that experience?

It was Kato at lightweight, Kimura at light-heavyweight, and Yamashita was a heavyweight. I watched his fight with Hélio Gracie at the Pacaembu Stadium.[6] Professor Kato fought and was strangled by Professor Hélio Gracie. Before the competition I trained with them at the Ogawa Academy and the technique presented by the Japanese team was extraordinary, both Kato and Kimura. That's why they were world champions.

After this challenge they accepted from Professor Hélio Gracie, they were expelled from the Kodokan of Japan because under Judo principles it was not allowed to accept challenges to profit financially. Long afterwards Professor Kimura challenged fighters from around the world to prove that he was the best Judoka in the world.[7]

---

[6] This was the second encounter between Kato and Hélio, which took place in São Paulo. Their first fight, which took place in Rio de Janeiro, ended in a draw.

[7] Shiguero might be repeating stories he heard here, but there is no evidence that Kimura and Kato were expelled from the Kodokan after their matches with Helio Gracie.

Could you tell us a little more about your early experience training Judo?

Between 1948 and 1949 I started training at Budokan. I was a green belt at another gym, but I started there as a white belt. The difference in training was that there was a lot of discipline about the time we began. It was well split, and the Black Belts trained on one side and the students with other belts trained on the other side. It was a well differentiated and well directed training. The training began with the "hai" greeting. Sensei Ogawa stood in the middle and everyone greeted kneeling with the Black Belts on one side and the other students on the other side. He began with only tachi-waza. Ne-waza was done after finishing the tachi-waza training. I had contact with Professor Octavio de Almeida (Sr). He taught at Rua Barão de Itapetininga at the invitation of Professor Fukaia, a Judo Black Belt. We went there every Sunday for Professor Almeida to teach ground-fighting classes, where he was very efficient. Then I came to meet his son, who is the current president of the Federation of São Paulo.

What were the dynamics of Judo and BJJ then?

After I received the Black Belt and was a teacher of Judo, I opened a gym on Rua Pamplona, in Oswaldo Cruz Square, and at that time I received many challenges through the neighborhood newspaper, challenging me to fight in an offensive way. The challenger would say that I was afraid to take up the challenge. Every Sunday this publication began to appear in the neighborhood newspaper. I attended the Judo federation meeting and told the president that I was being challenged weekly through the neighborhood newspaper by a Jiu-Jitsu teacher, and said I wanted to take up the challenge. The president said that I would not accept the challenge, and that I would be kicked out of Judo if I did. Between the '60s and '70s we founded eight academies in the city of São Paulo.

The challenger was a teacher, if I am not mistaken, of the region of Pamplona. He made the challenges through the newspaper and was *never in my gym. If he were in my gym, I would ask him to enter to train and not to make any kind of challenge, since the principles of Judo do not allow it. In those days, Jiu-Jitsu was starting and Judo already had a long tradition, and through these challenges, [Jiu-Jitsu practitioners] were trying to prove that Jiu-Jitsu was efficient. [But] because Judo cannot accept challenges, I had to keep to my place as a Judo coach and not accept the challenge coming from Jiu-Jitsu.*

What are the qualities of a good Judo teacher?

The first thing a Judo Master needs to do is to cultivate the trust of the students. It's no use imposing yourself with orders. You should gain the students' trust with simplicity so that you can teach them something about life, training, education, respect. You should do this as calmly as possible, to gain the confidence of the ones who come to train with you. To show humility, because its power is in showing simplicity and not imposing. Judo gave me mental agility, a monumental reflex, and a way to respect others with much love. If every Brazilian practiced Judo we would not have the sinking country we have today.

Upper left: Grandmaster Carnivalle and the author; Upper right: Group photo of Carnivalle and his students after the interview; Bottom: Grandmaster Oswaldo Carnivalle

OSWALDO CARNIVALLE

"I could say a number of things, but I will say two words: mutual respect. I believe this exemplifies what I can say about the role of Jiu-Jitsu in my life. Mutual respect. Because through this you respect and honor your opponent. Through mutual respect you become a better person. Mutual respect will bring you sincere and lasting friendships. This is what I think of our Jiu-Jitsu."

—Grandmaster Oswaldo Carnivalle, student of
George Gracie and the Ono Brothers

Fabio had spent a significant portion of our time in Brazil trying to convince Romeu Bertho to get in a car with his son and drive to São Paulo to be interviewed. Bertho was one of the last living students and Black Belts of George Gracie, and he still taught in the city of São Carlos, where Marcial and Fabio also lived. I felt it was extremely disrespectful to ask a Grandmaster in his late 70s to drive three hours to grant us an interview, but we didn't have a choice: our schedule didn't allow a trip to São Carlos to interview one person. Even Marcial, who was pretty much part of the team, had traveled to São Paulo by bus in order to be in our film.

Bertho's son had tried to convince him that the film was an important effort to help tell the story of George and the development of BJJ, but Bertho wouldn't budge no matter how much we insisted. We offered to pay for his transportation, but it made no difference. I regret not finding a way to make it happen: Bertho's voice was an important one that wouldn't be heard in our film—one of many I would come to regret not hearing during our production.

We did, however, have another one of George Gracie's students to interview, this one in São Paulo: Marcial Serrano's teacher Oswaldo Carnivalle was still actively teaching out of his home (with the help of his family). We arrived at the house and were led to the training area. The matted area was on the upper level and was, much like most mat spaces in Brazil, fairly small. Carnivalle was frail and Tuco, his son, warned us that he would not have a high tolerance for a long interview. Carnivalle himself seemed at once eager to tell his story and eager for the interview to end so he could rest. His family and students were admirably protective of him: they were a small group that trained daily under the eyes of their Master. Through the course of our brief interview Carnivalle would give us really interesting insights into the fixed fight scene in Brazil during his early days as a practitioner, his relationship to George Gracie and the Ono Brothers, as well as some of his opinions on how BJJ developed in relation to Judo.

Throughout most of our sport's history, the BJJ scene in São Paulo has been overshadowed by the much larger scene in Rio de Janeiro.

Still, as evidenced by the presence of Masters like Carnivalle, the São Paulo scene is an important chapter in the history of BJJ, and in this Carnivalle's role in our film was doubly important: not only was he a link to George Gracie, but he is one of the fathers—alongside Otávio Almeida Sr., Yassuiti and Naoiti Ono (the Ono Brothers), Nahum Rabay, and Orlando Saraiva—of the "Jiu-Jitsu Paulista." These men laid the groundwork for the growth the sport would experience in that state during the '90s (among other things, Carnivalle, alongside Otávio de Almeida, founded the first BJJ federation in São Paulo). All of this was of particular interest to me: having been raised in the state of São Paulo, I was keen to learn the history of our sport there as well as more about some of its main characters: it was, in fact, in the gym of Otávio de Almeida, Jr., current President of the Federação Paulista de Jiu-Jitsu and son of Otávio de Almeida, Sr., that I had my first experience with BJJ, back in 1998 (not counting my brief experience with a non-BJJ style called Morganti Ju-Jitsu in Itu the previous year). Needless to say, Carnivalle and Otávio de Almeida were two of the founding pillars of BJJ in São Paulo, and Carnivalle, being the only survivor of the pair, was revered by anyone who knew anything about the history of the sport in São Paulo. Though this group had become smaller over the years, it is now—thanks to Marcial and his efforts to revive his Master's memory—beginning to grow again.

It was interesting, too, to learn more about George Gracie from a man who knew him. George Gracie, unlike his brothers, lived a rather nomadic life, and never really put down roots anywhere. From Rio de Janeiro to the Brazilian Northeast to São Paulo, George wasn't a man to sit still for too long. Interestingly, many historians and members of the Gracie family we spoke to would describe George as a "rebel" within the family, due to his unruly nature and unwillingness to follow his brother Carlos' diet and instructions. Which may explain why so little has been said about George, despite his crucial role in spreading BJJ in Brazil as well as his being one of the founders of modern MMA (historians and people who knew him would refer to George as someone very similar in personality to his nephew, Carlson Gracie).

Either because he lacked the ambition to create a lasting legacy like his brothers or because he was the type to believe that the grass would always be greener on the other side or simply because, as I suspect, he was above all an adventurer, he always seemed to keep moving—much like the Japanese who came before him, and whose legacies he carried.

— **Oswaldo Carnivalle** —

Can you introduce yourself?

My name is Oswaldo Carnivalle, I'm 87 years old. I was born in São Paulo and I started in Jiu-Jitsu in 1950 with Master George Gracie.

Why do you believe George Gracie is less known than his brothers?

George Gracie is not known in the rest of the world like Hélio and Carlos because Hélio and Carlos made a greater marketing effort than George. But, in Brazil, George used to be as known or better known than they were.

Do you believe that George was the best fighter in the family at that time?

I have no doubt that George Gracie was the greatest fighter in the family. George faced a very large number of opponents. He won many. Many more than Hélio and much more than Carlos, without a doubt. George Gracie did not refuse challenges. He fought whenever there was an opportunity and he did not choose opponents. And usually he won the fights in which he was involved. I think with that he proved he really was the best one in the family.

What was George Gracie's relationship with his brothers like?

*George Gracie was rather reserved in speaking about his brothers.
I remember that sometimes he complained about Carlos. With Hélio
he sometimes had a problem, but he had a better relationship with
him. With Gastão he never complained. He got along well with
Gastão. His biggest problem was with Carlos.*

**Many believe George was the father of Vale Tudo [MMA]. What
are your thoughts?**

*I don't believe George was the inventor of Vale Tudo. Because
when I first met George, people already spoke about Vale Tudo. There
were even Vale Tudo fights in the circuses, that presented the fighters
in the arena of the circus. So it was not George who created Vale Tudo
here in São Paulo.*

When and why did you begin to train Judo?

*I became interested in Judo because I learned some standing
[techniques]. George taught some stand-up, self-defense, and Jiu-Jitsu on the ground, and I really enjoyed the standing part. So, since
George was not specialized at the takedown part of nage-waza, I
looked for someone to better prepare me for this part of nage-waza. I
trained with one of Ono's assistants. I trained for a long time with
Ono. I looked for the fight standing up because I think it's very important to know that part. I agree that Jiu-Jitsu is better on the ground,
but if you're going to start the fight standing up, you need to know the
part of nage-waza. That's why I went to look for Judo and started
training with the Ono people.*

What are the biggest differences between Judo and BJJ?

*Jiu-Jitsu does not practice standing. Judo does not train on the
ground. No. At that time, Judo was practiced on our feet, self-defense,
and a bit on the ground. Of course, the standing part was more important. Then seventy percent was nage-waza and thirty percent was*

ne-waza. Jiu-Jitsu was seventy percent ground training and thirty percent standing.

Why did the split between Judo and BJJ take place?

I think this split came after Judo became an Olympic sport and the Judo world championships took place. Because in those championships what won was the takedown, Judo was much more concerned with the part of nage-waza. They simply trained only the nage-waza. And Jiu-Jitsu was still training on the ground. It was there that there was a well characterized separation of Jiu-Jitsu on the ground and Judo standing. But many academies continued to train standing, on the ground, and self-defense.

What were the biggest names at the time?

At that time we'd heard of Ono, George, Hélio, Tatu, who fought Vale Tudo fights, and Takeo Yano. [They] were the fighters of the time. Beyond them I'd heard of Geo Omori. George faced Geo Omori a few times and said he was an exceptional fighter.

Can you tell us about Takeo Yano?

I first met Takeo Yano in the '70s. Takeo Yano was famous at that time mainly because he was also doing fixed fights. He was the idol of the Japanese colony here in São Paulo. Takeo Yano was a good fighter. He had a lot of technique, really. He even fought good fights against very good opponents and was a winner in many of those bouts.

Do you condemn these fixed fights?

No, I do not condemn them. What we have to consider is this: these individuals lived mostly exclusively from fights and they had a family to support. When there were no "real" fights, they had to do those fixed fights to make some money to support themselves. Sometimes in one of these fixed fights they made enough for them to sustain themselves for two or three months. So I do not condemn them, no.

Do you have any regrets in your career?

Of course. I think we all have something that leads us to think that we could have done something different in the past. Only the past we cannot change, so I do not think about it. I think that in the future I can do something so I focus on that, rather than the past. Have I always done the right thing? No. Have I done some things that were wrong? Perhaps. But I can't change the past. But I can evidently better my future and I can craft my present into having greater value through my actions.

Any final thoughts?

I could say a number of things, but I will say two words: mutual respect. I believe this exemplifies what I can say about the role of Jiu-Jitsu in my life. Mutual respect. Because through this you respect and honor your opponent. Through mutual respect you become a better person. Mutual respect will bring you sincere and lasting friendships. This is what I think of our Jiu-Jitsu.

—

We were finished with the São Paulo leg of our trip. I was already regretting not speaking to Romeu Bertho, but that regret was something I would have to get used to: as I became more and more familiar with the story I realized that there was no way we were going to be able to interview everyone, or to tell every bit of information worth telling. Even if we ended our story fairly early in the history, at the Masahiko Kimura vs. Hélio Gracie fight as we had planned, we would still fall short. In fact, it was becoming obvious that even a ten-episode series would be inadequate to do the story justice. Our script already contained a who's who of Grandmasters and BJJ legends and we were still leaving out Okura, Satake, Raku, Akitaro Ono, Pedro Hemetério, Carlson Gracie, Nahum Rabay, Capitão Souto, Rolls Gracie, and others. And these are only the characters that pertain to the Brazil chapter of this story: the list expands exponentially if we attempt to follow the journeys of the itinerant Japanese that left Japan looking for work and ended up becoming pioneers in the spread of Jiu-Jitsu/Judo in other places around the world.

Even our interview list was starting to seem woefully incomplete. During the course of production, I would be bombarded with suggestions for Grandmasters I should interview, nearly all of whom were left out for reasons pertaining to logistics and the limiting constraints of the documentary format. Of course we wanted to interview Vinicius Ruas (last living student of Satake, the man who helped spread Judo/Jiu-Jitsu in Manaus (the other major city in the Amazon, alongside Belém)), and drive to São Carlos to interview Romeu Bertho (instead of rudely asking him to drive to us), as well as speak to "Mestre Deo," one of the main students of the Fadda lineage. The simple fact of the matter was that there was more story than we could hope to get our arms around fully, and we were doing the best we could with the limited time we had. Even Fabio felt the pinch: we had planned on interviewing him before we left São Paulo, but in the time crunch that ensued we decided to push it back to another time.

São Paulo had been a sprint, and some of our team members were already showing signs of stress and discomfort. Some of this was the pace, but some of this was due to things that, looking back, could have been managed better. For example: attempting to maintain a tight budget, I only rented one car for the whole team and our equipment, and the hotels I booked were low budget and often lacked elevators, and the rooms were small (it hadn't occurred to me that our camera team would need more space to unload their equipment and work). Throughout our trip details like these would make things more stressful than they needed to be; at times, they would make things downright contentious. Still, we managed.

*Left: The team takes a break by the beach while Steve shows his drone to Fabio;
Right: The team collects B-roll on the beach in Ipanema. From left to right: Tufy,
Fabio, Jay, Steve, and the author.*

RIO DE JANEIRO

Rio would be equally hectic, but we were excited and inspired and
our energy levels were still high. I was looking forward to speaking
with members of the Fadda lineage, as well as the patriarch of the
Gracie family, Robson Gracie, not to mention Roberto Leitão, the father of Brazilian "Luta Livre" (or Brazilian "Catch Wrestling,"). Tufy
had joined us on this leg of the trip as well, and would continue to
work as a consultant in Rio before he left for home. We would be
staying at a hotel around the corner from the Palacio do Catete in the
historic neighborhood of Flamengo.

The Palacio do Catete was Brazil's Presidential Palace before the
capital of the country was moved to Brasilia, in 1960; it is also where
the then President Getúlio Vargas committed suicide.

Vargas remains, to this day, one of the most revered and controversial figures in Brazil's history. A populist leader who came to power in
1930 via a military coup, he enjoyed a strong base of support amongst
the masses and the working class, despite his strong anti-Communist
agenda. Under his leadership Brazil experienced unprecedented economic growth. Though he stepped down in 1945, he would be reelect-
ed to the presidency in 1951. He committed suicide in the palace in
1954, due to the political pressure coming from the military.

Unlike our time in São Paulo, the Rio de Janeiro portion of the trip

149

had an air of tourism to it. Being around these historical sites with people like Fabio and Tufy made for great conversation about Brazil's past and present. I had been to Rio many times but always as a competitor, never as a tourist (or a filmmaker, for that matter), and that made this trip all the more special for me. Still, our stay wasn't exactly leisurely: when we weren't conducting interviews, we were driving all over the place gathering B-Roll. Despite this hectic pace I was enjoying every second, and no amount of "caipirinhas" and "churrasquinhos" by the waters of Ipanema could come close to the thrill of being part of a documentary about the history of BJJ.

Upper left: Legendary BJJ and MMA coach Andre Pederneiras; Upper right: The "Marques de Abrantes #106" where the Academia de Jiu-Jitsu—later rebranded Academia Gracie— was founded; Lower left: Tufy, the author, Leitão, Jay, and Fabio; Lower right: Luta Livre Godfather Roberto Leitão

ROBERTO LEITÃO
AND
ANDRE PEDERNEIRAS

"All modalities have always grown parallel to one another. They do not evolve isolated. They are always interfering with one another."
—Roberto Leitão, Father of Brazilian Luta Livre

Our first stop would be the "Marques de Abrantes #106" building, once known as the "Academia de Jiu-Jitsu." Founded by Donato Pires dos Reis with Carlos and George Gracie and assistant instructors in 1930, the "Academia" is now most famous for being erroneously referred to as the "Academia Gracie" of 1925. The building symbolized an important moment in BJJ history and its split from Judo, and we took our time admiring it. The room where the Academy once existed is today a store that sells women's items. It's no larger than a small room or a big bathroom, though there may have been modifications to the building since those days; after all, it's been almost ninety years since a martial arts school operated there. At any rate, this picture would reinforce my hypothesis that BJJ became a ground-oriented art partially due to the fact that so many buildings in Brazil were unfit for an art like Judo, which requires special mats and adequate space for free movement on the feet and the safe execution of takedowns. The tight confines of so many BJJ training spaces, both historically and to this day, certainly limit the Brazilians' ability to practice takedowns. This, in my view, would help set BJJ on a course away from Judo and towards a style and practice particular to itself. Interestingly, this infrastructure issue would create a culture of "knee-Wrestling" that would severely and negatively impact the performance of BJJ fighters on the world stage of MMA years and decades later.

I hold a personal belief that "fighting" is in our nature. This belief is always reinforced when I see toddlers and even animals "play fighting" and attempting to pin each other down. Throughout history, "grappling"—under one name, banner, or ruleset or another—has made itself present in many places. From the Caucasus to Turkey to Japan, all of these grappling styles have one thing in common: being on your back is bad. And yet somehow BJJ escaped that notion, and in so doing opened up a world of technical possibilities. Apart from Kosen Judo, BJJ is the only grappling art to my knowledge in which being on your back can be tactically advantageous, making BJJ and Kosen Judo very unique grappling arts. Thinking of all of this while staring at the Marques de Abrantes building, and remembering all of the dozens of gyms with their small matted areas that I'd visited in Brazil over the course of my life, I wondered again if this simple fluke of infrastructure didn't play a key role in how BJJ developed away from the official Judo ruleset.

Coincidentally, this building is next door (literally next door, if it weren't for an empty lot between them) to "Upper," the academy owned and operated by our next interviewee, Andre Pederneiras, or simply "Dedé." Dedé is one of the founders (alongside Wendell Alexandre) of "Nova União," and is a legendary BJJ and MMA coach. I met Dedé once in my early days in BJJ: I had been a member of the Lewis-Pederneiras school in Las Vegas as a teenager during the two years I lived there (1999 and 2000). MMA was in its early days then (it was still called "No Holds Barred" at the time) and it was not unusual for people like Chuck Liddell, Tito Ortiz, Tsuyoshi Kohsaka, Maurice Smith, and Frank Shamrock to show up randomly for a training session. I'd met Pederneiras during my time there and it was nice to see him again, this time in Rio. On our way in we also bumped into UFC fighter Leonardo Santos, who greeted us warmly and seemed genuinely excited about our project: another good sign that we were on the right track and that there was an audience eager to hear the story, if we could just do it justice.

Pederneiras was a perfect fit for our idea of "not-so-old-school," alongside Mario Yamasaki and Chris Haueter, since Pederneiras' accomplishments as a BJJ and MMA coach needed no introduction. We would also be interviewing Roberto Leitão, and we couldn't have asked for a better venue: Upper was where he had spent much of his time defending his title of "Biggest Lover of Fighting in the World ("Não existe ninguém que goste mais da luta do que eu!"). A few years back I had exchanged emails with Roberto Leitão, as I was curious about the origins of Brazilian Luta Livre and its rivalry with BJJ, and I wanted to know the story from the man himself. Apparently it all went back to a man called "Tatu" ("Armadillo" in English), though where he originally learned Luta Livre remained unclear to me. I was hopeful that now, in our interview, I would get the full story.

In fact, I had a lot of questions for Master Leitão. I was curious about the custom, in some Luta Livre schools in Rio, for practitioners to wear gi pants and belts ranks. I wondered about what it meant that, in the 1967 Guanabara Federation handbook, "Luta Livre de Jiu-Jitsu" was the name given for the practice of BJJ without the gi. It seemed clear that there had been significant overlap between the two arts and that their terminology, much like with Judo and Jiu-Jitsu, had changed and morphed over time. I also wanted to ask about the well-known fact that both George and Hélio Gracie had trained with Catch Wrestlers, the style that would later—and through the efforts of men like Leitão—become known simply as Luta Livre. I wondered how much BJJ had influenced the development of Luta Livre, and vice-versa. We also wanted to learn about the rivalry between BJJ and Luta Livre. In my early years in BJJ I had heard that it was established that BJJ and Luta Livre were enemies; accordingly, even though I had never met any practitioners of that art, in my naive youth I came to view them as my enemies. I was also curious about Master Leitão's relationship with Takeo Yano, a Judoka and Japanese immigrant who would play a vital role in the history of BJJ, Luta Livre, and Pro Wrestling in Brazil, as well as start a lineage of his own in the Brazilian Northeast.

Leitão would also help us better understand the role of Capoeira in the bourgeoning fight scene in Rio de Janeiro (if Capoeira is seen today as a hybrid between dancing and fighting, practitioners in Leitão's heyday did not see it that way). I would later learn (through the research of Elton Silva in *Muitos Antes do MMA*) how Capoeira came to also influence BJJ: techniques like "the technical stand-up," so common in the warm-up of BJJ schools around the world and so unusual in Judo, the double-leg takedown, often referred to in Brazil as "Baiana" rather than its Judo name, "morote-gari," the "stomp" that precedes the takedown, so common in Royce Gracie's early fights in the UFC, as well as the up-kicks from the guard were all moves that were commonly taught and practiced in the old style of Capoeira; a style that was, in Roberto Leitão's time, much closer to MMA than the form now commonly practiced (Grandmaster João Alberto Barreto, in his book, also confirms the influence of Capoeira in BJJ).

Master Leitão was extremely charismatic and energetic for his age. When I asked him if he remembered exchanging emails with me years ago he told me that he did, though I suspect he was just being polite. His energy levels were astonishing, and he even got down and showed me a move or two on the mat. It was clear that everyone at

Pederneiras' gym had a deep respect and appreciation for him, and rightly so: he was, after all, one of the biggest exponents in the entire history of Brazilian martial arts.

But outside of his legendary status, the godfather of Brazilian Luta Livre seemed to me like a genuine person who was still simply in love with being on the mats. I wished I'd had the chance to spend more time with him, and a chance to learn more about the early days of Luta Livre. My curiosity would have to wait for another day, though—or perhaps another documentary. For now, we had our hands full with the task before us.

— Roberto Leitão —

Could you introduce yourself?

My name is Roberto Claudio das Neves Leitão, a long name for a little guy. I am now 80 years old. I was born in 1937, in the south of the country, in the state of Santa Catarina where the population is half German.

When did you begin training?

In Judo I started around 16 or 17 years old. By 1960 I was already a Black Belt. I dedicated myself continually. I had Japanese teachers: Professor Guengo Katayama, Yasu Yoshizawa, Ninomya, and Kihara. Later I became chief and owner of a gym, the Japanese-Brazilian Judo Academy. Also a detail: Kimura came to visit us once. A very good thing.

Did you train with Takeo Yano?

A lot. He was a great fighter. He even tied with Hélio Gracie in Jiu-Jitsu. I had my first contact with Takeo Yano around 1957. These are dates I do not forget because my father died that year, and so I remember it. Takeo Yano helped me a lot.

How was he technically?

Takeo Yano's technique was one of the best things I could find in my life. At that time he knew a lot, he fought well. But he had to live, so he even went over to Catch [Wrestling] and fought fixed fights.

Why did you switch from Judo to Luta Livre?

I started in Luta Livre, scorched by the heat. I used to do Judo, but here in Gávea where our gym was, it was really hot. Then I would take off my jacket and began to see that Luta Livre was smarter than other things, because it is more natural. The heat was too great and the first thing we did was take off our jackets. There we went from Judo to Luta Livre. The "free" [livre] is not free to do whatever you want, it is free of holds. I wear shorts and my problem is solved. I loved Luta Livre and I started to study it and to this day I'm in it.

Who taught you Luta Livre?

Always when they ask who I started training with, I have the impression that it was with myself, because there was no one who practiced Luta Livre exclusively. But I was picking up a little bit with one, a little bit with the other, a little bit with someone else. I was a pilgrim. If there was a good gym in the suburbs, I'd know who was there so I could learn something.

Many of those fights were fixed. Did the public know this?

It's a question I'm always asked, if I think the audience knew that those fights were staged. I do not know if they knew, but they cheered a lot. There was a crowd who liked those fights. The Vale Tudo fights were sometimes less applauded than the so-called fixed ones.

Where does the rivalry between Luta Livre and BJJ come from?

The rivalry between Luta Livre and Jiu-Jitsu comes from a very simple thing. When Jiu-Jitsu began to be introduced here in Brazil they needed to promote it somehow. And they did this by showing that it was effective in a direct confrontation, in free confrontation, really. So they were looking for people to fight them. And who would show up? The Luta Livre guys. That was it.

What were the dynamic between Luta Livre, BJJ, and Judo in your youth?

When I was in my youth and I was starting out in Wrestling, I used to do Judo and I knew many friends of better financial standing who did Jiu-Jitsu. I was friends with them and had free exchange of Jiu-Jitsu, free exchange of Wrestling. I've always tried to do that. When there was a question between the two, I tried to balance the situation to avoid that direct confrontation that was inevitable. I trained and became friends with many Jiu-Jitsu practitioners, I became friends with many in Judo, and became friends with many in Luta Livre.

When did you first meet Hélio Gracie?

The first contact I had with Hélio Gracie was at my house. [It was] in the late '70s. Hélio Gracie one day appeared at my house along with a friend we had in common to ask for a favor. This kindness was a very simple thing. Rickson was going to the United States and he did not have any paper credentials that would explain who he was and what his value was, because there was no Confederation of Jiu-Jitsu. I happened to be director of the fighting department of the Boxing Federation and the Brazilian Confederation of Boxing at the time. Very well, I said that I would write him a letter and I went to the confederation and grabbed a diploma and a paper saying that Rickson was a great fighter. Of course this caused me a lot of problems with the Luta Livre guys, who did not like it. But I said that the boy is worth it and we need to help. And he went with that certificate to the United States and he got there to do the things he had to do. Hélio was delighted with that favor and never forgot and he started to come to my house, invite me to watch the training of Rickson and Royler in Judo at Flamengo. And when he found out that I was a professor of mechanics at the university, that was even better. He liked to exchange ideas to show leverage theory because he was intuitive. Very practical, it was good, but he did not know what he was doing sometimes. So I helped him by showing the theory. I think I contributed a lot in helping Hélio understand leverage because he knew what a lever was, but I would say, "Hélio, that lever you're thinking of is a theoretical leverage. It simply does not exist. What we're using in the fight is something else. It's a bio-lever." That word is one I invented. Bio-lever is a lever made of living things. It does not always work the way a theoretical lever would work.

Tell us about Agenor Sampaio, "Sinhozinho"

I met Agenor Sampaio, Sinhozinho. He was a great Capoeira Master. He took his students to my gym. He trained in my gym. When he turned 69 I organized a party for him there. Then I found out that he knew a lot of Luta Livre and I went to try his technique. This is around 1958 or 1959. Every day Sinhozinho went there, he went a couple of times a week, he took his students, some were my friends. I was right there, watching and learning and I really learned how to kick with him. It was really interesting and the kicks were very strong. Sinhozinho's Capoeira did not have many acrobatics. It was more kicks. Side kick, stomps, frontal kicks, more sidekicks, all very strong. And once the late Waldemar Santana went there. The boys who were there simply demolished Waldemar. He wanted to grab them and he couldn't. The boys would just move back kicking, kicking very hard.

Could we credit any single person with having invented BJJ or Luta Livre?

We know that no one invented anything. All modalities have always grown parallel to one another. They do not evolve isolated. No, they

158

are parallel. Because they are always interfering with one another. You obviously cannot be a person who knows everything. That does not exist.

Do you have any regrets in life?

I don't think so. I am very satisfied with my life. I only miss the people who have left.

Could you live without Luta Livre?

I would die. I would die if I did not practice. Suffice it to say the following: I have a serious injury here whose solution is called pros-thesis. Very well, should I do it? I will not do it, because if I do pros-thesis I cannot train. So, you'll have to come up with another solution for me because I'm not going to do prosthetics because I want to train. There is no one who likes fighting more than I do. I love it and I'll keep training.

—

— André Pederneiras —

Could you tell us about the relationship among a teacher, stu-dent, and memory?

When you start to train, the first thing you think about is achieving the Black Belt. And the one who starts teaching you then is the person you want to be closest to. For example, I'm a Carlson Gracie Black Belt, but I trained from my white belt to my brown belt with a teacher named Rodrigo Vieira. In all the interviews I say that I got the Black Belt from Carlson, but the one who taught me from white to brown belt was Rodrigo Vieira. At the time I even competed for Rickson's academy, because [Vieira] was a student of Rolls and started to com-pete for Rickson's academy. So I think that remembering all of the people who gave you the knowledge right from the start or at any point in your career is the least you can do for those who have set aside the time to teach you. I was not financially well off. I started paying the gym fee, because my father enrolled me to work out there. I found Jiu-Jitsu and fell in love, so I left bodybuilding. However, after the first year my father, because he was retired, could not pay anymore. Then, Professor Rodrigo Vieira gave me a scholarship at the gym that is now mine and then I started to train Jiu-Jitsu until it got to the point where one day [Professor Vieira] moved far away. I was invited by Carlson to attend the classes he was giving, and I ended up going from being a brown belt to receiving my Black Belt from him. I stayed there for a long time. So in every interview I give, I always remember Rodrigo as my first teacher. So I think it's a very important thing to remember the ones who helped you.

What is the importance of telling history correctly?

When you want to tell a real story you have to tell the real story. Unless it's a fictional movie, because then you can mix it up and do it the way you want it done. When it's a real story of a sport, whatever it is, you have to tell it the right way. Can you forget? You are not required to remember all the details that have happened in your life to tell a story. You can forget João, Manuel, Zezinho, but you cannot forget all three. You have to remember someone and you have to tell a story for which someone in the future will not say that they were there at that time and that it was not quite like that. Because, as much as you have told this story with ninety-nine percent certainty, there will be at least one percent that you did not take into consideration or that you have told incorrectly. This will cast an unfavorable light on the ninety-nine percent of the story that is correct. Because, from the moment you cause mistrust because of that one percent, that one percent can end up mixed with the ninety-nine percent. Sometimes you tell the story, but you want to omit something. From the moment it is revealed that that part did not happen that way, everything that did happen the way you explained can be destroyed. People stop believing everything you say.

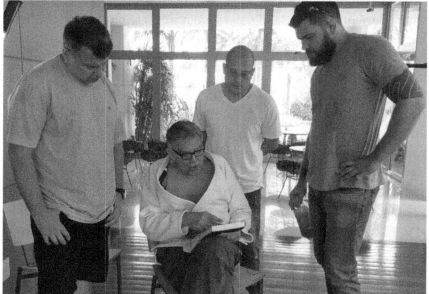

Upper left: The author and Grandmaster Barreto; Upper right: Grandmaster João Alberto Barreto; Bottom: Grandmaster Barreto kindly gifts our team an autographed copy of his book.

JOÃO ALBERTO BARRETO

"Existence is not measured by time. Existence is measured by the

*ways you have been finding and creating and writing your story. So
here, at the moment, I'm writing my story through this documentary."*
—Grandmaster João Alberto Barreto, student of
Hélio Gracie and author

Our team's next interviewee was João Alberto Barreto: author,
scholar, BJJ and MMA pioneer, one of Hélio's earliest Black Belts,
and currently a 9th degree Red Belt. We met him in the lobby of his
luxurious apartment complex in Rio de Janeiro. While Steve and Jay
collected B-Roll with their drone outside, Fabio and I set to work trying to get as much information out of our interviewee as possible.
This had become something of a method for us: even off-camera we
were constantly trying to dig stories out of these Grandmasters, hoping to discover something that would significantly impact not only
our documentary but our understanding of BJJ history overall. (This
tactic would prove very successful with other Grandmasters, particularly Armando Wriedt, who we found to be an open book free of any
filter and a lover of genuine conversations unrestricted by politics and
affiliations.) In the moments before the camera started rolling Fabio
and I would talk to the interviewee, vaguely touching on topics we
wanted to discuss while avoiding any direct questions or challenges.
The hope was always that an interviewee might take the bait and offer
something up themselves; Barreto, however, proved too savvy for this
approach. He masterfully avoided answering the tough questions and,
for the most part, stuck to the party line—all while keeping an enormous smile on his face (this, despite the fact that we all knew what
was being asked, and what was on the line). Finally, abandoning all
tact, I asked him directly what the issue was between the Gracie
Academy and Georges Mehdi. Even this proved fruitless, however:
Master Barreto gave me a long reply that was so devoid of any substance or revelatory insight that now I can't recall any of what he said.
He was running circles on us, and it was no accident: The Grandmaster, it seemed, was a Red Belt in more than just BJJ.

Perhaps this should have come as no surprise: Barreto is a Gracie
man in every sense of the word except for his surname. His undying

loyalty to Hélio was so obvious, in fact, that I was a little concerned we were merely going to be collecting soundbites belonging not in a documentary about BJJ's true history but rather in the *Gracie in Action* tapes Rorion Gracie produced to sell their brand of Jiu-Jitsu to the world. As it would turn out, though, even though Barreto never hid his affiliations, he did give us some great material, including some of the best soundbites about the importance of telling history accurately and Hélio's personality. This may have been due in part in his belief that "truth-telling" could not hurt the cause and history of Hélio Gracie in any way (I would later feel this same stance from the Valente Brothers).

Despite his fame, walking into this project I honestly hadn't known what to make of Hélio Gracie. Now, and slowly, he was becoming a character I both admired and disliked. In some ways he seemed to embody BJJ and its stubborn existence; it was in many ways his unwavering resolution to create a space in which he and his brother could be the leaders, during an era when the pressure to submit and return to Judo would have been great, that allowed Jiu-Jitsu to stand on its own. This resolution was a key ingredient in allowing our art to survive. I admired him for taking a short-notice fight against his former student—the much younger and heavier Waldemar Santana—and enduring a beating for over three hours (sources disagree on the exact duration of the fight), yet I despised his attacks on Santana, and I couldn't help but see him as the villain in their fight: a fight that went beyond a simple rivalry between student and teacher and went well into the social and racial tensions simmering in Brazil at the time. I admired the courage he displayed when (according to the story the family tells, at least) he jumped in shark-infested waters to save a total stranger,[8] but I couldn't respect the fact that he held two families simultaneously, one unbeknownst to the other, as well as the fact that he had three children with his maid and not his wife (even if his wife, Margarida, couldn't bear children, it is difficult not to disapprove of

---

[8] Though this story did appear in at least one newspaper, it is unclear whether the story was confirmed by or simply related to the article's author.

this). I am thankful for his stubborn leadership—leadership that in many ways created a space for this larval style to develop into something distinct from Judo—and thankful because, in this regard, it is because of him that I enjoy the job and the lifestyle I now have. Conversely, I despise his authoritarian tendencies, tendencies which led him to enroll in Integralismo, the Brazilian Fascist Party (though, to be fair, even *Time* magazine named Hitler their "Man of The Year" during this same period; this does not necessarily excuse the stance or the enrollment but does, perhaps, paint the man and his actions in the context of his time). I saw vanity in his insistence that he had "created" BJJ (a claim he would make towards the end of his life, probably due to Rorion's influence and ambition to become the heir to this "creation"). In short, he embodied BJJ history because he embodied the good and bad from which BJJ was born.

Judo, in my view, is infinitely more in tune with a moral, ethical, and just society; in this regard, it dwarfs BJJ by comparison. Yet I can't help but think that, in many ways, BJJ is a continuation from where Judo limited itself; interesting when we consider that, had it not been for this resistance to and cleaving from Judo, the UFC itself wouldn't exist, and the realistic approach to combat that is MMA may not have come to the forefront of the public eyes. I can't envision MMA without BJJ and I can't envision BJJ without Hélio. Regardless of what I think of him as a person, I strongly believe that, were it not for him, we would all be doing Judo today. His ambition, vanity, and even a degree of egomania helped carve the foundation for what would become BJJ, and I don't see a way around that.

I knew that some would feel that this book (and our film) were unfair to the Gracie Brothers. To this I would argue that, in my view, Carlos and Hélio in fact played a far more important role than even the one with which they credit themselves. Technical evolution and innovation are a natural progress of any martial art practice: given enough time and competitive space, this evolution is inevitable. The stubborn resistance to Judo was not a "natural" occurrence of time and space, but fruit of the obstinacy of the Gracie Brothers and their desire to shine. (One could also argue that BJJ would have been better off being reabsorbed by Judo, given the latter's superior moral and educational foundations... the jury remains out.)

Furthermore, in a strange way, I came to admire some of the elements of the upbringing of the Gracie Brothers' offspring. The purposeful and spartan education (the diet, the intense training, et cetera) is something I believe children can benefit from in some ways. This upbringing, so at odds with how most people are raised, had a sense of purpose (or "patrician ethos," if you prefer) within the realm of their niche martial arts practice, and thus was an element in the role played by the Gracie family and its development of Jiu-Jitsu in Brazil... yet another unexpected ingredient in this seemingly never-ending recipe of events, characters, and cultures.

— João Alberto Barreto —

Can you introduce yourself?

My name is João Alberto Barreto. As for age I have already deleted the age of my existence. I no longer have an age. You will ask me: "Why don't you measure yourself by time?" Because existence is not measured by time. Existence is measured by the ways you have been finding and creating and writing your story. So here at the moment I'm writing my story through this documentary.

How did you come to meet Hélio Gracie?

Hélio Gracie was challenged by a Bahia fighter named Caribé and my father let them use the gymnasium [at the school where my father taught]. My father was an educator, Antônio Carlos de Mello Barreto. He was an engineer and educator. And they were very grateful for being allowed to use the gymnasium. There was the fight. Hélio Gracie easily beat Caribé. My father invited me to watch this fight with him and I was amazed by that kind of sport I did not know. [Afterwards] they went to my house and my father received them and they thanked my father. My father was in the habit of saying, "My son, take off your shirt to show your physique to the Gracies." I took them out and they were amazed. I was a strong, tall boy, I liked sports, I did weightlifting at that time. Carlos Gracie said, "João Alberto, we will give you a Jiu-Jitsu scholarship, want it? Do you want to be a champion?" I said I was in. And that's where my story started.

What is the importance of retelling BJJ history in a more complete way?

The story of our Jiu-Jitsu needs to be told, but without any fantasies. Often society itself leads to a completely different story from what history is. The stories have to be truthful, real, and nothing fancy. Today Brazilian Jiu-Jitsu and the Brazilian Vale Tudo are all over the world. But the origins are being highlighted. Carlos and Hélio Gracie, their children, others such as myself, Hélio Vígio, Armando Wriedt, my brother Alvaro, my brother Sérgio, and all the others who made their academies and were promoting Brazilian Jiu-Jitsu.

But the story, we have to be very careful with it, because man, the human being is a being who likes to modify things. And incompetence often leads individuals, wanting to think they are doing good, to do evil. This is what happens today in Brazilian Jiu-Jitsu and in the whole Brazilian Vale Tudo. Man is a historical being, but history has to have a basis of truth. It cannot be false. The human being walks in both. Some are historically true, others create historical fantasies. How can I tell the story of one or the other? I can talk about my story. I can talk about other stories that I naturally have mastery and knowledge of.

But not that I need history to support me in the present. Once they asked Jean-Paul Sartre, this great existentialist, what he thought about the work he had written. "I have no further connection with what I wrote. I'm more worried about what I'm writing." So my life today is what I'm writing. Today I am writing about marital and family relationships. It has nothing to do with fighting. Because I want to help people in the society in which we live where families are being destroyed by the lack of humanization.

What do you think Carlos and Hélio would have to say about BJJ today?

Carlos Gracie died, Hélio Gracie passed away, and Brazilian Jiu-Jitsu became an art in deconstruction. If Hélio Gracie is up there watching us, he'd say that himself. "Wow, what have they done with my Jiu-Jitsu, which was a Jiu-Jitsu for the weakest and today is a Jiu-Jitsu for the strongest?" They created a gi that only with a steel gauntlet can you choke someone. Neither a girl nor a child can strangle with these gis. This is a way of creating a deconstruction of Jiu-Jitsu for the weakest. Why should we allow such a thing? Everyone started to make their own Jiu-Jitsu. Even the Gracie family. There are only a few who still practiced Hélio Gracie's Jiu-Jitsu.

How did Hélio learn Jiu-Jitsu?

Look, Hélio Gracie, he was a Jiu-Jitsu genius. He himself said, "Look Joao Alberto, my observations taught me Jiu-Jitsu. Watching Carlos give classes to his students. I went on learning. And once Carlos did not show up to teach, and his student and I were there, and the student asked me if I could teach him some lessons." That's when Hélio started teaching this boy. When Carlos arrived the student told Carlos that he wanted to continue taking classes with Hélio Gracie. Then Carlos, who was very intelligent, realized that Hélio had conquered the student by his way of being. Technical and knowledgeable of fighting. And never again has Hélio missed the opportunity to develop Gracie Jiu-Jitsu.

Was Hélio a natural leader? What was he like as a person?

Hélio Gracie led because he was a leader. Hélio Gracie had the intrinsic qualities of a great leader because he spoke truths. He was a critical man. With him, everything was the pursuit of truth with the critical process.

Hélio Gracie was in Ceará, and there the press went to do an in-

terview with him. They asked what the Brazilian hierarchy in Jiu-Jitsu
was. He said that first was Hélio Gracie, Carlson Gracie, João Alberto Barreto, and Pedro Hemetério, who was from Ceará. And he
added, "This implies that the above-mentioned names can be included
among the top fighters in the world. Such is the level achieved by our
national Jiu-Jitsu." Pedro Hemetério was annoyed [that he was listed
behind me] and complained to Hélio. Hélio replied that he had the
right to be upset, and he suggested that we train to see who the third
best one was. He did not accept. Hélio was like that. "Let's see, let's
go to the ring." In 1954 I was 18 years old and three years of Jiu-Jitsu
alone, and was third in the hierarchy. Hélio, Carlson, and me. And
Hélio never said that to anyone. Hélio was not one to praise. He was
more about criticizing you and putting you on the spot, to challenge
you. Hélio was like that.

**What was the ranking system like? What about early tourna-
ments?**

At that time the belt was not something taken into consideration,
because the belt came to be considered when Jiu-Jitsu became a competitive system. At that time we had no competitive system. The fights
took place through challenges. [In] 1950 the first Jiu-Jitsu championship took place. Carlson Gracie was the champion and Pedro
Hemetério was the runner-up. There was no federation [at that time].
Then Carlos and Hélio created a great gym on Avenida Rio Branco. It
was the Brazilian Kodokan. That's where we began to do in-house
competitions and we began to see the possibility of creating belts, because Hélio himself wore a blue belt. We teachers, a lighter blue belt.
[That was] until we created the first official Jiu-Jitsu Championship,
[which] I organized at Botafogo Futebol and Regatas. I created it,
because before that we created the Carioca Federation of Jiu-Jitsu.
This federation I created at the time through the National Sports
Council. Because at that time the Gracies, with that eagerness to
show their Gracie Jiu-Jitsu, they were in a certain way emperors and
said, "With my Jiu-Jitsu I face any guy stronger than me. Want to try

it, let's try it." That is, there was a principle of challenges in those days. These were isolated fights. So what happened, we had at a given historical moment created a federation. Hélio was the honorary president and I was the executive vice-president of the federation. Who created the first rules of fighting in the world? It was me and Hélio Gracie. [Note: Barreto here most likely means the first ruleset for Jiu-Jitsu competition].

Your father-in-law told you he met Carlos Gracie at Koma's academy. Can you tell us about it?

My father-in-law met the young Carlos Gracie. They were about 16 or 17 years old. Because my father-in-law liked sports. He met Carlos Gracie, a very intelligent young man, and was interested in the arrival of Count Koma in Belém do Pará. It was a revolution in the sportive society in Pará. Then the Japanese opened a gym, and Carlos Gracie and my father-in-law went to train with him. Another student was also Fernando Ferro [sic, likely Jacyntho] who was one of the forerunners and also a student of Count Koma there in Belém do Pará.

Who was Oscar Santa Maria?

Oscar Santa Maria was, let's say, one of the "patrons" of the Gracies. Oscar Santa Maria was a very intelligent man, prepared, lawyer, Minister of the Economy in the time of Getúlio. He was a very special man and was very close to Carlos and greatly admired Carlos Gracie. And he was Carlos' student. Oscar Santa Maria was a wealthy man, he had his own economic financial life and he became a member of the family. The Gracie family came to have him as a great brother. And he spent his entire life living with the Gracie family. And I lived with Oscar Santa Maria for awhile, because I lived with Hélio Gracie at Flamengo Beach, where Hélio lived in Copacabana, and Oscar stayed in Flamengo and I stayed with Oscar Santa Maria. Santa Maria was a gentleman, a highly educated guy. A formidable fellow.

But at the end of his life he had a problem with the Gracies. He had a sister who thought he had been exploited all his life by the Gracie family. But I do not see any exploitation in this. So much so that, at that moment that there was this problem, and the newspaper O Globo *began to post and distribute the news of this conflict between Carlos Gracie and Oscar Santa Maria, Oscar came to me along with his lawyer asking me to testify on his behalf against the Gracies. I said I could not do that against Carlos, and neither against Hélio, because I'm part of the family. I do not have any historical standing because I do not even know your problems with Carlos, in relation to religion, spiritualistic matters, these things. Then his lawyer realized and said that I was very young and had not participated in this process.*

What was it like to live in the Rio Branco Gracie Academy?

They set up a great gym on Rio Branco Avenue, number 151, and we all went to live there. Live on the mats. Everyone had their own laundry area because we woke up early and we had to clean the ring, the bathroom, et cetera. Each had its own designated area and Hélio arrived early to check that everything was clean. If it had any dirt, there was a fine. And at the end of the month he would tell us how many fines we had. And who had the most fines? Carlson Gracie. Then Carlson would say to Hélio, "Wow, Uncle Hélio, are you going to charge me this?" Hélio answered that he was going to charge because he had to improve. He said he would have to charge even more, because he should have had an interest in cleaning up even better his sector. It was me, Carlson Gracie, Hélio Vígio, and Armando Wriedt.

What was Waldemar Santana like?

Waldemar Santana was a formidable person. A simple but very brave man. He was a marble worker. I met Waldemar at Hélio Gracie's house doing a job for Hélio. And he liked fighting. So with the new gym he went there and stayed as a janitor and trained with us. I taught Waldemar every day. He was my student. At the time he had that fight with the Gracies, and it came out in the press that he could fight me instead of Carlson or Hélio, he said that he would not fight me. Because we had a great friendship. He was my student. He was not my paying student, he was a student friend. He had this gratitude towards me. Always had.

What was it like being the introducer of BJJ in the U.S.?

I do not want to toot my own horn, but I've always been an entrepreneur. I always wanted to advertise Gracie Jiu-Jitsu, and I had the opportunity to take it to America. I was the pioneer in taking the Brazilian Jiu-Jitsu—that was formerly Gracie Jiu-Jitsu—to show the Americans what we had here in terms of fighting. I was able to take two great friends who were Barrene and Flavio Behring. They went with me. They were my students and we did shows at the New York Athletic Club, a great club in New York, and we did the presentation of a movie that we did with Cesar Yazigi, who was a great English teacher who [had lived] in Brazil and who was my student in New York. We took it to the Naval Academy of Annapolis, for the American cadets. We did a demonstration to the FBI. I mean, to do a schedule like this you have to be an entrepreneur. If not, you won't do it. I was not getting anything out of it. I wanted to show what I did that would be good for everyone to do, especially Americans.

I had never been to America. I went to America and had the opportunity. It was around 1963. It was just when Kennedy died in November, and I was in October in the United States. I trained with a European Judo champion at the New York Athletic club. I went there to show Jiu-Jitsu. I fought a New York karate champion from the New York police. I did shows in [inaudible], a neighborhood of New York, in a public school there. We did a great schedule. I also took it to Europe. I exhibited in France, exhibited in England. I was the first Brazilian along with my brothers to make a great exhibition at Hyde Park in London. It was a formidable thing, I exhibited at various academies.

171

What was your relationship with Hélio like?

I am a fighting son of Hélio Gracie. He considered me family. He had a very special affection for me. So much so that I have always been with him for his whole life. Of course, there came a time in my life that I had to part with him. But I have never ceased to be bound by his history and its importance in its formation of [me as a] man and also as a practitioner of Gracie Jiu-Jitsu. I always defended the Gracie family. Carlos Gracie, who was the spiritual father and father of our diet, which I always followed. And Hélio, I always dedicated myself [to him], so much that in my book, where he made an endorsement, he says that the relationship with me has always been a very special relationship. And the interesting thing is that our other companions were very jealous. Because it really was all me. So that's part of the story. I do not mean that he did not treat others in the same way, but to me he had a very special affection. I would say that there was an identity relation. A relation of psychological son, not biological son. It is one of psychological son. That is to say, he saw in me qualities perhaps very similar to his own, because I was very dedicated to the Gracie Academy. I was the teacher who taught the most while I stayed there. No teacher gave as many lessons as me. I was dedicated to that. If Hélio had some students that he could not teach, the class was mine. I replaced him, no one else. So much so that I fought in the world competition of Hélio Gracie with Kato and with Kimura in Maracanãzinho. I was 15 years old, fighting. I fought with a Japanese and I drew and I fought with a Brazilian and won. At 15 years of age. How could I, with 15 years of age and 6 months of Jiu-Jitsu, be fighting in an international tournament I ask? I must have had some qualities, and Hélio saw these qualities in me. I mean, I had a very fast technical development, very fast. But I dedicated myself. In my life I have always done things with love, with affection, with dedication to become better and better. I've always been like this in my life. So much so that in the field of sport Jiu-Jitsu and in the field of psychology I succeeded. But I think that human success depends exactly on the truth you have before you. That's what I want, I believe

172

that, I'll do it, and I'll be the best. Win or win, that was our motto.

—

Following our interview, on our way out, Barreto gifted me with a copy of his book *Do Vale Tudo Brasileiro ao Mixed Martial Arts,* and signed it. A true gentleman and owner of a sharp mind, Barreto had made history; I was flattered to even be in the presence of a living part of BJJ and MMA history, and honored to receive the gift.

Upper left: Grandmaster Hélio Fadda; Upper right: The original Fadda Academy in 1950; Middle row left: Newspaper article depicting the charismatic Fadda favorite "Torpedo"; Middle row right: Grandmaster João Rezende; Bottom left: Our team visits one of the many "Fadda Projects" that teach underprivileged children in Rio de Janeiro; Bottom right: The Fadda Academy in 2018

HÉLIO FADDA AND JOÃO REZENDE

"[The Faddas] never sought out financial gain. The goal was always to get the kids off the streets. That was the work he taught us. I do this

in Ilha Bela with six hundred and fifty children. I do not have a salary. I'm Fadda to my core, from head to toe."
—Grandmaster João Rezende, student of Oswaldo Fadda

The "Carioca" (a term used to refer to someone or someplace in Rio de Janeiro) neighborhood of Bento Ribeiro isn't necessarily the "favelas" (slums) of Rio de Janeiro, but neither is it the "Zona Sul" (or "South Zone," where one can find the historic and touristy neighborhoods of Ipanema and Copacabana). Bento Ribeiro is a lower-middle-class neighborhood, and not particularly beautiful to look at; nor did we ever feel particularly safe there. Still, our visit was important because it would help us explain the Oswaldo Fadda lineage, and its relevance to the development of BJJ outside of the Gracie Academy.

When I began telling other BJJ practitioners that I was helping produce a documentary film about the history of BJJ, the most common question I received was, "Are you guys going to talk about the Faddas?" Awareness about the existence of a "non-Gracie" lineage in Brazil has been growing in recent years on internet forums, websites, and Wikipedia (quickly becoming the primary source of knowledge in the age of the internet), but the conversation actually started years earlier, with a claim made by Oswaldo Fadda's teacher, Luis França. (França's last living student, Antonio Vieira, in a later interview, would also testify to Luis França having made this claim; Oswaldo Fadda himself would repeat the claim in an article published in the '60s.) Now, however, I was learning that the story of the Fadda lineage was not only complex but—like the story of the Gracie lineage—clouded by mythologized accounts and unsubstantiated claims.

I have always found it interesting how, whether we are discussing government politics, the coronavirus, or BJJ history, people immediately assume that you hold a position on either side of the aisle. It is as if, to them, the world is binary in every way: a Disney cartoon where "good" and "evil" are locked in a battle to be resolved by the end, when the "right" side will win and everyone will "live happily ever after." Yet it is equally true that, for those holding this worldview, "evil" and "bad" seem to be designations reserved specifically for those with whom they don't agree; for those holding this binary worldview, Hell—in Sartre's words—is *other people.*

All of which is to say that, strangely enough, many people I spoke with early on in the production process seemed to assume that our documentary was going to champion the story of the Fadda lineage while casting stones at the narrative originating from the Gracie Academy. People simply assumed that our film was anti-Gracie and, by default, pro-Fadda. Personally I have always found this binary mentality, in all its manifestations, childish and ultimately self-defeating. Within the specific context of our project, however, it quickly became apparent to me that this polarized worldview of "teams" and "parties" was a force to be dealt with, and would require us to expend enormous amounts of energy in explaining that, really and truly, we sided with neither (a position which nevertheless elicited flak and criticism from interview and podcast listeners who, despite our best efforts, insisted that our film was either pro- or anti-Gracie).

Despite the potentially fraught waters into which we were wading, we were welcomed with open arms by the members of the Fadda Academy. The plan was to talk to two Red Belts of that lineage: Hélio Fadda, nephew of Oswaldo Fadda and current leader of the Fadda clan (Hélio Fadda was named, I was told, after Hélio Gracie, a man Oswaldo Fadda held in great esteem), and João Rezende, a student of Fadda since the early days of the Academy, which had been operating out of this same building since 1950 (it is certainly impressive that the Academy has remained in operation and in the same place for all these years, apart from a temporary closure due to a fire). Hélio Fadda ran the Academy while João Rezende carried on another Oswaldo Fadda's tradition: he ran a BJJ program for hundreds of underprivileged children in Ilha Bela, an island off the coast of the state of São Paulo. He had driven far to meet our team and tell his story.

What immediately struck me was how eager and happy these men were to tell the story of Oswaldo Fadda. I found it remarkable that they never tried to diminish Carlos or Hélio Gracie in any way, but, on the contrary, praised them, Hélio Gracie in particular, with whom

Oswaldo apparently had a good relationship. They were not bitter that their story had been largely overwhelmed by that of the Gracie family, though they clearly felt that they had a lot to say that was worth hearing. João Rezende went as far as bringing dozens of boxes of photos that told that story (though, unfortunately, these pictures were too recent to be relevant to our documentary).

I was struck, also, by their profound loyalty to Oswaldo, and the manner in which they spoke of him. It reminded me later of how some of Hélio Gracie's students spoke of him, in other interviews we conducted. They seemed eager to introduce the world to a man they considered admirable and worthy of historical note much more so than they were to talk about the alleged "non-Gracie" aspect of their lineage.

By now Fabio and I had agreed that the best way to get meaningful soundbites out of our interviewees was to appeal to their emotions as much as possible, especially with the Grandmasters for whom history was not called forth from newspaper articles and archives but from their own lives and memories. There is an enormous difference between the two, and—however more accurate the historians' accounts may prove—for the purpose of film you really can't beat a 90-year-old Grandmaster's deeply emotional retelling of his youth and involvement in the birth of BJJ. A message is often better heard when reason takes temporary leave and the messenger communicates through the less rational language of human sentiment; the spotlight of clinical inquiry can, by revealing all, sometimes obscure the beauty of the object pursued. Still, this approach has to be tempered, and Fabio and I had already (half-jokingly) wondered if eventually one of us was going to push it too far, and end up making one of our interviewees cry from nostalgia for a bygone era. It was never our intention but Fabio came close with Roberto Leitão, who became very emotional when recalling his youth. With João Rezende, however, I didn't even have to try: the mere mention of Oswaldo Fadda's name evoked in the man such emotion that we wondered whether if what had rallied that emotion was the fact that Fadda was no longer with us, or the fact that Rezende could no longer relive that golden age.

The interest in the Fadda lineage is well warranted: Oswaldo Fadda's teacher, Luis França, allegedly learned from Mitsuyo Maeda ("Conde Koma") himself. Researchers in Brazil have searched for years for anything that could verify this connection, but to no avail. To date, there is no evidence of Luis França having ever met or trained with Maeda. However, it is a possible that França, who began his training in the Brazilian Navy, met and learned from Takeo Yano, who taught for the Navy during the same period; Yano, although not a direct student of Maeda, did train with him in Belém for a time. Under this scenario, the hypothesis goes that França, much like Carlos Gracie, would eliminate the "middle-man" when describing his own lineage, favoring the more famous Maeda and claiming for himself the accordant credibility. The evidence available, however, suggests that França's true apprenticeship occurred at the Gracie Academy. If this is true, that would mean that much of what we thought we knew about the Fadda lineage is incorrect. This doesn't discredit them in my view, though it does change the whole discussion regarding their non-Gracie lineage... though at this point in the production I was more or less done with the topic. As far as I was concerned (and based on the evidence available), Luis França's initial education took place under the auspices of the Gracie Academy, but the story of the Faddas, and their role in spreading BJJ to a broader audience, was far more interesting than an alleged relationship between França and Maeda.

Viewed in this light, it began to dawn on me that, in fact, the Faddas' role in the development of BJJ is far more significant than that with which they have credited themselves. Competition is necessary for growth, and the rivalry between the Faddas and the Gracie Academy was undeniably beneficial to the sport, not to mention the teams themselves. And since they were not competing over clients, due to the distance between Bento Ribeiro and the South Zone, as well as the difference in income between the two clienteles, the two groups could coexist financially while pushing each other technically.

A "lineage" is an arbitrary concept, the product of a top-down sort of view of martial arts, and one which is too simplistic to do justice to the true nuances of history. We know that we don't learn just from "observing" or from "being taught": the things we observe and the things we are taught may broaden our horizons or help us rethink what we know, but true learning happens within us; a Master can show us to the door, but we have to walk through it ourselves. Deeper learning comes when we wrestle with ideas and, in the case of martial arts, bodies as well. Accordingly, a more accurate view might be that we learn from a wide variety of sources, our training partners—who challenge us and force us to reevaluate our technique—not the least among them. In light of this, the popular notion of a "lineage" as a single unbroken chain of knowledge transferred from teacher to student down through the ages seems arbitrary and ill-conceived, and adds very little to the conversation. In the case of the Faddas in particular this seems especially true: the questions surrounding the origin of their lineage do little to elevate or diminish their undeniable role as contributors to the art's development; further, they pale in importance when considered against the role the Faddas played in opening BJJ up to those who previously couldn't afford to learn it. (For example: one of the most touching moments in the whole production was when João Rezende vividly described to us how Oswaldo Fadda and his wife Zelia would manufacture gis out of flour sacks for the children who couldn't afford them. In light of stories like these, questions of lineage seemed beside the point.)

It is perhaps most important to remember that, while the Gracie Academy catered to the wealthier echelon of Carioca society (diplomats, politicians, actors, business men, et cetera), Fadda centered his work in the underprivileged neighborhood of Bento Ribeiro, teaching BJJ to children who couldn't afford to pay for lessons. (These "projetos" as Brazilians call them, spread everywhere, and it is unquestionable that they have had a positive impact in Brazilian society, even if in a currency that can't be quantified. Listening to Rezende talk about the work he was doing in Ilha Bela, and that other Fadda instructors were doing on the outskirts of Rio, I recalled the projeto ("Pequenos Samurais") in Itu where I grew up, where approximately fifty children trained for free. Unbeknownst to me, we were continuing a Fadda tradition; in this sense, I realized, the Pequenos Samurais and the thousands of programs like it in Brazil, and all who benefit from the training they offer—despite their various lineages—are all members of the Fadda lineage, only in a more significant way. In my mind, the positive impact of these efforts simply dwarfs all other considerations.

This initiative alone would have sufficed to establish Fadda in the hall of BJJ Greats; still, it wasn't all he would do. Fadda is remembered also for his efforts to open up BJJ training to the physically handicapped at a time where such a practice was, at best, uncommon. (When the older members of the Fadda gym spoke about "Torpedo," the charismatic handicapped practitioner who along with Fadda pioneered the practice of BJJ for the disabled, they spoke of him so vividly that you could almost feel his presence in the room, and it became clear that during his time there he was the life of the academy.) Again, when considered against all of this, I can't help but feel that the questions surrounding the Fadda lineage's true origin, and whether or not Luis França trained with Maeda, don't matter much at all.

Lastly, I won't hold it against Carlos and Hélio Gracie that they opted to teach the well-off and privileged classes of wealthier beaches. Most of us choose the greener pasture when the circumstances allow for it, and I'm not in a position to judge: many Brazilians left their home country to teach in affluent plazas across Southern California, New York, Europe, and Australia, and in this group I must include myself. I could have gone to Zimbabwe or to some village in El Salvador to teach BJJ, but instead I chose the more economically promising route and settled in the opulence of Las Vegas. Whether Fadda taught the poor purely out of altruism or because he had no access to the Brazilian elites, we will never know. In either case, his efforts changed BJJ forever, taking it from a boutique niche practice for the few and bringing it to the masses where it belongs, and for this Jiu-Jitsu itself and we who love it are forever in his debt.

— **João Rezende** —

Could you introduce yourself?

180

My name is João Rezende—with a "z"—de Sousa Filho. And I am 65 years old in Jiu-Jitsu, and 75 years of a well-lived life. The same time that this Fadda family has with Jiu-Jitsu. And I always trained at the Fadda Academy here in Bento Ribeiro.

How did you meet Oswaldo Fadda?

I met Fadda in a wonderful way, because when I was very young I got beat up a lot in the streets, and my parents thought that they would be able to help the situation if they put me in an academy that taught self-defense, and I found one in Bento Ribeiro. Later I also found several places with some students whose origin was in the Fadda Academy teaching classes in certain suburbs of the Fluminense region that goes all the way to Santa Cruz. This is very important.

What was Oswaldo Fadda like as a person?

Oswaldo Fadda was not just a friend, he was a father. He is a person we loved as a father in every way. He took in his students as his own children. If we were to classify him today, he would be a general. But a big-hearted general. He was a father, a friend, a brother, a cousin, an uncle. He always talked to the students to be credible because he knew the responsibility was great. There were many students who could not afford to pay, and this was one of the first gyms in Brazil to open its arms to people who could not afford to pay. Many students leave this place with great human warmth, and not only with Jiu-Jitsu.

Were there many difficulties?

He was always encouraging the student to seek some sponsorship, because at that time it was difficult to find gis available in stores. He himself sought to make the gis with flour sacks with his wife Dona Zélia, by coincidence the same name as my wife as well. Not only did he do this, he did the size adjustment of the gis according to the size of the child. There were not many sizes of gis available for sale. He measured the children and made various sizes according to age. The belts were all made in white and when the student was promoted, the belts were dyed. Mrs. Zelia, like my wife, dyed all belts. The mats were not the same as the modern ones we have today. They were made of rice straw.

Why did Fadda teach here in Bento Ribeiro?

His choice in staying here was because here was the center. This Academy has ranked many Black Belts, some already deceased. It is all something sacred. He never charged anyone to teach. He taught this to all of us. Speaking for myself, I have never charged anyone. Today I have six hundred and fifty students in Ilha Bela, and I never charged them for classes. And we're looking for people to donate gis. Master Fadda asked parents who were in better [financial] condition to help those who needed it. That is why he took the sacred name: Fadda, Grandmaster of suburban origin. Hélio Gracie, Grandmaster of South Zone origin. It was the Rich Master and the Poor Master.

This seems to be one of the biggest differences between the Fadda and the Gracie Academies. Could you tell us some more about this?

In many interviews we would say that they were the rich cousins and the poor cousins. The poor cousin was Fadda and the rich cousins were the Gracies. They were wonderful and came from a richer area that was the southern zone. In the northern zone, from Santa Cruz to Japeri, Master Fadda made all the Black Belts he promoted take the initiative of teaching in the suburbs in general. Everyone taught with pride and did not charge [for lessons], as Master Fadda didn't.

Oswaldo Baptista Fadda and this dignified family and now—thank God—his nephew, has embraced the cause and will carry it on, on behalf of the Fadda family. Because they never sought out financial gain. The goal was always to get the kids off the streets. That was the work he taught us. I do this in Ilha Bela with six hundred and fifty children. I do not have a salary. I'm Fadda to my core, from head to toe.

If Oswaldo Fadda could see your work today, what would he say?

I would not say "if" he was here. He is here. You can rest assured he's here. Hélio Fadda is happy because he is his blood. I respect him as the man who reeducated me and brought me to where I am today and—thanks to God—I am proud to bear the Fadda banner and teach my students to respect their fellow men. The Fadda family lives in my heart and in my blood.

I'm sure he's thanking us for what we're doing for him. I have in Ilha Bela thirty-five Black Belts with the biggest pride in the world. I've been living there for twenty years. I have in total three hundred and ninety registered Black Belts. Always Fadda.

Will the Fadda lineage ever end?

It never ends. This history will never end. The Fadda lineage will never end.

—

— Hélio Fadda —

Could you introduce yourself?

My name is Hélio Fadda, I am 69 years old, I started to train Jiu-Jitsu in 1956 with my Master Oswaldo Fadda. My name is Hélio because of the admiration and respect that my father Humberto Fadda had for the great Master Hélio Gracie, and in light of this consideration and this respect he decided to name me Hélio Fadda.

What do you know about Luis França?

About Professor Luis França, I know he was from the northeast and taught the knowledge of Jiu-Jitsu to my Uncle, Oswaldo Fadda, in the Marine Corps.

Is there a difference between the the Jiu-Jitsu taught by Hélio Gracie and Oswaldo Fadda?

The Jiu-Jitsu of Hélio Gracie and the Jiu-Jitsu of Oswaldo Fadda, in my opinion there is no difference at all.

What was the relationship between Hélio Gracie and Oswaldo Fadda like?

I am sure that the Master Hélio Gracie and Master Oswaldo Fadda had a great friendship and a great respect. Hélio Gracie and Oswaldo Fadda were always together at the Jiu-Jitsu events of the time. This is the reality.

What is the difference between them?

I will answer about Oswaldo Fadda. [He was] an irreverent, cheerful person. Master Hélio Gracie, although a gentle and educated person, was more serious, more focused, and did not have that behavior of my uncle, who was very irreverent. Master Oswaldo Fadda was a wonderful person, educated, irreverent, friendly, and always willing to help students, friends, and everyone around him.

What were Oswaldo Fadda's classes like?

I will describe the training of Oswaldo Fadda as a highly technical training, but he did not make it forceful or demanding. He made training deeply enjoyable.

What are the memories of your relationship with your uncle?

The memory I have of Oswaldo Fadda, of the Fadda Academy, is that being a boy, by the way, occasionally I had to be disciplined. That always happened. And it happened even with a certain frequency. The demands were about learning. When you did not assimilate, did not learn, he demanded and put you, let's use a word, placed corrections. He would remove you from training, take you out of that class or send you home. That was the most he did with the kids.

What was the clientele at the Fadda Academy like?

Oswaldo Fadda's students were the suburban students, the vast majority of whom were poor people. They had a totally different kind of life from Master Hélio Gracie's [students], who at the time were students from the center of Rio de Janeiro who had a purchasing power and were usually prominent figures in our society. That was the difference.

Why do you think Oswaldo Fadda is not better known internationally?

Master Oswaldo Fadda is not known in the rest of the world precisely because he did not invest in marketing and advertising in his lifetime. I'm sure that Master Oswaldo Fadda had great concern for society, and with that he forgot about propaganda and marketing that would have made him known all over the world.

Could you tell us a little more about this concern with reaching out to the under-privileged?

I am sure that Master Oswaldo Fadda had a very great concern with social issues, so much that I followed all this history and saw the number of non-paying students and the number of those participating and that today we denominate with special needs. Nothing was *charged. The ease he gave to anyone who had a problem, and who was not able to pay the gym: this was the demeanor of Master Oswaldo Fadda.*

Was he worried about establishing and making a name for himself?

I am sure that Master Oswaldo Fadda was not worried, although of course he appeared in the press, in the newspapers, in the magazines due to his work in the Fadda Academy. Oswaldo Fadda was not worried about this aspect of advertising, with that marketing part.

Could you tell us more about the work that Oswaldo Fadda did with the disabled?

Master Oswaldo Fadda was a pioneer in this adaptation of Jiu-Jitsu for those with special needs. I remember when Torpedo climbed those stairs from our gym where we are with his wheelchair and arrived here, my uncle realized that it was his moment to put into practice everything he already had in mind about Jiu-Jitsu for those with special needs.

Who was Torpedo?

The Torpedo was a wonderful character. Cheerful, well-to-do, calm, he worked in public squares selling jigsaw puzzles. He was a great jigsaw puzzle maker. He assimilated Jiu-Jitsu with great ease. Particularly, I had the opportunity to train a lot with Torpedo in the same space that we find ourselves in. Torpedo, from the moment he lost his legs, he could only fight on the ground. So, whoever was training with Torpedo knew perfectly well that the fight would start on the ground. And he would do all this work with excellence. He even had a technique of applying a choke using one of the legs that was smaller than the other in terms of amputation.

The Fadda logo is a triangle. Why?

The logo of the Fadda Academy, this triangular symbol, which means the balance that characterizes the triangle, the base and the angles facing upwards. This symbol was created by my uncle Guilherme Fadda who is a plastic artist. Today he is a man who is 88 years old now, January 6th. Guilherme Fadda was the one who made this symbol that still remains the symbol for Fadda Jiu-Jitsu. The symbol of the Fadda Jiu-Jitsu Academy was created in the 1950s.

Could you tell us a little more about the differences between the Fadda and Gracie Academies?

The Gracie Academy of the Master Hélio Gracie, at the beginning did not exist in the South Zone. The South Zone came later. Much later. The Gracie Academy was located on Avenida Rio Branco, downtown Rio de Janeiro, and it was attended precisely by businessmen, executives, and artists. Prominent people. The late Oscar Niemayer was his student. So they were figures of that level. Oswaldo Fadda, here in the suburb of Rio De Janeiro in Bento Ribeiro, was the worker. The factory worker, the railroad worker, had many military men. So it was a totally different crowd, the academy of Master Hélio Gracie and that of Master Oswaldo Fadda. Hence the general differences in terms of collection, investment, of everything. Even in terms of projection, because the Gracie Academy students had bigger visibility due to them being in the media, being artists, businessmen, and communicators. They made a point of emphasizing that they were students of Hélio Gracie. Very different from the students of Master Oswaldo Fadda, who felt the same way but did not have the same repercussion because they were workers who did not have such a strong voice for advertising, media, and marketing. That's it.

Was it intentional that he lived and taught here instead of other areas?

I think the Master Oswaldo Fadda had this characteristic and that was part of his personality. This work I mean, precisely with these classes. And the question about this location, he always liked Bento Ribeiro. He always liked and loved this neighborhood here and made it a point to stay here and attend precisely to those classes of workers. That's how I've witnessed it my whole life, from boyhood to manhood. This place has always been frequented by these social classes.

—

While at the Fadda Academy, we heard from one of their students that the Fadda family had the only footage available of Fadda teaching in a gi on an old CD-ROM. Needless to say, we jumped at the opportunity to include this in our film. With many emails between the family's lawyer and our team, we finally managed to get the footage. Below are the transcripts of a Q&A between Oswaldo Baptista Fadda and the students at the academy of Master "Deo," one of Fadda's Red Belts. This recording took place in November, 1997, in Brasilia.

— Oswaldo Fadda —

How old were you when you started training?

17 years, 17 and a half or so. I'm turning 57 today.

Why did you leave Boxing and go to Jiu-Jitsu?

The case is the following. When I was a boy I was chubby. I was a little ball. It was a disgraceful pejoration, what people did to me. And I would go and fight when they would piss me off. And when I got home, I had to wash my face so dad wouldn't see it. This has happened several times. And I became a reference: "Fadda? The fat Fadda..." That marked me deeply, but what am I going to do? When I was about 16 years old, almost 17 years old, I was not 17 years old, there was a call, a call by the newspapers for those who wanted to serve in the Navy. I was not 18 but I introduced myself. And to a sergeant who looked cooler I said, "Look, I'm not 18 years old, but see what you can do for me." Since there was always construction going on there, he said, "Do this, start helping there with construction until you turn 18."

So, I gravitated towards Boxing. Because I wanted to learn anything. And I'll tell you the real reason. Me getting beat up was normal, but one day I went to work at a firm and there was a guy who was a grown man and I was still a boy, and we went at it and fought. I do not know what was the reason that I was going to fight, I do not know, but the guy was handicapped, the fact that I fought and won the first fight.

The guy was a man and I was a kid. Two days later the guy waits for me at the exit with two more from the "morro da cachoeirinha" and said he was waiting for me. I said, "What do you want?" I had beaten him yesterday. He said, "Me and my friends want another go. I got mine! [Afterwards] it looked like I had been hit by a train. There I made a decision and said, "Gee, I need to learn anything, anything." Not to be brave, but I wanted to get beat up less. That was when I went to the Navy and there I fell in love with Boxing.

How was your beginning in Jiu-Jitsu?

[Note: Fadda here discusses events that took place after a Boxing sparring session that was witnessed by França.] *...Then França took me to the infirmary, where I was doing repair there in that workshop, another week of work. And at his insistence, he wanted me to try Jiu-Jitsu. "I'm not going to do that. What fight is this? Grabbing each other like that? I can't. It's not exciting, it's not what I want." He would say, "Do you know this? This is where you can dominate a man with the body. And you think that's all?" For me it was just that, nothing else. He said, "Then you show up here tomorrow that I'm going to introduce you to the class." His class was small at that time, about thirty or forty alone. Jiu-Jitsu was little publicized. Then I went to see. He asked me if I was willing. I said yes. He said, "So let's see. Want to*

189

spar?" I answered that it's all well and put on gloves. He said, "Come at me, try to kill me. Do whatever you want." I thought, it's now! I attacked him ferociously. A layman thinks he's going to take over the world. There, with the greatest delicacy, he dominated me. I said, "Wow!" He said, "Did you like it? What I did to you, you could do tomorrow to him, and not take so long and not get beat up so much. Now I'll show you that there is more to this."

He took off his kimono. Today everyone in karate put their leg here and there. At that time, he already did it with tremendous mastery. Then he would beat me with his feet [kicks], beat without hurting me, showing me. And I thought, "Wow! This is too good!" I said, "I'm in. I'm staying, I'm going to enroll." So, I stayed and I fell in love, I have been in love ever since and never left.

What kind of relationship do you have with the Gracies?

We've never gotten along in terms of fighting. We were always arguing with each other, there was no way. I've always been a pebble in their shoe. Just so you have an idea, I always led the west side [Zone Oeste] of Rio de Janeiro, and [Hélio and Carlos] wanted to put a show on television. The idea was that they would put a big clock so close to the ring and the clock would go off every five minutes. Come and Beat Us was the name of the program. And they invited me to a meeting. I arrived at his gym and they greeted me and it was late and the staff did not come. Hélio and Carlos said they were coming. Then I got tired of waiting and said to schedule another day. Then Hélio said, "Fadda, since you're here, give me your opinion on this here." That meeting did not exist, it was a meeting for me. He explained the program to me, which accumulated cash prizes and asked what I thought. I said I thought it was great. He then asked me if I would participate. Then I said, "I'm not going to, I'm thinking it's great for the Gracie Academy. Why don't they change that name from Come and Beat Us to Come Face Us at least or Come and Lose. Then get people to come lose. I said that this was my opinion and not my students, because although I lead, I was not the voice of others. And the program died at birth. They were always setting me up.

The man is so wild [Note: It is unclear here whether he is referring to Carlos or Hélio], *it always was, just so you have an idea of what it is like, one of the brothers, George Gracie, had a gym also in Cinelandia and had a student, such a very good [student] called Guanair Vidal, and George took him to the gym at Rio Branco [Gracie Academy] for Hélio and Carlos to test him with Carlson. When they made these invitations, they brought many people into the gym. They fought and the Guanair lost to Carlson, of course he had to lose. Do you know what old Carlos did with a full house, and his brother the one who brought the student? He said, "My friends, what you saw is the reflection of your teacher." My god, he was his brother! If he did this to his brother, he'd do it to everyone that defied him. He bullied them in the newspapers and put them in the ring to get beat up.*

Knowing this, I issued a challenge in a delicate way. I wanted him to reply in a way that I knew I could hear about it. Then this is what happened: Hélio, Carlson, and João Alberto in the picture: "The great Brazilian champion Hélio Gracie, impressed by the honorable way in which he was challenged by Master Fadda." And then he invited me to his gym. "Let's make this something casual, no publicity, what do you think?" And me, always conservative: "It is my intention to test my students and find out if I am on the right track." But when I get there it is a full house, filled with photographers. And then I said, "Hélio, I think I came on the wrong day." I did not know that that reception was for me. "Fadda, you know, students are terrible, and that thing leaked and everyone found out, and all of a sudden I see this place full of people and I'm even annoyed by it." And he went through with his dramatic scene. I said, "No problem, if we are here [inaudible] I only want to test my students. Then I went to talk to Xadu, a student of mine, [and I said], "They set us up here." And then [Hélio] called me back. "Fadda, since it is a full house, let's do this, get your students, your team, the strong ones last so we don't disappoint these people I have no idea from whence they came from." I said, "They set us up again, leave it to me."

The first student I put in there was called Jacó. Someone not so good, but he begged me so much to be on the team, I allowed him and threw him in there to lose. And so he entered the ring: "Jacó... from the Fadda Academy!" And he went and lost. And then everyone screamed, "Throw in another água de poço!" ["water from the well," derogative expression aimed at someone from the outskirts of Rio], because we were from the suburbs. I threw in the rest of my list.

We won the second, third, fourth, fifth, and sixth. We won five straight fights. Look, we didn't even tie with a student of them. We won five in a row. Then he went crazy. For the first time in their lives Hélio and Carlos Gracie opened up and got into the ring and gave the highest compliments to my academy. That the Fadda Academy was some sort of continuation of the Gracie Academy... Well, I was never a continuation from their academy, but I put up with everything. "The suburbs were represented with Master Fadda, congratulations." And acting clueless, with all the humility, but crazy to do a back flip of victory. The rest we drew some and won others.

In short, between wins and draws, we got the upper hand. We didn't lose a single match, only that first one. And then the journalist, you know what was the headline on his magazine? "Fadda Academy Ends the Gracie's Paradigm."

———

In 2019, I wrote an article for Roberto Pedreira's site GTR that I hoped would add substantively to the debate surrounding the Fadda lineage. This article draws on the interviews we conducted during our trip to Brazil, as well as the research material available at the time. Perhaps in the future some new evidence will come to light to reveal more of the story; for the time being, however, the conclusions expressed in the article represent what I feel to be the most natural conclusions based on the material at hand. You may judge for yourself. The article is included below:

Is the Fadda Lineage a Non-Gracie Lineage?
Originally published on GTR January 1, 2019

In recent articles and internet forums much attention has been given to Oswaldo Fadda and his students as members of a non-Gracie lineage. [1] Fadda was a student of Luis França (aka Luiz França Filho, Luiz França) who claimed to have learned directly from Mitsuyo Maeda (aka Conde Koma). For example, one of França's students, Antonio Vieira, testified that "O Luis de França falava que aprendeu o que ele sabia com o Maeda que usava o pseudonimo de Conde Koma. O Conde Koma morreu em 41, então ele ficou sem professor" [Luis de França said that he learned what he knew from Maeda, who was also known as Conde Koma. Conde Koma died in 1941, so after that he [França] was without a teacher]. [2]

This, obviously, is merely what França told Antonio Vieira (or more precisely, what Vieira said França told him).

Others claim that França's teacher was Geo Omori. [3]

Fadda absolutely deserves his place in BJJ's memory. Despite that, his lineage is unclear.

Two recent discoveries help us better understand the origins of the Fadda lineage.

The first one is an article of 1938 announcing a Luta Livre match between Gaúcho (C.R.F.) and Luis França (A. Gracie). The article in question clearly identifies Luis França as a representative of the Gracie Academy. [4]

A second article is even more revealing. In 1956 a fight was announced between Dupont Saraiva and a Luis França student named Talvanes Falão. Significantly, Luis França was described in the article as "um dos melhores alunos de Hélio Gracie" ["one of Hélio Gracie's best students"]. [5]

It is worthy of notice that Fadda, after a single news-worthy appearance (with França) in 1941, disappeared from the public eye until Carlos and Hélio Gracie revived their efforts to bring "Jiu-Jitsu" back into the public eye, in the 1950s. [6]

Luis França's affiliation with the Gracie Academy does not mean that he could not have also learned from others (although there is at present no evidence that he did). But to underline the point, the evidence that does exist suggests a close relationship with the Gracie Academy.

The plausibility of França being indeed a student of the Gracie Academy currently holds more weight than the widespread—but unsubstantiated—belief that França learned from Maeda himself, or even Omori or Yano for that matter.

Fadda went on to be an instructor in the neighborhood of Bento Ribeiro in Rio de Janeiro, as well as an early pioneer of the practice of grappling for the underprivileged and the handicapped. For this, Fadda is certainly worthy of commendation. But the claim that it is a lineage outside of the Gracie family, or that Luis França was a student of Takeo Yano, Geo Omori, and Mitsuyo Maeda, lacks any supporting evidence at the moment. Further research is necessary to determine the origins of the Fadda lineage. Nonetheless, the evidence available suggests that Luis França was a student of the Gracie Academy, and of Hélio Gracie in particular.

Article Notes:

1. See https://www.bjjheroes.com/bjj-fighters/luiz-franca; https://www.bjjee.com/bjj-news/valente-brothers-answer-article-from-tatame-magazine-criticizing-gracie-family/; https://www.bloodyelbow.com/2011/5/22/2184090/history-of-jiu-jitsu-oswaldo-fadda-nova-uniao-and-non-gracie-jiu-jitsu; for examples.

2. The Antonio Vieira interview was conducted during the filming of *Closed Guard: The Origins of Jiu-Jitsu in Brazil* in September, 2018

3. See http://global-training-report.com/cartas.htm. Readers will note that author Eduardo Pereira offers no evidence for his claim.

4. *Jornal do Brasil* (RJ), November 2, 1938.

5. *O Poti (Natal)*, November 14, 1956. This source was provided by Elton Silva. The credit for the discovery is entirely his.

6. See *Choque Vols. 1-3* for details.

Upper left: From left to right: Steve, Tufy, Jay, Grandmaster Robson Gracie, author, and Fabio; Upper right: Lunch with the charismatic Robson. From left to right: Steve, author, Robson, Tufy, Fabio, and Jay; Lower left: Fabio interviews Grandmaster Robson Gracie; Lower right: Patriarch of the Gracie Family, Grandmaster Robson Gracie

ROBSON GRACIE

"The memory is that we were seen, looked at, and judged as arrogant, bullies, even ruffians trained in the martial arts. What happened was you couldn't go anywhere where people, the tough-guys, the boys in those days, didn't naturally want to fight you. And fighting was a romantic deal, and so everywhere we went there was a scrap. So many times I would be drinking a soda or having lunch in a restaurant on the edge of Copacabana Beach, and groups of Capoeiristas making demonstrations to earn some money would stop, they would recognize me and want to fight me. They defied, they kept looking at you, calling you out. And one hundred percent of those times, we went, "Want to fight? OK." Stop it all, we left the girlfriends aside and got into it with the troublemakers. We fought then and there. We

would make a call, we had our brothers, we would make a circle, no
one interfered, only the two would fight. We would match about five
or six pairs and fight right there in the middle of the street. And the
beating would take place, right there and then. Wonderful, beautiful
thing."
—Grandmaster Robson Gracie, Patriarch of the Gracie Family

Our final interview in Rio de Janeiro was with Robson Gracie. We
met him in Ipanema, where we had arranged to conduct our interview
at a combination Aikido school and Yoga studio. The interior had an
oriental feel that we felt would make for a good backdrop for the interview, as well as offer us a change from the type of backgrounds
we'd had up to this point, but the venue fell through and we ended up
meeting in a building belonging to the Consulate of Sri-Lanka, with
whom Robson was in contact.

Robson's reputation preceded him in many ways. I would say that
he was the very image of an archetypical Carioca: smooth talking,
cunning, and "malandro" as can be. He was not scared to speak his
mind and he came across as a resolute man, full of life and certitude.
He had no qualms about being critical of his own family members,
and gave us his opinion about his cousin Rorion's two eldest sons,
Rener and Ryron Gracie, and their program for ranking people over
the internet.

After the interview we would spend another two to three hours
talking with him about life, women, BJJ, his family, and women (he
loved that topic). At 82 years of age the patriarch of the Gracie Family
displayed an impeccable pick-up game with the waitress at the restaurant. He kept us enthralled with the story of how, during the Brazilian
Dictatorship, he was arrested for his involvement with Brazilian Left-
ist Leonel Brizola and how, later, he would be the middle man for
money sent from Cuba for Brizola to start a guerrilla unit in Brazil
(and also how he was ready to "break" Brizola's face in case he dared
count the money and show that he doubted Robson's integrity). Being
interested in the history of the Cold War myself, I found all of this
fascinating. Still, he was such a great story-teller that it was hard to

tell where the story ended and where he was merely trying to entertain us.

I have always lived by the belief that we are well served to listen to our elders: if someone has lived much longer than me then it's a safe bet that they know better than I do, and throughout my adult life I have always thought it unwise to disregard their counsel (I would equate it to ignoring the advice of those whose time on the mat and rank far exceed your own in BJJ). Throughout the production of this film I always took as much time as I could to speak with the Grand-masters, not only because I wanted to learn from them but also because, in my view, they were me in the future. I wanted to know more about each of them so I could try to figure out which one I would be most like as I aged.

With all of them I found different shades of wisdom, but also sorrow and regret for mistakes made. Mostly I found men who seemed at peace and content with the lives they had lived as they prepared to close the book on life's final chapter. I found that admirable, and I hoped that in my old age I would also find that same peace, and as much wisdom as my experience would grant me. Of course the frantic pace of our production meant that I didn't have as much time as I would have liked with any of these men, but I tried my best to take advantage of this once-in-a-lifetime opportunity. I wanted wisdom I could remember and repeat to myself and absorb as a lesson. And while most would give me the advice that you would expect—enjoy life, spend more time with family, live in the moment, forgive and be a good person—Robson would go on a tangent.

I was drawn to Robson, not because I admired him or his actions, but because I found him to be incredibly charismatic, engaging, and possessed of a powerful talent for putting words together. I would say that his eloquence was even poetic at times. In fact, he was so good with his words that I began to wonder whether his speech was truly fruit of the moment or lines he had memorized in advance. In either case, he was without a doubt interesting. During our long chat over lunch, I asked him for life advice. He paused for a moment, thinking it over, and then he gave me the least expected of answers: "Na vida,

197

você tem que ser inconsequente" ("In life, you have to be inconsequential"; it should be noted, however, that in Portuguese the word "inconsequente" is more readily associated with "irresponsible" than with "unimportant"). I was a bit shocked: was this 82-year-old man advising me to be irresponsible and reckless in life? I didn't quite get it.

Over the next few weeks I would try to digest and make sense of it. I thought back on the stories he'd told us about his life, and his assertion that he never thought he would live long enough to be the patriarch of the Gracie family. Indeed, Robson seemed to have lived a fast and adventurous life, one that might even be called "reckless." This approach invited me to see my own life in retrospect: how so many of my best memories involved adventures and trips that arose from an impulse, with no planning or forethought. There was something stale about being overly responsible, while there was something energetic and powerful in the Dionysian mind that led to a memorable and colorful life. After all: my own journey into BJJ had been irresponsible, as my grandfather, father, and uncles repeatedly warned me against it. It was reckless... but it paid off. I have a living and a lifetime of incredible experiences and memories to look back on. Robson wasn't wrong, but I couldn't accept that he was exactly right, either. I found some wisdom there after all, even if not at the surface. At any rate, the BJJ poet had made his point and converged with Hamlet's sentiment that "conscience does make cowards of us all."

As far as the history of BJJ went, Robson was open to telling us all he knew, and I was hopeful that we could learn something from him. The truth of the matter is that everything we knew about the early history of BJJ, at least up until recently, leads back to Carlos Gracie's testimony. Websites, magazine articles, and testimonies have all recycled the narrative that now forms the cornerstone of BJJ's history: Carlos' apprenticeship under Maeda. A recent discovery in the Brazilian National Library challenges this, however, and sheds some light on the early days of Maeda in Belém. The article suggests that Carlos Gracie (most likely him) was indeed training Jiu-Jitsu/Judo in Belém, albeit under a different instructor. I was eager to ask Robson about this possibility, though I found that he didn't seem too concerned with any version of history that contradicted his father. In fact, to him the question of Maeda's tutelage seemed almost irrelevant while the legacy of the Gracie family stood paramount.

When I asked him about his father's role in the history of BJJ— asked him whether, if Carlos had not existed, BJJ itself would exist— Robson gave the following reply:

"[BJJ] would not have existed. Who would Count Koma be if it were not for Carlos Gracie? Of course he had his value—fantastic, sensational—but it would be another story of the pink dolphin ("boto-cor-de-rosa"). It would be another legend of the Amazon. Take Carlos Gracie out and what would there be left of Count Koma and Jiu-Jitsu in the whole world? He taught and he fought over a thousand times. But would you have heard of Count Koma? I doubt anyone would have heard of him except for some enthusiastic Japanese. Who did it? There he was, Professor Carlos Gracie, the Jiu-Jitsu man."

Agree with Robson or not, he does suggest an interesting possibility. Perhaps it wasn't Maeda who put Carlos on the map. Perhaps, in reality, it was the other way around.

— Robson Gracie —

Could you introduce yourself?

My name is Carlos Robson Gracie, I was born in 1935 in the city of Rio de Janeiro, thank God. I am the son of Carlos Gracie and Carmem Gracie and today I am the President of the Jiu-Jitsu Federation of the State of Rio de Janeiro, the first federation founded in the world. There was never a federation of this style of fighting founded before we founded one here, which in fact the founders were Carlos Gracie my father, Hélio Gracie my uncle, and I was one of the vice-presidents with Carlson also, João Alberto Barreto, Hélio Vígio, and the whole crew that was part of the team made up the administration of this federation.

Today you are the patriarch of the Gracie family, correct?

Today the patriarch is me, Robson Gracie, against all expectations. We have survived a good, sometimes cruel, world, but we are here.

What was it like getting the first federation started?

My friend, it was not easy, first because implementing Jiu-Jitsu here in Rio de Janeiro, in Brazil, was not an easy thing. It was a give and take kind of business. No one believed in the Jiu-Jitsu of Carlos, of Hélio, of George, of Oswaldo Gracie.

Do you know what the classes were like here? How the classes were taught, because nobody wanted to take classes? Dad, a blue-eyed blonde, a Scotsman or an Irishman, came here in the 1930s, and who knew what Japanese Jiu-Jitsu was? He had to put an ad on the street: "You want to get beat up? If you want me to break your face, go to this street at this number that I'm going to break your face. Carlos Gracie." That's how Jiu-Jitsu started.

How do you remember that era? What did people think of the Gracie family?

The memory is that we were seen, looked at, and judged as arrogant, bullies, even ruffians trained in the martial arts. What happened was you couldn't go anywhere where people, the tough-guys, the boys in those days, didn't naturally want to fight you. And fighting was a romantic deal, and so everywhere we went there was a scrap. So many times I would be drinking a soda or having lunch in a restaurant on the edge of Copacabana Beach, and groups of Capoeiristas making demonstrations to earn some money would stop, they would recognize me and want to fight me. They defied, they kept looking at you, calling you out. And one hundred percent of those times, we went, "Want to fight? OK." Stop it all, we left the girlfriends aside and got into it with the troublemakers. We fought then and there. We *would make a call, we had our brothers, we would make a circle, no one interfered, only the two would fight. We would match about five or six pairs and fight right there in the middle of the street. And the beating would take place, right there and then. Wonderful, beautiful thing.*

Can you tell us about the time your father caught thieves inside your house?

One day dad came home—he lived in Botafogo—and there were three or four thieves robbing the house. He said, "Do you guys want to be arrested by the police or do you guys want to fight us here? If you fight with us, no matter what happens, when the fight is over, you'll leave. If we call the police you will be arrested. What do you prefer?" As a rule they preferred to fight, and we would break their faces right there and then. Everyone would go away, the robbed items would stay home, and they would leave only with a black eye.

Can you tell us about the fight between Hélio Gracie and Waldemar Santana?

We make comparisons and we see the following: who are the heroes that exist in our history today that did what we did? You'll excuse me if it sounds rude. I watch these stories in schools about the great warriors, about the great battlers, and I wonder: who did what Professor Hélio did in his fight against Waldemar Santana? No training or anything that would allow him to fight three hours and forty-five minutes without rest, without water, without anything. Tell me. David and Goliath? He threw a rock, that wasn't a fight. I see those warriors of the round table and I will tell you that I'd walk past them with respect—a warrior is a warrior—but we owe them nothing. Champ, you know what happened in our family? With all those whities? In the old days we did not have creoles in the family. We were all blue-eyed blondies. You know what we did? We beat up the world. The whole world.

What about the incident where you fought Waldemar Santana's brother?

Once I was at the gym and Waldemar Santana, who had a falling out with us, came in. He was our wardrobe guy [Note: The word Grandmaster Robson uses here is "roupeiro," the person who handles the laundry], *he trained very well, he had fought with Professor Hélio. He came with a few more and said they wanted to fight us. Who was there was Carlson, Hélio Vigio, João Alberto Barreto, Robson, Georges Kastriot Mehdi the Algerian, and according to our weights we decided who would fight against whom. It fell on me to fight Waldo Santana, Waldemar Santana's brother who had been well trained. He had just arrived from Bahia. And here I was coming from the good life, dating, did not want to hear anything about fighting, I was in love with women.*

No problem. In a month, let's go! I stopped working, stopped teaching classes, I lost three kilos. Dad told me to stop training, otherwise I'd be leaner. I should be weighing about sixty-nine or seventy kilos and he was weighing about eighty kilos, but let's go. On the day of the fight, the TV auditorium was packed, the television station at the Posto 6. And Carlson quickly beat his opponent, who was a Frenchman. The French Georges won his fight, and everyone won. Joao Alberto, Guanair Gomes Vial also fought.

It's my turn. Three five-minute rounds. First round, a marvel. Enter Waldo. His corner was Waldemar, which worked in my favor. A beating took place in the first round. I broke two of his front teeth, burst an eardrum and then I gassed out. I couldn't raise my hands. Dead tired. Then Waldinho came up to me and beat my face. My face was huge. I got beat up a lot and in the break in between the second and the final round, my father looked at me and felt sorry.

My face looked swollen. He said he was going to throw in the towel. I said, "My father, you told me one thing once I took it very seriously. Something about giving up, retreating. Not even for a break!" He kept looking at me. I said, "If you throw the towel I'll lower my shorts and pee in the middle of the ring." He did not throw the towel and I kept fighting. Waldo caught me and threw me to the ground and fell into the middle of my guard and tried to pass my guard. When he tried to pass my guard, his brother told him not to try that he would not pass it. He had trained with me, Waldemar, back at the gym, and had not been able to get past my guard. Thanks to that I was able to take the fight to the end. But before that Waldo punched me in the chin and I felt something inside my mouth. It was my wisdom tooth that had come out with the punch. Then I thought, "Am I going to spit the tooth out here for everyone to see? Am I going to live with this shame? No way." You know what I did? I swallowed it. I'm not going to give this satisfaction to those bums, no. Result, he did not win and we drew. And I couldn't even have my arm raised with him and the judge, I had to hold on to the rope.

Who was Oscar Santa Maria?

Oscar Santa Maria Pereira was a very close person to my father, very. He was a very intelligent, very capable figure. I even lived a time in Urca in a house that was his that he ended up selling to my father. But then I do not know what happened. I think Carlos Gracie took his bride that was going to marry him and ended up marrying her, and the friendship did not work out. That was one of the big reasons.

Why did Georges Mehdi leave the Gracie Academy?

French Georges, who by the way is not French, he is Algerian. Georges Kastriot Mehdi of Algeria. I liked him. He left because we were going to move from the Gracie Academy of Rio Branco to the seventeenth floor and he had nowhere to go, he left to live his life. He left not to teach Jiu-Jitsu. He also taught Jiu-Jitsu, but he trained Judo. He became a Judo champion. He was living his life like any other. Same as the thousands who have passed through our gym.

Do you remember the first time you saw a triangle choke?

The triangle at Gracie Academy began to be used in 1958. The first time they used a triangle there I found it absurd because I did not know it until they did it to me, and I saw it was a very efficient move. Everyone has their tricks, each has a way. Foot-locks for example. I was an expert at them, and people did not have much love for it. It's a move like any other. Very good. If you know how to use it well, it works.

Did you learn the triangle from a Judoka?

No, he was a Jiu-Jitsu fighter. I think he was a Fadda fighter. He was a Fadda student. One day at a gym there in a class I was teaching, it was a collective class, one of Fadda's students applied a triangle on the other and he tapped. I asked him why he was tapping. I asked him to do it to me, and I saw that it worked. Then we took the triangle for ourselves. It worked, great.

Hélio's story of how he learned Jiu-Jitsu changed over time. First he learned from your father, then he learned by watching, and then he invented Jiu-Jitsu. How do you explain this?

It is easy. I took class with who? They never explained a single technique to me. I learned watching. Do I need more than to see? I don't. Hélio Gracie learned Jiu-Jitsu with whom? Hélio Gracie is like my father. He raised me. One time in my life he raised me. I have great regard for him to this day. For me he is a great and spectacular idol, but who taught him if not Carlos Gracie? Did he meet Count Koma? No. He was at the base of Jiu-Jitsu in Belém do Pará? No. When dad met Koma he was 17 and Uncle Hélio was 6 years old. Do you see? Do you understand? And I'll tell you more. My father was a visionary. He saw things no one could see. I believe he saw something in Count Koma.

Did Carlos and Hélio get along?

Look, the strength of the partnership between Carlos and Hélio Gracie was complete and total, it was twenty-four hours. The greatest proof of partnership between Carlos and Hélio Gracie, the total, existential proof: Hélio would not go around the corner if he did not ask [Carlos] if he could go. For you to have an idea, Uncle Hélio once bought a motorcycle and fell off the motorcycle. When dad found out, [Hélio] was at the hospital to amputate his leg. The old man ran there, he had some premonitions, fantastic things. He looked at him and asked to see, they let him see, and he said not to cut his leg. That leg does not have to be cut, he said. He said, "I sign any medical liability document if something happens, I am to blame. You will not need to cut your leg." Outcome, Professor Hélio died with his legs. And once I was talking to Professor Hélio at the Gracie Academy on Rio Branco Avenue, seventeenth floor, when my father arrived. They started talking and Uncle Hélio was a little upset with him. My father said, "Hélio, you're in some kind of trouble. You cannot hear me anymore. I say things to you and you are not giving much importance." And uncle Hélio got up, went to the window, seventeenth floor, sat by the window and said, "You think I do not obey you, Carlos? OK, see if I do not jump out of this window right now." He put both legs out. "Say it! Give the order!" Dad looked at him and asked him to stop and get off the window. He sat up a bit and asked, "Are not going to have me jump? Do you want to see if I obey you or not? Tell me to jump now." Then he left and nothing happened. So that was their relationship, get it?

What were the most outstanding qualities of Carlos and Hélio Gracie?

Carlos was just common sense. He had fantastic reasoning, a constructive way of thinking. And he had a premonition that was incredible. Normal human beings do not have that. He saw things and said things that you had not said or done and he said you were going to do. Do not do that, he said. With Uncle Hélio, this worked great because he guided Professor Hélio. He was our guide. This was Professor Carlos, my father. I still miss him a lot.

Hélio Gracie was my second father. He knew everything, too. He knew the things of life. He was always with us all, not only his children, but all the children he raised. And he raised most of my father's children from the second marriage and the first marriage of my father. To me they are a single figure. Divided in two, but a single figure.

Have you ever seen any martial arts books at the Gracie Academy?

No, Professor Hélio, to our terror and horror, do you know what he would scream at us? "I never read and I will never read a book!" He never read a book. What a situation...

Why did your father have so many children?

The fact that Carlos Gracie wanted to have children is that he believed that the function of the human being here, while alive, was to reproduce. So the more children he could have, the better for him. And it influenced a lot of people, including me. I have thirteen children, thanks to the influence of Professor Carlos Gracie. I lived with my brothers, we were twenty-one. So that was part of the existential idea of evolution of the human being. So there's the teacher with his offspring, and thank God everyone's out there. For me it was a festivity that he had with life.

Did he expect them all to be fighters?

I've never heard Professor Carlos Gracie speaking of an army, [but] there were a lot us. He had his children and everyone was going to be whatever they wanted. For me, he knew what each one was going to be. And most of all, for me, I believe he knew each other's lives before they even came here.

What was the rivalry amongst family members like?

This rivalry among the members of the Gracie family did not exist. Each was what they were. Each was what Master Carlos Gracie told them to be. There were not fights, or, "I'm going to get you." That was never the case. We trained; if you lost, you lost. He is better than you. And there was no training that could change that. Family was family.

BJJ barely survived the expansion of Judo. Why do you think it managed to resist?

Carlos commanded and commanded very well, coupled with Professor Hélio Gracie. But Jiu-Jitsu had a very great relevance because it was a fighting art of war, of combat. It was not a sport. It was defensive. When you saw a Jiu-Jitsu fighter you automatically wanted to be the same as him because he was efficient, he would not let himself be cowed, he would not be intimidated. He reacted. That's what elevated Jiu-Jitsu up there to this day.

This is Jiu-Jitsu. It's the whole world, you understand? We beat up the whole world. That's what got us up there. Very well.

Would BJJ exist without your father?

Jiu-Jitsu would not have existed. Who would Count Koma be if it were not for Carlos Gracie? Of course, he had his value—fantastic, sensational—but it would be another story of the pink dolphin ("boto-cor-de-rosa"). It would be another legend of the Amazon. The occupation of the gringos in the Amazon. Where would those stories be? They would be all gone. Take Carlos Gracie out and what would there be left of Count Koma and Jiu-Jitsu in the whole world? He taught and he fought over a thousand times. But would you have heard of Count Koma? I doubt anyone would have heard of him except for some enthusiastic Japanese. Who did it? There he was, Professor Carlos Gracie, the Jiu-Jitsu man.

Could you tell us a little bit about George Gracie?

Look, to talk about George Gracie, we're going to have to go back a little bit. How did Jiu-Jitsu come about, you know? Why did we stop in Pará? I'm going to explain to you. Gastão Gracie spoke sixteen languages. Our family was not of martial artists. Our family was from the Brazilian diplomatic corps. Gastão Gracie, my grandfather, made a contest and passed first place in Itamaraty, which was not Itamaraty at the time, it had another name. And he went to a position in Central America and took a ship that stopped in Pará to refuel with oil and food and he went down to a party. He was invited—gringo, beautiful, blue-eyed. Went to a party there in Pará. He met Dona Cesalina Pessoa, a beautiful woman. Her photo is a fantastic deal. And he fell in love with her. For you to have a notion: the boat left the next day at dawn, and he stayed in Para with the clothes on his body. He fell so much in love that he quit his profession, left everything, and stayed in Para with the clothes on his body. Jiu-Jitsu was born of love and there was no one more loving than the great George Gracie. Also good-looking, blond. He adored women. We love women. So Jiu-Jitsu was born of my grandfather's passion for Cesalina who later went from the Pessoa last name to Gracie. They fell in love, had all their children. This was George Gracie, brother of Carlos, younger of Carlos, of Hélio, of Oswaldo, of Gastão, Cesalina, and Ilka Gracie. So that's our story. We are born of love, thanks to the good God.

But did you ever train with your Uncle George Gracie?

Never, I've never seen anything from George Gracie. I've never seen a workout. I've never seen him in a kimono. I knew him from bumping into him on the streets. His wife [was] very beautiful, too. But I never saw him fighting.

Have you ever heard about Jacyntho Ferro?

Carlos Gracie talked a lot about Jacyntho Ferro. He was a fan of

Jacyntho Ferro. He was one of his instructors when he started learning with Koma there in Belém do Pará, so he was a fan of Jacyntho Ferro.

Your cousin Rorion has two sons, Ryron and Rener, who have a program for promoting people online. Do you agree with this?

Who's giving it? Who authorized this? Imagine tomorrow you go to an operating table and the comrade who will operate on you has earned a surgeon's title [that he earned] in such a way. Explain. Are you going to operate with the guy? Would you operate a heart, a liver, a kidney, whatever? There is no such thing, boy. I'm sorry, but these cousins of mine have to do a turnaround, have to a come back, because everything is wrong. Sorry my cousins, if you come here with this business you are lost.

What do you think Carlos and Hélio would say about this?

Carlos Gracie and Hélio Gracie about this internet promotion? They would not take this business seriously. What? Where are you doing it? Why doesn't he go ask his mother to promote him? That's what old Carlos Gracie would say, and Hélio Gracie too. I'm very surprised that this came from a relative of the great Hélio Gracie. There was a discussion before, because no one had belts. [Hélio] was a Black Belt and all of us teachers were blue belts, all of us. João Alberto, Hélio Vigio, Carlson, we were all blue belts. Stop it. Guys, stop with that, this is what Carlos Gracie would have said. And Hélio Gracie, too.

Any final thoughts about Jiu-Jitsu and life?

There is one thing I would not want to lose, and that is the hope in life and hope in God. I do not know if you know what is written on the door of hell. You know what's written there? "Lasciate ogni Speranza, o voi che entrate," ("Abandon hope, all ye who enter here"). Divine

Comedy, Dante Alighieri, canto three, line nine. I have not given up hope yet. We are here, let's live life. What God told me to live I'm living. I am aware of this and I have hope, and that is why I do not lose this hope that is there at the door of the dark place.

Is there anyone in the history of the world you would like to fight?

No one. I want everyone to go live their life, go where you want to go, because I have nothing to do with it. Everyone has to live their lives, which is the most important. I already fought what I had to fight. I fought, I did everything. The right thing for me now is to go back to the place I've been, it's the only dream I have. Do you know the French Polynesia? Have you been there? Where Marlon Brando died? You have to go there. There is no God and no devil there, nothing. There is the land of men. So I do not want to beat anyone up, I do not want to fight anyone, nobody owes me anything. I can die tomorrow morning, I'm at peace. I've lived what I had to live, I'm calm, I'm happy, my children, the exes that I've always loved, everything is fine.

Left to right: The author holds what he was told is the original picture of Maeda at the home where Maeda died; Our team is shown by Maeda's son-in-law a series of pictures and diplomas belonging to Maeda at their home; Our team captures B-roll of Maeda's grave. In the picture, author and Steve (in the background).

BELÉM DO PARÁ

The Rio de Janeiro leg of our trip was over. Our next stop would be Belém do Pará, the second-largest city in the Amazon and the epicenter of the rubber boom which brought thousands of Japanese immigrants to the Brazilian north in the early part of the 20th century.

It was becoming increasingly obvious to our team that historical events and circumstances of no apparent relevance to martial arts were in fact directly responsible for the events of the story we were trying to tell. Roberto Pedreira's *Craze: The Life and Times of Jiu-Jitsu* speaks of the process by which Japan first opened to the West, and how this opening greatly impacted not only Japan as a whole but also the formation of Kano's Judo as a method of moral and cultural education as much as a means of self-defense, and there was a discussion among the filmmakers that perhaps we should begin our story with the opening of Edo (modern Tokyo) at the hands—or better, cannons—of Commodore Perry's "diplomacy" in 1854. Other events, such as those of the Russo-Japanese War, would serve to boost Japan's standing in the West, and would eventually form the central theme of a marketing plot that is still employed by Judo and BJJ schools today: that the small may defeat the large by the application of superior skill and technique (I wonder whether any of these gyms realize that we have the then newly-formed and modernized Japanese army to thank

for that one). And, of course, there was the wave of Japanese expatria-
tion that would serve to spread Jiu-Jitsu/Judo all over the world, even
to places as far away as Brazil; the Amazon, the main provider of
rubber for the Allies during World War I, lured Japanese immigrants
with the promise of work and opportunity. Enter Mitsuyo Maeda.

Growing up in Brazil I visited few regions outside of the São
Paulo and Rio axis, and the Amazon always seemed to me as far away
and removed from my reality as Machu Picchu or Athens; because of
this, our visit to Belém—like our stay in Rio—would have an air of
tourism about it. Part of this had to do with the momentarily slack-
ened pace of production: in Belém, we only had one person to interview—Gotta Tsutsumi, the head of the Associação Pan Amazonica
Nipo-Brasileira.

Originally we'd had another interview scheduled. A researcher
named Rildo Eros de Medeiros had come highly recommended by
Tufy and Fabio. Rildo was from Manaus, the other large city in the
Amazon, and his research, I was told, focused largely on Maeda and
Satake, the man who pioneered Jiu-Jitsu/Judo in Manaus, and who
was a longtime friend of Maeda. Personally, I was interested in speaking to Rildo for two reasons: first, he had been researching the history
of BJJ since the '90s (at a time no one seemed to care about it, something I greatly admire); second, it was said that he had sources that
were not in the Brazilian National Library that he was holding onto,
unpublished. (I would later learn that, in their rivalry with each other,
many of these researchers will not publish their discoveries for fear
that someone else will "steal" them, and claim them for themselves.
Needless to say, this "stealing" is plagiarism, and the correct and ethical thing to do in research is to give credit to the person who made the
published discovery. At any rate, the way things are is not always the
way things should be, and it remains common practice for these researchers to withhold their discoveries from the public).

Rildo would, however, prove problematic for other reasons. Fabio
was our point of contact with him—it was Fabio who had originally
contacted Rildo about being interviewed by our team—but a few days
before our trip, Rildo and Fabio got into an argument over some old

rivalry that I didn't care to learn about. As far as I was concerned it was all irrelevant, anyway: telling the story of BJJ was the only thing that mattered. Rildo didn't see it that way, though: the argument with Fabio was enough to put him off the project. I reached out to him and told him that Fabio would not be coming with us to Belém (which was true: Fabio had stayed behind in Rio, and would reconnect with us later in Brasilia), so he had nothing to worry about. Rildo responded by asking me for money to be interviewed. He said his family needed it. I understand that everyone's situation is different and I try not to judge, but it didn't sit well with me that he wanted money to be interviewed. I denied his request. It was unfortunate: we wanted very much to feature him in the film, and to honor his efforts. From all accounts he is a dedicated researcher with a lot to share.

Much later I would learn that he had tight connections with a group of researchers in Brazil (called Goshinjutsukan) from which Marcial and Fabio had split off. I wish I had known about them earlier, as their interviews would have enriched our film. Towards the end of our production one of their members, a researcher named Elton Silva, author of *Muito Antes do MMA* (*Well Before MMA*), would kindly help us and provide us with sources and rare pictures (the only known picture of Luis França among them), all free of charge.

I will add that it didn't sit well with me either that Fabio had never made me aware of this group of researchers in Brazil. As I see it, his rivalry and disagreements with them should not have kept him from doing what was best for the film, namely to help us interview as many experts as we could. There was certainly a time constraint and we couldn't have interviewed everyone, but the right thing to do would have been to put all options on the table and let the team decide collectively, instead of effectively making the decision himself by not making us aware of their existence.

About a year after our trip to Belém I reached out to Rildo again and asked if he would share his research with our production. I told him that if he could show us anything that wasn't yet published I would pay for it and credit him for the discovery. He initially accepted but then later changed his mind, saying then that he would rather keep his research to himself. I left it at that.

Rildo wasn't the only person who asked to be paid for his appearance. Early on in the production I reached out to Rorion Gracie through his daughter, Rose. Our original plan was to have a few representatives for each of the relevant characters in our story: Carlos, George, Hélio, Fadda, and the Ono Brothers. Rorion was to have been a representative for his father, Hélio. Say what you want about Rorion, but he was instrumental in helping to spread BJJ in the U.S. His reputation is terrible, even within his own family, but we wanted to speak to him and see what he had to say about BJJ history. We felt that his image added a lot of value, given the nature of our project and his role as the source for so much of what was commonly known about BJJ's history.

He initially agreed to be interviewed for a fee (at that time unnamed) and on the condition that he needed to know more about our project. I sent him an email with all the relevant information, and asked how much his fee would be. His answer shocked me. Rorion Gracie wanted $15,000 to share pictures of his father with us and an additional $20,000 to be interviewed by our team. I couldn't believe what I was reading. I was tempted to reply that we had more pictures of his father than he did, and ask if he wanted to buy some of them from us... but in the end I let my better judgment rule the day. As with Rildo, I left it at that.

Rorion's request, however, would pale in comparison to the one later made by his cousin, Reila.

From the very beginning of the project, Reila had been at the top of our list of hoped-for interviewees for three reasons. She was the daughter of Carlos Gracie, Sr., she was Carlos' biographer, and she was a woman. This last one I didn't feel to be a necessity, since she belonged in our production because she had a story to tell and not because she was a woman, but the political correctness of our age demanded "diversity," and it was highly recommended that we have at least one woman in the movie to avoid any potential flak from the noisy minority. Either way, the overlap helped us.

I reached out to Reila (I can't recall how I got her number; possibly it was from my father) and introduced myself as a BJJ Black Belt and producer of a documentary about the history of BJJ. I honestly don't know whether she knew my name from my BJJ career (and the fact that I had lost two finals in the World Championship, and a semifinal in the open weight class at the same tournament to her son, Roger Gracie, widely regarded as the most dominant BJJ competitor of all time) or she was simply suspicious of a documentary about BJJ history (or maybe someone had tipped her off that I would be calling), but she was far from receptive. In fact, her coldness for the first thirty minutes of our conversation made it difficult to not give up the effort. It took a while for her to warm up to the idea that I genuinely wanted to have an honest discussion about BJJ's history.

Perhaps her coldness was warranted: after all, we were looking to give credit to other previously-unknown characters, effectively parceling out the credit traditionally enjoyed by her father and uncle alone. She finally became a little more communicative, but she was still far from agreeing to an interview. In fact, according to her, it sounded like we were making a movie adaptation of her book, and she wanted to be paid for the rights for this adaptation. My conversation with Rorion Gracie was still fresh on my mind, but I dared to ask, "How much?" Nothing could have prepared me for her answer. Reila Gracie wanted $250,000 dollars for the film rights and the interview.

Much like in my exchange with Rorion, I felt like taking her down a peg: I felt like telling her that our film wasn't an adaptation of her book but that, in many ways, we would be correcting the account given in the book... this time, with sources. Instead, I merely insisted that she do the interview for free, like everyone else, and that she would be acting as a representative for her father, providing an important voice and point of view. She didn't go for it, though, so again I left it at that.

Later it crossed my mind that perhaps her silence was a form of boycott: that, realizing the extent to which her biography was flawed and unsubstantiated, particularly in regards to the period of time we would be discussing in our film, she reasoned that fewer eyes on our film meant more credence to her biography as the sole version of that history. Accordingly, she certainly wasn't going to help put more eyes on our film by being in it.

Funnily enough, I would later receive militant messages from Reila regarding her opposition to the then-presidential candidate Jair Bolsonaro. Our views on the candidate converged in some ways, and we ended up spending some time on the phone in friendly conversation regarding Brazilian politics. Overall I found her to be an intelligent and driven woman; still, I can't help but feel that she would have done her father better service by granting us an interview, rather than boycotting us with her silence.

Rildo, Rorion, Reila, and the already-mentioned Romeu Bertho were not the only people we missed out on interviewing, unfortunately. Fabio tried to organize something with the descendants of the Ono Brothers in São Paulo, but it didn't work out for some reason. We were also unable to get an interview with Satake's only living student, Vinicius Ruas. Perhaps more regrettably, we also missed out on interviewing the legendary but reticent Georges Mehdi. It was a real shame since, according to some, Mehdi had played a key role in BJJ's development. He lived for some time in Japan, and trained with many elite Judokas there, and the knowledge he brought back to Brazil may have impacted BJJ and its progression into a more sophisticated ground-fighting style. His involvement with and eventual split from the Gracie Academy is discussed by Armando Wriedt in an interview we did with him not meant to be in part of the documentary (shared on our Instagram page, and included in Armando's chapter), and discussed in *Choque* as well. Everything I had heard about Mehdi made him ideal for our documentary, and I am still not sure why he wouldn't give us an interview. I suspect that he felt that his life's work was his "word," and that no amount of talking or interviewing could change, add to, or detract from that. Mehdi, if I understood his motives correctly, was a man of action and deeds, not words, all while being extremely humble and so at odds with so many of the things I found objectionable in BJJ and its history.

Mehdi's reclusiveness proved challenging, because we wanted to honor him in some way. Even finding a good picture of him was proving difficult. Fortunately, towards the end of our production, one of Mehdi's old-time students, Gilson Campos, reached out to me with a treasure trove of pictures of Mehdi. Interestingly, Mehdi was smiling in every one of the pictures where he wasn't training. One of them, my favorite, shows him rolling without the gi with none other than Carlson Gracie. In the picture, Mehdi, who from all accounts embodied the very essence of our film's purpose, is playing the open-guard with the Gracie prodigy.

Mehdi was also important to our project for another reason: he was Roberto Pedreira's inspiration for *Choque*, the book that—along with Marcial's *Geo Omori: O Guardião Samurai*—inspired our film. In this way I felt I owed even greater thanks to the man, and I truly regret never having the chance to sit down with him. I would have been content to just meet him and exchange a few words. I can't help but feel that his silence then meant an enormous loss for students of the history of both Judo and BJJ—a loss made both permanent and final by his death soon after, in late 2018. In hindsight, I should have been more persistent and found a way to interview him. In our haste I somehow felt it would be OK to let it pass. History seldom feels vital when it is happening, and I couldn't grasp at the time the enormous loss that this would mean for our film, as well as for the overall history of BJJ. An article I wrote for Roberto Pedreira's GTR, in which I attempt in some small way to draw attention and give credit to Mehdi, is included following this section.

Lastly, another interview we failed to get was with Roberto Pedreira himself, the writer whose works had in part inspired our project and which remain the most thorough and comprehensive works on the history of BJJ to date. I reached out to him with our request for an interview, but he politely declined. I wasn't offended: to be honest, I expected this answer. A part of me was disappointed—I felt that he had much to add to our film, but I already suspected that his answer to this would be that everything he had to say about BJJ history was already in his books (and if that would have been his answer, he would be correct). As it stood the film was never meant to be a replacement for serious historical inquiry, but always meant as a bridge between martial artists and that inquiry, and if our film brings readers to Pedreira's excellent work then our goal will have been achieved. Despite not sitting for an interview, throughout the three years of our production Roberto Pedreira would give us priceless advice, guidance, and suggestions for which our production will always be grateful. I did offer him payment on more than one occasion in exchange for the consulting, which he also respectfully declined. Such generosity from Pedreira and notable others stands in stark contrast to the response from those who saw our production as an opportunity to enrich themselves, and my opinions regarding these protagonists contrast in equal measure. We were not granted all the interviews we wanted for the film, but I am left with no doubts about the character and intentions of those who willingly aided our efforts to give credit where credit is due to all those upon whose shoulders we, in the BJJ world, now stand.

Remembering Georges Mehdi
Originally published on GTR November 6, 2019

It is difficult to credit the impact and depth of influence of someone who did so little self-promotion during his lifetime, and yet did so much in furthering the growth of martial arts in Brazil in a responsible and ethical manner. Georges Kastriot Mehdi was the prototypical martial arts Master whose teaching went well beyond throws and submissions. He witnessed and helped kickstart a revolution that would ultimately culminate in MMA and BJJ, yet he never wanted anything to do with any of it, let alone any credit for it.

Georges Mehdi moved to Rio de Janeiro as a teenager, and it would be here that he would begin his martial arts practice. The late Armando Wriedt tells the story:

"One day somebody asked, "Hey kid, have you got the courage? You said you're a fighter and so on." After all, he was really a strong kid. He would dance that, ya, ya, ya! He could dance that pretty well. He was good! Well, one day, he accepted. "I accept because I'm strong, and I'm not afraid of anyone." So, they took him over [to the Gracie Academy]. Getting there, the poor kid. Soon he faced off with

Carlson. So Carlson did what he wanted to Georges, and Georges didn't know what to do. So Hélio asked him, 'Kid, you said you just arrived in Brazil, come stay with us.' They didn't have a guy to take care of the clothes. Valdemar [Santana] had already left, and so they put Georges in charge of the clothes. And Georges trained. He was strong." [1]

Hélio Gracie, immediately recognizing the boy's potential, lauded him in the press as a French Champion with a long successful fight record overseas. According to Hélio's account, Georges had specifically moved to Brazil because he had heard tales of Hélio's feats from his homeland. This would all had been a normal marketing exploit typical of that era if it weren't for one thing: Mehdi, according to himself, was a beginner and never a champion when he moved to Brazil, nor did he move there to train martial arts.

Mehdi's journey was an unusual one for a beginner French Judoka-turned-Brazilian. Albeit having initiated his training in Brazil under the Gracie Academy, it wasn't long before he fell out with Carlos and Hélio, and committed the infamous betrayal of becoming a champion and an icon of their dreaded rival: Judo. In fact, Mehdi's "betrayal," and what some would call "creontagem," may not have bothered him at all, since he believed he had left the Gracie Academy for the right reasons.

Following Mehdi's departure from the Gracie Academy, he went to Japan. Here he practiced at the Kodokan, as well as at Tenri and Chuo Universities, and trained alongside World and Olympic Champion Isao Okano amongst other Japanese Judokas. He also met, and possibly trained with, Masahiko Kimura himself. After his experience training in Japan, Mehdi brought back an enormous treasure of knowledge to Brazil. His skills and knowledge helped initiate his career as one of Brazil's greatest Judoka at the time and, later, one of its most successful coaches. His exploits in Judo cemented his place in Judo's history, having placed second at the 1963 and third in the 1967 Pan-Am Games.

It was through Kano's philosophical approach to combat that Mehdi found his life's purpose. His trip to Japan forever impacted not only his personal growth as a martial artist, but may have impacted the technical growth of Brazilian Jiu-Jitsu as well: all of this occurred at a time when the arsenal of techniques available to BJJ's practitioners was limited. According to Roberto Pedreira, he asked Zoca [2] about Mehdi's role in BJJ's development, and this was his reply:

"Was it possible that many, possibly even most of the Jiu-Jitsu techniques used by the Gracies and their students were introduced by guys who learned them from Mehdi?" I asked Zoca.

"Very possible," he said.

In later years Mehdi became known as a critic of certain members of the Gracie family. But not all, however. The record indicates that his relationship with Carlson Gracie and Carlson's students was always a healthy one. He taught the likes of Murilo Bustamante, Ze Mario Sperry, Wallid Ismail, Marcelo Behring, and most of Carlson Gracie's students at the time. Mehdi's issues with the Gracie family, in particular with Carlos and Hélio, seem to stem from what he referred to as their "penchant for brawling and lying." [3]

The problem seemed to also rest in the differing approaches Judo and its offshoot—later known as BJJ—had to martial arts. The rapid worldwide growth of a sport-oriented approach to martial arts, embodied in Judo, from the 1950s onwards not only rallied Jiu-Jitsu and Kodokan instructors teaching across the globe under its banner but also created an avenue for civilians in Brazil to practice Jigoro Kano's method. The distancing of the Gracie family from its roots wasn't only on the grounds of their technical and rules disagreements: it was also on their approach on how to market the two franchises. Carlos and Hélio were at an enormous disadvantage in marketing reach compared to Judo, with its worldwide social-political acceptance as well as its prestige as an Olympic sport. Their approach to countering this wasn't always commendable, and often leaned on dishonest and thuggish tactics in order to keep their brand of Judo alive. An example of their differences is illustrated by an event that took place during a seminar in Brazil's northeast, where Mehdi allegedly claimed to have defeated Gracie Academy champion Pedro Hemetério (whether Mehdi actually made this claim is unclear). Hélio's reaction to what he believed (or wanted to believe) was a provocation is well recorded.

Following the event, Hélio brought Hemeterio and two other fighters to challenge Mehdi in his own gym in order to "disprove [Mehdi's] lie and show that any Jiu-Jitsu fighter is superior to Judo." Mehdi replied that he "[didn't] want to fight Hemeterio, because a Judoka isn't in a condition of equality with a Jiu-Jitsu fighter. One is a sport and one is a fight without rules" [4], making clear the Gracies' leaning at the time towards a more "martial" approach to martial arts than their Judo counterparts.

Mehdi was heavily influenced by and embodied Kano's teachings; Kano himself, in his turn, was heavily influenced by Western philosophers and particularly by Herbert Spencer. According to Pedreira, for Spencer, "education should do more than instill knowledge. It must also produce good citizens and it must build healthy bodies to house healthy brains and spirits." [5] Accordingly Kano envisioned his new Jiu-Jitsu school as a step into modernity and education while maintaining certain aspects of Japan's past. Whether Mehdi believed in and followed this philosophy due to his own character or martial arts upbringing is unknown; what is certain is that he was at odds with Carlos and Hélio's marketing-oriented approach. In his own words: "'I'm not here to certify bullies. I'm here to bring up people with healthy minds." Mehdi did not mention the Gracies by name but it is difficult to believe that he did not have them in mind. Hélio Gracie, at least, seemed to think so. [6] Mehdi was a Kodokan man all the way.

In a recent trip to Brazil for the filming of the documentary *Closed-Guard: The Origins of Jiu-Jitsu in Brazil*, our crew had the opportunity to interview many Grandmasters. Among them was Flavio Behring. Knowing of Mehdi's reputation for not liking to be interviewed or filmed, I asked Grandmaster Behring to call Mehdi on behalf of our production and request an interview. After a few minutes of friendly conversation with his old friend, I could overhear him on the phone: "But why do they want to talk to me?" I heard Mehdi say. "I'm no one." [7]

History tends to record the wretched and to remember the vain. Men like Georges Mehdi seldom have their legacies recorded. His distaste for self-promotion and for giving interviews certainly playing a role here. On November 6, 2018, it wasn't only Judo that lost one of its icons. Mehdi was a man that should be credited as a central figure in the development of BJJ away from its Kodokan roots; at the very least in regards to its takedowns; he deserves credit also for being ground zero for the legitimate historical study of BJJ history, this despite the fact that he wanted and sought no such credit. [8]

It is ironic that the man who was such a rival of the Gracie Brothers and such a stout supporter of sport Judo would have had such an impact in the growth of BJJ, particularly in Rio de Janeiro. According to Mehdi, it was "all Judo," and BJJ's distancing from its roots was in fact a perversion of Kano's teachings. Differences aside, it is unquestionable that he played a crucial role in the formation of BJJ. For these and many other reasons, Georges Kastriot Mehdi deserves to be remembered in the Pantheon of BJJ's Greats, not because he would have expected it, but because he belongs there.

Article Notes:

1. Interview with Armando Wriedt, January 18, 2018.

2. Zoca was a schoolmate to Rickson Gracie and a student of Georges Mehdi. Roberto Pedreira's encounter with him is described in *Jiu-Jitsu in the South Zone*, Chapter 25.

3. Pedreira, *Choque Vol. 2*, Chapter 4.

4. Pedreira, *Choque Vol. 3*, Chapter 8. The incident was described in a recent interview with Armando Wriedt.

5. Pedreira, *Craze Vol. 1*, Chapter 5.

6. Pedreira, *Choque Vol. 3*, Chapter 5.

7. The telephone conversation took place on January 9, 2018. To the best of the author's recollection, Flavio Behring's part went as follows:

Flavio Behring: *Oi meu amigo tudo bem* [Mehdi response inaudible]. *Tem uma equipe de filmagem dos EUA aqui e eles querem conversar com voce.* [Mehdi response inaudible] *É um documentario sobre a historia do jiu-jitsu no Brasil.* [Mehdi response inaudible] *Mas converse com eles...*

[After they hang up]

Robert Drysdale: *O que ele disse?*

Flavio Behring: *Ele disse, "Mas eu não sou ninguem, eu não tenho nada a dizer."*

8. Personal correspondence between the author and Roberto Pedreira in regards to this article.

*

Updated August 06, 2020.

Upper left: Gotta Tsutsumi and the author; Upper right: Yoshizo and Lyoto Machida visit Maeda's grave after their family has rebuilt it for the second time; Bottom: Director of the Pan-Amazonian-Nipo-Brazilian Association Gotta Tsutsumi

GOTTA TSUTSUMI

"At the time, [Maeda] helped a lot with the welcoming of Japanese immigrants to the Amazon. He knew many Brazilians from the government and police level. He facilitated it a lot. Mitsuyo Maeda had strength. He could speak directly to the governor and the military. He helped a lot in receiving immigrants at the time."

—Gotta Tsutsumi, Head of the Pan-Amazonian
Nipo-Brazilian Association

224

We interviewed Gotta in his office at the headquarters of the Associação Pan Amazonica Nipo-Brasileira. It was an interesting interview: Gotta was well versed in the history of the Japanese immigration to the Amazon, and provided a lot of context for the events we
were exploring. Though he had lived in Brazil for over thirty years at
this point, he still spoke with a heavy Japanese accent. We spent the
rest of the day with him and he showed us around Belém, helping us
gather B-Roll. He showed us the cemetery where Maeda was buried,
and the house that Maeda built and where his family still lived. The
cemetery shot was an easy one and Steve and Jay had it handled, so I
focused my attention on speaking with Gotta about various topics
(most of our conversation took place off camera, and I deeply regret
not recording them).[9]

While Steve and Jay did their thing Gotta told me how, in 1983,
former UFC champion Lyoto Machida's father, Yoshizo Machida, had
discovered Maeda's grave in shambles, and practically abandoned.
With the help of some students from Kokushikan University in Japan
he rebuilt the grave entirely (and again in February 2018) into the
structure that still stands today. I found it admirable that a co-immi-
grant would take the time to honor someone he had never met, and at
a time when Maeda's name had almost been forgotten in Brazil (it
wouldn't be revived until years later, when the UFC and Royce Gracie
put BJJ on the map).

Gotta took us to his home in Belém and showed us his sizable collection of documents and newspaper articles about Maeda and other
Japanese immigrants to the Amazon, which I proceeded to photo-
graph, as some of these were not in the Brazilian National Library. I
asked him if many researchers had sought him out over the years to

---

[9] Steve is an outstanding videographer and filmmaker who has shot all over the world,
including in war zones, and his dedication to his craft is truly noteworthy. Throughout our
trip he would randomly stop the car, often in very dangerous neighborhoods, pull out his
expensive camera, and begin to film, and no amount of asking him to "hurry it up" would
accelerate the process. At one point, in Belém, even the locals passing by were warning
us that we were in a lot of danger, and that we should put our camera equipment away
and leave. I had a lot of respect for his commitment and it worked in our favor: we collected some incredible B-Roll during this trip.

learn about Maeda, and he responded in the affirmative; I asked him if he indeed had Maeda's passport, as it had been suggested by Rildo and rumored on the internet that he did. He responded that I was the second person to ask him, but that he had never seen such document. I told him that I had also thought the rumor strange, since passports weren't common until after World War I. (It is widely propagated that Maeda arrived in Brazil through the city of Porto Alegre on November 14, 1914, but the reality is that he was already making appearances in São Paulo as early as September 23—and possibly as early as July 17—of that same year.)

Hearing from Gotta stories that circulated in the Belém about Maeda regarding his penchant for gambling, drinking, womanizing, and dressing fashionably made the character all the more colorful and human. These were my favorite stories about historical figures: not the blown-up heroic ones, so incongruent with our experiences with life and people, but the one that showed the human side, that showed these characters to be flawed, ambitious, vain, and normal, all too normal. Too often historical figures are presented as exaggerated heroes or villains. Speaking for myself, it is always in the accounts in which they are shown to be possessed of human failings that the character becomes relatable.

Our final stop with Gotta would be the house that Maeda built and in which he died, and where his daughter still lived. We arrived at the slightly-better-than-modest house and were received by Maeda's daughter's husband. He greeted us cordially, but it was soon clear that he and his wife had had enough of researchers and enthusiasts knocking on their door and asking about Maeda. She wasn't feeling well, or so we were told, so she stayed in bed while her husband showed us pictures of Maeda, many of which are widely available on the internet, and that he claimed were the originals. He also possessed some beautiful certificates that Maeda had received from his efforts as a host for Japanese immigrants in the Amazon: a treasure trove of documents that we were fortunate enough to capture on film.

Maeda is a mythical character to say the least: his fame during his time was undeniable, his experience and world travels just as remarkable, especially at a time when most people never left their home-towns. He was a successful Judoka with many professional victories, many fake fights, a brief experience in Catch Wrestling, and it is even rumored that he was some sort of agent for the Japanese Empire (a claim that, though still unsubstantiated, merits consideration, given that similar accusations were made in at least three different coun-tries—the U.S., Cuba, and Brazil).

However, all in all, it seems to me now that Maeda's role in the development and spread of Jiu-Jitsu/Judo in Brazil is grossly exag-gerated. By the time he reached the Amazon he was practically re-tired; evidence suggests he spent a short time teaching and then passed the ball to his five main students—Jacyntho Ferro, Waldemar Lopes, Raphael Gomes, Guilherme Dela Rocque and Dr. Matheus Pereira—and took on a more active role helping with Japanese immi-gration.

The great Judoka was claimed by many as the source of their knowledge: Donato Pires dos Reis, Carlos Gracie, Luis França, Bianor de Oliveira (who as early as 1915 was claiming apprenticeship under Maeda), Mario Aleixo, and Capitão Souto. It took me a long time to mature into this conclusion, but it seems to me now that Mae-da's true contribution to BJJ was unwillingly lending his name and credibility to these Brazilians. Because he has been at the heart of this discussion for so long, it is difficult to place him anywhere other than in the center of it. But, other than creating the environment in which Carlos Gracie would be introduced to Judo/Jiu-Jitsu, what did he ac-tually do to foster the creation of BJJ? He is undoubtedly interesting and important, but I don't see why he should be at the center of this history. In my view, if we feel bound by necessity to create a link be-tween Japan and Brazil, men like Geo Omori, Takeo Yano, and Yas-suiti Ono had a far more active role in spreading Judo/Jiu-Jitsu in Brazil than Maeda. Additionally, there is a stronger case to be made for Carlos' apprenticeship under Jacyntho Ferro or Geo Omori, for Donato having learned from Ferro, and for França having learned from the Gracie Academy rather than from Maeda.

Yet Maeda's name was crucial: it gave these Brazilians credibility at a time where they had none. Ironically, it was the usage of his name by these men that kept his name alive and relevant to this day. It is unlikely that his feats in Brazil, standing on their own, would have accomplished this. And if this is the case, as I believe it is, then it seems that Robson was right in his assessment that no one—outside the small circles of researchers and a few aging Japanese in the Amazon jungle—would have heard of Maeda today, were it not for the efforts of Carlos Gracie.

I have often wondered what Maeda would have thought if he knew how, a century later, his name would be at the center of a historical debate regarding an art called "Brazilian Jiu-Jitsu." My suspicion is that he would have thought it silly. We will never know. What we do know, however, is that Maeda did promote five Brazilians, possibly to the rank of Black Belt... this, at the very least, disqualifies Carlos Gracie as Maeda's favorite. I explored this topic in an article I wrote for Roberto Pedreira's site, GTR, which is included below:

Mitsuyo Maeda Promotes Five Brazilians
Originally published on GTR November 26, 2018

On June 19, 1920, in the Northern Brazilian city of Belém do Pará, Mitsuyo Maeda promoted five of his students to the rank of "primeiro galão."

The students were Jacyntho Ferro, Guilherme de La-Rocque, Dr. Matheus Pereira, Waldemar Lopes, and Raphael Gomes. The promotion of these five Brazilians is significant in that it is the only documented promotion ever made by Maeda. This is interesting in light of the fact that Maeda reportedly said (in 1928) that he "never awarded a Black Belt to any student in Brazil." [1]

The expression used in the article was "colação do primeiro galão," which translates as "promoting to first rank or stripe." [2]

The promotion occurred approximately four years after Maeda began teaching in Belém do Pará, which could lead to the interpretation that Maeda was promoting his five students to a "Black Belt" rank. [3] The article poses problems of both interpretation and translation of what Maeda, or the journalist, might have meant by "colação do primeiro galão."

The word "colação" is commonly used in the context of a promotion or award of a degree or certificate (i.e. a university level bachelor's degree ceremony in Brazil is referred to as "colação de grau"). One of the meanings of the word "galão" is a military stripe of rank typically placed on the sleeve of officers. The biggest problem of interpretation is what was meant by "primeiro" ("first" in Portuguese).

In Judo, "primeiro" can be either the first or last, contingent on it having taken place on the *mu-dan* (無段) or *yū-da*n (有段) ranks ("no dan" or "with dan," respectively). The *mu-dan* levels are referred to as *kyū*, first *kyū* also being the highest rank. At the dan level, it goes in reverse with the *sho-dan* being the first of an ascending order that goes all the way to tenth-dan. With this in mind it remains unclear, with the evidence currently available, what was meant by "primeiro galão."

There are a number of possibilities. For instance, Maeda could be copying the Kodokan grading system, and this would mean that the "colação do primeiro galão" was either a *kyū* or a *sho-dan* promotion. In other words, this could be either a last rank before the *sho-dan* level or *sho-dan* itself, the first dan rank. In case of a first-*kyū* level promotion, these five men would have been close to a rank that we would typically refer to today as a "Black Belt." In the case of a *sho-dan* (初段) level promotion, this would mean these men were being promoted to a rank of "Black Belt" (or, more accurately, *sho-dan*) indicating a certain degree of mastery of fundamental Judo skills.

Additionally Maeda, while isolated in the Amazon Jungle, could have plausibly created his own grading system; in this case the Kodokan's system cannot serve as a guide, and the only reference we are left with is that the rank was significant enough to warrant mention in the press, and that it was fitting considering the experience of the practitioners.

Lastly, it is possible that Maeda created some sort of hybrid ranking system that he thought to be appropriate.

The issue of Maeda having promoted Brazilians to any rank at all is relevant given that he is widely, albeit perhaps unjustly, considered to be the beginning of Brazilian Jiu-Jitsu's lineage. It was previously thought that Maeda had never promoted anyone in Brazil. [4] Jose Cairus, in a 2011 article, cites a 1928 interview with Hajime Otake, a Japanese immigrant, who was allegedly told by Maeda himself that he had never promoted anyone to "Black Belt." Unfortunately, no source was provided. This was subsequently repeated in a 2006 interview conducted by a researcher named Rildo Eros de Medeiros. When contacted by this author to produce the video footage of the interview, Medeiros declined to do so.

It is unlikely, however, that this sort of conversation would ever have taken place in 1928 or any other time given the lack of significance of a "Black Belt" within Kodokan Judo. It is possible that an error in translation led to such a conclusion. Maeda might have used the more accurate expression *sho-dan*, but without access to the original sources we cannot know. If any of the possibilities above are correct, this rewrites not only previously held assumptions regarding Maeda's promotion of Brazilians but also bears relevance in regards to Brazilian Jiu-Jitsu's lineage.

Article Notes:

1. Cairus, José. "Modernization, Nationalism And The Elite: The Genesis Of Brazilian Jiu-Jitsu, 1905-1920." Revista Tempo e Argumento. Jul-Dec. 2011. DOI: 10.5965/2175180303022011100 http://dx.doi.org/10.5965/2175180303022011100

2. *Estado do Pará*, June 19, 1920.

3. The wearing of Black Belts by dan level Judoka was an unofficial Kodokan tradition adopted in or around 1886 (Pedreira, *Craze Vol. 1*, pg. 108).

4. Cairus, 2011. In a personal communication (November 25, 2018), Cairus clarified that his source in both cases was Rildo Eros de Medeiros, who as noted above, declined to cooperate, thereby leaving some doubts as to what Maeda actually said (if anything).

— Gotta Tsutsumi —

Could you introduce yourself? And where are we?

My name is Gotta Tsutsumi, I am 69 years old. We are at the Pan-Amazon-Nipo-Brazilian Association. This association is for the community of forty thousand descendants of Japanese living in the state of Pará.

What led so many Japanese to migrate early in the 20th century to Pará [Amazon]?

There are two reasons for [Japanese] immigration to the Amazon region. The first part is the big earthquake in Japan in 1903. This earthquake destroyed Tokyo. It was all chaos and many people were forced out of Japan. The second reason is that the states of São Paulo and Paraná had an impediment to the entry of immigrants. The only states that received the immigrants were Pará and Amazonas.

What was the role martial arts played for these immigrants?

Strength also comes from martial arts thinking. Martial arts also served to amuse the Japanese colony, since at the time there was almost no amusement. They practiced Judo, Sumo, et cetera.

What was Maeda's role in the Amazon, beyond his teaching martial arts?

At the time, [Maeda] helped a lot with the welcoming of Japanese immigrants to the Amazon. He knew many Brazilians from the government and at the police level. He facilitated it a lot. Mitsuyo Maeda had strength. He could speak directly to the governor and the military. He helped a lot in receiving immigrants at the time.

Why were these martial artists migrating out of Japan?

Most of the Japanese were seeking a new life because in Japan of that time it was not developed like it is today. There were no jobs or houses. So it was necessary to seek opportunities outside of Japan. But in the midst of these Japanese there were the adventurers as well.

Approximately how many Japanese immigrants came to the Amazon?

From 1929 until the 1980s approximately thirty thousand Japanese immigrants came to the Amazon region.

Could you tell us a little bit about what Maeda's friend, who you knew, would say about Maeda?

About six years ago Mr. Hajime Otake, who met Maeda personally, told me that he was a gentleman, very calm, and did not talk much. He was a person that everyone liked and when he walked the streets he liked to greet everyone wearing a hat. He was always in a white coat and hat. Every time he was going to turn a corner, he would take a short detour as a precaution for someone who might be waiting leaning against the wall. It was his custom as a fighter. Even older he had a warrior spirit so he was always wary of any attack. He kept that spirit to his death.

What else did Hajime Otake say about Maeda?

Maeda liked to play cards. When he lost, he was annoyed. Although he was a gentleman, it was the only time he had lost his mind. Once on the tram ride, he forgot the money and the bill collector said he could pay later. He had great credibility.

Could you tell us a little bit about how Maeda's grave was rebuilt?

In 1979, a group of Japanese college students came to Belém.

They were looking for the tomb of Mitsuyo Maeda, but it was all destroyed. The father of Lyoto Machida, who is a Master of Karate, was helping to find the place, and when seeing the state of the tomb removed the bones and took them away to be able to clean bone by bone. After cleaning the bones, he built a new tomb and returned the remains of Maeda. Yoshizo Machida has a dojo of Karate and Jiu-Jitsu and so he respected him as a great ancestor of martial arts and so he did this restoration.

Could you tell us a little more about Maeda's role in mediating Japanese immigration to the Amazon?

He always sought out regions with potential to welcome Japanese immigrants and he fell in love with this city. He never returned to Japan because the immigrants were going through many difficulties. So he did not want to go back because of the immigrants' difficulties. He even received an invitation from the Japanese government to return, but declined.

Maeda helped in the Japanese colonization that went through many difficulties in the beginning. He received an invitation from the Japanese government to return, but because of these difficulties that the immigrants were experiencing he did not want to return to Japan.

How is Maeda perceived in Japan?

The Japanese people themselves only knew of Maeda's fame after he fought the world. After the victories of Royce in the UFC, the Gracie family said that their technique had originated from Maeda and it was then that the Japanese began to recognize Maeda.

What was the role of the Japanese in the Amazon?

The goal of Japanese immigration was not just agriculture. This was only at the beginning of the colonization. They influenced Brazil in sports, cooking, martial arts, anime, and in various areas. Martial arts are fundamental for the Japanese, because with the disappearance of the samurai the Japanese are concerned to keep alive this spirit. The Brazilian absorbed this spirit and I am satisfied with that.

Why did you never go back to Japan?

I'm still Japanese but I really like Brazil. The Brazilian people are very open and affectionate. I've never suffered prejudice. I especially like the people of Pará. They are very warm. I like the hot weather. I lived in São Paulo for three years, but now I'm living here.

Do you like martial arts?

I like martial arts because I was born in a place that traditionally men had to practice martial arts. My father trained Judo and influenced me. He believed that men should be tough and know how to defend themselves and defend the wife if needed. This is a natural thought in my homeland.

The Brazilian capital.

BRASÍLIA

At the time of its founding, Brasília was meant to represent the promise of a new Brazil. Built in the middle of the country (also in the middle of nowhere), it was meant to stand as the Capital of the future for what later propagandists would call "O País do futuro" ("The country of the future"). It is an architectural marvel, projected out of the mind of renowned architect Oscar Niemeyer, and it may be the most beautiful modern city I have ever seen. Lacking anything remotely organic, everything there was planned and designed to give it—and, by extension, the country—an air of grandeur, space, and progress. The people who live there however, have mixed feelings about the "infrastructure of the future": its streets and blocks were designed to accommodate a population on wheels, which has the effect of making everything seem far away. In some ways it reminded me of so many American cities: so friendly to cars, and so hostile to pedestrians. It was my first time visiting, though I had read much about it, and I was a bit disappointed that we had little time to experience it. There was simply no time for sightseeing: we had work to do.

Left to right: Researcher Carlos Loddo; Carlos Loddo and the team, from left to right: Steve, Jay, Fabio, Carlos Loddo, and the author.

CARLOS LODDO

"And as that phenomenon only occurred in Brazil, this ends up being known as Brazilian Jiu-Jitsu. We have it well documented that the principles leading that art were already developed, but the Gracies were the guys who put them into practice and resisted change."

—Carlos Loddo, researcher

Our first interviewee would be Carlos Loddo, a friend of Fabio's and—somewhat oddly, given his interest in BJJ—a practitioner of and Black Belt in Taekwondo. Nonetheless, according to Fabio and despite his choice of disciplines, Loddo was one of the most well-versed researchers in BJJ history. And—bonus for us—he spoke English. We met with him at a beautiful Country Club called "ASCADE" (Associação dos Servidores da Câmara dos Deputados; Association of Servers of the Chamber of Deputies), where a matted area would provide an appropriate setting for our interview.

Our interview with Loddo was probably the longest of the production, lasting approximately five hours. As I mentioned before, we had tailored our questions as the best we could to the abilities of our interviewees, and Fabio was confident that Loddo could speak knowledgeably about all of the themes we would be approaching in our film. I found this to be true, as the length of our interview indicates, and I relished the opportunity to speak with Loddo further after the interview over what I felt was some of the best pizza I have ever had (Steve and Jay disagreed: they hated Brazilian pizza). I liked Loddo, but in the end I found that I didn't always agree with his conclusions. Our differences seemed to relate to a difference in opinion about methodology and how one should approach history and evidence: I am not a professional historian, nor have I spent anywhere near the number of hours in research that some of the people we interviewed have. Still, I feel that those of us making these inquiries need to do a better job drawing a distinction between hypotheses and evidence-based conclusions (however difficult that may now be, given the years that the Maeda-Carlos-Hélio narrative has enjoyed being repeated by virtually every BJJ source and website that discusses the art's history). Skepticism, I feel, should be the keystone holding science and historical inquiry together. In other words the historian should begin by doubting, not believing.

All of which is to say that I was surprised to find that, of all our interviewees, Loddo was perhaps the staunchest supporter of Carlos' version of events. To him there was no question that Carlos had trained under Maeda for five long years. He remained unmoved by the fact that not only was Carlos the sole source of information regarding his own apprenticeship, historians simply couldn't verify that there was any Gracie family member training in Belém at the time of Maeda's residence there... That is: until recently, though the recent discovery perhaps does more to complicate the story than clarify events. The only mention of anyone with the name "Gracie" training in Jiu-Jitsu/Judo during that period in Belém is an "Oscar" Gracie who is referenced in an article recently found in the Brazilian National Library. It should be noted, however, that even if we are to assume that Oscar is Carlos, misnamed by mistake, this single mention of anyone bearing the Gracie name stands in stark contrast to repeated mentions of men such as Jacyntho Ferro, Guilherme de La Rocque, Dr. Mateus Pereira, Waldemar Lopes, and Raphael Gomes in the local press in association with Maeda. All of which suggests that, at the very least, and contrary to commonly held beliefs, Carlos/Oscar did not have a prominent standing in the hierarchy of Maeda's academy in Belém, a possibility made more likely by the fact of Carlos' young age (Carlos Gracie was born in 1902, so he would have been 14 years old when Maeda began teaching in Belém, in 1916).

I discussed the Oscar Gracie article in a piece first published on Roberto Pedreira's site GTR. That article is included below:

Who Was Oscar Gracie and Who Taught Him Jiu-Jitsu?
Originally published on GTR February 13, 2018

Did Carlos Gracie learn the Gentle Art of Jiu-Jitsu under the auspices and intimate "paternal supervision" of Mitsuyo Maeda, aka Conde Koma, as he and his supporters claimed (and still do), invariably without any substantiating evidence? A recent discovery throws important light on the question.

In 1921, an event took place in the Campo da Recreativa in the city of Belém do Pará in the Brazilian Amazon. It was announced in the June 26 edition of the local newspaper *Estado do Pará*. It read as follows: "Terminado esse numero seguir-se-ão jogos de jiu-jitsu entre os srs. Donato Pires dos Reis e Oscar Gracie, alumnus do prof. Jacyntho Ferro. Servirão de arbitros nessa lucta os profs. Conde Koma, Jacyntho Ferro e dr. Matheus L. Pereira." ["At the end of this act, Jiu-Jitsu games will follow between Mr. Donato Pires dos Reis and Mr. Oscar Gracie, students of the Professor Jacyntho Ferro. The referees for this fight will be Professors Conde Koma, Jacyntho Ferro, and Dr. Matheus L. Pereira."]

The article is important for several reasons. First, it is the first time that a "Gracie" was ever associated with the practice of Jiu-Jitsu. Second, there was no "Oscar" in that generation of the Gracie family, raising the question: Who was Oscar Gracie? More precisely, could he have been Carlos Gracie, possibly misnamed due to the sort of editorial errors that were very common during that period? Most likely it was Carlos: the other Gracie brothers were either too young, and in fact, with one highly atypical exception, none of them ever claimed to have trained with Maeda or even denied it.

Another reason for suspecting that Oscar was actually Carlos was a comment later made by one of Jacyntho Ferro's students, who trained with Oscar (Carlos) Gracie at the same time, namely Donato Pires dos Reis, to the effect that "some people" exaggerated their training with Maeda." By "some people," Donato was clearly referring to Carlos. A short time later, Donato clarified that Carlos not only did not receive a diploma from Conde Koma, he had never even met him. [1]

The article is also important because it refers to both Donato Pires dos Reis and "Oscar" Gracie as "alumnos do prof. Jacyntho Ferro" ["students of Jacyntho Ferro"], and not Mitsuyo Maeda, despite the fact that Maeda was present at the event.

Based on the evidence available, it seems that Carlos Gracie was a student of Jacyntho Ferro who, in his turn, was a student of Mitsuyo Maeda. Carlos may have taken a few classes from Maeda during his stay in Belém, although there has never been any evidence of it. At present, the best available evidence indicates that Carlos Gracie's Jiu-Jitsu teacher was fellow countryman Jacyntho Ferro.

Updated August 30, 2018: In 2013 Marcial Serrano referenced the news article discussed above in *O Livro Proibido do Jiu-Jitsu Vol. 1*. Serrano insisted that the switch of names between "Oscar" and "Carlos" was "inconceivable" if Carlos Gracie had been in Rio de Janeiro since 1918, a possibility for which he offered no evidence. According to Reila Gracie, Carlos and the family moved to Rio early in 1922, making Serrano's interpretation highly implausible.

Article Notes:
1. See Myths and Misconceptions, # 5. Donato's clarification was published in *O Globo*, September 2, 1931, as follows: "...Sr. Gracie nunca foi diplomada por Conde Koma (que nem ao menos o conhece)." The author wishes to thank Fabio Quio Takao for bringing this article to his attention.
© Robert Drysdale, 2018. All rights reserved.
Edit History:

Updated August 30, 2018.

Updated November 22, 2019.

Updated May 23, 2020.

Updated July 28, 2020 (date that Carlos arrived in Rio de Janeiro was (according to Reila 2008, p. 43) early 1922, not December 13, 1921 (Reila claimed that they family left Belém because Carlos' great-grandfather, Pedro Gracie, died in Rio on December 13, 1921. However, Reila was mistaken about that: Pedro died on February 13, 1921 (consult *Craze Vol. 3* (forthcoming 2020 or 2021), by Roberto Pedreira, chapters 5 and 7, for details).

These points take on a different shade when one considers all that Carlos had to gain from the association of his own name with Maeda's. Claiming in São Paulo in 1929 that he was a student of Maeda in Belém (the first time such a claim was made) would have given him much credibility in the epicenter of Japanese immigration in Brazil. Of course, there were many shades of truth to his assertions: he did live in Belém, his father was the owner of a circus in which Maeda fought, and he did mention by name other prominent members of the Judo/Jiu-Jitsu scene including "Sataki [sic], Okura, Shimiti [sic], Laku" (also written as "Raku"), and Conde Koma himself. The fact that he knew these names suggest that he was indeed familiar with the Judo/Jiu-Jitsu scene in Belém; additionally, Donato Pires dos Reis would later invite Carlos to be his assistant instructor at the police academy in Belo Horizonte in 1928, and he wouldn't have done that if he a) did not know Carlos from Belém, and b) did not know that Carlos was acquainted with Judo/Jiu-Jitsu. Still, though all of this suggests a degree of familiarity with Judo/Jiu-Jitsu, it says nothing about how much Carlos trained with Maeda. And, considering the "Oscar" Gracie article, which names Jacyntho Ferro as the instructor of both Donato Pires dos Reis and "Oscar" Gracie, (despite Maeda being present at the event) it seems far more likely that it was Ferro and the other apprentices of Maeda who taught Carlos. Furthermore, it is noteworthy that despite the renaissance of research that ensued after the digitization of the Brazilian National Library, researchers are yet to find any materials directly linking Carlos to Maeda. This simple fact has led some to believe that Carlos Gracie either never met Maeda or had very little training under the Japanese Master.

This claim would elicit some flak from researchers and enthusiasts alike after a few interviews I gave in the lead-up to the documentary's release. There is a clear distinction, to me at least, between saying that "Carlos Gracie never met Maeda" and saying "There is no evidence that Carlos Gracie ever met Maeda." Absence of evidence does NOT necessarily mean evidence of absence. Anything can change tomorrow, and new discoveries will prove not that the skeptic historian was incorrect but rather that he was following proper methodology in remaining skeptical until definitive evidence was made available. Serious inquiry begins with the assumption that "it is not," followed by conclusive evidence that suggests that "it is." The distinction is so clear, in fact, that it doesn't even merit discussion... but people get held up on these issues; hence my disagreement in methodology with so many researchers. At any rate, this issue is by no means a major player in the overall history of BJJ and the relevance, which is indisputable, of Carlos Gracie to this same history.

Loddo and I discussed the possibility that Carlos claimed Maeda as his instructor in the way a white belt in my gym's beginner class might claim to train under me because it is my gym, despite the fact that I haven't taught the beginner classes in many years. My personal opinion is that Carlos did meet Maeda at some point, and that the Japanese Master might have even taught classes on occasion; however, in terms of historical inquiry, such unverified hypotheses and personal opinions are irrelevant. The simple fact is that the evidence available points to Jacyntho Ferro as Carlos Gracie's real instructor.

As for Donato's claim that Carlos never met Maeda, it is important to remember that this was made at a time when Carlos and Donato were not on good terms; furthermore, I am not convinced that Donato—who made the equally unverified claim that he was the only instructor certified by Conde Koma—was the most reliable of characters.

Whatever the extent of Carlos Gracie's relationship to Maeda, in the broader scope of BJJ's history, it does not change the outcome in any significant way. Nor does it alter the fact of BJJ's departure from the Judo mothership. In fact, it is merely a curiosity. It is what Carlos Gracie did that matters at the end of it all, not who taught him.

As I have argued before, "lineages" are arbitrary and limiting constructs, the product of an overly-simplistic view of martial arts and its history. Carlos didn't have to learn anything from Maeda to be firmly planted as a central figure in BJJ's history, any more than Dana White had to put on MMA gloves and step into the Octagon.

— Carlos Loddo —

Can start by giving us your name, age and academic pedigree?

My name is Carlos Loddo. I studied philosophy in education and I have been researching the history of Vale Tudo, Jiu-Jitsu, and Brazilian martial arts for about thirty-four years.

Can you tell us about Jigoro Kano?

Jigoro Kano was from a noble family in Japan, and he was obsessed by the Jiu-Jitsu schools. He devoted his life to Jiu-Jitsu. He wanted a school of Jū-Jutsu that would encompass all the schools. And so he developed the Kodokan, his school. In his view he was taking the best from every Jū-Jutsu school. But, as he came from the Kito-Ryu himself, which was a school very much specialized in throwing, he devoted too much attention to throwing. He thought that ground grappling was an inferior aspect that should be worked, but if a student put too much attention to ground grappling they would not ever be good at throwing.

Many of the Kodokan representatives seemed to be well connected in regards to some of their students. Can you comment?

Those guys were more like representatives of a mentality, a Ja-

243

panese mentality, that they were elite fighters and they would only teach to elite members. So they traveled all around the Americas, teaching elite Americans—businessmen, politicians. Even Yamashita, before Maeda came to America, he taught President Roosevelt. And this idea that they should teach the elite, military elites, business elites, and social elites, was very strong all over the West. So [when] they went to Europe they would teach generals, not regular soldiers. Top elite members. And that mentality sort of matches the Brazilian patriarchal culture. So when they got to Brazil... Brazil's a very, has a very aristocratic culture, up to today.

Maeda was accused of working for the Japanese Empire. Can you comment?

There's a lot of talk about Maeda being a spy. Doing some informational sort of work to Japan's benefit. And this is very interesting. This talk goes back to Yamashita, who introduced Jiu-Jitsu or Judo—it was a Kodokan man who introduced Judo or Jiu-Jitsu with the name Jiu-Jitsu, at least—in the United States. And he taught President Roosevelt. He was invited by President Roosevelt to teach at The White House. And Roosevelt mentions him in many of his letters he writes to his kids. And Roosevelt wanted Yamashita to teach [Jiu-Jitsu] in the Annapolis Academy. But the military in the United States were against this, because they saw no purpose for a stranger to be inside a military academy. And they were suspicious that this was not a good deal. But as Maeda started to move around and get into many countries, he was accused of being a spy on many occasions. And I find it interesting that he came to Brazil after traveling all over the world, and settles in the Amazon. And as we know, Japan has a serious problem of a huge population in a small land. The Amazon would be a perfect place to establish a Japanese settlement. In Brazil, all that land given to the Japanese immigrants, that was the subject of many huge newspaper articles. People were saying, "Why is the Brazilian government giving that land to Japanese immigrants?" So, I think things were messy. I think that's a subject

244

that should be studied.
Why didn't Maeda use the term Judo?

Mitsuyo Maeda used to use the term Jiu-Jitsu. Sometimes in his life he used the term Judo in respect to the Kodokan school. But I think he used to think that Jiu-Jitsu was a term more encompassing to represent the martial art from Japan.

Is there evidence of Carlos Gracie training with Maeda?

I found a newspaper article on Carlos Gracie having trained in Maeda's school, in particular a competition in 1921 in which he fought against Donato Pires Reis where both were trained by Jacyntho Ferro. Well Jacyntho Ferro was a direct student of Mitsuyo Maeda. So it was the same school. And Carlos' father—this is very well documented—Gastão Gracie was Maeda's manager. And we have testimonials, independent testimonials, showing that he, Gastão, met Maeda because his son was training with Maeda. So, I think it's pretty objective and proven that Carlos practiced with Maeda from 1915 up to 1920 or '21 around there. We have a testimonial by Samuel Pinto, a doctor who is related to João Alberto Barreto, Carlos Gracie's student. And he was a friend of Carlos' father Gastão. And according to him, Gastão didn't have money for his son to practice with Maeda. So he asked Samuel to ask Maeda as a friend to accept Carlos. And Maeda did like Carlos, so we have this testimonial.

Donato also claimed to have been a direct student of Maeda. Was he?

As we know, Donato Pires dos Reis is claimed to have been a Maeda student. What was he doing being Jacyntho's student? The same thing as Carlos. If you are Jacyntho's student that means you are Maeda's student. That's the same school, that's the same thing. So he practiced under Maeda and Maeda's guidance, Maeda's student's guidance, from 1915 up to 1921, when Maeda left.

Did Carlos have other instructors?

I think a fighting artist learns with everybody, OK? It's impossible to say that Carlos only learned with Maeda. He had experience during his whole life. And of course being close to Geo Omori, as he was for a long time, he learned a lot from him.

Who was Jacyntho Ferro?

Jacyntho was a grown man, he was a strong man, under Maeda in Belém. And Carlos was a young student, so we have to imagine a 15-year-old kid and a grown man. So, Carlos was a 15-year-old kid who grew up around those guys. But the hero then was Jacyntho Ferro. But both were students at Maeda's school, that's the important point. At some point Maeda had a challenge and from some fighter, [a] Catch Wrestler fighter, and he said, "I am very tired, you fight with my student Jacyntho Ferro." And Jacyntho creamed the guy. But unfortunately Jacyntho died young, so he didn't become nationally known. He was more known only in Belém.

In the press at the time you see a constant debate over the length of the gis. The Gracie Brothers preferred shorter sleeves and pants while the Japanese preferred the longer uniforms. Why is that?

When the Japanese introduced Jiu-Jitsu in the West, in the first decades, it's clear that by evidence that the sort of gear they used was short sleeves, short pants. And that's how, we have evidence, they introduced [the gi] in Brazil. And the Gracies simply followed the pattern. But it's possible that helped them along the way, strategically. Maybe both because of tradition and because they would fight Japanese who were used to having long sleeves, that could give them some advantage. So I think both things could explain the fact that for a while [the Gracies] preferred short sleeves. But then they adapted to long sleeves.

246

Can you tell us about the Fadda lineage?

There's a tradition in BJJ coming from Master Oswaldo Fadda, who used to teach in the North Zone of Rio de Janeiro. He's very respected for his very important work with lower classes and people with special needs. And he's very much recognized for that. And he learned from a guy called Luis França in the '40s, during the '40s. And there's a tradition saying that Luis França was a student a direct student of Mitsuyo Maeda. I never saw evidence of that—only mentions of that, but never evidence. In interviews and searching in documents we sometimes see França listed as Geo Omori's student. We know for a fact that Luis França was teaching Jiu-Jitsu in the Brazilian Navy in Rio de Janeiro in the '40s. And who [else] used to teach in the Navy in the '30s? So probably who taught Luis França were first the Gracies, Carlos and George Gracie. And after they had a fight against Manuel Rufino dos Santos they were expelled from the Navy, and Geo Omori and Takeo Yano came to teach the Navy. Officially the Navy instructor was Takeo Yano. So I think the best hypothesis is that Luis França was a student of the Gracies, from Geo Omori and from Takeo Yano.

Can you tell us a little bit about Geo Omori and his importance?

Geo Omori was very important for the development of Vale Tudo because he was one of the first Japanese accepting to fight against Capoeira fighters, against Boxers, against all sorts of Wrestlers. I mean Conde Koma and his generation all did that, but Geo Omori did that for longer. And he stood in the market, in the Vale Tudo market, for longer. He fought many strong men, and he was the great name in the late twenties and early thirties. Unfortunately, he didn't last for the whole decade. But he was pretty influential, even before the Gracies.

Can you tell us about George Gracie?

George Gracie was a phenomenon, "the Red Cat" Gracie. He fought a lot more than any other Gracie. Even if you sum up all the Gracie fights, from all the Gracies, we would maybe not reach the number of fights that George Gracie had. But in around 1940 George Gracie came himself to the press saying that after his 1934 fight against Geo Omori he started to participate in fixed fights. So some Gracies feel that it's not fair to compare the number of fights George Gracie had with those of Hélio Gracie, because all of the Hélio Gracie fights were actual real fights. But anyway George Gracie was an amazing fighter. He won lots of real fights. He fought people much heavier than him. He lost some fights too. And he was a hot head, he didn't follow Carlos Gracie's advice, as opposed to Hélio Gracie who was like a soldier, very disciplined. So we have those two aspects in the Gracie family. George Gracie didn't follow the diet, he didn't follow Carlos' advice. For a while he was trained by Catch Wrestlers, so he trained Catch Wrestlers to learn more Jiu-Jitsu. So I think he was very important both to bringing elements of Catch Wrestling to Jiu-Jitsu and also to bringing Jiu-Jitsu elements to Catch Wrestling for what we now call Luta Livre in Brazil.

Another interesting thing about George is that he fought all over. Hélio Gracie was more fixed in Rio de Janeiro. George Gracie really followed the tradition of the Jiu-Jitsu fighters. He fought all around Brazil. He fought in the south of Brazil, in the north of Brazil, the northeast, wherever. So maybe he did lots of fixed fights, but he brought Jiu-Jitsu and Vale Tudo all over. And another interesting thing about him, he became a great friend of Takeo Yano. So for a while he was closer to Takeo Yano than to his brothers.

Can you tell us more about his relationship to Takeo Yano?

I think the reason for that is that when they fought, Takeo Yano was surprised. He threw George many times, many times, but he couldn't submit him. And when the press came to Takeo Yano to ask, "Oh, you didn't submit him because you didn't want to, right?" And Takeo Yano was such a nice man, he said, "No, I didn't submit him because I couldn't. He's really a good fighter on the ground." And they became friends and they fought for real. They also fought fixed fights, because they fought all over. And his friendship with Takeo Yano was very much relevant to the development of Vale Tudo in the northeast of Brazil, where they had lots of influence.

Why would they get involved in fixed fights?

Because actual fights between two experts tend not to be very interesting to the general public. So, they start to [say], "OK I'll throw you, or you help me throw you, so that the fight becomes more interesting to a great public."

Can you tell us more about Takeo Yano?

Takeo Yano was one of the great names [that] we have to recover. Much like George Gracie, he had a similar profile. He fought all around. He fought from Rio Grande do Sul, the southern tip of Brazil, to Belém de Pará in Manaus. He was an assistant to Maeda, to Mitsuyo Maeda. Before he came to Brazil he was a Judo champion in his town, same town as Kimura. He's mentioned in Kimura's biography. And he was a champion grappler, ground grappling, because then Judo was much more focused on ground grappling. When he came to Belém de Pará and he met Maeda he jumped to Jiu-Jitsu in Brazil. He came to Rio de Janeiro, he started to fight in Catch Wrestling, Vale Tudo, and Jiu-Jitsu, and he fought all over.

What happened in the fights between Carlos Gracie and Geo Omori?

Geo Omori fought Carlos Gracie actually twice in 1930. And those fights are controversial. In the Gracie version, in the first fight Carlos caught Geo Omori in an arm-lock juji-gatame and Geo Omori refused to tap and [Carlos] broke his arm. But in the second fight they had another draw, which was not so spectacular, nobody talks much about it. But then in 1934, when Geo Omori was waiting to fight George Gracie, it was a time of great competition between Omori and the Gracies. Omori came to the press and said, "Now I'm going to speak the truth about the fight with Carlos Gracie in 1930. The fact is that his father came to me and asked me to help him in the fight." So that's Geo Omori's version which was told in 1934, when there was a lot of hate between the Gracies and Omori.

Can you tell us about the fights between Hélio Gracie and Kato and Kimura?

Kato was not the vice champion of the world, that was more of marketing game to attract attention to the fight. That was normal in professional fighting. The fighters always came with titles to attract the public. That was not something Hélio Gracie did himself. That was a normal deal in professional fighting, you always promote the fight to the extreme. Kimura was not a Jiu-Jitsu world champion, he was a Judo world champion. There was not a Jiu-Jitsu world championship. But during the times of Mitsuyo Maeda and all those fighters they always came with those titles. World Jiu-Jitsu champion, many Japanese came to Brazil with this world Jiu-Jitsu champion title. That was a normal marketing strategy to attract more people to the fight.

Can you tell us about Oscar Santa Maria?

Oscar Santa Maria was a sort of partner of the Gracies. And according to some he was their sponsor, and he was a very influental man. He was a public servant in the Brazilian government. And he started to help the Gracies out. And he was also linked to the Rosacrucianism, and so he had this whole esoteric approach. And he was fascinated by Carlos Gracie. And he started to see Carlos as a sort of prophet or sacred person, and Carlos just played the role. And they became associates, and some people think that he was the main guy responsible for the whole economic, financial success of the Gra-

cies. So they ended up having a disagreement during the '60s and they broke and the Gracies tried to get out and get for themselves most of the houses and households that they all had. But during a long time, especially in the '50s, he was even for a while the Minister of Finance in Brazil. So he was a very influential guy, who did help the Gracies a lot.

Does Vale Tudo have a "creator"?

I think that's a sort of collective work. The development of Vale Tudo in Brazil didn't happen at once. It happened over decades. So it's a collective work, it's not something done by one or another person. We have main actors—we have the Gracies establishing a tradition of fighting other arts. But we have also their opponents, some people from Catch Wrestling, having to adapt their style to fight Jiu-Jitsu.

What was the overall role of the Gracie family in regards to the development of what we now call "BJJ," and its resistance to Kodokan Judo?

I believe that the principles, the basic principles of the art, were already given to the Gracie family. But the merit, the value of the Gracie family, was in understanding those and sticking to those principles against all attempts to change [them]. In the '50s everybody was saying, "They're crazy, what they're doing. They're crippled, they only want to fight on the ground." The phenomenon only occurred in Brazil, this ends up being known as Brazilian Jiu-Jitsu. But we have [it] well documented that the principles leading that art were already developed. But the Gracies were the guys who put it into practice and resisted change.

Why is it so difficult to tell history accurately?

History is a very complex matter. Some people find it so complex that they attempt to say that there are not facts, only versions. Those are the relativists. They say, "Well, if you have a version, that's it." I think there are facts. There are facts. I'm a realist, I believe history is out there. But the facts are so complex that in order to understand them, we need versions to learn what a complex object it is. We have to see it from all angles.

Upper row: The cheerful Grandmaster Armando Wriedt; Bottom: From left to right: Fabio, Jay, Armando, the author, and Steve

ARMANDO WRIEDT

"You see, we all have a religion, and almost always you will or won't do certain things for this religion. So Jiu-Jitsu, to me, became a religion."

—Grandmaster Armando Wriedt, student of Hélio Gracie

Armando Wriedt might have been, next to Mehdi, the old-timer with whom I was most eager to speak. I didn't know much about him beyond his reputation for being truthful, intelligent, and friendly. And, although he was one of Hélio Gracie's oldest students, and still loyal to that relationship, he differed from João Alberto Barreto in that he seemed ambivalent about the party line. At various moments during our meeting he was even critical of Hélio: he told us that, when he was first shown a copy of the book put together by Hélio and his son Royler, he was astounded that Hélio was—according to him—showing the techniques incorrectly.

Fabio had been in touch with Armando and some of his students for many years, and it was easy to set up a meeting. Armando's students were eager for their beloved Master to tell his story, and they facilitated everything for our team. We met at Armando's ranch, an hour or so outside the Brazilian capital, where he still taught classes daily to a few loyal students.

His advanced age (he was 92 when we interviewed him) didn't seem to slow him down at all, and he seemed both lucid and energetic when interacting with us (I was surprised, for example, that he drove his car alone to the outdoor tatami where he and his students practiced daily). I was also impressed with his mastery of the Portuguese language and his extensive vocabulary; in fact, I would say that Armando had the best vocabulary I have ever heard in any Portuguese speaker, a trait that his students insisted was only one among his many hidden talents. All this made him even more interesting to me.

I am often suspicious of people's affect, and suspect that they are "playing a part," behaving in a way that befits their own aspirational perceptions of themselves (or those they aspire for others to have of them). This couldn't have been farther from the case with Armando. He was genuine and generous as could be. A lifelong admirer of Mahatma Gandhi, Armando professed an abhorrence for violence, ascribing his experience as a fighter to peer pressure rather than his own inherent nature. It was all very genuine, and I didn't have to wait for the right moment to ask for a piece of life wisdom. The answer had already been plainly given: Armando embodied a lesson of peaceful happiness and serenity at having lived a good life as well as saluting its final chapter with a smile.

We knew that, of all of our interviewees, Armando would be the one most willing to speak to us at length about anything—and that he wouldn't filter his words. He joked that he didn't have much time left, and would tell us everything we wanted to know. "A verdade não tem partido," ("The truth, can't have affiliation") he told us, in perfect harmony with the spirit of our film (though we came to feel that at times Armando's frankness managed to go beyond the realm of historical inquiry).

Our team had learned that the best strategy with the Grandmasters was to get to the interview immediately before they got tired and, though we would later learn that Armando's energy was seemingly endless, we didn't want to risk losing him to the fatigue that accompanies advanced age. While Steve and Jay got set, Fabio and I took the opportunity to talk to Armando, sensing that he would give us valuable information even in casual conversation, and I pulled out my phone and, with his permission, began recording. After our interview I would continue to record our "off" conversations with Armando (of course, as before, with his permission). The man was a living piece of BJJ history, as well as an open book. At the time, I wasn't thinking about using this material for any other reason than to satisfy my own curiosity; however, after further consideration, it was clear that there was enough of historical relevance in these conversations to merit them being transcribed and made available to the public. I would do this through Roberto Pedreira's site, GTR, and later through our film's Instagram account after a few minor edits. (I was concerned that the means by which I had recorded this conversation—holding the phone with my arm down because holding it up was too tiresome—would lead people to believe that I had recorded all this secretly and without permission, which wasn't the case. This was my only hesitation in releasing the material). Excepts of these informal "interviews" are included below:

Robert Drysdale talking to Armando Wriedt, regarding a conversation Armando had with Reila Gracie. The conversation concerns the biography of Carlos Gracie, Sr., written by Carlos' daughter Reila Gracie, who interviewed Armando for the book.

Armando: *It's the way I watched them and saw them... I'm not going to say or do like Joao Alberto and Hélio Vigio did, they did not go against you... Well, it's just that your father was a very good man... I liked him but your father was not a saint... Your father had lots of faults.*

Author: *Did you say that to Reila!?*

Armando: *Yes, and I told Reila, but she asked me a question. . . "Well, that's not true, because of this, this, and this... But my father always said... But that's not true!" The story that I know is this, this, and this. Well, she got really upset with that. "Armando didn't like my father". When she came to Rio, she went to see Joao Alberto. "Joao Alberto, I regret going to talk to Armando, because he told me a lot of things that I had never heard of!" And João Alberto said, "It's just that Armando is someone who tries to be truthful. You asked me certain things that I didn't tell you, because I knew that you would get irritated..." And I said to her, "My child, I saw an interview of yours, and you said lots of things that are not true! If you put that in your book, those who know the family will think you are lying. So, I would like you to be more authentic." She asked me a question, and I pointed out what I knew, but she didn't want to hear it... She didn't...*

Author: *She wanted to hear what she wanted to hear.*

Armando: *Exactly! And I even thought she would not put my name in the book...*

Fabio Takao: *But she did, she put it in there...*

Armando: *So, that's the way it is... The whole thing is like that. The way I always saw it...*

The production team speaking with Armando Wriedt about Georges Mehdi, and incidents surrounding Mehdi's departure from the Gracie Academy:

Armando: *When I was in Teresopolis, every Sunday I would train on Hélio's grass, right? Hemeterio, Carlson, João Alberto. It's like I said, the questions they had weren't resolved at the Academy. They were resolved in Teresopolis. Because the Academy was where the classes were held. Well, that's the way it was. Now it was really important, you know why? Because it was simple, since the Academy was huge and the Gracies were famous, it's just what I said...* [Note: Teresopolis was the city where the Gracie family had a weekend/holiday ranch; it was common then for their martial arts practice to continue on their ranch during the weekends.] *There was always someone coming to put Capoeira against Jiu-Jitsu. And Hélio did things that way, you see. He would ask, "Who doesn't have a class now?" Armando doesn't! Armando, come over to the gym. When that happened...*

Fabio Takao: *He already knew what it was!*

Armando: *And he would say, "Armando, this Capoeira guy wants to show his Capoeira against Jiu-Jitsu." Then he would ask, "How many minutes?" No, it was quick and over. You could beat him easily, because Capoeira... if you got close, it was over.*

Fabio Takao: *Over. Right.*

Armando: *So that's the way it was. [If] it wasn't Armando it was someone else. That's how he did it. So come with me!*

Fabio Takao: *It was a surprise, like that?*

Armando: *Yes. Almost every week it was call Armando, call João Alberto. Who doesn't have a class now? Armando? So, it was Armando! Who doesn't have class? Vigio, come over here...* [Note: Here Armando describes some of the "challenges" that took place during the period between the representatives of the Gracie Academy and other martial arts.]

Author: *Teacher, there was a fight between Georges Mehdi and the Gracie Academy, what happened? Georges Mehdi, Georges Frances?*

Armando: *Look, you see, here's the story... Let me sit down...*

Fabio Takao: *Have a seat, Master.*

Armando: *The butt doesn't hurt much, but the knee hurts. You see,* *this was pretty funny, because Georges Mehdi, how did he show up at the Academy? Georges showed up, because he came from France, I guess! Because Georges wasn't French.*

Author: *Algerian?*

Armando: *Algerian. So he went to France, and from France to Brazil. Since he was a strong kid, because Georges was a strong kid, right? Well, this is what happened. One day somebody asked, "Hey kid, have you got the courage? You said you're a fighter and so on." After all, he was really a strong kid. He would dance that, ya, ya, ya!*

Fabio Takao: *Rock.*

Armando: *He could dance that pretty well. He was good! Well, one day, he accepted. "I accept because I'm strong, and I'm not afraid of anyone." So, they took him over there. Getting there, the poor kid. Soon he faced off with Carlson. On that day Carlson got on the mat, Carlson was about to fight Passarito. Carlson said, "You keep on insisting on that position. Don't dare use that position, for this reason, and that reason." He just might, then he grabbed and boom he broke his clavicle. Hélio said, "Carlson, are you stupid? You know, you hurt your dad!?" "I don't care, if you are on the mat, you're an opponent." That's how Carlson was!*

Elton Brasil: *Carlson broke his clavicle?*

Armando: *The clavicle, just boom, threw dad on the ground, and dad wasn't expecting that. Well, anyway, you can see how he was. Fighting against Carlson, your life was in danger. Well, it turned out, the guy went back again. So Carlson did what he wanted to Georges, and Georges didn't know what to do. So, Hélio asked him, "Kid, you said you just arrived in Brazil." "No, I'm really struggling, with no money, and I have to look for work." So Hélio invited him, "Come stay with us." They didn't have a guy to take care of the clothes. Waldemar had already left, and so they put Georges taking care of the clothes. And Georges trained. He was strong. He trained and took care of the clothes, but actually he learned, he wasn't really interested. When you looked at Georges, he was sleeping. Georges was tired, he was just sleeping, OK!* [Note: The "roupeiro" position, or the person who handles the clothes, was previously occupied by Waldemar Santana, who left the Gracie Academy in a series of dramatic events that would culminate in the fight between Hélio and his former student. See *Choque Vol. 2*, Chapter 6, for details and documentation.] *But what happened was, one day, he would play around with certain students. One day he almost killed a student. He strangled the student and shoved him against the edge of the stairway. He grabbed the student and he fell from the stairs. Hélio found out about it and told him that if he did it again, he would fire him! He said, "I don't know, it wasn't my fault, it was the student's fault, and he challenged me," and so on!*

On another occasion he messed up, [Hélio] said to fire him. He could eat a whole can of guava and cream cheese. He ate like a lion. Well, it turned out, not just because of that. So, Hélio, Georges, and I told him, "If you don't solve this, I don't want you here anymore. You can leave, I helped you all I could, but you don't want to be helped." Hélio was right. So that's it, he didn't want to be helped. Hélio wanted him to learn.

Fabio Takao: *He was undisciplined?*

Armando: *Undisciplined! Exactly, that is how he was like. Georges, like—they said—George Gracie. So he left the Academy. So, what happened? He didn't have anywhere to go. He started putting on shows in clubs. He began presenting in clubs around Rio de Janeiro. He was invited to dance there.*

Fabio Takao: *For the dancing thing?*

[Note: Mehdi's career as a rock dancer/promoter is described in *Jiu-Jitsu in the South Zone*, Chapter 14.]

Armando: *Yes. So anyway, one day, he did something different. A guy from the police caught his attention. "Hey, who are you?" He punched him and the guy fell to the ground. So, what did the guy do? He called his buddies over. All three came over. "Who did this here? Get that guy, arrest the guy!" They really beat up Georges, and I don't even want to talk about it because it's sad. They told him that if he did it again, you won't be back, you will be dead. Well, he was scared. So what did he do? He looked for Hermani from Judo and said, "Hermani can you [help me?]" So Hermani suggested, "You know what? Georges, I am going to take you to Japan. I can,* *because I've got friends in Japan and you can spend some time there."*

Fabio Takao: *Hermani told him that?*

Armando: *Rodolfo Hermani. [He told George,] "You are better off in Japan." And he stayed there for five years. It was good for him, because he learned to speak Japanese and Judo. Georges spent all that time there. But he left the Academy because he was lazy and undisciplined! Instead of...*

Fabio Takao: *Master, you know what is strange about that is how he stayed in Japan? Japan is tough! They are really tough in Japan.*

Armando: *My son, you know what?*

Fabio Takao: *To adapt?*

Armando: *After he went through all that in Rio, he could make it through anything! Right? So they sent him to Japan. Actually, they didn't send him, he left for Japan. Well, in Japan, what happened was, he had to get used to Japanese discipline, right? So after spending time there, when he came back to Brazil, he began teaching. And he did what he learned in Japan to his students. He would hit them with the bamboo.*

[Note: Armando is probably recycling rumors about when Mehdi went to Japan, and how long he stayed there. According to the sources cited in *Jiu-Jitsu in the South Zone*, Chapter 13, it is more likely that Mehdi went to São Paulo during the period in question, although he later did spend several months in Japan, in 1966.]

Fabio Takao: *Shinai.*

Armando: *And then, hitting them with the bamboo, the student said, "Hey!" So, there was some construction nearby and the student threw a bunch of bricks in the academy, and so on! He said, "Pai, this guy is hitting me, and so on!" So Pai had the guy arrested, since Pai was really the authority out there, and [George] went back to Japan again.*

Fabio Takao: *So he always had a discipline problem?*

Armando: *He always did. Now, why did he fight against the Gracies? You see, there are some things that many don't know. So, he was in São Paulo, and there was a competition in São Paulo. Well, I don't know if he was going to compete or if he was invited to be a referee.*

So he left, and what happened was, he went to visit Hemeterio. And Hemeterio said, "Georges, since you are here, let's do some training." So, what happened was he grabbed Hemeterio, and just held him at least two or three times. Hemeterio couldn't get away. Hemeterio was getting up there in his age. Georges was training and Hemeterio wasn't. He took Hemeterio down and held him. Hemeterio couldn't get out. Then he said, "Georges, I don't consider myself beat! I didn't tap!" He said, "No, but these are the Judo rules. I beat you in the Judo rules. I am a Judoka, and not Jiu-Jitsu. See you later." So, what did he do? Hemeterio talked to Hélio. "Hélio, this, this, and this happened." Hélio said, "Let's go get this kid!" So what did they do? They got Mauricio, Carlson, Hemeterio, and we went to Georges' academy. Look how funny this is, you can see that I always tried to calm things down. I knew, I already had my own academy. And in my academy Hermani would always come to visit, because I didn't have any reason to be against anyone, against Cordeiro, Hermani or Haroldo. I wanted to be a friend to everyone. In fact, I wanted to learn from them. Well, that's the way it was. So, they said, "Hey, the Gracies said they are going to take the guys and kick Georges' ass in his academy." Wow. So I called Hélio and told him I know about this and that.

[Note: Cordeiro, Hermani, and Haroldo were Arturo Cordeiro, Rudolf Hermanny, and Haroldo Brito. Cordeiro was a self-taught Jiu-Jitsu man who embraced Judo. Hermanny was one of his students. Brito studied Jiu-Jitsu with Carlos and Hélio briefly before also transferring his loyalties to Judo. He taught, or at least provided training opportunities to, several important Jiu-Jitsu personalities including Waldemar Santana, Carlson Gracie, and Oswaldo Alves, among others (See *Jiu-Jitsu in the South Zone*, Chapter 13, *Choque Vol. 2*, and *Choque Vol. 3* for details.]

Armando (continues): *Yes, that's true, Georges is very stuck up and he challenged me. I said, "Hélio, this is a student thing. You know that students are dangerous." "No, no, leave Georges alone." "No, you know that's not how we do things." "No! Either he is our friend or our enemy. I'm going to go beat up Georges." So he left, and so did I. But I didn't want them to fight!*

Well, something really funny happened. When [Hélio] Vigio got there, Vigio was part of the police. He took Jacare, Mariel, the cop, and Georges was scared to death of them... And you know what? Fortunately, they didn't get into a fight. Do you know why? Hermani stood at the door and didn't let anyone in. Georges stepped out of the academy and stood in the hallway. So, something really funny happened. Inside the academy there were two guys with guns. If Hélio ran in, they would have shot him.

Fabio Takao: *Were these guys Georges' students or what?*

Armando: *Yes, at Georges' academy.*

Author: *Were the two guys with guns his students?*

Armando: *They were Georges'.*

Author: *Were they the police?*

Armando: *No, they took two body guards. Hermani took them and put them there. "If Gracie comes in here, shoot him!" Because they are breaking into the academy. Hermani set everything up and let it happen.*

Author: *Do you think someone told Hélio not to go because of that?*

Armando: *Hélio took reporters, because wherever they went they took reporters.*

Fabio Takao: *Always, right?*

Armando: *They took them because the next day they left the academy. "Georges, you have to say that Jiu-Jitsu is best, and me at age 90 with my Jiu-Jitsu can beat judo. Did you say that?" "Yes!" He said it, and it's in the newspaper. Georges Mehdi said it that way, so Hélio felt like he won!*

Author: *But good thing he didn't go into the academy, because he would have been shot!*

Armando: *Because if he had come in, it's possible that they could have shot the guy! Let me tell you something. What if a guy breaks into your house? In my house nobody ever wanted to break in, because I never had problems with anyone. When the guy is OK I can invite you to go there.*

[Note: Armando's recollection of some of the details is questionable. The incident took place in 1968, so Hélio wouldn't have been 90 years old at the time. Refer to *Choque Vol. 3*, Chapter 8, for details and sources.]

Fabio Takao: *Master, did you ever meet Austregesilo de Athayde?*
Armando: *Yes.*
Fabio Takao: *His time was a little after yours, right?*
Armando: *He learned from a student, and not from a teacher.*
Fabio Takao: *He didn't know much?*
Armando: *Right! You see, that's what's funny. Austregesilo de Athayde, his family were all writers, right? Well, this guy had no business teaching classes. What he learned...*
Fabio Takao: *Master, you know there's a video that was out not too long ago. In fact, he was showing off his academy. Did you see the inauguration of his academy, near the end of the '50s or '60s?*
Armando: *In that building in Copacabana, right? I visited his academy. A very nice-looking academy, well decorated.*
Fabio Takao: *Apparently it seems like even Carlos and Hélio approved.*
Armando: *Sure, of course. Do you know why?*
Fabio Takao: *Why do you think so?*
Armando: *My son, it's what I've been telling you. His family is powerful, right? A family full of writers and so on.*
Fabio Takao: *Yes.*
Armando: *So the question is, Why would they be enemies of the kid? He already had his own academy. When he went to set up his academy, for example, imagine if Elton had said, "You give me something, and I tell Elton that I'm not going to give it!" It's not that I can't give it, I'm just afraid of you! My son, when I left Gracie Academy I was afraid to open my own academy. First, Hélio told me I would have to ask to come back, because I would go hungry! He told me I had left the nucleus, left the source. That I would forget everything. Well, I was already ready for that, right? Well, I told him, no problem, I can go back to making furniture. I never—and I mean never—worried the Gracies. When Hélio saw my academy, he was impressed! He said, "Do you want to trade your academy for an apartment I've got*

in Flamengo?" I told him I didn't want to! He was amazed by my academy, because I didn't build a large academy like his, but I made it as nice or better decorated than his. I gave kimonos to the students as well.

Fabio Takao: *Same system?*

Armando: *The same system, because I believed that [it] was good. Can you imagine if you had to take your kimono, wash, and that was too much work!*

Fabio Takao: *Master, do you think Athayde was not well prepared?*

Armando: *I don't think so. No, he wasn't! Do you know why?*

Fabio Takao: *I think he was around during the time of Mansur.*

Armando: *Right! What does Mansur know about Jiu-Jitsu? Mansur took me to his academy to see a self-defense class.*

Fabio Takao: *In Rio?*

Armando: *Yes, Tijuca. I went over to his academy and what I saw was guys breaking boards with their head or whatever. My son, this is self-defense? "Armando, they're learning to defend themselves." He didn't say it was Jiu-Jitsu, it was self-defense. So, that's how it was.*

Fabio Takao: *There's a question, as I always hear things. You are the only one who knew these people, right?*

Armando: *Do you want to hear something interesting? Behring. How did Behring teach Jiu-Jitsu? He knew it well, but he never took a course on how to be a teacher.*

Fabio Takao: *I see!*

Armando: *He was a good student. So you may not have seen what I was demonstrating about the base, hold on, and so on. What I was demonstrating to the students, without that position, nothing happened. You can even get hurt. So I was always careful.*

—

After the formal and informal interviews were completed we had the opportunity to spend some time with Armando on the mat, going over techniques. Armando continued with his advocacy of a self-defense approach to BJJ, as opposed to the sport-oriented form it has taken in recent decades, and demonstrated many self-defense techniques (he also corrected what he insisted was my incorrect guillotine defense). Following this impromptu self-defense seminar Armando left to go back home, and we hung around so that Jay and Steve could collect more B-Roll with their drone. Fabio and I were speaking with Elton Brasil, one of Armando's students, and walking back towards Jay and Steve, when we spotted Armando coming back out of his house: he'd taken off his gi, and was now decked out in a flowered speedo and sporting a walking cane. The curious spectacle, we were told by Elton, was unusual only in that Armando usually walked around naked on his ranch; even the neighbors had to become accustomed to the sight.

Armando had so much charisma and life to him, and I felt it a shame that this was our last day in Brasilia. I would have liked to have spent more time with the man. I understood why his students were so protective and proud of him. He was a soft-spoken man, critical when need be, but also gentle. He had no quarrel with our project and its avowed purpose to retell BJJ history in a different light. It seemed to be almost a theme among our elder interviewees: they seemed to share a common sense and belief that history needed to be told accurately. They did not seem concerned in any way that this new (old) narrative might change public perception of BJJ, either because they were confident in the veracity of what they were telling us or because they felt that it was time for what they knew to come to light. Or, perhaps, because they were simply too old to care. Whatever the case, their collective demeanor stood in stark contrast to that of our younger interviewees: with them there was a perceptible fear and concern that rewriting the past might affect their present.

Approximately two years after our interview, Armando would pass away at 94 years of age. Despite his humble standing in the broad BJJ world (he had few students, no physical school, no thriving affiliation program, no great financial success), his passing nevertheless seemed to leave a void in BJJ. I have previously compared the IBJJF to the Kodokan in that IBJJF came to give BJJ (almost too late) the structure, organization and well-defined hierarchy that BJJ needed to become what its practitioners aspired for it to be: the most practiced martial art in the world. Nevertheless, I can't help but think that BJJ still lacks the "DO" in Kano's "JU-DO" ("do" means "the way" in Japanese, and is meant to symbolize a more edifying approach to combat: one that places less emphasis on the "martial" and more emphasis on the educational and moral aspects of the "art"). Despite its proliferation, we still lack the philosophical foundation that would underpin and augment such a beautiful art by giving its practitioners values to uphold. Instead, we have the surf culture of Rio de Janeiro, with its açai and its relaxed manners. This, however appealing it may be, simply isn't enough. It lacks the steadfast quality of a true philosophy. It doesn't hold together in the face of the practitioners' need to relate and connect on a deeper and more mature level. All in all, BJJ seems to me to be the rebel child of an art of superior moral values, the orphan of a philosophy that goes beyond effective combat. And, regardless of the revisionist attempts made by those who were closest to them to make it seem otherwise, I don't see in either Carlos or Hélio Gracie the wisdom necessary to give BJJ what it lacks (though, admittedly, I never met them).

In many ways—though not entirely—our leadership—past and present—has been composed of hooligans, surfers, charlatans, or egomaniacs (and sometimes a combination of all of these). Nonetheless, if we are willing to look closer, there have also been men who shone a brighter light worthy of emulation. I never met Georges Mehdi, but from the accounts of those who knew this Algerian/French-turned-Carioca, his teachings surpassed the lower levels of learning. There were others I would never meet and about whom I could only draw assumptions: Fadda, from all accounts, inspired respect out of love more than fear from those whose lives he touched. But the one I did meet, albeit briefly, and who I feel best embodied that which BJJ lacks, is Armando. I can't help but feel that the vacuum his death created left BJJ more orphaned than ever.

— Armando Wriedt —

BRAZIL - ARMANDO WRIEDT

What is your name, date of birth, and when did you start practicing Jiu-Jitsu?

My name is Armando Wriedt. I was born on October 17, 1924, in Teresópolis, Rio de Janeiro. In fact, I started practicing [Jiu-Jitsu] in the late 1950s, when I met Hélio Gracie in Teresópolis.

What was the first thing you did when you heard about Jiu-Jitsu?

As I had never heard of it, I went to look for the word Jiu-Jitsu in a dictionary. There what I found was: Japanese fighting style. That was it. You didn't find anything else. Is there any literature that talks about Jiu-Jitsu? I do not know. I mean, all the books I found were in English, French, Japanese. The best book I found was published in Portugal in 1950. Did you hear about Minoru's book? Since the author of the book, Professor Antonio, he studied chemistry in Germany and he watched a demonstration by Jigoro Kano, and was enchanted by the technique. And he then started to learn from several Masters, and made this book one of the best. It was even praised by the Japanese themselves.

Why did you go to train Jiu-Jitsu? How did you go to train with Hélio Gracie?

This casual encounter with Hélio Gracie was what obviously made us closer. As I said, I met him on a Saturday night and on Sunday morning—I cannot specify the date, but it was towards the end of the year 1950—I went to Hélio Gracie's house. There we rode horses with him and on the way back he put a tarp on the grass and trained with everyone. He trained with students because at the Gracie Academy you learned the following: the teacher trained the student at the Academy, but there [at Teresópolis] it wasn't a gym, there it was a place for training. So I started to learn from Hélio Gracie in Teresópolis.

267

Why do you think Hélio Gracie invited you to train?

This is why, because from the start there was an empathy between myself and Hélio. And these are things… for example, I wouldn't be able to explain the reason for this empathy with Hélio, but the fact is that it happened to my joy, because this is what I always say: the best years of my life I spent with the Gracie family at the Gracie Academy.

Master, why did you leave the Gracie Academy?

Well, you see that it is always this story of the darn money. One time I had a dislocation in my collarbone, and was immobilized for a few days. Let me make a parenthesis. Hélio said to us, to me, to João Alberto, to Vigio and Carlson, that we were also owners of the Academy. And in reality we had a fraction of the Academy, because he did not want to pay the labor rights and as I am the owner, obviously I was exempt. It is obvious that the Academy would guarantee the future of each one. But when I got hurt I went to take care of myself, of course, with Doctor George, who was the doctor at the Academy. At the end of the day he said, "Armando, it is you who pays for the doctor." I didn't think it was fair and I told him, "Hélio, but I got hurt in a class while working at the gym." He said to me, "You got hurt because you weren't paying attention, and I'm not going to pay for your inattention." Well, he left me a little disoriented with what he had said to me. A student of mine said, "Hélio was not fair to you. You can no longer trust what he says about the gym taking care of you up to old age, so you better open your own gym." This guy was a cashier, and they hired me to teach at the cashier's association. And there I stayed with him for about three years, until I started my gym in Copacabana. So I left for that. Of course, I was fine with them and I told Hélio that I was not going to stay at the gym anymore and that was the reason.

Did you ever see a book that inspired the Gracie diet?

Yes, the book that inspired Carlos Gracie is from an Argentine doc-

tor named Dulin, Juan Steves Dulin. This book is called Human Rational Food. *It was in this book that Carlos learned to make this diet that is really very good, and I recommend everyone to do it. But the diet was not created by them, because there also has a history. Have you heard of Oscar Santa Maria? Oscar Santa Maria was the man who most helped the Gracies on the social side, because Oscar was a very well-known person. At the time, I knew the powerful press that was Chateaubriand, the Marines, so Oscar helped the Gracies a lot. I don't know if today they are grateful to Oscar, but Oscar had a treatment with this doctor in Argentina and the treatment was successful so he recommended, "Carlos, why don't you use this regimen for you, who have a great physical exhaustion." But this regime I believe is very, very good. Now that's it. Carlos praised himself [with] Dr. Dulin's book.*

Did you ever see the book at the Gracie Academy?

I have this book, so much so that when [Reila Gracie] was here and said that the regime belonged to her father, I said, "Darling it is not, you were born yesterday and it is not." I showed it to her and gave it to her. I gave it to her. I had the book up there on my desk where she went to interview me, and said that the book her father had based on was the one. So her father is not the creator. Now it is clear that he had merit, because without him nobody would know Dulin's book. I mean he had a good merit, which through him many knew and started to make the regime and many were cured with that regime. Then he went on to say that the regime was his, but in reality the regime that he preaches is from Dr. Juan Steves Dulin. And the book I have until today, because I was interested and Oscar even gave [it to] me. Santa Maria himself.

So you saw this book at the Gracie Academy?

Yes, I saw. Now it's like I said: Oscar Santa Maria gave me this book.

How important is Oscar Santa Maria for Jiu-Jitsu?

Son, I think he was very important, since the Gracie Academy was always very skimpy. When they passed to Avenida Rio Branco they bought the entire seventeenth floor and half of the eighteenth. So on the seventeenth the male academy worked and on the top the female part worked, and all this was done thanks to Oscar's performance. They don't say that because they are, as I say, very personalistic. Of course, everyone has to have help, an advisor... And Oscar was a great advisor for them. Carlos himself recognized this, in a book made by him. Carlos himself recognized it.

Hélio said for a long time that he was the only creator of Jiu-Jitsu. Do you agree?

Jiu-Jitsu gained a lot of momentum with the creation of the Avenida Rio Branco academy, because until then there was only Hélio. Their first academy—you know where it was, you said. It was at Rua Marques de Abrantes. 106, if I'm not mistaken. When did he open this academy, did they tell you? It was in the year 1925. I was 1 year old. From there, Hélio started teaching in an apartment in Flamengo. For a long time he taught there, but they always had the idea of growing Jiu-Jitsu and obviously they needed a good school. That was when they created the gym on Avenida Rio Branco.

Who promoted Carlos Gracie to a teacher or Black Belt?

It was Carlos himself, because at that time there was no one who knew Jiu-Jitsu. Jiu-Jitsu was strange to everyone, so Carlos promoted himself. Since when he set up the Academy he was doing the wrong advertisement. He used to say, "You want to be beaten, you want to have a broken arm, you want to have a broken face, enroll at the Gracie Academy on Marques de Abrantes street." Did you know he said that? Then it changed because, in reality, when they met Oscar, Oscar was a spiritual guide for Rosa Cruz, and they started to live a life, let's say, more spiritual. Both Carlos and Hélio. They were always very nice people, good people. Now when it came to Jiu-Jitsu they became wild. Now nobody promoted because at that time there was only Carlos. Who spoke of Jiu-Jitsu in Rio de Janeiro? For example, I didn't know anyone. So it was he who promoted himself. They started to teach Jiu-Jitsu on Rua Marques de Abrantes, which was the first school known.

Were the Gracies good at marketing?

Marketing? Yes, they were good at that. That's what I'm saying to you, is that they later had the press all in their favor and Santa Maria made it easier for them. Santa Maria knew all these people and the Gracies were still there in the early days, so much so, you see, Hélio was 17 or 18 years old. Carlos was the mentor of everything. And how did [Oscar] meet the Gracies? Have they told you? He met Carlos in a fight that Carlos held in a place that he calls, if I'm not mistaken, Ponta do Calabouço, and he accepted the challenge of a Japanese whose name I don't remember now. And everyone was amazed how a Brazilian dared to challenge a Japanese fighter. So when they saw Carlos, a slight man, they thought, "That poor Brazilian." It was to everyone's surprise that Carlos won from the Japanese. [Note: Armando here repeats the story as he heard it; this fight is probably one of Carlos' fights against Geo Omori, and was probably a fixed fight]. *On that occasion, that hat was [worn] a lot—you know, that little hat called cata ovo, the straw hat. When the Brazilian won [everyone] threw the straw hat, applauded the Japanese. So Carlos was not well known. Oscar was amazed to see that small, unknown Brazilian beat a Japanese man and went looking for him. So even Carlos apologized because [Oscar] was feeling dizzy, because until that time he had only eaten vermicelli. Vermicelli is a type of pasta and [Carlos] said it was weak and [Oscar] needed to eat something. From then on Oscar started to have an intimacy, a bigger conversation with Carlos and started to help him. That's the deal. They owe Oscar a lot for their knowledge and their rise.*

Was the Rio Branco academy an elite academy? For rich people?

The Rio Branco Avenue academy was an elitist academy because only those who had purchasing power enrolled there. The class was very expensive. For you to have an idea, a class at that time in 1950 cost a base of 250 reais [sic]. It wasn't just anyone who could afford it. It turned out that the academy made a selection.

The children of Rorion, Ryron and Rener, created an online promotion system. Do you agree with that practice?

I do not agree with this distance graduation, because it is humanly impossible to learn self-defense without the guidance of a good teacher. And I doubt that Carlos and Hélio would agree with that. I don't believe it.

How did Jiu-Jitsu influence you as a human being?

You see, we all have a religion, and you almost always do or don't do certain things for religion. So Jiu-Jitsu for me became a religion. [How] do I explain Jiu-Jitsu? Jiu-Jitsu is a science, a philosophy, and an art, with which you learn to profit by flexing. Isn't that what you learned in Jiu-Jitsu? So I see Jiu-Jitsu... For that reason, Jiu-Jitsu is a religion for me. So my life is all based on the philosophy of Jiu-Jitsu, which always asks you to be a lhano in the treatment... that treats people with nobility, even if they are the people who come with a certain aggressive attitude against you. There is even a beautiful thing in Jiu-Jitsu that the Japanese teach the Jiu-Jitsuka, if he has to fight, he punishes the evil that harbors [in] the individual, and not the individual itself. Because the human being must always be preserved from any violence. I see the thing in that light. So I spend my whole life on this philosophy of Jiu-Jitsu. It is you being a lhano when dealing with people. I am sorry that there are no good Jiu-Jitsu schools that allow people to be well trained. That's what Jigoro Kano wanted. Why did he create the Kodokan? The name Kodokan, do you remember what it *is? [The] place where you learn the process. And there people learn for life. A learning process for life is not for the individual itself. This makes the individual perhaps better, because he has a better understanding of life.*

If Jiu-Jitsu is a religion for you, would you consider yourself a missionary?

It could even. Why see, there on the mat, what do I ask people for? May they be better in every moment of time. If you are good now, tomorrow you have to be great, and the day after tomorrow, good quality people. That is my principle. I always ask the student to be good at every moment of time.

Can you tell us about one of your best moments in your life in Jiu-Jitsu?

My son, I say again: the best moments of my life were exactly at the Gracie gym. So clear and evident who provided this was Jiu-Jitsu. Because in the gym everyone had the same thought. To work for Jiu-Jitsu, to have a good diet, to have a good life conduct. So the best moments for me were lived with Hélio, Carlos and the Gracie family, and the gym.

Describe Hélio Gracie in a nutshell.

Hélio Gracie was a second father to me. He was the one who guided me the most and gave me the chance to learn Jiu-Jitsu well, if I learned well. So I don't see it any other way. [He] was my palinuro, my guide, the person I used to take as my advisor in Jiu-Jitsu.

What motivates you to continue teaching Jiu-Jitsu classes?

What exactly motivates me is the following: the good education and the good tranquility that Jiu-Jitsu brings to people. Because all the people who start to live with Jiu-Jitsu are more straightforward, more gentle people when dealing with their fellow man. So what motivates me is this: to make people good every moment of time. This is what I try to do.

Have you ever fought Vale Tudo?

Already, I fought Vale Tudo once in Maracanã, when Carlson fought with Passarito. I fought, João Alberto, Hélio Vígio, and Carlson Gracie [fought]. It was the only fight that registered my presence and that of João Alberto. The others are not going to talk because they were one-on-one fights.

Did you like to fight Vale Tudo?

I didn't like fighting Vale Tudo, because in reality I never liked the fight itself. What always attracted me was to learn Jiu-Jitsu to pass on to others. That's why I say, when I went to the Gracie Academy Hélio said that he wanted me to teach Jiu-Jitsu and not to fight, so I was never a fighter and I never saw myself as a fighter because in reality I am averse to that. So much so that Ganhdi once said that the law of love is the law of men, and the law of violence is of beasts. He is against me and I am also against these struggles, mainly Vale Tudo, which leads to nothing.

The first time you entered the Rio Branco academy, did you imagine that you would do so much for Jiu-Jitsu?

I wondered why, when I left my carpentry shop to come and do Jiu-Jitsu, I imagined making Jiu-Jitsu my profession now, as a teacher [but] never as a fighter. I've always been averse to fighting, that's the truth. It is incredible that you teach the fight, but you are averse to the fight. Because when you learn Jiu-Jitsu, you learn to fight so you don't have to fight. Because the guy doesn't fight because he's brave. He almost always fights more for being fearful.

There it is already a very complex thing, but this is how it works.

What was one of the moments that most marked your life?

In reality, there was no more striking passage. For me, what was remarkable was my life at the gym. Because we lived in the gym, [as] I told you. [The] principle you have to live [by was]: eat, live, sleep, live Jiu-Jitsu, and that's what we used to do. And the most pleasant thing in the Academy was the symbiosis that existed among the teachers. Everyone was there as brothers and there was great concern there for each other. Let's imagine that João Alberto had a little problem. His problem was everyone's. If I had a problem, my problem was everyone's. So this symbiosis, this beautiful thing, was what marked the Academy, and that is [why] it can leave some nostalgia that it was a very good environment. Everyone lived for Jiu-Jitsu. And that was what I say. It was food, the way of life, the way you treat your partner, friend, colleague, and that is what really marked my time at the gym. This good symbiosis that existed among teachers.

How do you want to be remembered by the next generations of Jiu-Jitsu practitioners?

It's difficult. Of course, I always wanted to be remembered for the kindness I try to impress on my friends. Being a lhano when dealing with people, and obviously what I do in favor of Jiu-Jitsu, which is very little, in [terms of] what I would like to do. If I don't do more it is because I can't, and I don't know, and so I always apologize to people for not being as good as I would like to be. So I would like to be remembered as that, that friendly person, that person who has a concern for others. That would be ideal. And I fight for it in all sectors of my life. It is not only inside the mat. But inside the mat it manifests itself even more.

What is the importance of telling the complete Jiu-Jitsu story?

Son, it is very important for you to do this because you still don't know much about Jiu-Jitsu. Is it like I was saying to you, if you asked Hélio what Jiu-Jitsu was, what did he answer? "It is the weapon of the weak against the strong." But when the strong man learned Jiu-Jitsu it changed everything, didn't it? So you know the ethos of the word Jiu-Jitsu don't you? Ju means smooth and technical Jitsu. Softness technique. Then Jigoro Kano came and changed the name... and you also know why he changed, right? He said that he also practiced an art, but it was more of a doctrine, the Do, so they changed the name. So you see that the name Jiu-Jitsu, few people know. Even more today, there are a lot of people out there who do Jiu-Jitsu but never learned Jiu-Jitsu. Question: Does Minotauro know Jiu-Jitsu? No! That criolo, what's his name? Does Anderson know Jiu-Jitsu? No! If they knew Jiu-Jitsu they would have won many fights that they lost precisely because they did not know Jiu-Jitsu. Then, if you want, I can even show you two or three fight positions that they could have won, but for not knowing Jiu-Jitsu they didn't win. I think what you are doing is a very good job, very commendable, because you want people, with some delay, to know the history of Jiu-Jitsu, especially in Brazil. Of course if you talk about Jiu-Jitsu in Brazil, you have to talk about Gracie. And Gracie has to be more like Hélio and Carlos, because Gastão and George were isolated. Whoever stayed in the center that drew attention was exactly Carlos and Hélio. When I met, I only knew both, so much that I didn't know Gastão, I didn't know George. Whoever stayed in the center and the person most responsible for the greater dissemination of Jiu-Jitsu is exactly Carlos and Hélio Gracie, because George and Gastão isolated themselves from the great center that was the capital. They moved away from Rio de Janeiro. So who was there? Carlos and Hélio, and they started working for Jiu-Jitsu to make Jiu-Jitsu known. Now here's how I told you. They created many enemies, because in reality they were the best and people did not tolerate it. The human being is bad. So they started showing up and made a lot of friends, but they also made a lot of enemies for it. And deep down, as they were the best, they always won.

Why did you choose to live and train here, and not in the city?

In reality my choice was more to live here exactly because I always liked the tranquility and to live with nature and to live with and in peace with nature. The classes here were a fluke. The only place I found for classes was here, because there is no gym here in Brasilia anymore that cares about self-defense, which is exactly what I emphasize. Because I don't want to prepare fighters, I want to prepare men for life, so I think that showing self-defense gives the subject that tranquility in this way of life. So my option here was this. I like life in nature. Here is life. You see a bird, you see a snake, you see a beak. It has life. There isn't in the city, that's why I chose to live here. Now the class was a consequence of my stay here. You see I'm not even ready for classes. Here we create something improvised because there is no gym here.

Upper left: From left to right, Fabio (front), Steve, Kyra Gracie and the author;
Upper right: Steve and the author about to begin interview with Kyra Gracie;
Bottom: BJJ Hall of Famer Kyra Gracie

KYRA GRACIE

"In my opinion, I do not see Jiu-Jitsu existing without Carlos and Hélio and without the Gracie family... The Gracie family preserved ground-fighting. My [great] grandfather had twenty-one children to make sure they would take this forward."

—Kyra Gracie, BJJ Hall of Famer

Our final interviews during the Brazil trip would be with Kyra Gracie and Fabio Takao. Kyra is the great-granddaughter of Carlos

Gracie, granddaughter to Robson, and a BJJ Hall of Famer. After interviewing so many aged Masters, we were eager to hear from a young representative of the family that had, to a large extent, become the face of women's BJJ around the world. We also felt, as a successful modern-day BJJ practitioner and competitor, she would help us bridge the enormous gap between the past and the present BJJ scene.

Kyra was kind enough to receive us at her apartment in São Paulo. We rushed to set up and get going: it was getting late by the time we got there, and Kyra and her friends were giving us cues that they were hungry and wanted to leave to go eat. The interview went as expected and Kyra gave us all the soundbites we needed about the importance of her family in the history of BJJ, and the state of BJJ in the world today.

At this point in our production I had interacted with many members of the Gracie family, and I was cultivating a growing awareness of obvious divisions within the family. It was becoming increasingly clear to me that the sense of unity the family fostered in the public eye (and from which they benefited) was far from the whole truth. It put me in mind of a time years back when, while in Japan for a fight, I bumped into Kron Gracie, Rickson's son, who to my surprise told me that he had met his uncle Royce only twice in his life. This was, I was learning, typical of the family in general: Kyra was clearly very close to her grandfather, Robson, based on the warmth with which they interacted on the phone, while she seemed to have little to no relationship with some of her cousins. I was particularly curious about these apparent divisions in the family as they related to the question of who the true "godfather of BJJ" was, and whether it was Carlos or Hélio—a question to which Kyra had a somewhat conciliatory and but nonetheless reasonable answer.

At some point, out of curiosity, I asked her about the fact that she was the first prominent female fighter in a family with solely male adherents to BJJ. She told me of the one time she met Hélio Gracie on a cruise, and how open he was to her being an active BJJ competitor. As the man says, "The times they are a-changin'..."; someone who, thirty years ago, would have had to keep a lid on her talent and ambition was now able to rise to the top as one of the most successful female competitors in the history of the sport (far more successful in terms of BJJ, it should be noted, than any other member of the Gracie family, female or male, with the notable exceptions of Royler and Roger).

— Kyra Gracie —

Could you introduce yourself and tell us about your beginnings in BJJ?

My name is Kyra Gracie, I am the first female Black Belt in the Gracie family, a five-time Jiu-Jitsu world champion, three-time Abu Dhabi champion. Today I teach Jiu-Jitsu and work at SporTV and Canal Combate channels as a sports commentator.

I started [training BJJ] when I was small, age 11. I competed in all the championships in Rio de Janeiro. And my mother was my biggest supporter. Because she suffered this prejudice and cannot continue in Jiu-Jitsu, she said, "Come on, go fight, go be cool, I'm here!" She encouraged me and took me to the tournaments.

Was it hard for you to be a BJJ fighter inside the Gracie family?

The Gracie family was very sexist; in fact, the world was very sexist when my family started teaching Jiu-Jitsu. The women in the family practiced a bit of self-defense, but then were not encouraged to continue the practice of fighting. I remember my mother. She reached the blue belt in Jiu-Jitsu and at one point she said she wanted to compete and dedicate herself to Jiu-Jitsu, and my uncles said, "You can't do it, this is for men. Get out." And to this day my mother thinks, "If I had continued, today I could be a Black Belt." It was really important to break this paradigm inside the Gracie family. It was important for Women's BJJ in general because it needed a Gracie woman to show them that Jiu-Jitsu is for everyone and that a woman could also carry the family's name and being a woman able to inspire women all over the world.

Can you imagine BJJ today without the Gracie family?

In my opinion I do not see Jiu-Jitsu existing without Carlos and Hélio and without the Gracie family. Not the Jiu-Jitsu we know today worldwide. We would have a little here and there, but not the boom we have today. The Gracie family preserved ground-fighting. My [great] grandfather had twenty-one children to make sure they would take this forward. And since then: we are in the fifth generation of the family, and most of them work with Jiu-Jitsu, either by directly being fighters and teachers, or indirectly with clothes, gis, or championships.

Why do we know so little of the other Gracie Brothers?

Why not talk about the other brothers, George, Gastão? Because they had no one to tell their story. The stories of Uncle George, in reality, I came to know very recently. I grew up and became a Black Belt and had no idea who George and the other brothers of Grandpa Carlos were. When I heard I asked, "Why does no one speak of them?" I went and asked Grandpa Robson who they were and how they were. My grandpa only spoke highly of George, saying that he was tough, that he fought and had no opposition, but that he didn't want to follow orders from Grandpa Carlos and that he was a rebel.

Who, after all, is the leader of the Gracie family?

There is a question between Carlos Gracie and Hélio Gracie because of the history of Jiu-Jitsu and how it was told. The first that had a world voice in the family was Rorion, when he went to the United States and the story he told was that my Uncle Hélio had created Jiu-Jitsu because he was the skinniest and that he learned by observing his brothers and so he created levers and Gracie Jiu-Jitsu came from there. Based on this story, the children and grandchildren of my great-grandfather Carlos began to ask, "Why are you telling this story if the story was never like this? The family was always united and everyone always trained together and they were all there."

What is the importance of retelling BJJ history?

This issue of rescuing Jiu-Jitsu's history is very important so we can tell what really happened. Even for myself, so I can know the history of Jiu-Jitsu and where everything came from so we can pass on to our students and the next generation of the family. I think this will be essential to our story.

Upper left: Team member Fabio Quio Takao; Upper right, from left to right: Tufy, Grandmaster Robson Gracie, and Fabio

FABIO TAKAO

"The importance of telling the full story of Jiu-Jitsu and Vale Tudo in Brazil is enormous because it reveals new characters, new events, and makes it clear how this story was really evolving. This was a long process that cannot be explained simply and punctually. We need to show all the characters and how they developed. It is a collective and evolutionary process."

—Fabio Takao, BJJ Black Belt and researcher

Fabio was instrumental in the Brazil phase of our documentary: not only did he help bring the team together by introducing me to Jay, but his knowledge and connections made everything much easier. This was only the beginning, though, as he went well beyond his role of advisor and interviewee and ended up actually working as our production's manager in Brazil, organizing flights, transport, and hotels for the whole team.

We never really stressed over his interview because he was with us the whole time (with the brief exception of our trip to Belém), but in the end the tight schedule on that last day meant we almost missed our chance. Still, leaving his interview for last worked in our favor: we knew that he could speak knowledgeably on most of the topics we'd covered, and speaking with him last allowed us to use him as a "wild-card" to fill in where coverage was incomplete or other researchers had answered poorly.

I'd quickly learned that, in the context of a documentary, a good answer isn't just what reads well on paper: a good answer also has to sound and look right. Stuttering, posture, affect, body language, and tone are just as important as the answer itself, which puts a much higher burden on an interview meant for a documentary film than one meant to appear only in print. With this in mind we needed to make sure that we not only had the answers we were looking for but also that those answers were said in a way that could be used in the film. Steve and Jay were proving crucial here, given my lack of experience in filmmaking and my hyper-focus on the relevance of the answers given in terms of the history, and not in terms of the technical requirements of our film... a key divergence of perspectives to which we will return later.

Fabio had made arrangements with the managers of an apartment complex where a friend lived, and we were allowed to set up in their conference room for a few hours. The interview went well: we modified it a little from our original script to make sure that he covered aspects on which we needed more information, or about which we simply needed better soundbites for the film. In the end Fabio had to leave in a rush to get back to his hometown of São Carlos; we said our goodbyes and then I said goodbye to Steve and Jay as well, who were heading back to the U.S. with all the footage. I was going to stay on for another week to commentate for the São Paulo edition of ACB-JJ, and to make a trip to visit my maternal family.

— Fabio Quio Takao —

Can you introduce yourself?

My name is Fabio Quio Takao, I'm 46 years old, I'm a Black Belt in Jiu-Jitsu, I've been a teacher, I've been practicing Jiu-Jitsu since 1996, and I have been researching the origins of Vale Tudo for about fifteen years.

What is the role of Oswaldo Fadda in BJJ?

The role of Oswaldo Fadda in the development of Jiu-Jitsu was important mainly in the city of Rio de Janeiro, because Oswaldo Fadda popularized it there among the lower classes, the poorest, those in need. Because until then [the] Gracie family's Jiu-Jitsu was aimed more at the people of the South Zone and at people who had a better financial condition.

Is there evidence of the relationship between Luis França and Maeda?

[Currently] there is no clear evidence that Luis França had direct contact with Count Koma. The name Luis França is a somewhat common name, and this makes searching difficult. The few references that exist say the opposite. We have some references that speak of a student named Luis França who even fought for the Gracie Academy.

What is Kosen Judo?

Kosen Judo was a very sophisticated Judo, it had a very large [arsenal] of techniques. I would say even more sophisticated than the Jiu-Jitsu practiced at the same time [in Brazil], but it had no direct relation to the Jiu-Jitsu practiced here in Brazil.

What is the origin of the triangle choke in BJJ?

The triangle, like other techniques made with the back on the ground, probably must have come by the influence of Judo. Through various interviews with Masters who trained in the 1950s, they confirmed that the triangle, for example, sankaku jime, they had through contact with Judo practitioners.

Who were the Ono brothers?

The Ono brothers were opponents of the Gracie family in the 1930s. They were Yassuiti Ono, the eldest, and Naoiti Ono. They were Judo practitioners, only they had the characteristic of practicing the standing Judo and the ne-waza. They were very good at ground techniques.

Can you talk about the fight between Hélio Gracie and Yassuiti Ono?

The confrontation between Hélio Gracie and Yassuiti Ono was a confrontation that made very clear the technical differences between the Gracie family and the Onos. [The] Onos, besides practicing the ground game as the Gracie family did, they were also very good at takedowns. So we could even say that technically the Ono family had an advantage over the Gracie family. But I believe that Hélio Gracie, through his defensive technique, somehow managed to nullify this. Although he had taken several falls, his defensive guard managed to prevent Yassuiti Ono from finishing him.

Who were Carlos Gracie's teachers?

Carlos Gracie did not have as his only teacher Count Koma. Most likely he learned from Jacyntho Ferro, who was Count Koma's instructor, and later he came to learn also from Donato Pires, who was a contemporary practitioner of [Jiu-Jitsu] in Belém, but who probably had a little more knowledge.

Did Carlos have other sources of knowledge?

There is a possibility that Carlos Gracie also learned from some books published at the time. Some books had already been published before the time of Carlos, in Manaus. They were translations of the book of Irving Hancock. A book specifically from Captain Bonorino was also circulating at the time that Carlos Gracie was getting started. So this was constantly reported in the press. As we know that Car-

los Gracie used the press as a tool to spread Jiu-Jitsu, it is very possible that Carlos also followed this type of news and consequently knew about the release of these books. So it is possible that Carlos absorbed something through books.

Was Carlos Gracie Maeda's main student?

There is a statement that Carlos was Count Koma's favorite student. This probably did not happen. Why? Several pieces of evidence lead us to believe this. During an initial period where Count Koma mentions in the newspapers of Belém his students, Carlos Gracie never appears on any of these lists.

What was the extent of Carlos Gracie's relationship to Maeda?

The relationship between Carlos Gracie as a favorite student of Maeda, for example, I believe is a bit exaggerated for marketing purposes. At the time it was very important for any practitioner of Jiu-Jitsu to maintain a direct connection with the Japanese. And even more, a Japanese who already had a certain name in the Brazilian press, as [did] Count Koma. So it was very interesting for any practitioner of Jiu-Jitsu to have his name linked to Count Koma.

When was the first "Gracie Academy" founded?

Contrary to what everyone thinks, the Gracie Academy was founded in São Paulo in the region of Perdizes in the early 1930s. Carlos Gracie already had a gym there and even organized an in-house tournament to promote this academy. The academy of Rua Marques de Abrantes, which all credit as the first Gracie Academy, is actually an academy of Donato Pires dos Reis. It was he who founded it and Carlos and George were his assistants. The academy of Rua Marques de Abrantes 106, it only came to be of the family Gracie a period later, when Donato Pires dos Reis was transferred as civil servant to Minas Gerais. It was only then that Carlos Gracie took over the academy.

Who did Hélio Gracie learn from?

The versions of Hélio, on with whom and when he learned Jiu-Jitsu, changed throughout the development of Brazilian Jiu-Jitsu. Initially Hélio Gracie states that he learned his Jiu-Jitsu with Carlos Gracie. He later states that he learned Jiu-Jitsu just by watching his brother teach classes, and later, in a more recent period, he states that he created Brazilian Jiu-Jitsu.

Why did this change?

Changing the historical versions of how Hélio Gracie learned Jiu-Jitsu is most likely due to personal issues such as vanity or even financial issues to attract more students, or anything of the sort.

What is the importance of George Gracie for BJJ?

The importance of George Gracie to Jiu-Jitsu and Vale Tudo in Brazil is enormous. George Gracie was probably one of the brothers who fought the most. Despite having participated in some fixed fights, George Gracie did many fights for real or "in the hard," as they spoke at the time, and he was also responsible for the greater exchange of techniques between the fighters of other modalities, especially Luta Livre. George Gracie was so important to the Brazilian Vale Tudo that he was probably the first fighter to participate in a "Bilateral" Vale Tudo, we can say, where he faced Tico Soledade and used both Jiu-Jitsu techniques and Wrestling as well as punches, kicks, and elbows.

Why was he forgotten?

George Gracie was omitted from the official history of Jiu-Jitsu for several reasons. One of these reasons was that the story was not told by him. Another reason that George Gracie was omitted from the story was that he did not leave direct descendants who practiced Jiu-Jitsu. We can also credit George Gracie's omission in history for his challenging nature. He did not readily accept Carlos Gracie's directions, and this made him relinquish his family over the years. This, consequently, erased his name from the official story.

What was the relationship between Donato Pires dos Reis and Carlos Gracie like?

Donato Pires dos Reis was the first person to give Carlos Gracie the chance to teach Jiu-Jitsu. Donato Pires invited Carlos in 1928 to be his assistant in Belo Horizonte. In 1930 Donato again invites Carlos Gracie and George to be his assistants in the academy that Donato opened in the Street Marques de Abrantes in Rio de Janeiro. Donato Pires dos Reis... I would not say that he was Carlos Gracie's teacher in a way we know him today, but quite possibly he had more experience than Carlos Gracie. It is possible to deduce this because in the two times where Carlos interacts with Donato, Carlos Gracie acts as an assistant to Donato Pires dos Reis.

Who was Geo Omori?

Geo Omori was a Japanese Judo practitioner who came to Brazil around 1928 and played a very important role in the development of Jiu-Jitsu and Vale Tudo in Brazil. The role of Geo Omori for this development was even to influence Carlos Gracie. Geo Omori since 1928 participated in challenges, Vale Tudo fights, and fights against other modalities in circuses in São Paulo, and had the first contact with Carlos Gracie in a demonstration fight made in São Paulo in 1929.

What was his relationship with Carlos Gracie like?

Geo Omori and Carlos Gracie had three fights. The first fight was actually a demonstration. It was published in newspaper articles as a simple demonstration of Jiu-Jitsu techniques. From this, the next *fights were eventually serious fights [grappling] or real confrontations, but there are doubts if these confrontations were totally real or [were] some kind of fixed matches, since Carlos and Geo Omori came to meet again after that period in Rio de Janeiro [as manager and fighter, respectively].*

Who was Oscar Santa Maria?

Oscar Santa Maria was a personal friend of Carlos Gracie who had a fundamental importance [in] the development of Jiu-Jitsu in Brazil. Oscar Santa Maria provided Carlos Gracie with the economic structure of the academies, contact with influential people teaching Jiu-Jitsu, and in this way propagating the art. So I think the importance of Oscar Santa Maria is somehow even minimized, when in fact he was a kind of financier of Brazilian Jiu-Jitsu.

Who was Jacyntho Ferro?

Jacyntho Ferro was a prominent sportsman in Belém, in northern Brazil. Jacyntho Ferro already practiced cycling, weightlifting, and other sports, and he for having already that athletic ability was one of the main students of Count Koma. He was considered and was even credited by Count Koma himself as his assistant in the classes he taught in Belém.

Who was Sada Miyako?

Sada Miyako was a Japanese who arrived on the ship Benjamin Constant at the end of 1908 in Rio de Janeiro. He already taught Jiu-Jitsu to the crew of Benjamin Constant and he was probably the protagonist in the first [style-versus-style] fight in Brazil. He faced Capoeira Francisco Ciríaco, but he was knocked out after being surprised with a kick in the head.

What is the importance of the Gracie family?

The importance of the Gracie family was precisely to maintain their resistance against the Judo that had expanded in Brazil between the decades of 1950 and 1980. If it were not for the Gracies, Jiu-Jitsu probably would have been absorbed by Judo today.

In the matches against the Judokas, was there a debate in relation to the gis?

The gis had always been a point of contention between fights and styles in the 1930s, '40s and '50s. Carlos Gracie claimed that the type of kimono they wore was a tradition inherited from Count Koma, but we know from Judo that already practiced at the time that the kimono had evolved and the sleeves and the pants were longer. It is possible that Carlos' demand for wearing kimonos with shorter sleeves and legs was a tradition inherited from Count Koma, but it is also possible that it was a strategy so that the Judokas of the time did not have so many handles to grip and so could not play their game.

What is the origin of the argument that the weak can defeat the strong with technique?

The rhetoric used by the Gracie family, where the weakest defeats the strongest, is not their exclusivity. This same type of argument has been used since 1904 in New York through advertisements made by a Japanese named Yae Kichi Yabe. In these ads he placed a text almost identical to the one that the Gracie family used from the 80s, where he talked about the possibility of the weak beating the strong, of Jiu-Jitsu being something forbidden.

Who was Takeo Yano?

Takeo Yano was a Judo practitioner who arrived in Brazil around 1931 and had a great importance, because besides teaching Jiu-Jitsu and Judo he left many students on his trips. He traveled extensively in the northeast of Brazil and the southeast, and during these trips he left students who started practicing Jiu-Jitsu and even Vale Tudo.

Why do you research history?

The reason I research the history of Jiu-Jitsu and Vale Tudo is first, because I am a Jiu-Jitsu practitioner, so Jiu-Jitsu is part of my life, and second, because I have an obsession, a passion for history and an obsession with search for the truth. Even if it does not bring me any kind of advantage or benefit, and even against the world around us today, I cannot accept that the facts are not told clearly and truthfully. That's why I started researching. The importance of telling the full story of Jiu-Jitsu and Vale Tudo in Brazil is enormous because it reveals new characters, new events, and makes it clear how this story was really evolving. This was a long process that cannot be explained simply and punctually. We need to show all the characters and how they developed. It is a collective and evolutionary process.

—

We'd covered a lot of ground, and at this point our team was exhausted and ready for a break. I have a high tolerance for work I enjoy (and an equally low tolerance for the opposite), and I don't mind the discomfort, rush, and lack of sleep that a heavy workload brings, but by now even I was at a breaking point. For two weeks straight we'd been averaging four to five hours of sleep a night, eating whenever we had time and whatever was available (a combination which doesn't always make for a healthy or tasty diet). Packing and unpacking, carrying equipment up flights of stairs, cramming into tight spaces and cars—and knowing that we would have to do it again in a few hours—had taken a toll on our enthusiasm, and our team was at each other's throats. (At one point at the Fadda Academy Steve and Fabio had been on the brink of testing each other's Vale Tudo skills over Fabio not wanting to throw something in the garbage for Steve, who was packing up the camera equipment all by himself.)

Little episodes like this one had been steadily accumulating during the trip, and at some point everyone on the team had to take a deep breath and remind himself of what we were doing, and why (I'm not innocent, here: I'm no angel and I know I'm not always the easiest person to deal with). We relied heavily on Jay who, with the least confrontational of all the personalities involved, took on the role of resident pacifier. Still, I was able to write all of this off as understandable, given our team's lack of any connection outside of our collective desire to make this film a reality. People's personalities, goals, and tolerance differ, and some conflict is inevitable when strangers are thrown together in tight quarters and put on a frantic schedule. I was hopeful that these differences would prove insignificant once we escaped the confined and heightened conditions of our trip, and were through the grind of interviewing. Many of them did. I would find, however, that other—and more problematic—differences remained.

Much like Fabio, I tend to think like a historian: my baseline attitude is that the information should take precedence over everything else. Steve, Brad, and Daniel came to the project from a filmmaking background, and tended to err on the side of entertainment and aesthetics (Jay, for his part, was somewhere in the middle). During the interview phase of production these differences took the form of an ongoing but a minor background conversation; during the editing and post-production phase, however, they would become a point of near constant contention.

Steve collecting B-Roll in Kyoto; The author at a temple in Kyoto.

JAPAN

A month after our Brazil trip, in February of 2018, we would travel to Japan for the last portion of the interview phase of production. This trip would be shorter and less rushed than our trip to Brazil, but would prove to be just as rich an experience. It wasn't my first time in Japan: I had been to Tokyo on three other occasions either cornering friends for MMA fights or teaching seminars, but I had no experience traveling outside of Tokyo, Yokohama, and the tourist town of Kamakura. I was excited to see Kyoto and Okayama, excited to see the pagoda-style architecture I'd always found so beautiful, and excited to learn from the Japanese themselves how they felt about an art they created now being referred to worldwide as "Brazilian Jiu-Jitsu."

I had always liked Japan: even in my brief visits I'd felt and observed social features that Brazil and the U.S., in my view, sorely lack. "Order and Progress" aren't just positivist propositions in Japan but rather the cultural norm, and make their way into everyday life naturally (the reason for this certainly has to do with the formation of their traditions throughout their history, and goes well beyond the martial arts... perhaps a topic for future studies). I also wanted to learn how this deeply hierarchical and structured culture helped shape Judo (and, subsequently BJJ). Our investigation, after all, wasn't looking for just a simplistic lineage-based explanation of "who taught (or didn't teach) whom," but rather an understanding of the events and attitudes that had played crucial roles in the formation of our art (and that had always been neglected by the lineage-based view of our history).

One example: my first time in Tokyo, while exploring the city alone on a public bus, I took a seat and let my mind wander, as it always does. I was vaguely aware of someone standing near me, but in my distraction I didn't bother looking up. When I finally did I found myself looking into the eyes of an elderly woman: she was standing right next to me and staring me down. She wasn't alone, either: looking around I noticed (to my embarrassment) that the entire bus was doing the same thing, wondering why the absent-minded foreigner didn't do the obvious thing and offer this woman his seat. Experiences like this one managed to be both embarrassing, refreshing, and informative at the same time, and I was eager and curious to learn more about the rich cultural understanding that seemed to inform every aspect and moment of Japanese life.

It goes without saying that Japan had a lot to offer our film. No film about the history of BJJ can call itself complete without a visit to the Kodokan, and its location in central Tokyo put it practically on our doorstep. The Kosen schools were of interest as well: they resembled so much the practice of BJJ, yet we knew that there had been no exchange of influence between the two (except, perhaps, through Judokas like Mehdi); further we wanted to present the possibility that, contrary to popular belief, the groundwork practiced in Brazil was actually less sophisticated than the style practiced in the Kosen schools in Japan for most of the 20th century (in my opinion as a coach and practitioner, this was true up until the inception of IBJJF, in 1994; a quick peek at YouTube videos contrasting groundwork in Brazil and in Japan through the '50s, '60s, and '70s presents strong evidence that this was indeed the case). Not to mention the fact that, in this beautiful country, it was staggeringly easy to collect stunning B-roll footage.

We had discussed bringing Fabio along but, given the fact that he spoke neither English nor Japanese, we decided that he wasn't going to be of much help and we wanted to save on the budget. This left us in need of someone who could fulfill the role Fabio had played in Brazil. I suggested Max Masuzawa, an old friend in Tokyo and fellow BJJ Black Belt who spoke fluent English. Luckily for us, Max was willing. His presence would prove to be invaluable as he would take on the role of designated interviewer, prompting the interviewees with questions carefully formulated by me, Fabio, and Jay (neither Jay, Steve, nor I speak a word in Japanese).

The building where Kosen Judo practice takes place at Tokyo University; The author and Sensei Matsubara; Group picture after the Kosen Judo practice at Tokyo University

RYUICHIRO MATSUBARA

TOKYO UNIVERSITY

"So if you look at Gracie Jiu-Jitsu, they have a lot of techniques related to self-defense. Unlike Judo, which developed as a sport... I think that's why [BJJ] and MMA were combined and developed."

—Sensei Ryuichiro Matsubara, Professor at
Tokyo University and Kosen Judo Instructor

Our first stop was Tokyo University, where Sensei Ryuichiro Matsubara teaches the Kosen Judo style I had heard so much about but had never actually seen. (Matsubara is also an Economist and Sociology Professor at Tokyo University). Matsubara greeted us respectfully and warmly, and showed us to the training area. The building in which they practiced was absolutely beautiful: I remember thinking to myself that, if I could ever choose a building in which to teach every day, it would be one exactly like this. We arrived thirty minutes before class was set to begin in order to unpack equipment and pick the best spots for the interview. However, we were not early enough to have the place to ourselves. A couple of students were already there, and these few were soon followed by others. The room began to fill with a young and jovial energy: Sensei Matsubara and his students all seemed genuinely excited at the prospect of us filming their practice. My guess would be that the average age of the students there was no more than 19, but I was struck by their traditional and respectful manners. I was also surprised to find that a few of them seemed to know me from the grappling world.

This first interaction with a Judo school in Japan was something of a shock for me. I had been to other Judo schools before, and had always noted the differences between the Judo culture and the one to be found in most BJJ schools; what I encountered at Tokyo University, however, was on a whole other level. The students (who, if memory serves me well, were all Black Belts, though it should be noted that the Kosen style uses the tradition of two belt system, white for juniors and Black for senior), were all sweeping the mats before class, and in unison. No one had asked them; it was simply what they did every day before practice. The noise the brooms made on the mats were music to me, and it was as I watched them that I noticed something else: all of their gis were spotless white, as though brand new. This was all in stark contrast to what I am accustomed in both Brazil and the U.S., in terms of the humility of a paying student (and a Black Belt at that) showing up so early and sweeping the mats before class. These small gestures spoke volumes to me about the values and respect that are so ingrained in these practitioners, and made me wonder if, in the end, the Brazilian practice would have been better off being absorbed by Judo after all... Though, selfishly, I would have preferred it to be this Kosen style, which I was amazed to see was incredibly similar to BJJ in technical terms. I was surprised, but it made sense: human anatomy is the same everywhere, and if people spend enough time doing the same thing—and, in this case, while wearing uniforms that are virtually identical—they will eventually and inevitably reach the same conclusions. The "Brabo" choke, for example, which I thought I had invented, apparently had already been discovered and used by a student of Renzo Gracie in NY, who the move is named after. No surprises there: after all, the wheel was also invented in more than one place at different times.

After practice and our interview with Sensei Matsubara, the students asked if I would show them a few moves. I was happy to oblige, adding as many details as possible. The student who volunteered for the moves, Max explained to me, walked away smiling and telling his friends about the "pressure" he'd felt in my side control, which made me smile and miss training at the same time.

I was surprised to learn how familiar they were with the BJJ scene. Even though their movement and demeanor were very Judoka-like, they referenced the high-level BJJ competition scene and many known BJJ practitioners. I found it strange and somewhat ironic that BJJ would be exported back to Japan after something of a makeover in Brazil, such that now Brazilians would serve as a reference for students practicing halfway across the world. This was the first, but not the last, time I would have this thought during our Japan trip.

— Ryuichiro Matsubara —

Can you introduce yourself?

My name is Ryuichiro Matsubara. I'm 61 years old. I am the head of the Judo club at the University of Tokyo.

What is Kosen Judo?

Kosen Judo is a rule[set]. The reason why that rule[set] was made was for those who started to practice Judo for three years or less and were white belts to be able to compete against those who had been practicing Judo with tachi-waza [throws], they needed the ne-waza time to be longer and to be able to pull them in hikikomi ["guard-pull"]. That's why they needed those rules. On the other hand, Jigoro Kano wanted Judo with a focus on tachi-waza. According to him, if you are fighting against multiple people alone and rely heavily on ne-waza, you would be kicked or punched from above. So he thought ne-waza should be a maximum of thirty seconds if used. Jigoro Kano did not like the idea of doing ne-waza for an extended period of time

Who is the founder of Kosen Judo?

I don't think there was a founder for it. If you had been doing Judo since you were a child, you would probably be strong with tachi-waza. In comparison, if you start practicing and competing in Judo from the age of 17 for three years, ne-waza is much easier to master. I think this is why rules, such as hikikomi, were made. I don't think there was a founder for all of this. Rather, Kyoto University pushed for it because it was a way to win against those who had been practicing Judo from a young age with tachi-waza. Personally speaking, I think this is why more time started to be used for ne-waza. However, the founder of Judo, Jigoro Kano, did not accept the idea of creating a new rule. There are stories of how he visited from Tokyo to talk about how he did not want those kinds of rules in Judo. However, Kyoto University argued that they were doing it for the purpose of education, so they could not accept his request. That's why, under the Kodokan rule, they didn't do ne-waza for a long time.

Were there other schools—other than the Kodokan—teaching ne-waza?

There were Grandmasters in each higher professional school, and Tokyo had the Kodokan as well. But there were other schools that per-

formed their own Jiu-Jitsu kata, especially in the Kansai area. Yaechihyouei Kanemitsu in Okayama, who was at the sixth higher professional school, was probably the one who had the most influence. He had originally been doing ne-waza from Jū-Jutsu, and he had the 9th dan from Kodokan. Techniques like triangle choke, or sankaku jime, were created when he was teaching Judo. It's been said that he created it with his students.

Why did Judo become so stand-up oriented?

One reason might be that Grandmaster Kano had been practicing Kito-Ryu, and those individual ways of performing Jū-Jutsu were focused on tachi-waza. Another reason he is talking about might be that when you think about the actual practice, and you have to fight alone against many others, or group versus group... and if you're pinning someone down for about thirty seconds, there's a chance you would be kicked or punched from above. I think this is the reason. Jigoro Kano has also written about this. I think this is why Kodokan was not very interested in ne-waza. However, towards the end of the Meiji era... probably after the Sino-Japanese war, there was a big organization of individuals who were not from the Kodokan. This was Dai Nippon Butokukai. This organization had a mix of Jū-Jutsu and Judo, so Jigoro Kano sent Grandmasters from the Kodokan to that organization. It was in Kyoto, so there was a lot of involvement with Kosen Judo. I actually think it's accurate to say that that was around the time ne-waza was introduced to Kodokan.

Why are the ideas of self-defense in Kano's Judo so different from those of BJJ?

This is my take on it, but I think it was because there was the idea that the actual practice would be one-on-one. There was a confrontation or fight that Rickson had at the beach. It was clearly a one-on-one match, and people surrounding them were just watching. However, Jigoro Kano did not see that as actual practice. He saw that group versus group was more of an actual practice, so he understood it as if you throw someone with tachi-waza, you could escape. In Brazil, a one-on-one match was more manlike.

What are the similarities between Kosen Judo and BJJ? And has BJJ impacted Kosen Judo in some way?

The similarity would be the techniques you use when you attack. I think it was around the year 2000 when the techniques of Brazilian Jiu-Jitsu actually started coming into the nanatei (seven university competition). Prior to that, we were practicing regular ne-waza techniques from Judo. However, ever since then, players use De la Riva or spider, which has more guarding elements to the technique. These are guarding techniques aiming for a draw. I believe this is how we've been influenced from the other side... For example, you're just hanging on with deep-half. The technique of deep-half is the same, but with this technique, you're basically only hanging on to your opponent. You don't really attack, and that's the biggest difference. There are a lot of similarities in terms of techniques nowadays.

Did the Kodokan spread Judo to the world alone?

My opinion is very different from the Kodokan's. Actually, it's not that it is different, but my opinion is the truth. As I mentioned before, the Kodokan had sent players to the organization of Dai Nippon Butokukai. However, after WWII, GHQ of America recognized the organization as something that started the war. That's why they banned it. By that time, Butokukai had already established a different school. They had a different dan [system] from the Kodokan, and there were many Judo players who were not a part of the Kodokan. These were the ones who went to Europe. France actually has many teachers (senseis) from Butokukai. All in all, they've had a big influence on the World Judo Organization. This is an organization that is not within the Kodokan. So I think there is a case that the Japanese from the Butokukai had a big influence on Judo in the world. The Kodokan has not recognized or accepted this. The Kodokan argues that they were the ones who spread Judo to the world, but I don't think this is true.

What were Kano's thoughts on pre-Meiji Jū-Jutsu?

Kano sensei actually said that the individual ways of Jū-Jutsu was not compatible to the Meiji Restoration. He saw that when they failed they became "professionals" who gathered audiences. He thought this was not right because he wanted [the art] to become a part of education. So, for him, Judo was for education and never a profession. He repeatedly said this in the Kodokan, so whoever wanted to become professionals in the Kodokan left to become one.

Why do you think BJJ moved away from Judo instead of being absorbed by it?

This is completely my guess and imagination, [but] if you look at Gracie Jiu-Jitsu, they have a lot of techniques related to self-defense. Unlike Judo, which developed as a sport, I think it had a different reason to develop. I think that's why BJJ and MMA were combined and developed.

How did the Japanese perceive the introduction of BJJ in Japan?

This came to Japan as something that was not related to Judo, especially Gracie Jiu-Jitsu. This did not come to Japan as Jū-Jutsu, but as Mixed Martial Arts. It was seen as a base of Mixed Martial Arts that would make you stronger, and it had a great impact on Japanese people

Has this introduction of BJJ and MMA changed how the Japanese see Kosen Judo?

303

Kosen Judo was ignored for a long time in the Judo world, but I think it's starting to be recognized again.

Upper left, from left to right: Max Masuzawa, Steve, the author and Jay outside the Kodokan; Upper right: Sensei Naoki Murata, 8th degree Judo Black Belt and curator for the Kodokan museum; Bottom: The author, Sensei Murata, Jay, and Steve inside the Kodokan museum.

SENSEI MURATA
THE KODOKAN

"The first reason why Judo was established or created was for physical education. This was for the Japanese people during the Meiji era.

People wanted to create healthier bodies, and that was one of the goals. Judo was created from a martial art called Jū-Jutsu."
—Sensei Naoki Murata, 8th degree Judo Black Belt
and Curator of the Kodokan Museum

I had been to the Kodokan once before (and with Max) to see for myself the institution where it all began. A beautiful life-size bronze statue of Jigoro Kano greets the visitors as they walk into the Kodokan and off the busy Tokyo street; inside there is a small store where visitors can buy souvenirs and equipment (and where I bought my own Judo coach and Cuban national, Jose Carricarte, a poster showing some of Kodokan Judo's fundamental moves).

Max had handled the arrangements. We were set to interview Sensei Murata, the curator of the Kodokan's museum and an 8th degree Black Belt in Judo. We had been told that there were no pictures or filming allowed in the museum but that they would make an exception for our film, which surprised me: I knew how strict the Japanese are about rules. That same day, while Steve was looking for a restroom, he ended up on a floor where he was not permitted and security was called (the incident was defused when Steve complied with their request that he immediately return to the floor where he was permitted to be). It is easy for someone unacquainted with Japanese customs and strict rules to make these mistakes, and we would make many throughout our trip there.

The museum wasn't large—it consisted of one main room and two smaller ones, if memory serves me well—but it was filled with treasures from the early days of Kodokan: old gis, manuscripts, paintings, books, et cetera. One prominently-displayed photo showed Mitsuyo Maeda, Akitaro Ono, Satake, and Tokugoro Ito as Kodokan representatives in the distant land of Brazil, and seemed designed to establish a clear and unspoken link between BJJ and Judo; I couldn't help but wonder whether that photo would have been so prominently displayed were it not for the marketing efforts of Carlos Gracie. Would the Kodokan acknowledge and proudly present this piece of its history if it were not for the explosion of BJJ around the world? (An explosion for which they were, to a very large extent, responsible, but one that, one way or another, was credited largely to Carlos and Hélio Gracie?) Robson Gracie's words regarding Maeda, and his father's role in making the Judoka a household name, echoed in my head as I considered the framed picture.

I was curious to hear Sensei Naoki Murata's views on BJJ, and how he felt about the Brazilian rebranding of Judo. I wondered if there was any bitterness at BJJ having taken so much from them without ever giving them the proper recognition. I was also curious to learn if he knew anything at all about BJJ, the Gracie family, and the creation of the UFC. Did the rivalry of the 1930s and '40s between Judo and BJJ live on in the hearts and minds of these Judoka? Or did they even know about it? Did they even care?

Murata began by giving us a brief tour of the museum, answering any questions Max or I had, while Jay and Steve set up the equipment for the interview. Once everything was arranged the interview began... as did my mounting frustration with the fact that I couldn't understand a single word of it. Part of the fun in Brazil was being able to jump in on the interview and ask questions, either to expand on anything I felt was interesting for the film or simply to satisfy my own curiosity. I trusted Max to get as much information out of our interviewees as possible, but it was frustrating to know that I would have to wait for the transcripts and translation to be finished before I could appreciate what was being said, and have my questions answered.

After the interview, our team continued our conversation with Sensei Murata. Despite the ground we'd covered in the interview it was still somewhat unclear how he and the Kodokan felt about BJJ. My sense was that there was no bitterness or resentment... but I also had the distinct sense that they felt that there hadn't been a technical revolution sufficient to justify the claim that this Brazilian style was something "new." To them, the Brazilians had merely become specialists in an aspect of Judo (one that, I would add, Judokas had increasingly—and to their own detriment—neglected over time).

I was surprised to learn, however, that the history that Murata was telling Max was essentially the same Maeda-Carlos-Hélio story so widely repeated in BJJ circles around the world (certainly unaware of recent discoveries regarding this past). In my understanding, he only differed with the "official narrative" in his assertion that Brazilians were practicing "Judo" and not "Jiu-Jitsu," in the original sense of the word. With so much lost in translation, it was difficult to clarify these points and get definitive answers. I will say, however, that his overall remarks seemed couched in a larger ambivalence: I was left with the impression that, to the Kodokan, this history didn't matter very much; that BJJ was a minor side story to the main line of the Kodokan's history, one to which they hadn't paid very much attention, if any.

I don't mean to give the impression that Sensei Murata or the Kodokan staff were dismissive of us in any way. Rather they greeted us warmly and respectfully, and did us a tremendous favor by allowing us to film in the museum. The Kodokan staff members asked that we give them credit in the film but this, along with a slight rewording of our "release" agreement, was the only request they made of us (the writing style of a Western attorney being, perhaps, too demanding, given that they were the ones doing us a favor. Fair enough: these are the differences in etiquette that one needs to learn when traveling abroad, particularly Japan).

We finished our Kodokan trip collecting some B-Roll in their main training room, where children and beginner adults were training (this surprised me, as I had imagined the Kodokan as a place where only elite competitors trained).

I was left again to wonder at the differences between the two styles. As I have said, the largest and most noticeable differences between Judo and BJJ are not only technical but also cultural. I had visited a few Judo gyms in Brazil in the course of my life, and even so far from the Kodokan it was obvious that Judo retained a different energy on the mats. Still, it would be unfair to say that Judo had not left a cultural legacy in BJJ. Brazilians bow to each other, the hierarchy of respecting the elders and higher-ranked practitioners is still there; the hierarchy within the culture is still one of "Master" and "student" rather than "customer" and "seller." The throws are all still named in Japanese (with the exception of throws that were made illegal in Judo such as the "single-leg" and "double-leg" or "Baiana" takedowns, whose name Brazilians borrowed from Wrestling—pronounced with a heavy Brazilian accent—and Capoeira, respectively) but, interestingly enough, this didn't happen with the ground techniques (though I imagine that some of these were borrowed from Catch Wrestling, and so bear their Catch Wrestling names: "armlock," "leg-lock," "Americana," all English words pronounced with a heavy Brazilian accent, and whose origins certainly aren't Brazilian or Japanese). Still other moves in BJJ's arsenal don't really have names, a curious feature that is slowly changing as the art spreads around the world. And, strangely, many English words use to describe situations that do not have a name in Brazil are making their way into the vocabulary of Brazilians practitioners, such as the "whizzer" and the "fifty-fifty" position (also pronounced with a heavy Brazilian accent).

This recent Americanization of BJJ is interesting to me. I recall how, as a blue and purple belt, the term "marqueteiro" (marketeer) was used as an insult for anyone who behaved in an excessively vain manner after tournament results, or who was constantly trying to get their name and picture into the press. The insult doesn't translate well in the U.S., where making sure you profit from your competitive exploits is the norm. Brazilians tend to see Americans as older brothers to be emulated and, though this view isn't universal, I believe many Brazilians suffer from a complex of inferiority in this relationship: a phenomenon which is manifested in Brazilians' habit of copying Americans in so many things—even in things that Americans learned from Brazilians themselves.

I can remember how, growing up in Brazil, the Brazilian children would refer to anything that came from a foreign country as "importado," a word meant to convey both that the item was imported and that, accordingly, the toy or gadget was of superior quality. "Importado" as opposed to what was produced nationally, which clearly didn't merit bragging rights. I also remember well the public perception in Brazil towards Vale Tudo in the '90s and early 2000s. There was a general attitude that the art was brutish and uncivilized, something that only lower animals would venture into; I found it truly shocking how quickly average Brazilians changed their views on the sport once it was rebranded, anglicized as "MMA," and accepted in the U.S. mainstream. The barbarians were turned into heroes overnight, the long history of Brazilian Vale Tudo was forgotten, and a new history began with Dana White and the UFC. "Importado" was better, even when the raw ingredients were indigenous. As it turns out, the colonial mind doesn't disappear with the emergence of a Republic, or a Constitution.

A martial art isn't only expressed through its techniques and rules of engagement, but also through the culture in which it is practiced. In this regard BJJ had absorbed much from Brazil and, more recently, from the U.S. In the U.S. in particular it seems that not much is left from the Japanese matrix other than the gi itself: not even the bowing to enter the mats is emphasized in most schools in the U.S. anymore. I wonder what derivation will rise next, in the age of the internet, as BJJ continues to reshape itself with algorithms as its guiding north. I suspect, however, that the "DO" won't be in it.

— Sensei Naoki Murata —

Could you introduce yourself?

My name is Professor Naoki Murata, I work at the Kodokan, and I am in charge of the Kodokan museum and library. I am a Kodokan Judo 8th dan grade. And I am also an international judge of kata competition in the International Judo Federation.

How did Judo begin?

It started from a room in one of the temples called Eishoji, which is located in Ueno. This is where Kodokan Judo started. This is because Jigoro Kano, who was a young man at the time, established Judo after he graduated from the University of Tokyo, gave himself in to Eishoji to study there, and that's how he propagated the name of Judo. This is why Eishoji is said to be the birthplace of Judo.

What were the biggest differences between Jū-Jutsu and Judo?

In the past, the biggest difference between Jū-Jutsu and Judo was that Jū-Jutsu was a martial art. This is a skill or art to kill people. On the other hand, Judo has not had the same understanding from the past: it's a way to create or educate people. However, it has the traditional skills from Jū-Jutsu, so it is possible to kill someone with Judo. But that is not the goal of Judo. As I said before, Jū-Jutsu was a skill to kill people. Judo was an educational way to create people. The educational end-goal was Jita-Kyoei, or a way to create peace, so that's obviously the difference between Jū-Jutsu and Judo. The end-goal is completely different. The time of Jū-Jutsu has ended now, because the time of samurais is also over. Jū-Jutsu exists in Japan as the cultural asset of Japan. Judo is used the same way it has been in the past, which is to educate people. For example, in education, police training, and many other places.

But why was Judo created?

The first reason why Judo was established or created was for physical education. This was for the Japanese people during the Meiji era. People wanted to create healthier bodies, and that was one of the goals. Judo was created from a martial art called Jū-Jutsu, and people wanted to protect the tradition of fighting. This "fighting" does not equate to the meaning of fighting in sports, but more brutal. They would kill the other people if they wanted to, and if someone attacked you for that purpose, you would be able to protect yourself. This all comes from martial arts philosophy. This was the "fighting," and that was the goal. I guess a modern way of talking about it is that it was for self-defense. Another reason was for shushin, which expressed the heart of a Japanese. There was a long history and tradition of bushido, so they did not want to forget that spirit of bushido. So, physical education, fighting, and shushin, which also means to let your heart rest. These three were the main goals or aims for Kodokan Judo when it first started.

Can you tell us a little bit about Mitsuyo Maeda?

He studied at Waseda University, and he was extremely good at Judo. I have heard that he was quite famous within the Kodokan. The first person the Kodokan decided to send to America to instruct Judo was Yamashita sensei. Afterwards they sent Tomita sensei, and that was when Mitsuyo Maeda also went to America with him. Tomita sensei went around and instructed Judo at different places in America for eight years. Maeda sensei was also with him, but they parted midway. Tomita sensei came back to Japan. On the other hand, Mitsuyo Maeda went to Europe, Cuba, and Brazil after that, and he never returned to Japan.

Can you tell us a little bit about Sensei Jigoro Kano and his role in Judo?

Jigoro Kano was the founder of Judo, but he was an educator. He was very fond of Japan. Since the era of bushi, or warriors, had ended, he felt the need to do something... He felt that they should not forget that tradition. OK, then we have to improve and develop a new one. We just need to take out the dangerous techniques, and keep the safer ones. This was how Judo was created. So why did they go out to the world? When Japan was going through modernization around the Meiji era, he understood that Japan needed and was being helped by the world. Japan learned various cultures, literature, education, military affairs, and industrial technology from the world, especially from the West. Jigoro Kano understood that it was Japan's turn to give back so that they can continue the relationship with the world. If they wanted to give back to the world, they couldn't copy what others had done. It had to be something original from Japan, and something very valuable. This was Judo for them. This was actually written by Jigoro Kano himself. In addition, Judo trains your mind and body. It seeks for the way to use your energy in the most effective way. The goal for this was Jita-Kyoei. This notion has no borders with other countries. He thought this should not be kept within the Japanese, but should be spread to the world. It would be giving back to the world, and people around the world would be able to enjoy it. This is the origin to why it was spread to the world.

Why did Judo deemphasize ne-waza over the years?

For Kano sensei, Judo had the element of martial arts. So when you say martial arts, it would naturally be one on one, one versus two, one versus three, or one versus many more. When you had to fight in those kinds of situations, you had to deal with it. With that in mind, it was better to use techniques that were in the standing position. Ne-waza would be fine if it were one on one, but with multiple people you would be defeated. Because of this, beginners were suggested to practice tachi-waza, which were the techniques in standing position. After you had gone through different dans, like 4 dan, 5 dan, and 6 dan, people would start practicing ne-waza and tachi-waza with a fifty-fifty balance. Overall, tachi-waza was prioritized, and the reason was because of martial arts. The reason why it was martial arts was because whether it be one on one or one versus many, you would have to be able to deal with it, and defeat them. [Note: Here Sensei Murata uses the term "martial arts" as we would use the term "self-defense."]

Why did the Kodokan dislike professional fights?

The reason is very clear for this one. The techniques of Judo isn't something to show others or to earn money. The skills of Judo is to train your body and your mind. It's nothing more, nothing less. It is acceptable to compete against each other with those techniques or skills, but getting money from that is completely different from the goals of Judo. I think Kano sensei had this in mind. Therefore, he was not thinking of it to become professional, but purely saw it as a way of education. Thus, money was not allowed.

Was Sensei Jigoro Kano aware of the deviation from his Judo that was taking place in Brazil?

Jigoro Kano sensei passed away in 1938. Unfortunately, we're not sure if there was any kind of information like that. However, Mitsuyo Maeda sensei was in Belém, Brazil, for a long time, and he had been writing letters to the Kodokan. I have seen those, too. I don't think there has been any letters found related to the Gracies. I actually don't think there is anything. After Kano sensei passed away, and I'm talking about after the war... I think around Showa 26 or 27. The very famous Masahiko Kimura sensei went to Brazil, and he actually had a match. Ever since then I think many people became aware of Judo in Brazil.

Upper left: Takeshi Itani; Upper middle: The author and Takeshi Itani after their Kosen Judo practice; Upper right: Yuuhei Unno; Bottom left: The team gets ready to interview Yuuhei Unno; Bottom right: Students warm up for Kosen Judo practice at Kyoto University.

TAKESHI ITANI AND YUUHEI UNNO
KYOTO UNIVERSITY

"Kosen Judo has more than one hundred years of history, and it's been said that Kyoto University is the place of origin for Kosen Judo. We still try to keep the tradition by remembering those one hundred years, and we practice many different types of Kosen Judo techniques every day."

—Sensei Takeshi Itani, Kosen Judo Instructor

Our next stop would be another Kosen Judo practice, this time at

315

Kyoto University. I had heard much about Kyoto, and wished we had more time to explore it. Gathering B-Roll there was a breeze: Kyoto is known as a very traditional part of Japan, and its architecture is full of beautiful temples and buildings of the pagoda style (we would find that this traditionalism extended beyond the architecture to the natives, who were far less hospitable to foreigners than the inhabitants of Tokyo). Still, the area was undeniably beautiful, so much so that I joked that we didn't even need Steve's talents to collect good B-Roll in Kyoto.

We only had two days there, so the days would be split between the interviews at the University and collecting B-Roll. Our first interview was with Kyoto University's head Kosen instructor, Takeshi Itani, who was much younger than I expected him to be, and who greeted us enthusiastically. Takeshi was very familiar with not only Kosen Judo but also BJJ and no-gi grappling; months later he would visit me in Las Vegas and I would be impressed by his skills, particularly his Wrestling, which surprised us all. During this same trip he and his traveling companion Ken would introduce me to Shodo, the art of Japanese Calligraphy, which I had always been curious about and was surprised to learn was practiced by these young students as a hobby. I gave it more than a few attempts and quickly came to appreciate how much skill went into it, as well as its meditative and relaxing properties.

Our team arrived early to collect some B-Roll at the University, and happened on a Kendo practice already in full swing. We stopped to watch, and managed to get some excellent B-roll footage, before moving on with our setup.

Like in Tokyo, the Kosen Judo practice in Kyoto had a room filled with youngsters and even a foreigner—from Holland, I was told—who was the only student in the room wearing a brown belt. I told myself I would try to make conversation with him after practice, but it ended up not happening. I was happy to learn, however, that one of the Black Belts in practice, Yuuhei Unno, was writing his dissertation on the history of Kosen: I hastily put together some questions and we improvised a short interview on the spot. We knew little about the history of Kosen, and we were excited by the chance to illustrate the art to our film's viewers.

We spent some time after the interviews discussing BJJ and Kosen with Takeshi and Yuuhei. Like at the University in Tokyo, the Kosen students at Kyoto University were very familiar with the BJJ competition scene, and frequently used famous competitors as technical references. It was clear that the BJJ scene had surpassed Kosen Judo in terms of its technical sophistication; still, to me, the question remained: When did this happen? Personally, as I mentioned previously, I felt that moment was the inception of the CBJJ (later the IBJJF) in 1994, but I wanted to know if the Kosen practitioners here felt that same way.

Interviews and B-Roll collecting done, Takeshi started asking me questions. We ended up exchanging information for the next thirty minutes or so. I was itching to get on the mats and feel what it was like rolling with the Kosen practitioners. I had trained with traditional Judokas before, and had a sense for where they were strong and where they were weak in terms of their ground-fighting skills, but with Kosen I knew it would be different. I wondered how well they would fair against a "spider guard" or a "half-guard," or how good their guards would be in general. I didn't bring a gi, we didn't have the time, and we weren't there to train, so it didn't happen. Still, I wish I'd had that experience. I deeply regretted not bringing a gi with me on this trip.

Watching them "roll," what kept jumping out at me was that the conclusions were the same, but that the Kosen Judokas had reached them much earlier than their Brazilian counterparts. We felt it was important to show this to our viewers: important for them to realize that Brazilians would not revolutionize the ground until many decades after BJJ had split from Judo, long after such "revolutionary" techniques were being practiced in Japan.

I am not very familiar with the history of Kosen, but my understanding is that it was essentially begun by the efforts of Judo practitioners resisting the official Kodokan ruleset and who refused to neglect the ground techniques (*ne-waza*) of Judo. Possibly this was due to their recognition of its importance, but it seems equally likely that many practitioners in Japan simply enjoyed the ground aspect of it, and were loath to give it up. Of course this is speculation on my part, but seeing the way people emphasize and grow skilled in the areas they enjoy (and conversely deemphasize and lack skills in the areas they don't enjoy—hence the difficulty when trying to get someone to train without the gi after they have spent many years in the gi, and vice versa; the same is true for takedown practice, and more recently, the introduction of heel hooks and other leg-locks in more traditional BJJ schools), it seems fair to assume—based on the high level of ground-fighting skill present in Kosen Judo—that these practitioners (and their forebearers) love (and loved) ground-fighting as much as any BJJ practitioner today.

And it is here that Kosen and BJJ share a commonality: though perhaps for slightly different reasons and in opposite ends of the world, practitioners of the styles that would come to be known as Kosen and BJJ both disagreed with the official Kodokan ruleset and its emphasis on takedowns and its lack of emphasis on ground-fighting.

Perhaps unsurprisingly, I sympathize with their position. Barring catastrophic injury, it is inevitable, after all, that a fight will continue on the ground following a takedown. Only the intervention of a referee can prevent this, a construct which detracts from the development of a full and complete martial art and creates instead what can only be called a martial sport.

It is my view that Jigoro Kano and the Kodokan made a tactical error in eliminating prolonged groundwork, wrist locks, leg-locks, and shoulder-locks from its arsenal. Kano's rationale for these changes ranged from the self-defense argument (multiple attackers can be thrown but not controlled and defeated on the ground) to emphasizing that "humans [walk] upright and the ground [is] meant for animals" to safety concerns (the argument being that submissions are particularly injurious, an argument that to me seems fundamentally flawed, as I have seen more injuries from takedowns than from submissions in both practice and competition). I also suspect that Kano was influenced by the Western idea of being a "gentleman" that was so in vogue at the time. We must remember that, despite his brilliance, Kano was a man of his time, and lived during a moment in Japanese history where Western values were to be upheld, and the ground thought of as a place of filth unfit for dignified people.

Regardless of what one thinks of the Kodokan's rules and its reasons for them (speaking for myself, I acknowledge the importance of takedowns as well as BJJ's deficiency in that realm), it is clear that the technical void those rules created is what made BJJ's existence possible. Had the Kodokan allowed these joint-locks and time for extended groundwork, how would BJJ have existed? There would have been no room for a new art to be carved out of Judo, nor would it have made any sense for anyone to try: Judo (the art itself, if not the competitive practice) would have been technically indistinguishable from what we today call BJJ.

—

Months after Takeshi and his friend Ken visited me in Las Vegas, I came across an article in the Brazilian National Library: Takaharu Saigo, the article said, was teaching "Jiu-Jitsu" in São Paulo in 1922, and claimed to be the grandson of Takamori Saigo, the leader of the Satsuma Rebellion of 1877 (the man who would become known in the West as "The Last Samurai"). I found it unlikely that someone in 1922 would have fabricated something like that at a time when no one in Brazil would have had any idea who Takamori Saigo was, or of his relevance to Japanese history; the story, I sensed, must have had some merit to it, and with Fabio's and Roberto Pedreira's assistance, I decided to chase it down. I knew that Takaharu's parentage didn't have much to do with the history of BJJ but it was interesting nonetheless, and I was curious to learn more. I reached out and asked Ken for help chasing down the story back in Kyoto, a request to which he promptly agreed.

As it turned out, Takaharu's father, Kikujiro Saigo, not only fought in the Satsuma Rebellion alongside his father (according to his family), but later became the Mayor of Kyoto. The prominence of the family made it easy enough for Ken to track down his descendants, in particular a woman named Takako, who maintained a collection of family pictures and a family tree that confirmed the story. Kikujiro's son had indeed gone to Brazil for a few years in the early 1920s to teach "Jiu-Jitsu." Takaharu was telling the truth, and finding records in both Brazil and Japan of a Kodokan man who had traveled across the world to teach Jiu-Jitsu almost one hundred years ago was pretty exciting, even if he didn't directly impact the development of BJJ. Takaharu was another one of the many Japanese immigrants who taught in Brazil; his story, at the very least, enriched the already rich history of Japanese immigration and cultural fusion we were beginning to better understand.

— Takeshi Itani —

Could you introduce yourself?

My name is Takeshi Itani. I am the instructor of Kosen Judo at Kyoto University.

Can you tell us about the similarities between Kosen Judo and BJJ?

The similarity between Kosen Judo and Brazilian Jiu-Jitsu is the fact that they both emphasize the use of ne-waza. The difference would be that you win or lose with ippon in Kosen Judo, whereas BJJ is point-based. I think that's the biggest difference. Katame-waza, or grappling technique, is the biggest similarity Kosen Judo has with BJJ. In addition, BJJ has also had some influence on Kosen Judo.

What is the origin of Kosen Judo?

Kosen Judo has more than one hundred years of history, and it's been said that Kyoto University is the place of origin for Kosen Judo. We still try to keep the tradition by remembering those one hundred years, and we practice many different types of Kosen Judo techniques every day.

—

— Yuuhei Unno —

Can you introduce yourself?

My name is Yuuhei Unno. I am a senior at Kyoto University majoring in educational sociology. My area of study is Kosen Judo. I am studying the characteristics that Kosen Judo has, but Kodokan Judo doesn't. I'm researching how the Japanese martial arts can also be related, and how the unique characteristics of Japanese martial arts has been influencing sports itself.

Can you tell us a little bit about the beginning of Kosen Judo?

Yes. The origin of Kosen Judo started from around Taisho period [1912] when there were competitions in the old system, in high school. Unlike the Kodokan Judo performed in many areas of Japan, Kosen Judo has a lot of techniques related to the ones used in Jū-Jutsu, especially the ne-waza. The variety of techniques, such as those, is the major difference between these two Judos.

Why is it important to preserve Kosen Judo?

The reason why we want to preserve the history and techniques of Kosen Judo is because Kodokan Judo has lost the techniques that had been used in Jū-Jutsu. We want to pass it down to future generations. Another reason is because Kosen Judo used to always be a team competition, and not an individual match. In that process, you sacrifice yourself for the victory of the team. Not win just for yourself. This kind of characteristic is not found in Kodokan Judo, and we want to respect that part, too.

How long have you been practicing Kosen Judo?

I've been practicing Kosen Judo since I entered university. I've genuinely felt that it has helped me grow by understanding and doing my best to win for my team, and fighting as a team to win the competition. I'm hoping to spread Kosen Judo because it's not something that is widely known around the world or Japan. I guess that's why I am researching and studying about Kosen Judo.

OKAYAMA

Sensei Inoue from the Fusen-Ryu style during interview; From left to right: Jay, Max Masuzawa, Sensei Inoue, author, two of Sensei Inoue's students, and Steve.

SENSEI INOUE

"Kano sensei was very smart, so he knew that he had to avoid a situation where he would lose when he was in the stages of preparing to spread Kodokan in Japan."

—Sensei Inoue, Fusen-Ryu Stylist

Fabio felt it would be helpful to our documentary to introduce the story of Fusen-Ryu, a style that had rivaled the Kodokan's in its early days and that had actually defeated the Kodokan in a school-versus-school competition. He did a search online and found a Fusen-Ryu school that had survived all these years out in the Japanese countryside, and he suggested that we visit them. I liked the idea, and felt it would be a great way to illustrate the martial arts culture out of which Kodokan Judo was formed. If anything, I hoped that this would help the viewer understand how similar Judo and BJJ truly were. Beyond this, however, I knew little to nothing about the Fusen-Ryu style, and was going primarily on Fabio's suggestion.

As I was to learn, Fusen-Ryu is the style some believe helped introduce the ground-fighting elements to the then almost exclusively throwing-based art of Judo. Mataemon Tanabe, Fusen-Ryu's highest exponent (though not its founder), was a renowned ground-fighting specialist, and the Kodokan's loss to the Fusen-Ryu school's superior ground-fighting abilities, at a time when the Kodokan was beginning to overshadow other Jū-Jutsu schools, is said to have caused Kano to consider Judo's deficiencies and incorporate many of the holds and joint-locks that would later become so characteristic of BJJ.

A feature of any martial art is that it is constantly changing: new cultural norms, new rules, and changes in preferences in the art's leadership all cause (and, in fact, require) an art to adapt over time. The very existence of BJJ is a testament to this. Even Judo has evolved, changing its ruleset over time to ban certain locks, as well as the single- and double-leg takedowns. Closer to home, I have witnessed firsthand the technical revolution that has taken place in BJJ due to the freedom allowed by the ruleset and the savviness of its competitors. To illustrate this evolution, I often recommend that people watch footage of BJJ from the '80s and '90s (or prior), and point out the techniques with which a traditional Judoka would be completely unfamiliar (I'll save you the trouble: there aren't any). Next, I tell them to try the same experiment with footage from the late 2010s and point out which techniques would be completely unknown to a traditional Judoka (I can think of more than a few, in the modern age of "lapel guards," the "50/50," and the "berimbolo"). Any practitioner will quickly observe that the IBJJF's ruleset, combined with a high level of intelligence and cunning on the part of its competitors, has increasingly distanced BJJ from Judo to the point that now it is much harder to recognize Judo in BJJ.

Undoubtedly Fusen-Ryu had experienced many changes over the years as well, but these have occurred without the advantages offered by a high-level competition scene, like the ones present in Judo and BJJ, in which a "natural selection" process filters out the art's inferior moves. The absence of this refining process was on full display in our visit to the Fusen-Ryu school in Okayama. Sensei Inoue, along with two of his students, welcomed us into his gym, which was located on the bottom floor of his home in Okayama. The matted area reminded me of the gyms I'd been brought up in back in Brazil: tight, inadequate for live sparring, and improvised in a room not built for the practice of martial arts. The infrastructure here, like in Brazil, stood in stark contrast to the facilities at the Kodokan and Kosen schools in both Tokyo and Kyoto. Here the walls were covered with blades, spears, and other weapons associated with the practice of martial arts, as well as many certificates of Sensei Inoue's achievements and commendations. After the interview Sensei Inoue took our team upstairs into his home, where he had a hefty collection of books and manuscripts (which I, unfortunately, being too uneducated on the matter and being unable to read Japanese, was unable to judge as to their value to our research). His younger student served us tea and a biscuit while we went through some of the books and discussed martial arts, with Max translating everything.

— Sensei Inoue —

Can you introduce yourself?

My name is Yoshinori Daisaku Inoue, and I am the head of Fusen-Ryu Seibukan Main dojo.

Can you tell us about the history of Fusen-Ryu?

The history of Fusen-Ryu starts from around the end of the Edo period. It was the last period of the samurais. It was a little bit before the Meiji era. It started around that time. Back then it was not really the Kodokan, but the Butokukai which was the biggest organization in Japan. After that, the Kodokan was established by Jigoro Kano, which he started from a town dojo. The time was around the beginning of the Meiji era, and the fourth generation of Fusen-Ryu. There was a man named Mataemon Tanabe in the fourth generation, and he knew ne-waza. It's been said that Kodokan struggled to win against him during this time. Also, Kodokan, tachi-waza and ne-waza existed from a bit earlier than that time... I think it already existed from around the time Jū-Jutsu was established.

325

Kano created a distinct style of Jū-Jutsu, but did he preserve the martial side of Jū-Jutsu?

No, I don't think so. Kano did appreciate the modern idea of sports, like the Olympics. He wasn't focused on the martial arts that the samurais used to do back in those days. It was more of a modern sport where men and women of all ages and even children could take part. I think that was the kind of direction it had.

Why don't we hear more about the challenges in which Fusen-Ryu defeated the Kodokan?

Well, it was because the Kodokan did not want to spread the story or legend of losing. If they wanted to make the Kodokan bigger, I don't think they would use or keep the legends that talk about their losses... Kano sensei was the one who avoided it. Kano sensei was very smart, so he knew that he had to avoid a situation where he would lose when he was in the stages of preparing to spread Kodokan in Japan.

Tell us more about the matches between Mataemon Tanabe and the Kodokan representatives.

I believe Mataemon had a match with Shuichi Nagaoka. In his memoirs, Shuichi Nagaoka notes that Mataemon sensei was skilled, and that he could not win. So, he actually lost. After that was Hajime Isogai, who was [from the] Kodokan. Back then, Shuichi Nagaoka and Sakujiro Yokoyama had the 10th degree or 10th dan level in Kodokan. They were the successful ones. Hajime Isogai was the strongest one out of the people who had the 10th dan. In the later years, it's been told in a famous story that he fought for the fate of the Kodokan. However, even in that match, Tanabe sensei was the stronger one. It seems like they had a match with mostly ne-waza. The reason why the Kodokan used ne-waza in the match was because they could not defeat Tanabe with only tachi-waza. Later, Shuichi Nagaoka *and Hajime Isogai practiced for three nights and three days in the dojo. The story says that it was just them with the doors locked, and they practiced until they "sweat blood." They had a strong motivation to defeat Mataemon Sensei. Another reason was because Jigoro Kano of the Kodokan was wondering how to defeat Tanabe with the Butokukai members. It's said that he thought about it really hard, and came to the conclusion that they should approach with the most dangerous ne-waza, which was ashi-garami (entangled leg-lock). Jigoro Kano understood that these kinds of techniques were dangerous, so they agreed to ban them. This is why it became a designated style of fighting. It has been said that the Kodokan members aggressively used ashi-garami, and dislocated someone's bones. And this all happened at a reception meal time in front of the Taisho Emperor, when the Judo player dislocated the other's leg. This is all in the books. Ever since then it has been recognized as a dangerous technique. Mataemon would ask Kano sensei why those techniques were so dangerous, and pointed out that there are other dangerous techniques in martial arts. He asked these kinds of questions one on one, and had some arguments.*

What happened to the other Ryū and Jū-Jutsu schools in Japan?

There used to be a couple thousand schools for Japanese martial arts. There are only a few dozen of those left in Japan. In addition, the reality is that there are fewer and fewer successors. So we are not thinking that the organization or Fusen-Ryu needs to or wants to appeal to other members. I don't think that's a problem. However, we want the current techniques to be as close to the traditional techniques as possible, and there are some that we can use. It is true that the techniques they used in the past were to kill people or protect yourself, and they developed from that time. Back then was a time when they either had to kill or protect. Now, it isn't. Having said that, I would like to consider the modern needs and ways, but also leave or use the traditional ways of doing techniques.

—

We knew from the outset that we had set ourselves up with a herculean task: we were trying to tell over one hundred years of complex history—from the pre-Meiji era through the formation of the Kodokan, the Russo-Japanese War, the Japanese immigration to Brazil, the rubber boom and the changes in Judo that would eventually lead to the creation of a new martial art that was also heavily influenced by Catch Wrestling, Capoeira, the circus, and fixed fights—all while introducing new characters, drawing conclusions, presenting and correcting the prior erroneous narrative; all of this accomplished by bringing together a team of strangers with very different backgrounds and skill sets to produce a movie that was educational, archival, and entertaining at the same time, and that clocked in at under ninety minutes. At this point in the production, however, success on all of these fronts was beginning to seem unlikely. I had an increasing awareness that I had bitten off more than I could chew, and that our goal was far too ambitious for a ninety-minute documentary. We couldn't decide on what to leave out and so we'd decided to touch on everything, and in ways that weren't always the most effective: in hindsight, I wish I'd spent more time looking for and speaking with professional historians on these topics; the practitioners, though certainly old and wise, often simply repeated conventional notions about the history of martial arts and seldom had the knowledge to correct the popular history—the very thing our film was hoping to do—which ultimately left me (with help) with the task of mining out and cutting anything that was factually incorrect.

I was slowly coming to terms with the realization that we weren't going to please everyone. Still, I thought, we could do our best to remain impartial and introduce the viewer to a new view on BJJ and its history. I was comfortable at least that our film would provide a jumping-off point for anyone interested and willing to make the effort of further inquiry. And I comforted myself with the thought that, at any rate, the information we had collected and would present was leagues beyond the widely-known narrative of BJJ's history.

BACK TO TOKYO

Max Masuzawa, Yuki Nakai, author, Jay, and Steve; Sensei Yuki Nakai and the author.

YUKI NAKAI

"The difference between Japanese martial arts and Brazilian Jiu-Jitsu... there is cultural difference. I think Brazilian Jiu-Jitsu has elements of Japanese culture that lived within [the] foreign culture. There are parts that are very similar... The manners, frankness, and the relaxed ways are probably from foreign culture. I think these kinds of ways make us feel comfortable or friendly with them. I think Japan is a bit stricter in terms of mannerisms. I think this is another reason why foreign Jiu-Jitsu has more flexibility. In other words, Japan values the kata, whereas foreign cultures seek and accept creative Judo. Looking at it from a world perspective, I think Japan is learning to compromise with foreign culture, and they are trying to have the world understand the importance of Japanese culture."

—Sensei Yuki Nakai, President of the
Japan Brazilian Jiu-Jitsu Federation

I wanted to interview Yuki Nakai for a number of reasons. He had practiced in Kosen Judo, fought in Shooto, and later in the Vale Tudo Japan (in which he permanently lost vision in one eye). He had, over the years and to a large extent, become an ambassador of BJJ in Japan, and was now President of the Japan Brazilian Jiu-Jitsu Federation (my second favorite set of words throughout all of this, after "patrician ethos"). In other words: he was the perfect connection between the present and the past.

We visited his gym, Paraestra (the name comes from ancient Greece, and means "a school for fighting"), in Tokyo. We intended to show up before their scheduled class—throughout our trips to both Brazil and Japan, Steve and Jay always tried to show up as early as possible to gather B-Roll—but this time we weren't as early as we would have liked. We accidentally walked for thirty minutes (carrying our luggage and equipment) to the wrong train station, and barely made it to the school at the scheduled time.[10]

Nakai's school was known for having high-level competitors in BJJ, and its mats reminded me of a lot of the places I trained while in Brazil, as well as the Fusen-Ryu school in Okayama. BJJ had largely developed without the benefit of government or private funds—these were normally allocated towards Olympic sports, which explains the size of the mats in Wrestling and Judo training centers. Still, it wasn't only the smaller mats in Nakai's gym that reminded me of my experiences in Brazil. The memory of the Kosen Judo schools was still fresh on my mind, and the contrast was pronounced.

However similar to BJJ in its approach to grappling, the manners of the students at the Kosen schools was a world removed from what I had become accustomed to in Brazil and the U.S. Kosen Black Belts showed up thirty minutes early for class, their gis were immaculately clean, they bowed deeply as a show of respect for myself and my team, and—perhaps my favorite part—they voluntarily and spontaneously swept the mats before practice. Like at most BJJ schools I'd visited, Paraestra differed in notable ways from this model. Nakai's students were all extremely respectful and welcoming, but their de-

---

[10] I had actually visited Paraestra in 2008 on my first trip to Japan, and had some fun rolls with some of the students there (though Yuki Nakai was not there at the time). They were all much smaller and less experienced than me, so we weren't going to war. At one point, after submitting one of their top students a couple of times, I "turtled-up" defensively and let the student get my back and wrap my neck. At this point a local reporter snapped a picture. I noticed, but didn't think much of it; I proceeded to escape the position and tap the student again before the round ended. I went on with my life until, months later, someone sent me a screen shot of me in a Japanese magazine getting, apparently, mauled. It left a bad taste in my mouth, but I brushed it off.

meanor lacked the formality of the Kosen schools. Also, and more tellingly, many students showed up a little late for class (possibly due to traffic and work-related reasons not indifference; after all, these weren't college students, they were adults), took their time putting on their gis, and, while others were already going at it, some took their time taping their fingers while sitting casually on the edge of the mats and joking and laughing with their other teammates.

What was so interesting to me was the fact that, while traveling the world teaching seminars, it had not occurred to me until we began filming the documentary just how much of Brazilian culture had traveled throughout the world with BJJ as its vehicle. It may go largely unnoticed, but I strongly believe that the "surf culture" (or the "Hakuna Matata" philosophy, as I prefer to call it) that is so ingrained in BJJ is a major and under-looked factor in its spread around the world. It is in the fist-bump, the açai after practice, the relaxed manners on and off the mats, the streetwear, the flip-flops, and the laid-back demeanor. These manners and this energy, imported from the beaches of Rio de Janeiro (and, in fact, borrowed largely from the beach culture in Southern California) have made their way to places as far away as Chechnya, Australia, Germany, Scandinavia, Africa, and, finally, after a long and unanticipated makeover in an unlikely destination, back to Japan.

All of this was on my mind as Max got down to interviewing Nakai, and made me kick myself even more for being unable to understand and join in. I would have loved to have heard Nakai's thoughts on these ideas. Instead I would have to wait for months for the transcripts to get a peek at Nakai's mind.

Even after all the travel and the interviews, I could only see BJJ from the perspective of an American-Brazilian practitioner (and, now, documentary producer). We wanted to add the perspective of a Japanese practitioner and observer, and there was no one more suited to this role than Yuki Nakai. When asked how the Japanese perceived BJJ when they first had heard about it, Nakai summarized it beautifully:

"I think there are three elements to the [reaction to the] fact that techniques that were already in Japan from Judo came back to Japan again as Brazilian Jiu-Jitsu: surprise, respect, and a sense of threat. The biggest part is the core of Judo—which is the *ne-waza*—this was not valued after Kosen Judo disappeared. The Judo world did not value *ne-waza* that much, but people around the world saw the value in it and brought it to Japan. That's why they were surprised. We were surprised by how the element that was valued before the War was still kept. This was also a threat to us. Unfortunately, even though Kosen Judo has been around for a while, it wasn't anything major or big in Japan. It was like we could not understand the true value of it if it was not reverse imported like this."

— **Yuki Nakai** —

Can you introduce yourself?

My name is Yuki Nakai. I'm the president of the Japanese Brazilian Jiu-Jitsu Federation. I'm also the president of a martial arts dojo, Paraestra.

Can you tell us about your beginnings in martial arts?

I started Wrestling first when I was in high school. I learned and built my basics there, and I entered a Judo club at the university. The Judo there was Kosen Judo. There were a lot of ne-waza techniques. After that I moved on to practicing Shooto, which is a type of Mixed Martial Arts, and joined the world's first MMA team that practiced it as a sport. I became a professional fighter, and I also became a champion. Vale Tudo was starting to become popular around the world at that time, and along with that movement, I fought against Rickson Gracie in a competition in Japan. I got injured in that competition, so I had to rest for some time. After a while, I decided to try Brazilian Jiu-Jitsu. I decided to wear the Judo uniform to try Jiu-Jitsu once more. I continued to pursue it after that, and this is where I am now.

How did the development of BJJ in Japan take place?

The development of Brazilian Jiu-Jitsu in Japan started around the mid-1990s when the Japanese Brazilian Federation was created. I think that's when the history starts. However, I've also heard that there were Japanese-Brazilians who came before that, too. The official time the federation was created was towards the end of the '90s. Several Brazilians came and competitions were held. At the same time dojos were established all around Japan, like my dojo as well, and there were competitions held by them, too.

What are the similarities between Kosen Judo and BJJ?

The similarity between Kosen Judo and Brazilian Jiu-Jitsu would probably be ne-waza, or groundwork. The ne-waza in Japan before Brazilian Jiu-Jitsu was introduced were parts of Kosen Judo, and was practiced under the rules in sophisticated ways. However, from Brazilian Jiu-Jitsu's point of view, I think it is a fact that there are ne-waza that are based on the rules of Judo. Although Brazilian Jiu-Jitsu has rules supposing that anything could pretty much happen in combat sports, Judo is based on the fights from the past. From that, the Judo rule that was recognized was osaekomi, or the pinning technique. There are other techniques, even though it is limited, for example shime-waza [choking techniques] or kansetsu-waza [joint-locking techniques]. But you use them based on the rules in a sophisticated or refined way. I think the rules create the difference in quality.

How was the introduction of BJJ seen in Japan?

I think there are three elements to the [reaction to the] fact that techniques that were already in Japan from Judo came back to Japan again as Brazilian Jiu-Jitsu: surprise, respect, and a sense of threat. The biggest part is the core of Judo—which is the ne-waza—this was not valued after Kosen Judo disappeared. The Judo world did not value ne-waza that much, but people around the world saw the value *in it and brought it to Japan. That's why they were surprised. We were surprised by how the element that was valued before the War was still kept. This was also a threat to us. Unfortunately, even though Kosen Judo has been around for a while, it wasn't anything major or big in Japan. It was like we could not understand the true value of it if it was not reverse imported like this. In addition, the ne-waza from Judo has the Judo rules, so people questioned how it was being used for self-defense, but there was no problem because they were [competing and training under] Judo rules. I think this is how new techniques are created, but the realistic reaction to the actual practice in Brazilian Jiu-Jitsu/Gracie Jiu-Jitsu was nothing other than surprise.*

Can you point out some other differences between Japanese martial arts and BJJ?

The difference between Japanese martial arts and BJJ... there is a cultural difference. I think BJJ has elements of Japanese culture that lived within foreign culture. There are parts that are very similar... The manners, frankness, and the relaxed ways are probably from foreign culture. I think these kinds of ways make us feel comfortable or friendly with them. I think Japan is a bit stricter in terms of mannerisms. I think this is another reason why foreign Jiu-Jitsu has more flexibility. In other words, Japan values the kata, whereas foreign cultures seek and accept creative Judo. Looking at it from a world perspective, I think Japan is learning to compromise with foreign culture, and they are trying to have the world understand the importance of Japanese culture. Now that Brazilian Jiu-Jitsu has developed, I think Japan sees it as an opportunity to learn and take in what they can, rather than feeling threatened. I also think Japanese martial arts are fantastic. However, it is also true that the Jiu-Jitsu that was created outside of Japan is bringing in new cultures. I think Japan had a late start when the world was already paying attention to it. Japanese martial arts have horizontal ties with the world now, and our generation is trying to push that. We're trying to have more communication with others, and I think we're trying to create something new. So, I don't think it is a threat that we are feeling, but stimulation to move forward.

What do you think the future of BJJ will be like in Japan?

I think Brazilian Jiu-Jitsu will become more popular in Japan, and start collaborating with other combat sports or sports. Brazilian Jiu-Jitsu has the culture of ne-waza, or they heavily rely on groundwork. However, I think many people are starting to realize that something is missing if it is only that. This is why we need to start mixing and collaborating with other arts. For example, the biggest movement right now is to collaborate with Judo. Obviously, with this movement, Judo players and other combat sports players are starting to practice different techniques.

Why do you think BJJ has spread so quickly around the world?

I think Brazilian Jiu-Jitsu has a way of attracting people in ways that Budo, martial arts, or other combat sports couldn't do. I've heard of cases where people who couldn't continue playing one sport for a long time are continuing to practice Brazilian Jiu-Jitsu. A new way in which people are starting to take it in as part of their lives, like surfing or hiking up a mountain. I personally thought it wouldn't take long for Brazilian Jiu-Jitsu to become popular in Japan because they use ne-waza a lot. Even if you are a late beginner, it's very easy to master ne-waza. I understood that it was quite easy to master it even if you are not very athletic. That's why I decided to use Brazilian Jiu-Jitsu as the core when I started to spread martial arts to the world. I'm trying to say that you can basically go anywhere from here if you master it. I think this is a lifestyle.

You became blind in one eye during a fight at the Vale Tudo Japan in 1995, but came back to fight that same night anyway. What happened?

335

I injured my eye in a match in 1995. It really hurt at that moment, but it was during the match... so I had to go on with it, and I won the match. I also went on to the final [against Rickson Gracie]. I don't remember much about that day. I actually found out the day after. I was supposed to get it treated on that same day, but I don't think of it as anything big now. I just think, "Yes. That kind of thing happened in the past." Because that happened, things changed, and I was able to grow. I appreciate what happened because I am what I am from that, and I have what I have now.

I can't see. I still wanted to continue Mixed Martial Arts, but people around me stopped me. That's why I moved on to spreading martial arts to the world. I think that's why I have my path now. I wondered what I should do after knowing I wasn't able to do certain things. I know there were times when I was uncertain, but I knew my path would naturally be found and made. I always try to think positively about the current situation and move on.

—

Our brief experience in Japan had not only given our team new friends, new experiences, and great interviews: it had expanded our own understanding of the development of BJJ as an art, as well as its spread around the world.

It would come as a welcome surprise that some of the greatest takeaways from this process—besides the interview and B-Roll footage we were gathering—were the conclusions I was reaching and the lessons I was learning. It was becoming clear, for example, that BJJ and Judo differed not only in technique but also in purpose. My previous trips to Japan and experiences with Judo had not granted me these same feelings—perhaps because I was looking with eyes that were not critical and thoughtful enough to grasp what was right in front of me.

I left Japan even with a certain nostalgia for something I had never experienced in my BJJ journey. This feeling would grow on me over the next three years, and I would come to envy Judo in many ways.

Deep down I'd always felt that BJJ and MMA lacked what I now understood Judo to possess—and I'm not speaking of the throws. Beyond skills and accomplishments, there are more significant lessons we should all endeavor to learn in the course of our martial arts journey. The Gracie Brothers were undoubtedly committed to their dream, and the effort to turn this dream into a reality. This commitment is something I can admire, to some degree, and even be grateful for—even if I don't always agree with the methods and demeanor they used to realize their vision. But I can't help notice that Kano's vision, even if not perfect, was more in tune with the values I would like to see myself and people around me uphold.

When we think of martial arts we don't usually associate them with marketing, rivalry, and ambition, but these were certainly key ingredients in the making of BJJ and, later, MMA. Kosen Judo and BJJ might be similar in terms of their techniques and even in their opposition to the official Kodokan ruleset, but what the Brazilians added to it gave it a whole new flavor—for better or for worse, according to one's own palate.

Nonetheless, I won't discount what the Brazilians added to the old Japanese recipe. I appreciate, for example, the happy and energetic demeanor practitioners are inclined to carry, on and off the mats. BJJ did not captivate the world accidentally: its energetic and cheerful culture played a pivotal role in its success, in my view—well beyond its borrowed surf-culture and technical arsenal. Furthermore, I am convinced that the creativity and appreciation for artistic improvisation (or "ginga" if you will: a word of African origin used to describe creative movement, and often used to describe the creative playing of soccer, and movement in Capoeira) so ingrained in the Brazilian culture played a key role in BJJ's rapid technical development (that is: after an organized tournament circuit was created, a move which, as I said before, created a condition in which the art was able to evolve and manifest itself). This constant improvisation and adaptation to new circumstances would create what I refer to as the culture of open-software (this, as opposed to doing things exactly how your coach taught you, and passing along to future generations a fixed canon of techniques). This phenomenon is perhaps best expressed in the total lack of a "curriculum" in Brazil for BJJ. This freedom for all to adapt, redact, and alter at will and according to one's abilities and needs is one of BJJ's most endearing qualities, in my view. In fact, this "grappling intelligence" is so at odds with our standard view of "intelligence" that it has made me, over the years, rethink entirely the meaning of the word.

BACK TO THE U.S.

Upper left: The author interviews Pedro Valente; Upper right: The author with Guilherme Valente; Bottom: The beautiful Valente Brothers Academy

VALENTE BROTHERS

"When Royce Gracie lost to Matt Hughes, two days later Hélio Gracie was in our school in Miami. And during the class—there were a lot of students that night—people were doubting Jiu-Jitsu. That Jiu-Jitsu lost its power, its effectiveness. And Hélio Gracie felt that doubt in the room... He asked me to translate accurately the following the

statement, in front of the whole class: 'If anyone here doubts the effectiveness of Jiu-Jitsu, I'm willing to fight you right now.' It wasn't that he expected to win the fight, at 91 years old... he wanted to show this courage that he had, to prove that Jiu-Jitsu is a source of confidence that's so great that a man in his nineties can stand in front of the room and challenge the whole class to a fight."
—Pedro Valente, Hélio Gracie student and Black Belt

Following our return from Japan the plan was to focus on the script, work on reenactments, and begin some rough cut of the tens of thousands of gigabytes we had collected of A- and B-Roll. I began writing a rough script based on the soundbites we had while Jay and Steve worked on the reenactments and Brad helped organize the footage.

That wasn't all, though: we still had three more interviews left to do. The Valente Brothers, Royce Gracie, and Daniele Bolelli would all have the chance to give their take on the history of BJJ.

From the beginning, we knew that our movie would ruffle feathers in the BJJ world. For starters we would be diving into the already-simmering controversy around the question of whether Carlos or Hélio was the true "godfather" of BJJ. Even to an outside observer, it was obvious that there was a split in the family in this regard: a division to which Reila refers repeatedly in her biography of her father, and which is played out in lockstep on gym walls—where either Carlos or Hélio's picture is hung—all over the world.

As far as this controversy was concerned, it now seemed clear to us that Carlos had played a leading role in the early days of the family's involvement with Judo/Jiu-Jitsu, and that Hélio was in fact a late comer in all of this, busying himself instead with swimming and rowing for an elite club in Rio de Janeiro. Rorion's carefully-constructed marketing gimmick—and Hélio's later participation in and confirmation of it—re-branded this high-level swimmer a weakling, and what ensued was one of the most successful marketing ploys the martial arts world has ever seen. (The exploit actually built on a much older pitch, one that dated back at least to Kano's youth in the 19th century:

340

"From my childhood," Kano wrote, "I had heard that in Japan there was a thing called Jū-Jutsu by which even a weak person could defeat a strong person. I definitely thought about learning it." (Cited from *Craze: The Life and Times of Jiu-Jitsu* by Roberto Pedreira.)

The outcome of the Russo-Japanese War itself was presented as a large-scale proof-of-concept, and was central to the pitch used during the original Jiu-Jitsu boom of the early 20th century. It is part of BJJ's central pitch to this day, and to the benefit of many gym owners—myself included.)

Of course, it wasn't all marketing: with good technique, the weak can defeat the strong. It's just that Hélio wasn't exactly weak... nor was he the first to make that claim. And, although Carlos undeniably learned the art first and probably fit better the description of a weak individual (he at least looks to have been less athletic than Hélio, although—admittedly—athletic ability has little to nothing to do with how one looks), Rorion chose to emphasize the role his father played in the art's development, making Hélio the center of the narrative (and making him, as Hélio's eldest son, the heir apparent to the family's legacy).

We knew that by adding a third element to this controversy—the possibility that, really, Carlos and Hélio had not created anything new, but were essentially idiosyncratic Brazilian Judokas—we would be seen as "haters" out to whitewash history; accordingly, we wanted to bring as many representatives from both sides of the family feud as possible to (hopefully) make the point that we were welcoming as many different perspectives as possible. This strategy would prove to be only partially successful, though, as it turns out that being a member of a world-renowned family does not necessarily make you an expert in that family's history, true or otherwise. Luckily for us there are people who, though they don't share the Gracie name, know more about the family's history than maybe all of the family's members combined.

The Valente Brothers' school in Miami is one of the most successful schools in the world, and operates on the model first employed by the Gracie Academy in Rio: catering largely to students of higher economic status, focusing mostly on private lessons, and advocating a self-defense approach to martial arts, their school and style is said to closely resemble the approach and culture of the original Gracie Academy as led by Carlos, Hélio, and their disciples. But beyond this, brothers Pedro and Guilherme Valente also research the art and the Gracie family, and accordingly could (we hoped) offer us some further insight into the story we were exploring. Fabio knew Pedro Valente from previous discussions and made the connection, and we set up an interview.

I knew that the Valente Brothers had strong ties to Hélio, having trained under him and enjoyed a close relationship to him; accordingly, and to be frank, I wasn't sure what to expect from them. I was even prepared for some degree of hostility. As it turned out, though, my concern was completely unwarranted. In fact, throughout post-production I would exchange many messages and information with Pedro, who on more than one occasion assisted us with valuable information. Although it was always clear that he, like João Alberto Barreto, was a Hélio Gracie man to the bone, this never stopped him from listening to diverging opinions and interpretations of Hélio's role in all of this.

Steve and Jay couldn't make it to this shoot, so I flew down to Miami alone. I was to meet up with a camera man named Alfredo who Brad found on a work-for-hire website for videographers. We met up at the Valente Brother's gym, which is arguably the most beautiful martial arts gym I have ever seen in my life. I had come straight from the airport, with only a backpack and my laptop for the interview. Alfredo had no idea whatsoever what he had been hired to do, and I spent the next thirty minutes explaining the job while we waited for the Valente Brothers.

Pedro and Guilherme Valente arrived and welcomed us inside. Pedro took me on a tour of the gym while Alfredo got set up. He proudly talked about the school's growth and its recent move from a much smaller location to this new facility, in a building that he and his brother had built from the ground up. The facility was truly impressive and reminded me very much of the Kodokan, and I was happy but unsurprised to learn later that the Kodokan had indeed been their inspiration in the design and construction of the new academy. I'd met Guilherme Valente a few years earlier through a mutual friend, and it made me happy to see his and his brother's growth and success as businessmen and instructors.

I was also happy to discover that, not only was there no animosity or hostility towards our project, our presence and questions were welcomed. Overall, the brothers seemed confident that whatever came out could neither harm nor diminish Hélio Gracie's legacy. Of course, that had never been our intention, and I believe that came across in our discussion of BJJ and its history. I was excited to learn that the brothers had quite a library of old books regarding martial arts, as well as the Gracie family's history. In fact, I doubt anyone in the family has such an archive or could speak on the history of the family so knowledgeably.

We agreed that Hélio's role in the development of BJJ was indisputable, though our interpretations as to the nature of his importance differed in some ways. In my view Hélio was central in that he stubbornly and pridefully resisted the expansion of Judo and, in so doing, helped carve out a space in which this variant of Judo could thrive… and in which he and his family could stand at the forefront. Hélio was a leader, and to fall in lockstep with the ranks of Judo simply would not have been fitting with his personality. I can't actually imagine him ever admitting that what he practiced was Judo, can't imagine him admitting that it was anything but his own style, even if that style itself was changing through time; Robson Gracie privately confessed to our team that Hélio commonly referred to Judo as a practice for "viados" (in Portuguese, a derogatory term for homosexuals), and ballet dancers.

Pedro Valente presented Hélio as having rescued the martial aspect of Judo as that art became more sport-oriented and less practical for self-defense. I had to agree to some extent: regardless of what one thinks of self-defense, there was clearly an effort to teach it at the Gracie Academy at a time when Judo was increasingly becoming a sport. Still, I can't help but feel that this distinction pales in comparison with the many structural similarities between the two arts. It seems obvious to me that at some point the leaders of the Gracie Academy understood that, regardless of what they thought of Judo, the Kodokan model worked and Judo far outshone what the Gracie Brothers, their art, and their academy had been able to achieve. So many of the elements that were introduced to BJJ and that, in large part, define its modern practice—the ranking system, the formation of a federation tracking and standardizing those ranks, the tournaments organized by that federation—are, in effect, an imitation of what Judo was already doing. The so-called differences between the arts, if anything, highlight how similar they really are.

I asked Pedro what he thought of Hélio's claim that he had "invented BJJ." To me it had always seemed a bold and selfish claim, not to mention an inaccurate one, as most damningly evidenced by the simple fact that his versions changed over time: first he learned the art from Carlos who, according to him, was "the legitimate and perseverant introducer of pure Jiu-Jitsu in our country"; then he learned the art from watching Carlos teach it and adapted it to his limited athletic abilities; then, finally, he "invented BJJ" altogether. When I brought this up, however, Pedro defended Hélio. Hélio, he pointed out, had been the leading force behind the Federação de Jiu-Jitsu do Estado da Guanabara in 1967 (alongside João Alberto Barreto), whose ruleset would go on to become the basis for the IBJJF's ruleset. In this sense, by codifying its practice and articulating its priorities, he did help "invent BJJ." Though I had to admit this was a good point, I can't help but feel that Hélio, at the very least, worded the claim rather poorly. Still, perhaps he can be excused for this, given his advanced age when he began to make the claim.[11]

The whole conversation made me consider anew the question of what constituted a "beginning." Everyone agreed that BJJ had evolved out of Judo, but an evolution—by its very nature—defies the identification of a moment where one thing definitively stops and another is

---

[11] In a 2001 Playboy interview Hélio said that he never invented anything. Visit http://www.global-training-report.com/helio2.htm to read the interview.

definitively created. If anything, an evolution is revealed by events whose outcomes stand as evidence that an evolution has occurred at some prior moment: perhaps this, after all, is the best (and only) way to mark BJJ's split from Judo.

Thinking this, I began to consider which events served as those evolutionary markers. I identify three key moments for this split:

1) The two fights between Hélio Gracie and Yassuiti Ono in 1935 and 1936 seemed like an obvious choice: though both matches were conclusively dominated by Ono, both were ruled a draw because there was no point system in place—a divergence from the internationally-accepted Judo rules, and one insisted upon by the Gracie camp (this stipulation would be employed over and over again throughout the course of the family's long and storied career). Also, the length of the gis (the Gracie Brothers preferred shorter sleeves) and the length of the matches (the Gracie Brothers preferred longer matches) not only diverged from the Japanese norm but also seemed designed to bring the fight to where the Gracie camp had a better chance of winning (or, at least, forcing a draw). Whatever the reason, these deviations from the Judo norm could be seen as the first definitive and legislated assertions of the forming split.

2) The formation of the Guanabara Federation in 1967, and the creation of an official competition ruleset (one that would, much later, become the foundation for the IBJJF's ruleset), also came to mind. As any practitioner knows, the rules define the boundaries as well as the hierarchies of the techniques to be practiced; by clearly breaking with Judo's ruleset and laying down its own, the Guanabara Federation effectively codified the practice of the art. Even if, for a long time after, the practice of BJJ still resembled Judo, and even if the overall technical ability of the Brazilians was far behind that of the Japanese, both in terms of takedowns and ground-fighting skills, the emphasis placed on the ground techniques by the Guanabara Federation's ruleset effectively defined this Brazilian style as a distinct style of Judo. What is interesting to note here is that Hélio, who had always preferred longer

matches and no point system for his own fights, would concede to a point system and shorter matches under this ruleset. Whether this was because he accepted the need for points and time limits, or because he was no longer fighting himself and didn't care as much what rulesets were in place for others, is impossible to say. On a side note, these rules were not created in 1967 but in 1954 for an in-house tournament at the Gracie Academy, at which, curiously, Pedro Valente's father— Pedro Gomes Valente—was the first fight, making him technically the first ever "BJJ" competitor. Also worthy of note is the fact that Amaury Bitetti, Sr., father to the first two-time IBJJF Absolute Champion Amaury Bitetti, Jr., fought in the seventh fight at that same event.

3) Finally, I identify Carlos Gracie, Jr.'s creation of the CBJJ (Confederação Brasileira de Jiu-Jitsu, later known internationally as the IBJJF) in 1994. It seemed clear that this, due to the high-level competition, the more frequent and well-organized tournaments, and the resultant growth of practitioners in Brazil and later the world (fueled in part by Royce Gracie's performances in the UFC) created a condition that would serve to boost tremendously the skills and repertoire of techniques of BJJ as a sport. I would venture the claim, though it is not something we can factually verify, that the birth of this federation marks the moment Brazilians took a technical leap above their counterparts in Japan (at least in terms of ground-fighting, since the collective takedown abilities would remain technically inferior) and BJJ became a truly distinct martial art.

Still, and despite all of this, I was having a harder and harder time thinking of BJJ as "Jiu-Jitsu." The name seemed expressly designed to draw a distinction between itself and Judo—a distinction that now seemed both false and ill-intentioned. Accordingly, shortly after the editing process of the film, I began referring to Brazilian Jiu-Jitsu as "Brazilian Judo" in interviews. I did this for many reasons, not the least of which was the fact that this art was clearly not "Jiu-Jitsu," as was understood in the pre-Meiji sense of the kanjis. There had been attempts made to link what Brazilians did to this period through Maeda, who allegedly shared the secrets of "real Jiu-Jitsu" with Carlos Gracie, but—as with so many other claims in this history—there is nothing to support this story, and Carlos and Hélio's interpretation of "Jiu-Jitsu" as defined in this pre-Meiji period sense would have been little more than an invention of their imaginations: they simply would have had no way of knowing what Jū-Jutsu/Jiu-Jitsu looked like prior to Kano's school; Maeda, to our knowledge, at least, had no experience outside of Kodokan Judo, Sumo, and a brief experience with Catch Wrestling in England. Rather, the truth seemed increasingly obvious: Carlos and Hélio, and subsequently all of the BJJ practitioners who followed them, were teaching their own Judo preferences with their own preferred ruleset and erroneously (and misleadingly) calling it "Jiu-Jitsu."

Nonetheless, this is an inconsequential discussion of nomenclature. BJJ is a variation of Judo and there is no way out of that. But there was also no way out of the fact that they are practiced completely differently today. The IBJJF circuit has elevated BJJ beyond its Judo past (solely in terms of ground-fighting) and what is now being practiced resembles, to me at least, less Judo than Taekwondo resembles Karate. The technical revolution, regardless of what one thinks of it, has been undeniable, and the most knowledgeable of Kosen Judokas, during any period, would be entirely lost inside the guard of modern BJJ competitors. It has become idiosyncratic over time, both technically and culturally, and these differences are by now too severe to ignore. Even if the matrix and raw ingredients remain the same, for better or for worse, BJJ is now on an entirely different course of evolution.

— **Pedro Valente** —

What is your definition of "Jiu-Jitsu"?

My definition of Jiu-Jitsu is a complete fighting system that includes stand up and ground, throwing, grappling, and striking, in addition to a philosophy, a way of life.

347

What did Maeda teach in Brazil? Was it Judo or Jiu-Jitsu?

When Maeda came to Brazil he was practicing the Japanese martial art that can be called Jiu-Jitsu or Judo. At that time, both words were practically synonyms. When Jigoro Kano first created the art of Judo, he didn't consider Judo to be an independent art from Jiu-Jitsu. He considered it to be a teaching methodology. In his words, a scientific teaching methodology. A way to teach Jiu-Jitsu. But he was still teaching Jiu-Jitsu. So I believe that Maeda was teaching Jiu-Jitsu, even though he was a student of the Kodokan and a student of Kodokan Judo.

What was Maeda's role in the development of BJJ?

I think Maeda's role in the development of Jiu-Jitsu in Brazil was extremely important, even though there were some Japanese teachers who arrived before him. His world prominence made him an authority in Jiu-Jitsu. The community, the Brazilian community, knew of Maeda's feats around the world, in Europe and other countries in South America. And he was considered to be a world champion. If you read the newspaper articles from the time, he was very respected, very well respected as a Jiu-Jitsu teacher. So he gave Jiu-Jitsu credibility in Brazil. And the fact that he taught Jiu-Jitsu in so many places, first in São Paulo then in Rio... A lot of people don't know that he even taught law enforcement. He was teaching specific law enforcement classes to the police in Rio, which used to be the capital of Brazil at the time.

What is the relevance of Donato Pires dos Reis and Jacyntho Ferro in BJJ history?

Donato Pires dos Reis is relevant in the history of Jiu-Jitsu in Brazil because when the Academy Gracie—which at the time was not called Academy Gracie, it was called Academy of Jiu-Jitsu—was inaugurated on September 7, 1930, the newspapers depicted him as the main Professor in that school. Carlos Gracie was also described as a Professor, and George as an assistant. But you could see that the prominent role as a teacher in that school was Donato's. And I think that in itself is very important. Later Donato leaves, and it becomes the Academy Gracie, in the same location.

The first connection between Donato Pires dos Reis and Jiu-Jitsu that we can find is in 1921. Donato is also from Belém do Pará, the same city where Carlos Gracie was born. And they are introduced as students of Jacyntho Ferro. Jacyntho Ferro was an instructor at Maeda's school. And they were going to do an exhibition match. In fact, Maeda was to be the referee in that exhibition match. And so Donato and Carlos trained together in Belém. Donato was the one who actually invited Carlos to teach Jiu-Jitsu in Belo Horizonte, to train the police. Firstly as his assistant, and then Donato left and Carlos continued. So Donato gave Carlos the opportunity to become a Jiu-Jitsu teacher full-time. And so his role is undeniably important.

What was the Jiu-Jitsu scene in Brazil like at that time? Were there other practitioners worthy of note?

When we analyze the beginnings of Jiu-Jitsu in Brazil, especially the beginnings of the Gracie family, we must understand that it was not only Carlos' lessons within Maeda's school that allowed the Gracies to become so proficient. They benefited tremendously from Jiu-Jitsu being prominent in Rio Janeiro during the 1930s. There were other Jiu-Jitsu teachers, Geo Omori for example, he's a very prominent Jiu-Jitsu instructor, who started training when he was eight years old in Japan. With a very very strong lineage. Same as Mitsuyo Maeda. And the fact that he was in Brazil, the fact that the newspapers were covering him, the fact that the Gracies—specifically Carlos Gracie—had a chance to fight with him, to grapple with him, two times, I am sure was extremely beneficial for them, to be able to develop their amazing abilities in Jiu-Jitsu. Yano, Takeo Yano, as well, he taught Judo to the Marines In Brazil, to the Navy I should say. In fact he was competing for that job with the Gracie brothers in the

1930s. And because they had that problem where they were arrested after the fight with Manuel Rufino Santos, the Navy decided to give the contract to Takeo Yano instead of the Gracie Brothers. So I would say that Geo Omori, the Ono brothers, and Takeo Yano, they have a prominent role in the development of Jiu-Jitsu in Brazil. And I believe that not only they benefited from what the Gracie Brothers did—Carlos and Hélio—but also that the Gracie brothers benefited from them.

Can you tell us about Hélio's fights with Yassuiti Ono?

You have the Ono brothers, for example. It's important to mention the Ono brothers because especially Yassuiti, the older brother, who also comes from a very very important lineage in Japan, who actually was the first person that we saw doing the triangle choke at a time when we know that the Brazilians did not yet know the triangle choke. He was already doing it. And Grandmaster Hélio Gracie would often tell us about his match with Yassuiti Ono. He fought Yassuiti Ono two times. Grappling matches. Each match went the distance. Five twenty-minute rounds. One hundred minutes. And Grandmaster Hélio was very honest about it. Yassuiti Ono and Grandmaster Hélio weighed the same, around sixty-three kilograms. However, Grandmaster Hélio described the first couple of rounds as [being as] if he was in a blender. That's the analogy that he used. He said, "Ono was amazing, and I was lucky to survive. If it wasn't for my defense, he would have caught me. And I didn't even know what was happening. When I got back to the corner, Carlos had to put ammonia in my nose for me to be able to wake up and understand what was happening. And then towards the end, as Ono got tired, then I was able to even things out." So I think Ono—who had a school, a very prominent school in São Paulo, with a lot of students—I think he had a very important role.

What are your thoughts on George Gracie and his role in the development of Jiu-Jitsu?

When Carlos Gracie came to Rio his two younger brothers, George and Hélio, were still very young. They were the two who did not train Jiu-Jitsu in Belém do Pará [at] Mitsuyo Maeda's school. When Carlos moves to São Paulo in 1929, he becomes the tutor for George. Hélio was still in Rio when George started helping Carlos in São Paulo. George learns Jiu-Jitsu in São Paulo. He even had some fights against Boxers. And he learned very quickly. And George, in that generation, was the one who had the most extensive record when it comes to fights. He had more fights than his brothers. If you ask me about his contribution, I think you cannot compare his contribution, his contribution was as a fighter. He was a good fighter who was fighting to make money. He was a professional fighter. He has a lineage, he did have some students. He was traveling from state to state, from city to city. But there's no comparison of his contributions to the contribution of his brothers Carlos and Hélio. There's no question that George Gracie was a very, very courageous fighter and person. And even though he was not an idealist, and that's why some of the fights that he participated in had pre-arranged results, he understood his brother's role in the art of Jiu-Jitsu and his brother's idealism. And when he came out with the truth of some of those fights that he took [part] in and some of those fights that were happening in Brazil, that some of those fights were fake, he made sure to say that his brother's fights were always one hundred percent real and that Hélio Gracie would never take part in a fight with a pre-arranged result. And that was laudable, because the relationship between George and his brother Carlos and Hélio was always a difficult one. So for him to say that was a huge compliment to his brother Hélio Gracie, and I think it stands as clear proof that Hélio Gracie's fights were always honest. One of Hélio Gracie's greatest passions was to protect the truth in fighting and the truth in Jiu-Jitsu. So he was really, really critical of fake fights. Especially when they claimed to be real. And he did not want any involvement with any fighter that was participating in fixed fights.

We know that there was no such thing as a "Gracie Academy" in 1925. Where does that date come from?

351

One of the things that's not easy to do in my opinion is to pinpoint a precise date for when a school begins. The Gracie Academy in California utilizes the date of 1925 as the establishment of the Gracie Academy, of the Academy of Gracie. We know that an official academy was inaugurated in Rio de Janeiro for the first time in 1930. And it used to be Academy de Jiu-Jitsu. The name "Academy Gracie" started to be used in Rio in 1932. And we can see this very clearly through the newspapers. Now, was 1925 the year when Carlos on his own started practicing Jiu-Jitsu with his brothers, and is that the reason why they used that date? I'm not sure. But if you want to be precise about when the Academy Gracie was established in Rio de Janeiro, the correct date is 1930.

But Carlos already had opened a school in São Paulo the previous year. In your opinion, what is the relevance of this?

I believe that the fact that Carlos Gracie opened a school in São Paulo in 1929 is important for us to see the sequence of events that occurred before the art of Jiu-Jitsu was established in Rio de Janeiro by the brothers Carlos and Hélio Gracie. When they established their school, I should say. It started in Belo Horizonte with his work with the police. Then it went to São Paulo, where [Carlos] opened his school for a few months. And then he moved to Rio. When he moves to Rio with Donato Pires dos Reis he opens an academy, which in 1932 becomes the Academy Gracie.

Tell us more about Hélio as a person.

Grandmaster Hélio Gracie was an idealist, and a man of great conviction. He believed in Jiu-Jitsu, and he believed in himself. He was a true samurai of the modern era. And he felt a very strong connection with the samurai spirit and with Japan. And he believed that his most important mission was to preserve the essence of Jiu-Jitsu. And what did he consider to be the essence of Jiu-Jitsu? He considered Jiu-Jitsu to be the best way to give somebody true confidence. He felt that courage could be developed in people through the art of Jiu-Jitsu. And that was his life's mission. I think that he felt the benefits of Jiu-Jitsu in himself, and he wanted to give that to as many people as possible. So when the Japanese changed the way Jiu-Jitsu was to be practiced with the introduction of Olympic Judo, of sport Judo, he gave it a chance, he experimented—he actually participated in a tournament in São Paulo with Sumiyuki Kotani, who actually gave him a Black Belt[12]—but even then he said, "This is not the Jiu-Jitsu that I know. I don't believe this is real Jiu-Jitsu, I don't believe this is the true Jiu-Jitsu that was practiced in Japan. I believe this is a mutation. I believe this is a limited system." He believed the Japanese were trying to hide the essence of Jiu-Jitsu. And he would not go for that. So he dedicated his life to preserve Jiu-Jitsu and to protect the truth about fighting and about self-defense.

When Royce Gracie lost to Matt Hughes, two days later Hélio Gracie was in our school in Miami. And during the class—there were a lot of students that night—people were doubting Jiu-Jitsu. That Jiu-Jitsu lost its power, its effectiveness, and Hélio Gracie felt that doubt in the room. And the most important thing to him was to teach that Jiu-Jitsu gives you the confidence to achieve anything. And he had so much confidence, and it was so important for him to teach this lesson, that he asked me to translate accurately the following statement in front of the whole class: "If anyone here doubts the effectiveness of Jiu-Jitsu, I'm willing to fight you right now." It wasn't that he expected to win the fight, at 91 years old, even though he was absolutely courageous. But he wanted to show this courage that he had. That Jiu-Jitsu made him able to look at this whole room and challenge and be ready to fight. To prove that Jiu-Jitsu is a source of confidence that's so great, that a man in his nineties can stand in front of the room and challenge the whole class to a fight.

When did Hélio begin training?

---

[12] As of the publication of this book, there is no published evidence of this promotion ever taking place.

Grandmaster Hélio told me that he started training Jiu-Jitsu when he was 16 years old. Carlos Gracie in an interview also said that he started training Jiu-Jitsu when he was 16 years old. He was 16 years old from October 1, 1929, to October 1, 1930. 1930, September 7, is when Carlos opens the school under Donato Pires dos Reis. So I believe that's when Hélio Gracie starts training Jiu-Jitsu.

The Gracie Brothers and their Jiu-Jitsu was largely overshadowed by Judo for many years. How did they manage to carve out a name for themselves in this environment, and overcome all of this?

If you look at the history of the Gracie family in Brazil, they chose to promote Jiu-Jitsu through fights. Sometimes these fights had rules, sometimes these fights were with the Jiu-Jitsu kimono, only grappling, sometimes with strikes. The rules changed, but they always liked to promote the art of Jiu-Jitsu through fights. And when Rorion Gracie created the UFC in America, he took this concept to the rest of the world. He always saw America as a bridge to the rest of the world. And so it worked: Jiu-Jitsu became extremely popular throughout the world because of the UFC and because of Royce's victories in the UFC.

Were the Gracie Brothers competitive amongst one another?

The Gracie brothers were very competitive individuals, and that's why they chose to promote Jiu-Jitsu through fights, through demonstrations of the effectiveness of Jiu-Jitsu in the ring. And they were not only competitive with these fights. You could see it through their habits and their hobbies, they competed in everything they did. They competed with each other, and that's something that was promoted inside the Gracie family. Competition with each other. And so when you talk about the Gracie style of teaching Jiu-Jitsu, especially the way that it's taught today, it has a lot to do with that competitiveness that you find in the Gracie family.

Hélio was presented to the world as a weak individual, but we now

know that he was a successful swimmer and rower to an elite club in Rio de Janeiro prior to training Jiu-Jitsu. Can you comment?

He went to live in Botafogo, in a rowing club. And they had a swimming team, and he became a member of that swim team. It's not something that he talked a lot about, but he told my brother Gui about his experiences as a swimmer. And he was actually swimming competitively. And so when Carlos opens a school in 1930 this was already after Hélio Gracie had become proficient in the sport of swimming, which I'm sure helped him become so good at Jiu-Jitsu so quickly.

What did Hélio teach then? Judo or Jiu-Jitsu? And did he create BJJ?

Grandmaster Hélio always told me that he taught Jiu-Jitsu, and that Jiu-Jitsu was a Japanese art, and that he did not invent a new martial art. He had his own teaching methodology, but he did not create a different style of martial arts. So I believe he taught Japanese Jiu-Jitsu. That's what he taught. As far as something new being created, I would point to the federation in 1967. That when they create a new rule set for the practice of Jiu-Jitsu as a sport, that's something that was original from Brazil. There's a big misconception nowadays about different statements by Grandmaster Hélio which might seem that he contradicted himself, but in my opinion he did not. He always said that he did not invent the art of Jiu-Jitsu. That's something that he always made very clear. But he also said that he is the father or the creator of Brazilian Jiu-Jitsu.

Can you tell us about the fight with Masahiko Kimura?

Hélio Gracie considered his fight with Kimura to be one of the most important, if not the most important one, in his career. Because it was a chance for him to measure himself against the true Japanese champion... His objective was to survive. And so he spent the entire match defending himself. And the fact that he was able to go all the way to the

355

end of the first round, ten minutes, was a great victory for him. And then in the second round Kimura threw him again, and this time after attacking the same lock—and people sometimes forget that in the newspaper O Globo, *on the day of the fight, October 23,1951, there's a picture of Hélio Gracie showing the Kimura lock; he knew that Kimura was going to try to get that move and he practiced the defense—but Kimura insisted so much, so technical and so persistent, that he was able to catch it.*

In the first round Kimura actually caught Hélio in a choke, a very technical choke by the way. But Hélio refused to tap. He said that Kimura was only applying scissor pressure with his legs on the chest and that was not a real move. But the fact is that if you look at the picture, Kimura's hand was in the collar. And it was a great choke. And Hélio Gracie told us that he fell asleep. He fainted from the choke, but Kimura didn't realize it.... [And he was] impressed that Hélio Gracie did not tap to that choke. In the second round Kimura caught him in the ude garami, which in Brazil they started calling it "Kimura" lock because of that incident. And Hélio Grace still did not tap. And Carlos... Many people think he threw a towel, [but] that's a figure of speech. He didn't throw a towel. He walked into the ring, onto the mat, and pushed Kimura off, thus interrupting the fight. And Kimura was the winner.

Growing up having classes with Grandmaster Hélio, many times we heard from him, of course, the stories of his fight with Masahiko Kimura. And many times he told us that after the fight he was invited by the Japanese to teach at the Kodokan.[13] *At the time he told us that he always felt a little bit suspicious about the Japanese plans, and that's why he never went. Today, even though there are no formal historical traces that lead us to understand exactly how that invitation happened, yes, he told us that many times.*

---

[13] As Pedro says, there is currently no evidence that this invitation ever took place.

Rodrigo Gracie, Royce Gracie, and the author; Author eating açai after the interview with Royce and Rodrigo Gracie.

ROYCE GRACIE

"[Hélio Gracie] was persistent, stubborn. He wants to do it, he's going to do it. And he will stay up all day doing it. There was no such a thing as, 'I'll do it tomorrow.' No. We're going to do it now."

—Royce Gracie, UFC Hall of Famer

In 1993 the world was shocked by a skinny Brazilian in a gi practicing a Japanese martial art and representing a family tradition of fighting without many rules. Pay-per-view, the cage, and the proposition that "anything goes" were all ingredients of a recipe destined to make history and improve martial arts forever; the key ingredient, however, was the unassuming yet confident youth we had scheduled as our next interview.

We met and interviewed Royce Gracie in Los Angeles, where he lives. It was around the time of the IBJJF 2018 World Championship in Long Beach, where I would be cornering my students, and I flew in early to interview the man who got me into BJJ. We met at Rodrigo Gracie's academy and, like in my recent experience at the Valente Brothers' academy, I had an entirely new film crew with me; it just didn't make financial sense to fly out Steve and Jay for just this one interview.

I don't typically get starstruck when I meet famous people, and for the most part I have been disappointed in meeting people I admired. People are people, and fame, money, and success (however we choose to define "success") can't change this. "If we're to come to love a man, the man himself should stay hidden, because as soon as he shows his face, love vanishes," wrote Dostoyevsky, with dreadful wisdom. Nonetheless Royce had been a hero of mine during my youth, and for a second I forgot that I was also a Black Belt, forgot my own accomplishments, forgot even the documentary and was staring down the man who had set my 16-year-old self on his life's path.

Royce, like his father later in life, wore a Navy Blue belt. Hélio, I understood, wore his in protest of what he saw as falling standards in the BJJ community and the speed with which practitioners were being promoted to Black Belt. It was a return to the original belt rank system employed by the Gracie Academy before the Guanabara Federation was created: originally, and prior to the creation of the belt ranking system used today, instructors and older practitioners at the Gracie Academy wore a Navy Blue Belt as the only colored rank; all other students wore white belts. I wondered why Royce wore his, and I thought back to an article I had written about Rorion's sons, Rener and Ryron, selling belts online. Hélio would have turned over in his grave, I thought at the time. Now I wondered if he didn't have to: if Royce, by wearing the Navy Blue Belt, was making the statement of protest for him.

This interview was important to us not only because of what Royce might have to say about BJJ's history but also because of the role he'd played in it. Simply put, he is an icon of a martial arts revolution that, in my view, rivals the creation of Kano's Judo in its impact. Hollywood had inserted martial arts into pop culture and the public psyche with screen idols like Bruce Lee, but even if we consider Bruce Lee a pioneer and a visionary we must admit that his role is dwarfed by what Royce did in the UFC. Royce's success fundamentally changed the way the world understood fighting. Rorion's marketing scheme could not have worked better, and hand-to-hand combat would never be the same.

In reality, Royce would spearhead not one but two revolutions. It may have been a coincidence that the UFC and the CBJJ/IBJJF were founded in 1993 and 1994 respectively, but the fact remains that neither of these organizations would have made a dent in the martial arts world without the right poster boy. Royce's performances in those early UFCs would mark the beginning of not one but two new brands of martial arts that would become not only my two main life passions but also those of millions of practitioners in the coming years.

Of course, he could not have done any of this on his own: it is, perhaps, more accurate to see Royce as the first wave of a swell that was a long time coming to the world's shores. History is too complex, and events too intertwined, for any one person or event to stand on their own: our interviewee, to us at least, represented the culmination of a long and complex history full of unlikely turns, bitter rivalries, aggressive marketing campaigns, and cunning retellings.

Cordial and eager to speak, Royce was easy to get along with; I did, however, sense an initial edge of suspicion in his demeanor. Perhaps he was concerned that we would attempt to belittle his father's legacy. We knew he wouldn't tell us anything we didn't already know in terms of BJJ history, as he would merely be repeating what he had heard from his father (which wouldn't be much, since Hélio had "invented" BJJ, and thus by definition it didn't have a history that predated himself). Like with the Valente Brothers, our initial concern was that we would encounter hostility; like with the Valente Brothers, this concern was unwarranted. Though at times Royce would be a bit defensive in his answers, the overall vibe was pleasant and the interview went well.

Naturally we were aware that our project might be viewed with suspicion. After all: if we were setting out to tell a new narrative then we must stand in opposition to the prevailing one, right? Our team went to great pains in our effort to counter this perception. Nonetheless, the problem remains that there is no way to tell this story without correcting misconceptions, pointing out omissions, and clarifying outright exaggerations. At times this put us at odds with our interviewees and the stories they told. Throughout the process we held to the principle that facts can't be biased, and that if anyone dislikes them then it's their issue. Despite our preferences, our outrage, or our denial, the facts remain unscathed.

After the interview Royce, Rodrigo Gracie, and I went to a local açaí spot together. It was a nice break from the interview mode, and great to be able to talk in a relaxed manner to a living piece of history, and the man who'd helped steer me onto my life's course.

—

Coincidentally, as I finish writing this chapter, it's been exactly two years (to the day) since my interview with Royce. Thinking back on it and looking over old pictures, I find myself wondering again about my own journey. I'd gone from renting a VHS tape in the mid-'90s with Royce and Dan Severn on the cover to taking my friend's recommendation that I should try it out myself to actually showing up to practice and getting tapped (twice) by a girl to living the BJJ competition life for so many years to fighting MMA to getting involved in this film to finally being able to buy the man who'd inspired my life's journey an açaí bowl. Who would have thought?

— Royce Gracie —

Could you introduce yourself?

I am Royce Gracie. And I'm a product of my father's work, son of Hélio Gracie, the famous Gracie family from Brazil. And I came to America in 1984. And in 1993 my brother, Rorion created the UFC. And I was the representative of the Gracie family there, representing Gracie Jiu-Jitsu.

In what way did your family help to spread BJJ around the world?

The Jiu-Jitsu growth all over the world, it was a quest that my family had. A lot of people thought, "Oh my God, the Gracies are arro-

gant. They're trying to put down the other styles of martial arts." No. It was a quest that my family had to find out which style of martial art is the best. And there's only one way to find out: by taking all the rules out, taking all the time limits, weight divisions. Put two men in the ring or a cage and put it to the test. So that quest, it started a long time ago with my family in Brazil. Once they learned Jiu-Jitsu, that was the quest. And my brother brought the concept to America, Rorion did. And he created the UFC.

What was the role of your father, Hélio Gracie, in the development of BJJ?

The main contribution that my father gave to Jiu-Jitsu was the growth of the sport or of the Gracie family, to the Gracie family. It was that he was persistent, stubborn. He wants to do it, he's going to do it. And he will stay up all day doing it. There was no such a thing as, "I'll do it tomorrow." No. We're going to do it now.

How did your father first come in contact with Jiu-Jitsu?

What I learned from my father is that he learned... I mean, Esai Maeda came to Brazil, taught my uncles. And he was doing business in Brazil... with my grandfather, [and in the good faith of business] he taught my uncles the art of Jiu-Jitsu. And my father learned by watching my uncles teach class. So yes, Uncle Carlos was the main instructor that my father had visually. You see, that was his example to follow. So I think that's, I mean, that's what I heard all my life from him. He learned by watching my uncles teach class and studying. He was too weak to do it. He was a smaller person, so he had to develop this style. Or not develop, but adapt the style for himself so he can defend himself against somebody bigger and stronger. So yes, he was the main tool for the development of Jiu-Jitsu in Brazil. And the world.

Do you recognize names such as Yassuiti Ono and Oswaldo Fadda? If so, what did your father think of them?

Yes, I recognize the name Ono, Fadda. Yes. They were opponents for my father. I'm trying to think over here. My father was a type of person that never put no opponent down. So as far as I remember, when he'd talk about Ono and Fadda, they were tough guys, but again, it was a quest. It was a challenge. He would be like, "I cannot see how they're going to beat me. Let's do it. They're good. So I want to see how good their Jiu-Jitsu is, if they can beat me." That was my father's mentality, instead of putting somebody down. I never heard him saying anything bad about an opponent.

Today we know that the Gracie Academy was not founded in 1925. Do you believe this will change anything in our history?

The historical dates of who found, who created the first Gracie Academy in Brazil, with Uncle Carlos and Gastão and George and the brothers, the Gracie brothers, it doesn't really matter to me. It doesn't change who I am today. I learned Gracie Jiu-Jitsu from my father, Hélio Gracie. That's what I say all the time. I'm a product of my father's work.

Your father has the reputation for having been very strict. How was he?

My father was like... People like to say that my father kept a very military schedule. And yes, he was very much like this. Man, have you seen the size of this family? You have to be somehow a military. I am like this today. I try to be on time every time, try to get my kids up and on time. And everybody makes their bed. And everybody is organized. And yes, my father was like this. But not in a mean way. He was very much of a "I'll do it myself" type of person. So it's not like he was trying to militarize everybody in the family.

Your father, towards the end of his life, wore a Navy Blue Belt in protest. What was he protesting?

My father, he was not critical about people that got promoted to Black Belt fast, but he was critical about the way they were promoted. You see? I say that all the time. Say you get a very good Boxer. They'll walk into [a] Karate school and he will knock everybody out. Would that make him a Black Belt in Karate? He doesn't know the system. But then people [say], "Well, but he knocked everybody out." He still doesn't know the system. Because he's a talented athlete, young, fast, and because he is able to fight, doesn't make him a Black Belt in Karate. Same thing with Jiu-Jitsu. It became a young man's sport and people got promoted because they are athletes, because they are good fighters, because they have heart and not because they know the self-defense system. That was my father's criticism to people that got promoted. It's not because of the timing. It's because of knowledge.

Why is your father more known than your other uncles?

It doesn't mean that the other uncles were less or they did less, but they did not follow Uncle Carlos' vision as much as my father. My father was more attached to Uncle Carlos and follow[ed] his leadership more than the other uncles. So yes, that's why it was almost like we don't have much history on them, their fighting career, and academies, and the following that they had wasn't as big as Uncle Carlos and Hélio's.

What were the early days of BJJ in the U.S. like?

Rorion, when he came to America, like when I first came to America in 1984, nobody knows Gracie family, Jiu-Jitsu. You open up any martial arts magazine in America it was all about Hapkido, Taekwondo, Aikido. There was no grappling at all. Grapplers. I'm talking Judo and Wrestlers. They tell me all the time, "Hey, thanks [to] your family we are considered to be martial artists now." Because in 1984, '85, when I first came over here, they were not in any martial arts maga-

zine. They were not considered to be martial artists. Martial arts were Kung Fu, Karate, Taekwondo. Those are martial arts.

What was your brother Rorion's role in all of this?

He brought the concept to America and created the first UFC. It was more of a quest again when he did the eight-man tournament, a sixteen-man tournament. And by putting me to fight, people would say, "Well, what if you would have lost?" I don't think it would have changed what my family's done in Brazil, where Gracie Jiu-Jitsu would have continued to be what it is. Maybe the development of Gracie Jiu-Jitsu wouldn't be as fast all over the world, because what happens in Brazil nobody knows. Today it's a little easier with the technology, [the] internet, but back then nobody knew what was happening in Brazil. Nobody knew who Hélio Gracie was. Only in Brazil. But then, once America found out, the whole world found out. It took a few years, but the whole world found out what's the style that's superior to all the other styles, to be able to choke them out and you don't have to beat the opponent up. You can just take them down, control the opponent, and apply the submission. And who creates this stuff again? Hold on, where you came from? So, yes. Rorion was very important on developing Jiu-Jitsu all over the world.

What was the role of your cousin Carlos Gracie, Jr.?

Carlinhos Gracie, or Carlos Gracie, Jr., created the federation [IBJJF]. It helped explode the sport of Jiu-Jitsu all over the world. So people today come from all corners of the world to compete in Jiu-Jitsu. Again, it's a challenge—a personal challenge to test themselves out with the best. The competition, the tournaments. I'm personally against competition in general. My point of view, the martial art was made for you to defend yourself in a street confrontation, for you to defend yourself. Not to score a point. But when Carlos create the federation, it exploded all over the world. There're schools all over practicing Jiu-Jitsu.

Do you know if anyone ever promoted your father or Carlos Gracie to Black Belt?

I don't think they ever got a Black Belt. I think, I mean... The way I heard from my father, the way I heard from my father was [in] the beginning the belt system was white belt, a light blue, and a royal dark Navy Blue for the instructors. When they create the federation, the Jiu-Jitsu federation in Rio in Brazil, then they award to my father and Uncle Carlos a Red Belt, being that's the highest rank. So I don't think my father ever put a Black Belt on. He went from royal Navy Blue, dark blue, straight to Red Belt.

What about your other uncles?

Same thing. Yeah. I don't know, the uncles... Honestly I can't say about the other uncles because I have almost none, never met some of the uncles. George, Gastão, and Oswaldo, I don't even remember if I met them. If I did it was [when I was] very young, very little. Don't remember. But Uncle Carlos and my father, I never saw them with a Black Belt.

Some historians believe your Uncle Carlos had little or no contact with Maeda. Does this bother you?

It doesn't matter to me. It doesn't matter how long Uncle Carlos and George, Gastão, Oswaldo, and my father, how long they met Esai Maeda, how long they trained with him for. Look what they did. If it was six months, oh my God. He only trained with him six months. Credit for Esai Maeda because look what he created. Look what he was able to do. That means he was a good teacher. "Oh, they trained for two years, three years." Awesome. Look at what they did. Even three years is nothing. A student that trains three years today is not much. It's just a beginner. And somebody he was be able to train for a little amount of time, and able to develop all this? Wow.

What is the importance of completing BJJ history?

It's very important that people like you are doing this documentary to complete the missing pieces of the history, pieces that I don't know. The history, the little that I know, is what my father told us [at] the dinner table, let's say. So yes, I'm glad somebody's doing this.

*Upper left: The author with Bolelli and his girlfriend, professional fighter Sovan-nahry Em; Upper right: Daniele Bolelli with his daughter; Bottom: Author, schol-ar, and martial artist Daniele Bolelli and his **History on Fire** podcast.*

DANIELE BOLELLI

"[I]nitially, what the Gracies practiced was Judo. Was that old-time Judo. So, different from Judo today. It was Judo pre- all the changes in rules. So there was a lot of ground-fighting. There were things like leg-locks, which don't exist in Judo now."

—Daniele Bolelli, Professor and Author

A documentary production differs from a scripted film in more than a few ways. In the latter the director tells the actors what they will say and how they will act their lines; in the former the questions are asked of those who can best answer them according to the story the documentary is planning to tell and based on the interviewee's knowledge and ability to answer. The emphasis here is on "planning," because all we could do was guess where the questions would take us.

With this in mind, we had focused our questions on what we saw as the most relevant events in Brazil as well as the characters who had played a central role in BJJ's development. We knew we wouldn't be able to tackle the entire history of the sport all the way up to the UFC and the formation of the CBJJ/IBJJF, and had decided early on that the Kimura versus Hélio fight decisively marked an end to an era and the beginning of a new one that was less controversial, and with which the average practitioner was more likely to be familiar. Further, the Kimura fight seemed to illustrate the nature of the growing rift between the Brazilians and the Japanese in terms of how they practiced Judo, and took place during a time in which Judo was growing rapidly worldwide while the niche practice centered around the Gracie Academy remained small by comparison.

We had an ending: the problem was that we didn't know where to begin. Originally we'd thought to start off with Maeda's arrival in Brazil, and use this as a vehicle for discussing the phenomenon and impact of Japanese immigration. As we learned more, however, it seemed clear that this approach would skip over too much rich history: if, after all, these Japanese immigrants were practicing and teaching Judo, then that meant that the story began elsewhere. We couldn't just skip over the history of Judo. If we told the history of Judo, however, we opened the door to the history of the arts that preceded it and from which it is derived. It was, as the story goes, "turtles all the way down."

One of the most commonly held beliefs regarding Jiu-Jitsu is that it had its origins in India: traveling Buddhists monks, the story goes, being both vulnerable to attack by bandits and religiously averse to violence, needed to develop a system of martial arts by which they could defend themselves without injuring or killing their attackers. Still, regardless of how loosely one defines "Jiu-Jitsu," I have never seen any conclusive evidence linking it to India (or China, for that matter).

I actually spent quite a bit of time trying to figure out where the origins of the "Jiu-Jitsu in India" myth started, but I never had any luck until Pedro Valente emailed me screenshots of a booklet from the Federação do Estado do Rio de Janeiro dating from approximately 1975 that gives the "Buddhist Monks in India" origin story. If there is something older, I don't know of it. Interestingly, that document states that, "Apesar de contraditórias versões, a origem do Jiu-Jitsu é in-egavelmente, atribuída à Índia, bêrço das religiões e de cultura inigualável." ("Despite contradictory versions, the origin of Jiu-Jitsu is undeniably attributed to India, birth place of the religions and of unmatched culture.") The combination of the certitude of the text and the complete lack of sources put me in mind of the official narrative of BJJ history.

Further on, the booklet presents more of the commonly-known mythology about the origins of the Gentle Art: it discusses Maeda's role while also making the claim that Kano's Judo was no more than a crass attempt to sell a "Jiu-Jitsu falsificado" (a "false Jiu-Jitsu," i.e. a Jiu-Jitsu from which the true secrets of the ancient art had been re-moved) to curious Westerners. Needless to say, this heavily biased and limited explanation makes no attempt to explain that, in creating Judo, Jigoro Kano was attempting to create a new school more in tune with the modern times and the changes Japan was going through. Not to mention that, like other Brazilians of the time, the writer would have had no way of knowing what "non-falsified Jiu-Jitsu" would have looked like, and thus no contrast on which to base his claim.

This booklet—which might well be the origin of at least some of the myths surrounding BJJ—didn't get everything wrong, however: it did mark the opening of Japan to the West as the catalyst for the cre-ation of Judo and, subsequently, BJJ many decades later. Japan suf-fered forced and rapid modernization from 1854 onwards: it went

369

from being a feudal society to defeating a modern European army just fifty years later. An impressive feat, but one that came at the cost of many of Japan's traditional ways of being. All peoples go through (suffer?) changes, this goes without saying, but the forced integration of Western ideas and values, many of which the traditional Japanese found offensive, certainly took its toll on this country's sense of identity—while helping to form a new one.

For better or for worse is not the point here: our purpose is to understand what happened, and what came as a result. Jigoro Kano was born into this changing world, and what is perhaps most interesting is the way in which he assimilated those changes and absorbed what he felt was valuable. He absorbed Western ideas of physical education and sport which are not indigenously Japanese. He was influenced by British philosopher and evolutionary theorist Herbert Spencer, the man who first coined the term "survival of the fittest"; his art would also borrow a move or two from Western Wrestling. It is easy, then, to see Judo as a product of the changing world in which it was codified, and not merely a product of Japan's traditions.

Starting out, we did not understand any of this: when we sat down to write our original questions for our interviewees we had close to nothing addressing the history of Judo. Nor did we seek out anyone who could speak on it with the degree of authority we wanted, except Sensei Murata. It was late in the production when we realized that the formation of Judo, and its fusion of Eastern and Western matrixes, was too rich a story and too important an element to completely leave out. The problem was that we had little to no A-Roll regarding this history. Still, we were now convinced that it had to be told, one way or the other.

It was around this time that Jay Coleman introduced me to Daniele Bolelli. A UCLA Professor and a lifelong student of the martial arts and its history, as well as an author and host of the *Drunken Taoist* and *History on Fire* podcasts, Bolelli was already on our radar: at one point we'd even considered asking him to be our film's narrator. In the end, though, we decided we could make better use of him as an interviewee. We were counting on Bolelli to deliver the soundbites necessary to finish the segment of the film we were struggling with the most.

I met up with Bolleli at a Thai restaurant in Hollywood. We talked about history, politics, parenthood, and other topics in which we shared a common interest, as well as his role in our documentary. I immediately developed a liking for Bolelli: I found him to be intelligent, charismatic, and full of life. We had a lot in common: so much, in fact, in terms of our interests and the authors we liked, that I felt we had enough to talk about for many dinners.

I explained to him the difficulty we were having with the pre-Meiji era in Japan, and our goal of completing BJJ history and introducing it to an entirely new audience. He was very supportive and enthusiastic about the prospect of helping in any way he could. I was happy also to learn that he was familiar with *Choque* by Roberto Pedreira, and to find that we were on the same page in regards to our views on the martial arts in general, well beyond the history of BJJ.

That first meeting would be the beginning of a friendship that would extend beyond our shared interest in martial arts. Our conversations would range over life and its challenges, and I dare say that in our encounters he taught me something of great value. Introspection and insight often come from psychological stress and strife, and many great thinkers have a reputation for having suffered for their aptitude. Still, despite his undeniable wisdom, Bolelli seemed to me rather cheerful about life: a man content and at peace with his differences with the world. The martial arts journey, I was learning, isn't exclusively about self-defense and/or fitness, but also about self-development and spiritual growth. Though I have disliked and avoided the word "spiritual" for most of my life, I can understand it today within the context of my martial arts journey and our need for balance in everything we do in life. This I am learning thanks, to a large extent, to the perspective given to me by Daniele Bolelli.

Bolelli's interview would be at his home in Southern California. Unfortunately I was unable to make the trip, and the work ended up being done by a local camera crew. It worried me not being there, but at the same time I had heard Bolelli speak many times and I knew that he could deliver. I just hoped that the camera crew would too and, after many long phone calls with the hired team carefully explaining our needs and going over our instructions, the interview went well.

— Daniele Bolelli —

Could you introduce yourself?

My name is Daniele Bolelli, I teach history in college, I host a couple of podcasts, and I write books.

Who was Jigoro Kano?

Anybody who practices any type of martial art today owes a huge debt to a Japanese man who lived between the latter part of the 1800s and the early 1900s. That's Kano Jigoro. He was the creator of Judo. Now, if you don't practice Judo, why would you feel a debt to this guy? Well, he was more than the creator of Judo. He's the guy who in many ways created a space for the very existence of martial arts in the modern world.

Kano started training as a young boy. It's the classic Karate Kid story, right? Young weaker boy who starts training like crazy, gains the strength, gets empowered. [And he's] unlike most people who practice martial arts at the time... They were more thugs than anything. Kano was an intellectual. He was a really bright guy. He was really smart.

How did the creation of Judo take place?

What happened was this: in the late 1800s in Japan they were going [through] a period of very fast modernization, where a lot of their traditional past didn't seem to apply to modern circumstances anymore. So what happened was that the West had the same problem. You know there were many schools of martial arts in the West that died out because there was no point to them anymore, from a practical stand-

point. The only reason why we have martial arts is because Kano fig-ured out a way—at least for Asian martial arts—to justify their exis-tence. He wanted to make an argument for why people should train them. Even at the time when, from a practical standpoint, it didn't make sense to train martial arts. And what Kano argues [is] that training martial arts was a form of education. Now that's a bit of a stretch on the surface. It's like, let's try that again. How exactly [is] training to choke each other out, or punch each other in the face, a form of education? Kano managed to provide a good answer to that. He started arguing how, through training, people learn lessons that can be applied not just to physical combat. They can apply to everything else in life. How physical combat is basically just a specif-ic area, a specific context, in which you can apply some principles. But the principles can be applied in life. So Kano [played] a bit of a game, because he's like, "Oh, you think martial arts are about fight-ing? No no, no, martial arts are about life and education, and your spiritual development." Which is not exactly an easy argument to make, but he made it well. And so suddenly what happened is that, at a time when in Japan they were ready to get rid of all their martial arts, and [the martial arts] would die a slow death, Kano provided a rationale [for] why martial arts should be taught in school. And he eventually became an educator and played a big role in the develop-ment of the education curriculum in Japan.

How did the creation of the Kodokan take place?

So here is what happens. The martial art that Kano started was called Jū-Jutsu. When he opened the Kodokan, which was his first school, which is… it's kind of funny when you think about it. Because his first school was a tiny space, probably slightly bigger than most people's garages today. That was the birth of Judo. That was the birth of modern martial arts. He was 22 years old, and he was doing it in a tiny space. And what happened in that space changed the world.

Why did he call his art "Judo"?

He wanted to use the term "do," which means "the way." He was trying to emphasize that his martial art was a way of life, not just a series of techniques.

Why did Judo practitioners in Brazil refer to it as Jiu-Jitsu?

When Judo arrived in Brazil people initially used the terms Judo and Jiu-Jitsu kind of interchangeably, because Kano had started [in] Jiu-Jitsu. His art was based on traditional Japanese schools of Jū-Jutsu. He modified the curriculum a little bit. So he kind of revamped the Jū-Jutsu curriculum, gave it a philosophical grounding, called it Judo. But of course there was a lot of overlap. A lot of his best students were coming from Jū-Jutsu and just happened to like some of the Judo philosophy, so they switched to Judo.

Were the Gracies practicing Jiu-Jitsu or Judo?

No, initially what the Gracies practiced was Judo. Was that old-time Judo. So, different from Judo today. It was Judo pre- all the changes in rules. So there was a lot of ground-fighting. There were things like leg-locks, which don't exist in Judo. There were all sorts of techniques that were part of the Judo curriculum. But what we know as Judo today is a bonsai version of what it used to be, because so much of the curriculum has been cut down for the sake of making it fit within a sport format. That's what you see in the Olympics.

How did the split between Judo in BJJ occur?

Brazilian Jiu-Jitsu started focusing less and less on the throws that characterized Judo, and emphasized primarily the ground-fighting aspect of the art. Judo went the exact opposite way. As time went by they started reducing the ground techniques to favor the stand up, because it was more spectacular for the average person who doesn't know anything about the sport.

How was Judo/Jiu-Jitsu becoming popular around the world at that time?

Teddy Roosevelt, the President of the United States, started Judo under some of the guys that Kano sent to him. Plus there were also people who were just traveling because they were traveling, period. There were people who [were] migrating to other countries. There was a lot of Japanese migration to South America, Brazil in particular. Some of these guys [had studied] Judo. So there were a few of them who started bringing the art with them.

Who was Mitsuyo Maeda "Count Koma"?

One of the guys who was most famous is Mitsuyo Maeda. Or, the Japanese way: Maeda Mitsuyo. He was who arrived early on and kind of created the mythology of Brazilian Jiu-Jitsu as being the guy to bring what [would] become Brazilian Jiu-Jitsu. And then the Gracie family studied under him, and they developed Brazilian Jiu-Jitsu. Well, that's a bit of a simplified version of the story. First, [he] wasn't the only guy in Brazil teaching—there were people who were already teaching before him—[and] second, there are debates about exactly how much time he spent teaching people in general, or the Gracies specifically. But the point being: he was part of this wave of migration from Japan to Brazil that brought the art there. And then the modifications over time led to what we now know as Brazilian Jiu-Jitsu.

Why did these Japanese immigrants go to Brazil?

I think it was just economics. It was just economic opportunities.

How did the spread of Judo/Jiu-Jitsu take place in Brazil?

One of the ways in which martial arts seemed to spread in Brazil [is] it seems to kind of go back. Whereas Kano had taken the art from the tough gangsters and [brought] it to a more educated crowd, once it arrived in Brazil it started going the other way in a lot of ways. It went back to, "Yeah, the philosophy is great and all, but can you fight?" Let's throw those two guys on the mat and let's see what happens. In Brazil there was a lot more of this tradition of challenge fights.

What was the role of the Gracie Brothers in all of this?

Well, the role of the Gracies is tricky to say the least. Because they certainly marketed themselves better than any other Brazilian Jiu-Jitsu family. In the early days of [the] Ultimate Fighting Championship, the Gracie name was almost synonymous with Brazilian Jiu-Jitsu. [But it's] not that simple. There were many other people who practiced Jiu-Jitsu in Brazil. There were other schools that did very well for themselves.

Who were the students of the Gracie Academy?

Now the Gracies, unlike other practitioners of Jiu-Jitsu in Brazil, they were more catering to the upper classes. A lot of the Gracie clientele was upper class, richer Brazilian crowd. There are other schools of Jiu-Jitsu [that] were very much from the lower classes of Brazil. And that's why sometimes some of the clashes didn't just have a school against school aspect, [they] also had a class aspect to [them]. And an ethnic one, [too], because of course the rich and poor —there was definitely a color element to that story.

Can you talk about the match between Hélio and Kimura?

So the fight between Hélio Gracie and Kimura Masahiko was pretty funny. Because in the Gracie mythology the fight was this moral victory for Hélio: who was the smaller guy; who resisted for thirteen minutes against this big, huge guy. So even though he lost, he really won. Kimura kicked his ass from pillar to post for the entire thirteen *minutes. He threw him with just about every throw in the Kodokan book. So technically there really wasn't much of a match. Kimura just rolled over him. And eventually he broke [Hélio's] arm. He got him in the technique that will take his name, [that] will become known as the Kimura. Hélio didn't tap so Kimura kept applying it [and] popped his arm. Hélio still didn't tap, [Kimura] kept applying it [and] popped his arm a second time. [Hélio] still didn't tap. Eventually one of Hélio's brothers came in and threw in the towel and that was that. So the one thing that Hélio demonstrated was being monstrously tough. He took a beating like few people would be able to. So totally hats off for that. Really tough individual. In terms of the match, Kimura dominated. [It] wasn't even close. But of course, that—in the Gracie [public relations] machine—got spun a little bit to make it a cooler story for the Gracie family.*

Upper left: Reenactment of Maeda teaching self-defense for his book; Upper right: Reenactment of the opening of the Academia de Jiu-Jitsu, from left to right: actors portraying Carlos Gracie, Donato Pires dos Reis, and George Gracie; Lower left: Brad and Jay film the George Gracie Vale Tudo reenactment; Lower right: Actor portraying as Geo Omori

POST-PRODUCTION

Coming into this project, the only experience I had with film was watching them; accordingly, just about everything about the production was a new lesson for me. For example: I had no idea how much a film cost, or that post-production was exponentially more expensive than filming and traveling; nor did I have any idea how difficult it would be to write a script for what would turn out to be such a wide-ranging and complex topic. Conscious of all of this, I walked into my new role with an open mind about the things I didn't know, but a confidence that I could learn them. One thing fighting will do is make

378

you confident that you can do just about anything in life because there is nothing in life more challenging than fighting. Neither chess nor physics nor CrossFit nor film production compares to the emotional, physical, technical, and intellectual effort required in a fight. I know I am biased here, and that some will disagree, but this is how I feel about it. Unfortunately my habit of stepping confidently into totally unknown circumstances often has the side effect of irritating those around me, as it often falls to them to pick up the pieces when I inevitably make a mess starting out in a new endeavor; our film's production would prove to be no exception.

As soon as we came back from Japan it was obvious that our team had lost momentum. I agreed that we needed a little break, but in my mind I still imagined us getting into the reenactments, the final interviews, and the editing process right away. I was mostly speaking to Brad, as our post-production manager, during this time, and he explained to me that a film is like a layered cake in which "A" (for example, the editing) could not precede "B" (for example, filming the reenactments). Fair enough. Still, even though I was busy with my academies, team, seminars, commentating, parenting, and a master's program, I wanted to make our film a priority, and I wasn't too happy that our team was involved in many other projects, and that our film was taking a backseat to them. I had given our investor a schedule, and I wanted to meet it at any cost.

This wasn't the only point of contention, however. Brad and I had reached a point where we disagreed on pretty much everything, and we decided it was best for him to leave the production. Unfortunately, though, even this drastic change would prove insufficient to get our project back on track. Other members of the team had concerns. They were worried that the film we were making would be boring, or that we would come across as "haters," and that I was acting out of some sort of personal "vendetta" I held against the Gracie family. At some point during production I started receiving hate mail citing my losses to Roger Gracie as my motivation for this film, all of which I thought to be absolutely ridiculous. I had entered this project with the intention to be informative and impartial: if people interpreted the intentions behind our film incorrectly then as far as I was concerned that was their prerogative, a symptom of their own ignorance and bias, and I couldn't be held accountable. The team, however, did not share my indifference: they worried that this sentiment among the BJJ community would negatively affect the film's reception and reach. By the time this conversation came to a head it was just a drop in the bucket, however: the team disagreed on just about everything and we were nearing an impasse.

During my early exchanges with Jay he had sent me a short trailer Steve had shot for a film titled *The Architect*. The film told the story of a man who built prosthetic legs with rudimentary materials for children victims of land mines in Africa. In about two minutes that trailer had me on the verge of tears, and I felt certain I had found the team who could help me forever change how the history of Jiu-Jitsu in Brazil would be understood. It wasn't just that they had the film experience I lacked: it was clear from the trailer that they were passionate and good at what they did. Now, however, we were butting up against a funda-mental lack of agreement about what film we were making. Fabio and I wanted to make an archival film: to us popularity and acceptance were beside the point; it was all about the facts. The rest of the team wanted something that would reach a broad audience, something that even a non-practitioner could and would appreciate, something aesthetically pleasing to the viewer. A somewhat ironic conflict, given that normally it is the executive producer who is worried about sales and reception and the filmmakers who have to fight for the more niche elements. My initial script was loaded with all the information I considered to be rele-vant to the story, and skipped any colloquial language; the Virginia team wanted something that focused on the beauty of BJJ rather than its unknown historical events and characters. This all came as a shock to me, since I felt we were clear on what we were doing from the begin-ning. At one point, while going over Brad's notes on my script, I came across a comment that seemed to cut right to the very heart of our mis-aligned priorities. It was written in the margin beside the segment talk-ing about how Jacyntho Ferro was Carlos Gracie's main instructor, and not Maeda. The note read, "Who cares?"

I rarely get emotional when dealing with people, especially in business, and I don't have an issue responding to an insult with a compliment as long as they are both true (the opposite hold equally true). I am also perfectly capable of maintaining a professional and productive work environment focused on the mission at hand with people who are willing to do the same, regardless of our differences. But I don't relent on things I feel right and passionate about, and, in terms of this film, I was not ready to surrender my original intent of retelling BJJ history, nor the promise I'd made to Mairbek Khasiev, simply because people didn't understand the film's mission. Nor was I open to making a film that was completely devoid of any meaningful historical substance out of a concern that one of the Gracies might sue us.

I felt that I had to put my foot down: otherwise, I feared, we would end up with a film consisting of beautiful B-Roll wrapped around re-cycled propaganda. The team, to their credit, shared my fear, but in the opposite direction: they worried that if things were done entirely my and Fabio's way we would have made something incredibly bor-ing that only researchers and the most hard-core of martial arts stu-dents would appreciate. In the end I relented more than I ever thought I would, and acknowledged that if something were too monotonous then it would drag on, and that if only the most knowledgeable and dedicated viewers watched the film and appreciated the end result then we would have failed in our mission to tell the story to the mass-es. As before it was clear that our differences, if properly balanced, could be an asset rather than a source of intractable conflict... the trick was finding this balance.

Issues were also cropping up around the pace at which we were moving forward. Fabio is far less patient than I am, and after a year of post-production, with three reenactments filmed (the George Gracie, Donato, and Maeda ones) and a lot of arguments over the script, he left the production in protest. Prior to this Jay and I had been working as buffers between Fabio and Steve to keep the whole thing together: at various points during this period I was close to replacing the team myself due to their tardiness and procrastination. In the end, though, given that I had already paid them for half the work, it didn't make financial sense. Beyond this, I truly appreciated Steve's passion, and I'd been impressed by his work ethic and talent while we were in Brazil and Japan. He was good at what he did, he'd worked hard during those days, and I felt a sense of loyalty to his talent and his effort. I felt similarly about Jay, who not once throughout our travels and production raised his voice to complain about anything. Fabio didn't feel the same way and, even though we never had a direct issue about it, I know he was angry at me for not having a more confrontational stance towards the rest of the team.

Fabio's departure left me in a complicated position. Fabio was supposed to do any further research the film required, and provide whatever documents we needed to corroborate our narration. Now it fell to me to fulfill this role as well. Not that this was such a burden: research is time-consuming, and some people find it tedious, but I enjoyed the "the needle in a haystack" process. After finding a few original articles in the Brazilian National Library I felt like I could actually do this for a living (that is: if I had the time, and if it paid well enough. Unfortunately I don't, and it doesn't).

The upshot of all of this is that, by the final phases, a production that really needed a team of twenty or more experts was down to a rookie executive producer and historian, Jay, Steve, and Daniel, who was just beginning in his role as editor. For my part, I knew my limitations: I knew that I didn't know everything about this history and would need assistance. I reached out to Roberto Pedreira, who graciously agreed to help. Roberto would prove vital to the process that followed, not only correcting our scripts but also giving me sound and reasonable advice, all while refusing to be paid. Later on Marcial, Elton Silva, and even Fabio would assist me as well, all free of charge.

Though we were managing as best we could, at times things seemed to grind to a halt. I wanted to move forward faster, wanted more done sooner, and I got frustrated. The team's "You don't know what you're talking about" argument—their go-to saying whenever there was any contention between our views—was getting old, and didn't hold water anymore. During these times it was Jay who held things together, and who pulled the film back from the brink of collapse.

The solution to all of this was—of course—balance. There was a part of me that wished I had acted decisively and in a more assertive fashion from the start, as Fabio repeatedly requested: this would have undoubtedly expedited the film, as well as caused me less stress, but I knew that it would also have hurt the end result. I had to keep reminding myself that I was the one who was new to film, while these were talented experts who knew their craft. Deadlines are deadlines, though, and experience of any level doesn't (or shouldn't) exempt anyone.

Still, the length of the post-production process had its upsides: shortly before leaving the team late in 2018, Fabio had found the last living student of Luis França, a man named Antonio Vieira (1930-2020). We all agreed that he was certainly worth interviewing, and Fabio took the lead with a crew we hired in Brazil. Meanwhile, Jay paid a visit to his coach's son, Darlynson Lira from the Francisco Sá lineage, and interviewed him as well. Also during this period I made a trip to Cuba (not with funds from the film), where I had both my knees treated and taught a seminar for their Olympic Judo team (interestingly enough, their head Judo coach insisted on calling what I taught "Brazilian Judo"). While in Cuba I took the opportunity to hire a local historian, Nileyan Rodriguez, to help me research in their National Archives (this *was* paid for with funds from the film). I was looking for anything related to Maeda and his visits to that country and, though we found less than expected, we still came across some exclusive pictures of Maeda that made the effort more than worth it. (We shared everything we found with Roberto Pedreira for *Craze: Volume 3*, the book he was working on at that time.) Had the post-production not taken so long, we would not have been able to include these elements.

My original goal was to finish the movie within a year; instead it would be almost three years from the beginning of the process to the film's completion. Though it was ambitious, I still think my original goal would have been possible… if everyone on our team had made our project a top priority.

At any rate, as I was still learning, life is about balance and balance is about dialogue, concession, and the effort to understand the other side's point of view, as well as your own flaws and shortcomings. The problem with having a single mind heading any operation is that, no matter how experienced, intelligent, capable, principled, and righteous that person may be, any endeavor will be subjected to unknown unknowns. How can a single mind know or see it all? Because of this grave mistakes are almost inevitable, and history is filled with examples of the failures and blind-spots of authoritarian rule. While the committee's balanced and democratic approach can be challenging, stressful, frustrating, and slow, the wisdom derived from informed, pragmatic, and rational debate is less subject to the fatal errors that lead to total collapse: a lesson we all need to heed beyond BJJ history and filmmaking, in a world of increasingly binary views.

— Antonio Vieira —

Could you introduce yourself?

My name is Antônio Vieira da Silva, I was born on February 5, 1930, and I am 88 years old. Married, father of four children, and I live in Rio de Janeiro

Tell us about your beginnings in Judo/Jiu-Jitsu.

I have been playing sports since 1948. I started in Natal, Rio Grande do Norte, on the occasion of my entry into the Marine Corps, and there I met a Marine Corporal named Luis França and took my first steps with him training during our physical education class. In 1949 I was transferred to Rio de Janeiro and brought with me the address of a man called Oswaldo Fadda from Jiu-Jitsu here in Rio de Janeiro, who was a student of Luis França.

Who did Luis França learn Jiu-Jitsu from?

Luis de França said he learned what he knew from Maeda, who used the pseudonym of Count Koma. Count Koma died in '41, so he was left without a teacher. Then Corporal Luis França was deployed to Natal and later came to Rio de Janeiro, where he met Oswaldo Fadda.

Was your first teacher Luis França?

Yes, but he was not a trained teacher and did not have the rank to promote anyone. My real teacher was here in Rio de Janeiro, Yushi-maza Nagashima, at YMCA in 1949

How long did França train with Count Koma?

Luis de França had little instruction with Count Koma, with Professor Maeda. In reality, [Maeda] was not a teacher: he was a fighter who passed through Brazil and for survival reasons he threw himself into fights because he was a fighter. He came from Japan a 3rd da[14]n from the Kodokan, and he didn't want to face the crops. At that time there was no radio [or] TV, and the great fun for people at the time was the circus. And he would appear in the circus and launch the challenge against the strong.

How was Luis França physically, and how old was he when you met him?

He was of medium height, between the ages of 50 and 60, and had white hair and was deaf (laughs). And he liked to train using the name he received from Maeda. And Maeda said it was "Jū-Jutsu" and not "Jiu-Jitsu," as they say here. But this has changed over time.

What were Luis França's classes like?

---

[14] According to the records we found, Maeda was promoted to 4th dan before he left Japan for the U.S. in 1904.

385

Luis de França taught the form of the old Jiu-Jitsu, but with the practical form of modern Judo, because he taught the nage-waza, that is, the throws, in addition to the katame-waza part that deals with immobilizations, arm-locks, chokes, and submissions. So he taught everything but kicks, which [would have made it] an MMA fight.

—

— Darlynson Lira —

Can you introduce yourself?

My name is Darlynson Lira, Im the oldest son of master Darcio Lira from Fortaleza, Brazil. I'm a Black Belt, 6th dan, in Jiu-Jitsu.

You come from a different lineage in Brazil, yes?

Well, my father comes from a lineage that it goes back to Takeo Yano and his teacher, Master Sá, that already passed away. I think he passed away in 2005. Master Sá trained directly with Takeo Yano for several years, and he actually received a Black Belt from the hands of the Japanese, and my father learned Jiu-Jitsu from Master Sá. So that's our lineage. Even though Master Sá had some contact with the Gracie lineage—like he trained some guys like Pedro Hemetério, [and] some other guys that in northwest of Brazil had some contact with the Gracies. But Master Sá received his Black Belt from Takeo Yano, so we are from that lineage.

How did Master Sá begin his journey in Jiu-Jitsu?

Master Sá worked at the Air Force base in northwest of Brazil. They hired Takeo Yano to go and train some of the military people there. And then, because Master Sá was part of the military personnel, so he got to train with Takeo Yano.

Who were Jose and Ivan Gomes, and what is their importance?

Jose Gomes—Master Jose Gomes—he was a younger brother of Ivan Gomes, and Ivan Gomes had a huge importance on the martial art Jiu-Jitsu, at the beginning of the history of Jiu-Jitsu in Brazil. Because he was a great fighter, and actually he was undefeated for a long time. Very strong guy, he was about like 100 kilos, you know 220 pounds. And Master Jose Gomes, his brother, followed his steps. I met Master Jose Gomes, too. Him and Master Sá, they gave my father the Red Belt. So I was present on the day that that happened, and was a great day. So Master Jose Gomes, he's in the north of Brazil, now. He's kind of like a little bit forgotten, you know. People don't care too much about him. But he's a great person, taking Jiu-Jitsu through the years. I think his importance was because he kept a different lineage from the Gracies. And Ivan Gomes, he did his own thing. He fought some of the Gracies and he did very well. I know some stories about Ivan Gomes, and he was a very tough fighter.

Why weren't they assimilated by Judo or the Gracies?

As far as I know, they never actually wanted to get attached to the Gracies. And they had their own thing, even though they were in different places in Brazil. You know the Gracies, they focus more on Rio de Janeiro [and] São Paulo, and Jose Gomes and Ivan Gomes were more in the north of Brazil. So the distance back then wasn't so easy to be traveling and going [from one] place to another, to do that cross-training stuff. But I know that Ivan Gomes, he did a tour in Brazil with the Gracies. They call[ed] him because—if I'm not wrong—he had a really tough fight with Carlson Gracie, and he did really well. Carlson was beating everybody back then, and he couldn't do much to Ivan Gomes.

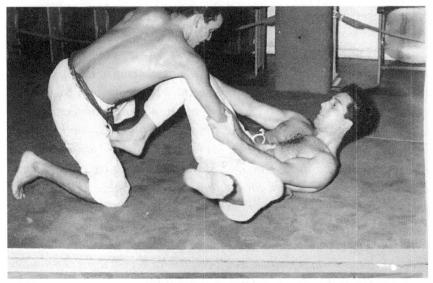

Carlson Gracie and Georges Mehdi train without the gi in the Open Guard position. Source: Mehdi Academy Archives

CONCLUSION

The internet, like other technological developments before it, has at the same time the astounding power of democratizing information and opinions (as well as creating the tools for the research that facilitated our film) while flooding our senses with everything that an open forum of opinions brings. Unable (and/or unwilling), to filter through all the sounds and images fired at us daily, our natural demeanor is not the one of avowed skepticism, but rather one of "follow the leader" or, in other words, "do and believe what others do and believe." Or more simply put: fashionable behavior.

Fittingly, it has remained so with the history of BJJ. Fortunately, however, facts are not subject to the desires or beliefs of the majority. Our inherent tendency to follow mass-psychology is at times sensible and at times severely flawed. It would be plausible to assume that this behavior may have played a role in our evolutionary past, saving our ancestors from life-threatening situations. Conversely, we don't have to look too far back into history to learn about the dangers and repercussions of herd-mentality and allowing others to do the thinking for us. This is the human odyssey in a nutshell.

It requires an enormous and continuous effort to develop the ability to filter through it all and not follow tendencies but rather learn how to think critically and judge for ourselves. Recently I found myself in a discussion with a student who insisted that "books are useless because the internet provides all the answers at the tip of your fingers" (by "all the answers" I can only assume he meant the top of the page of a Google search... which is invariably Wikipedia). With this same "top of the page" dynamic the history of BJJ continues to be written daily (and inaccurately), and those responsible for shaping these new narratives never cease from shrewdly sensing the favorable changes in the wind, and just as quickly make their stand.

Who would have thought that the expansion and democratization of information would make us less informed and more confident in our ignorance? And that history from now on would be written not by the great skeptic minds but rather by computer algorithms with coding to reinforce the will of the majority. Or perhaps it has always been that way, and the world has just gotten better (worse?) at it. Has anything changed really? Or has the speed of (mis)information simply followed pace with the technology that spreads it? "Who controls the past controls the future. Who controls the present controls the past..." Orwell remains more relevant than ever, reminding us how the past carves our identity—which in its turn defines our future. Accurate historical telling isn't merely an act to correct the past, but rather one that guides our future in a more fulfilling and purposeful way. Ultimately, it is a service to future generations of practitioners of the art... a service we owe them.

—

And while we try to navigate these questions and understand the process by which BJJ evolved from Judo, we remain hopeful that we can learn lessons that can educate our future. I can't say for certain what the lesson is in all of this—or if there even is a lesson to be learned—but out of the many questions we could ask regarding the history of BJJ, the one that most vigorously jumps at me is an old one: Does the end justify the means?

The process by which BJJ evolved from Kodokan's Judo wasn't always a righteous one. The events that made the evolution of BJJ a reality were at times dishonest, vain, egotistical, and destructive. To be fair, there was also passion, ambition, dedication, resilience, and courage. There is nothing saintly or heroic about the motives that led Brazilians to carve a style from the Judo matrix, but neither is there anything that we aren't all responsible for at some point in our lives, if not daily. Ultimately, all of these ingredients led to the crafting of an art that impacts hundreds of thousands around the world.

It is easy to condemn, but condemnation without comprehension and context is plain ignorance. There were moments in which the Gracie Brothers undoubtedly behaved as hooligans. On three separate occasions they were accused of jointly attacking Oswaldo Baldi, Donato Pires dos Reis, and Manuel Rufino dos Santos (they were tried, convicted, and pardoned for this last one). "Dojo Storming" rival gyms was common practice, as was fighting in public to prove the superiority of their art, as when Rickson Gracie attacked Hugo Duarte on the beaches of Rio de Janeiro. Still, though these methods weren't exactly noble, these tactics and rivalries ultimately led not only to BJJ but also to the creation of Valendo Tudo as a means for these practitioners to survive during a time where rivaling Judo in organization and numbers was unthinkable.

My own sense of these events and practices changed over time, and —despite my objection to these practices—I found myself wondering: Are we any better? Even if attacking rivals on the streets is no longer customary, I can't help but notice that our motivations and ambitions have remained the same throughout. Talking trash on forums may not be the same as attacking someone on the beach, but is it any less distant from Kano's lofty ambition? We all want to stand tall in the world, often at any cost and in detriment of an honorable demeanor. Again, we all err—we differ only to which degree we err, and for what reasons.

Our production team was maturing into all of this over the course of making the film. These weren't conclusions we had reached when we first began our pursuit. Our views and interpretations were obviously changing over time while we were attempting to find a common thread for our film that would unite all these characters and events.

At some point, while thinking about all this, I found myself thinking back on Robson Gracie's life advice to me. "Inconsequente" seemed the perfect word, a fitting way to describe BJJ's winding history. Little had been planned, it seemed: there had been no vision for the future beyond the desire of creating a legacy. Now, with the process of our production behind us, I could only see this fact in light of its contrast with the art that gave it birth.

Regardless of what one thinks of Judo, it is astonishing how it has managed to remain consistently cohesive and organized over the last century, all while expanding to every corner of the world. Certainly, this growth was not the product of being "inconsequente" through this length of time. Although, to be fair, this cohesiveness is likely more a product of Japanese society than Kano's mind in particular; conversely, the same is true of Brazil and its impact on BJJ. If Brazilians are to BJJ as Kano is to Judo, then certainly the cultural matrix into which each art was planted owns a share of the credit—and the blame. Differences aside, Judo is not only the technical matrix from which BJJ evolved, but also the mark in the horizon with whom the Gracie Brothers persistently rivaled: the rivalry that would give BJJ the impetus to be.[15]

Despite its technical merits, its broad appeal, and its cultural significance (sparking the rise of MMA and the UFC), I now can't help but see the ways in which the art of Brazilian Jiu-Jitsu lacks a central code or morality for its students to uphold on and off the mats; can't

---

[15] On a more current note, the burgeoning rivalry between "BJJ" and "AJJ" has stirred in me the notion that the people that were most well positioned to make a claim for "JJJ" were not only silent in all of this, but were also perfectly willing to call the Brazilian version of their Judo, "Brazilian Jiu-Jitsu," including using it in the name of their national federation. Whatever acronym you choose to brand yourself with, they are both in their infancy in terms of more relevant matters that apparently were unable to make the voyage across the Pacific, unlike its more easily appreciated technical canon.

help but see it as a martial art orphan of a higher morality: a warrior's way without a "way." This phenomenon may in fact be getting worse, as the economic pressure to engage and entertain shapes and drives BJJ's competitive (and therefore—as the competition culture inevitably trickles out to the broader culture—general) future. And perhaps this is the lesson we were all searching for. As Kano would have it, martial arts ought to be a means of not only learning the truth about combat, but also of moral education.

But did Judo achieve this portrayed goal? It is unquestionable to me that Kano and the Kodokan made a tactical error by deemphasizing the ground-game (perhaps leaving strikes out was also a mistake) in preference of throws. These two aspects of grappling are two sides of the same coin and for the purposes of true combat, they are equally useless without one another. The result of Kodokan's ruleset being so stringent on the fight developing on the ground, followed by its emphasis on the sportive aspect of its practice, wasn't a more reality oriented art, but rather one that was impoverished by self-regulation.

Can anyone argue that Judo, for the purposes of self-defense and combat, would not be a more comprehensive art had it incorporated a more wide-ranging arsenal of techniques on the ground with which to follow its throws? Can it be debated that eliminating the "single-leg" and "double-leg" takedowns made it less reality-oriented and efficient? Martial arts ought to be a means of not only moral education, but also one for learning the truth about combat.

For maintaining the reality of combat as the guiding north of our martial arts experience, we have protagonists and events in Brazil to thank. They were the ones who nourished the seed of what would later become the most sophisticated and realistic form of hand-to-hand combat ever devised. Even if the seed of MMA had been also sown on other grounds, it was in Brazil that men such as George Gracie, Tico Soledade, Waldemar Santana, Euclides Pereira, and Ivan Gomes kept it alive long enough to have Rorion Gracie and Art Davie repackage it and present it to the world in 1993, live from Denver, Colorado.

CONCLUSION

—

Out of these names however, there is one that deserves special comment and commendation: Carlos Gracie's eldest son Carlson. Born Eduardo Gracie (later having his name changed by his father) he is arguably the most important Gracie of all time, if not the most likable one as well. I had the opportunity to take a photo with him at a tournament in California when I was 17 years old and just getting started in BJJ. I remember well what I told him when I asked for a picture: "Você é meu Gracie favorito" ("You are my favorite Gracie").

At that time, I knew nothing of BJJ history; I didn't even know anything about the history of the man himself, for that matter. But I knew he was my favorite because his students were the best fighters in the world, in my eyes, and because he took the time to take a picture with me and seemed genuinely happy about it. It doesn't seem like a lot today, but at the time it meant the world to an aspiring BJJ teenage competitor. My impression of him never changed over the years, and the more I learned about him the more I came to admire him.

He had a reputation for being bad with money, but was loved by all who knew him. For standing up to any challenge but not riding for long on any victory, instead immersing himself in the next challenge. Charismatic when most were acting tough, tough when others shied away from combat, a visionary when others thought they had it all figured out and above all, open-minded enough to understand that you are never done learning, Carlson was a revolutionary martial-artist.

I came to deeply regret not being able to insert his conquests as a fighter and coach into the film, but that would have extended our scope even more broadly and it wouldn't have done the man justice anyway. Carlson deserves a documentary just about him and the role he played in helping sow the seed of MMA unto the world. His legacy was not one of amassed fortune, a large academy, or world fame. His legacy was his work and his work was playing the leading role in creating the most applicable adaptation of Jiu-Jitsu/Judo for MMA. If it weren't for him, I doubt the UFC would have been the vehicle for BJJ to catapult itself to the world, and without the UFC, would BJJ be a global phenom? I seriously doubt it.

But not even Carlson could fill the void that the absence of the "DO" left in BJJ. In some ways, I came to think of Carlson as the man who completed Kano's vision by taking a limited practice and expanding it to cover the full spectrum of possibilities present in hand-to-hand combat. Beyond this, he was a singular figure, loved by many, who dedicated his life to Jiu-Jitsu, Vale Tudo, and his students.

Living now in the forest these men and others have planted and cultivated over the past one hundred and forty years, it would do us all well to reflect on what we have all achieved today and what is still missing. Followed by considering whether what is missing in BJJ and MMA can coexist, without contradictions, with show business.

—

There are so many elements to this story: far too many, it turned out, to tell and explain in a ninety-minute film. This book is an attempt to expand on what we were able to show onscreen: to offer a more in-depth view and analysis of the characters and events that shaped the BJJ world in which we live and the practice we all enjoy. These endless and intertwining events enriched our history, but at the same time made it all the more complex. Yet no matter how we feel about these events, I can't see the present now without seeing also every element of the past. I can't see BJJ or MMA existing without all the ingredients that we were learning about and discussing. After all, if the key ingredient had been only the ne-waza techniques, why didn't Kosen Judo spread like wild-fire in Southern California, and then to the world? If Carlos and Hélio Gracie had no role to play in all of this, why was there no such thing as Peruvian Jiu-Jitsu, when there are so many Japanese immigrants in Peru? Had Carlson not played a pivotal role in crafting Jiu-Jitsu for real fighting, would Royce have stood a chance in the UFC? Had Rorion Gracie not helped create the UFC with an old Brazilian formula called "Vale Tudo" would Dana White have a job today and would so many people around the world have MMA as a favorite sport to watch? I seriously doubt it. The truth matters, but its recording seems half-done already: every moment of the past is written into every moment in the present, whether those moments are acknowledged or not.

Does the end justify the means? The final outcome of our past behaviors is the only vantage point from which we view and interpret our world. Other possibilities will never be known to us and, for this reason, to judge the past based solely on its positive outcomes while ignoring the deceitful means by which this outcome is achieved is to overlook the endless other possibilities of our actions, and thus it is "inconsequente." Perhaps we could have been better. Perhaps we should have been. And perhaps, if we had, we—and the world we occupy—would be all the better for it. Nonetheless, I am grateful that events unraveled as they did: these events led me to find that which gives my life purpose and meaning. This simple fact remains despite my disagreement with so many of the actions undertaken in BJJ's service. Perhaps this is selfish and contradictory, but I can't help it. As I wrote in the beginning: in historical inquiry, one must be aware of one's own bias. I know now if I didn't know before: I am biased by my love for Jiu-Jitsu.

I am proud of our film. Regardless of its reception, I can rest assured that I played a small role in helping correct and complete BJJ history. But this pride didn't come without a cost. I have spent the last three years of my life working on being the best and most honest historian, film producer, and writer I could be to help bring this story to light—all without any reward in sight, other than the satisfaction that I have done my part. But, as I often tell my students, "The hard-work is the reward," and my peace is made with the film's impact or reception, whatever they may be.

Other costs don't find their peace so easily and give me pause to wonder whether it was all worth it or not. In this pursuit of telling this history, never could I have imagined that my work schedule would be dishonestly used as a weapon against me and cost me the most valuable currency in the world: priceless time with the two people I love most dearly. Suffice it to say that I have suffered major personal losses that can't be quantified and that, at any rate, are too personal to make it into this book.

But whatever the nature or background of injustices, they should be challenged with work and a defiant smile grounded in the knowledge (hope?) that time is the only judge that matters. And while it is discouraging that history is often written (and repeated) without scrutiny, and as an expression of the prevailing bias of the one who holds the pen, let us remind ourselves that when we stand with justice we stand with hope for a more righteous future—hope that the cheerful poet was right in his assertion that "you can fool some people sometimes, but you can't fool all the people all the time." Until that day, we can only work and hope.

The author with Carlson Gracie at a tournament in Southern California, 1999.

ROBERT DRYSDALE

Born in the U.S. from a Brazilian mother and American father, and having spent his life between these two countries, Robert Drysdale remains the only American competitor to have ever won both the IB-JJF and ADCC World Championships, the two most prestigious tournaments in all of Jiu-Jitsu. Furthermore, he has also cultivated a career in MMA, both as a fighter and as a coach. The author also holds a Bachelor's Degree in History, as well as a long-held passion for this discipline. He lives in Las Vegas, Nevada, where he teaches Brazilian Jiu-Jitsu and MMA. He is also the co-founder of the international team Zenith Jiu-Jitsu, and is the father of two girls.

Author photo credit: Piotr Pędziszewski

APPENDIX I

Included below and in the following pages are some additional images of the historical figures discussed in this book. (Note: In the captions U/B refers to Upper/Bottom and L/R refers to Left/Right.)

UL: Hélio Gracie. Source: Brazilian National Library; UR: Hélio taking his brother Carlos down. Source: Brazilian National Library; BL: Brazilian Judo/ Jiu-Jitsu pioneer Mario Aleixo. Source: Brazilian National Library; BR: Hélio Gracie's nemesis, Yassuiti Ono. Source: Brazilian National Library.

UL: Gracie Brothers from left to right: Hélio, Carlos, and Oswaldo. Source: Brazilian National Library; UR: George Gracie Source: Brazilian National Library; BL: Jigoro Kano. Source: Unknown; BR: Takeo Yano. Source: Source: Brazilian National Library.

APPENDIX I

U: From left to right: Akitaro Ono, Mitsuyo Maeda, Tokugoro Ito, and Satake (sitting down) Source: Brazilian National Library; BL: Maeda's right hand man in Belém, Jacyntho Ferro. Source: Brazilian National Library; BR: Mitsuyo Maeda in Cuba. Source Biblioteca Nacional Cubana José Martí.

UL: Signed picture by Geo Omori. Source: Brazilian National Library; UR: From left to right: Carlos Gracie, Donato Pires dos Reis, and George Gracie at the founding of the Jiu-Jitsu Academy in 1930. Source: Brazilian National Library; B: Geo Omori and Carlos Gracie in Rio de Janeiro. In the article accompanying this picture Carlos is identified as Geo Omori's manager. This article appeared after their alleged real fights in São Paulo, making it clear that they weren't rivals, but rather had a working partnership. Source: Brazilian National Library

Promotional images for the documentary featuring, from top to bottom: Armando Wriedt; actor playing Mitsuyo Maeda a.k.a. "Count Koma"; actor playing Carlos Gracie.

APPENDIX I

Propaganda and immigration posters regarding the voyage from Japan to Brazil.
Posters available for purchase at www.ClosedGuardFilm.com.

APPENDIX II

As I argued in the book, lineages are overly simplistic and arbitrary ways of recounting history. For these reasons, I was hesitant to publish one. I decided, however, that simplistic as they may be, they can help tell the narrative of Jiu-Jitsu in Brazil in a more complete way.

What I have included below may prove incomplete (and perhaps incorrect) in the future. Also, as it would be impossible to name all of the instructors, we decided to stick to the ones whose lineages were most influential. Additionally it should be noted that the size of the rectangles or the order of names does not reflect the relevance of these characters in the overall history of Jiu-Jitsu in Brazil. Lastly, given what is available in print, this is as close to an accurate Jiu-Jitsu lineage as we can get.

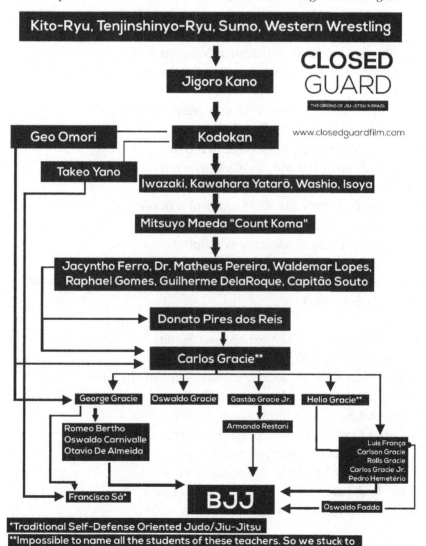

Kito-Ryu, Tenjinshinyo-Ryu, Sumo, Western Wrestling

Jigoro Kano

CLOSED GUARD
THE ORIGINS OF JIU-JITSU IN BRAZIL

Geo Omori

Kodokan

www.closedguardfilm.com

Takeo Yano

Iwazaki, Kawahara Yatarō, Washio, Isoya

Mitsuyo Maeda "Count Koma"

Jacyntho Ferro, Dr. Matheus Pereira, Waldemar Lopes, Raphael Gomes, Guilherme DelaRoque, Capitão Souto

Donato Pires dos Reis

Carlos Gracie**

George Gracie   Oswaldo Gracie   Gastão Gracie Jr.   Helio Gracie**

Romeo Bertho
Oswaldo Carnivalle
Otavio De Almeida

Armando Restani

Luis França
Carlson Gracie
Rolls Gracie
Carlos Gracie Jr.
Pedro Hemetério

Francisco Sá*

BJJ

Oswaldo Fadda

*Traditional Self-Defense Oriented Judo/Jiu-Jitsu
**Impossible to name all the students of these teachers. So we stuck to the main ones.

APPENDIX III

Front cover images, clockwise from upper left:

1. Statue of Jigoro Kano in front of the Kodokan Museum. © *Message in a Bottle*
2. Mitsuyo Maeda. *Source: Nileyan Rodriguez, Biblioteca Nacional José Martí, Havana, Cuba*
3. Geo Omori. *Source: Brazilian National Library*
4. Jacyntho Ferro. *Source: Brazilian National Library*
5. Carlos Gracie. *Source: Brazilian National Library*
6. Donato Pires dos Reis. *Source: Brazilian National Library*
7. Hélio Gracie. *Source: Brazilian National Library*
8. Oswaldo Fadda. *Source: Luis Carlos Guedes de Castro personal archives*
9. George Gracie. *Source: Brazilian National Library*
10. Luis França. *Source: Brazilian Navy*
11. Armando Wriedt. © *Message in a Bottle*
12. João Alberto Barreto. © *Message in a Bottle*
13. Flávio Behring. © *Message in a Bottle*
14. Oswaldo Carnivalle. © *Message in a Bottle*
15. Robson Gracie. © *Message in a Bottle*
16. Naoki Murata. © *Message in a Bottle*

Back cover images, clockwise from upper left (uncovered / partially covered photos only):

1. Armando Restani. © *Message in a Bottle*
2. Roberto Leitão. © *Message in a Bottle*
3. Masahiko Kimura. *Source: Mehdi Academy Archives*
4. Inoue Daisaku. © *Message in a Bottle*
5. Marcial Serrano. © *Message in a Bottle*
6. Carlos Gracie, Jr. © *Message in a Bottle*
7. João Rezende. © *Message in a Bottle*
8. Ryyuchiro Matsubara. © *Message in a Bottle*
9. Dr. José Tufy Cairus. © *Message in a Bottle*
10. Hélio Fadda. © *Message in a Bottle*

11. Takeo Yano. *Source: Brazilian National Library*
12. Yuki Nakai. © *Message in a Bottle*
13. Royce Gracie. © *Message in a Bottle*
14. Shiguero Yamasaki. © *Message in a Bottle*
15. Yassuiti Ono. *Source: Brazilian National Library*

RECOMMENDED READING

Portuguese

Géo Omori: O Guardião Samurai by Marcial Serrano

O Livro Proibido do Jiu-Jitsu: A História que os Gracie não contaram, Volumes 1-7, by Marcial Serrano

Jiu-Jitsu: O TÚNEL DO TEMPO: A Marinha trouxe o Jiu-Jitsu para o Brasil, Volumes 1 and 2, by Marcial Serrano

Muito Antes do MMA, Volumes 1-3, by Elton Silva

English

Choque: The Untold Story of Jiu-Jitsu in Brazil, Volumes 1-3, by Roberto Pedreira

Craze: The Life and Times of Jiu-Jitsu, Volumes 1 and 2, by Roberto Pedreira

The Gracie Clan and the Making of Brazilian Jiu-Jitsu: National Identity, Performance and Culture: 1905-1993 by Dr. José Tufy Cairus

Modernization, Nationalism, and the Elite: The Genesis of Brazilian Jiu-Jitsu 1905-1920 by Dr. José Tufy Cairus

Made in the USA
Las Vegas, NV
12 February 2024

85702424R00233